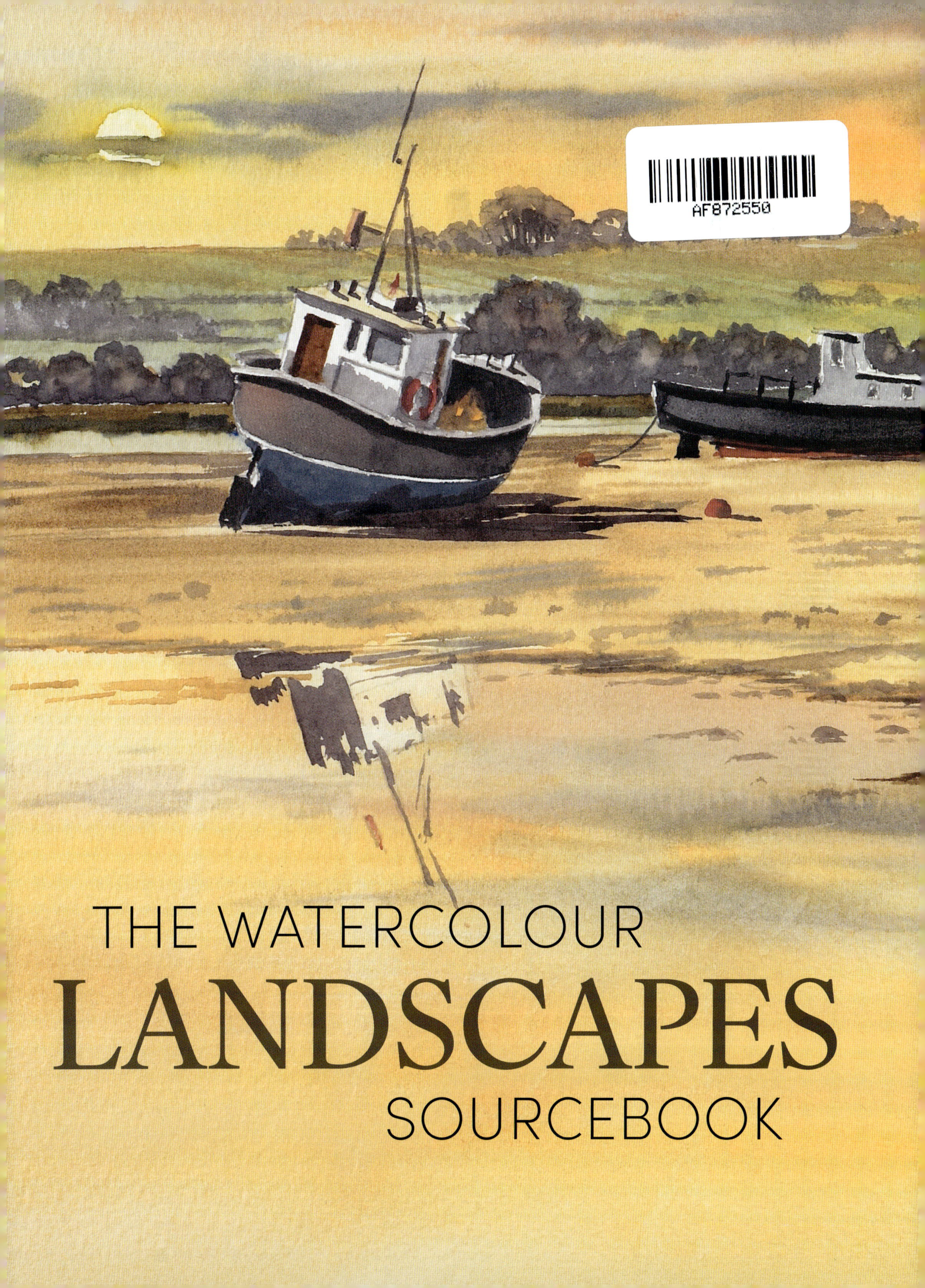

THE WATERCOLOUR

LANDSCAPES

SOURCEBOOK

First published in 2027

Search Press Limited
Wellwood, North Farm Road,
Tunbridge Wells, Kent TN2 3DR

1 2 3 4 5 6 7 8 9 10

Including material previously published by Search Press as:

- *Watercolour Tips & Techniques: Painting Landscapes & Nature* by Richard Bolton, 2003
- *Ready to Paint: Country Landscapes in Watercolour* by Terry Harrison, 2011
- *Ready to Paint: Watercolour Hills & Mountains* by Arnold Lowrey, 2009
- *Ready to Paint: Coastal Landscapes in Watercolour* by Tony Cowlishaw, 2011
- *Ready to Paint: Irish Landscapes in Watercolour* by Dermot Cavanagh, 2014
- *Ready to Paint: Watercolour Boats & Harbours* by Charles Evans, 2008
- *Ready to Paint: Watercolour Landscapes* by Terry Harrison, 2007
- *Ready to Paint: Watercolour Rivers & Streams* by Keith Fenwick, 2010

ISBN: 978-1-80092-384-3
ebook ISBN: 978-1-80093-363-7

Bookmarked Hub
Extra copies of the outlines are available to download free from the Bookmarked Hub. Search for this book by title or ISBN: the files can be found under 'Book Extras'. Membership of the Bookmarked online community is free: www.bookmarkedhub.com

Publishers' notes
The Publishers and author can accept no responsibility for any consequences arising from the information, advice or instructions given in this publication.

For errata, please visit our website (www.searchpress.com) or the Bookmarked Hub (www.bookmarkedhub.com).

GPSR information can be found at www.searchpress.com
Printed in China, AP082026

FSC www.fsc.org MIX Paper | Supporting responsible forestry FSC® C136333

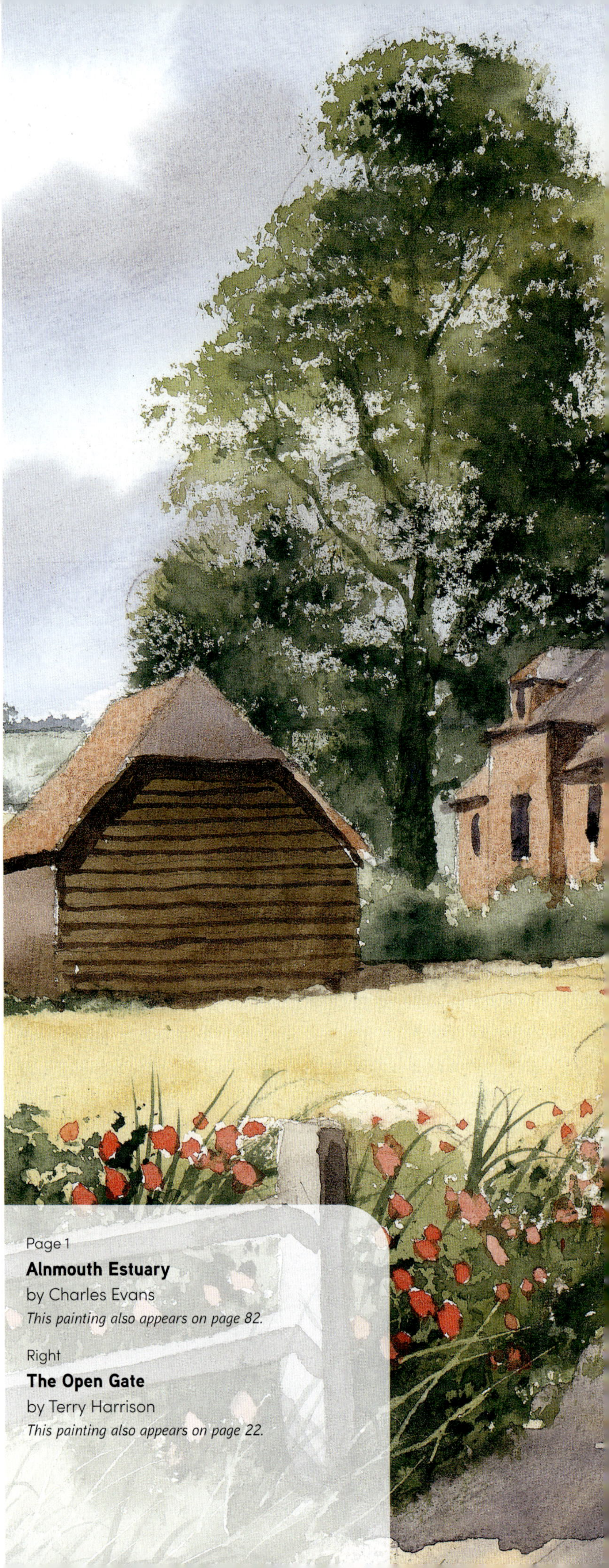

Page 1
Alnmouth Estuary
by Charles Evans
This painting also appears on page 82.

Right
The Open Gate
by Terry Harrison
This painting also appears on page 22.

THE WATERCOLOUR LANDSCAPES SOURCEBOOK

50 beautiful pictures to trace & paint, with full-size outlines

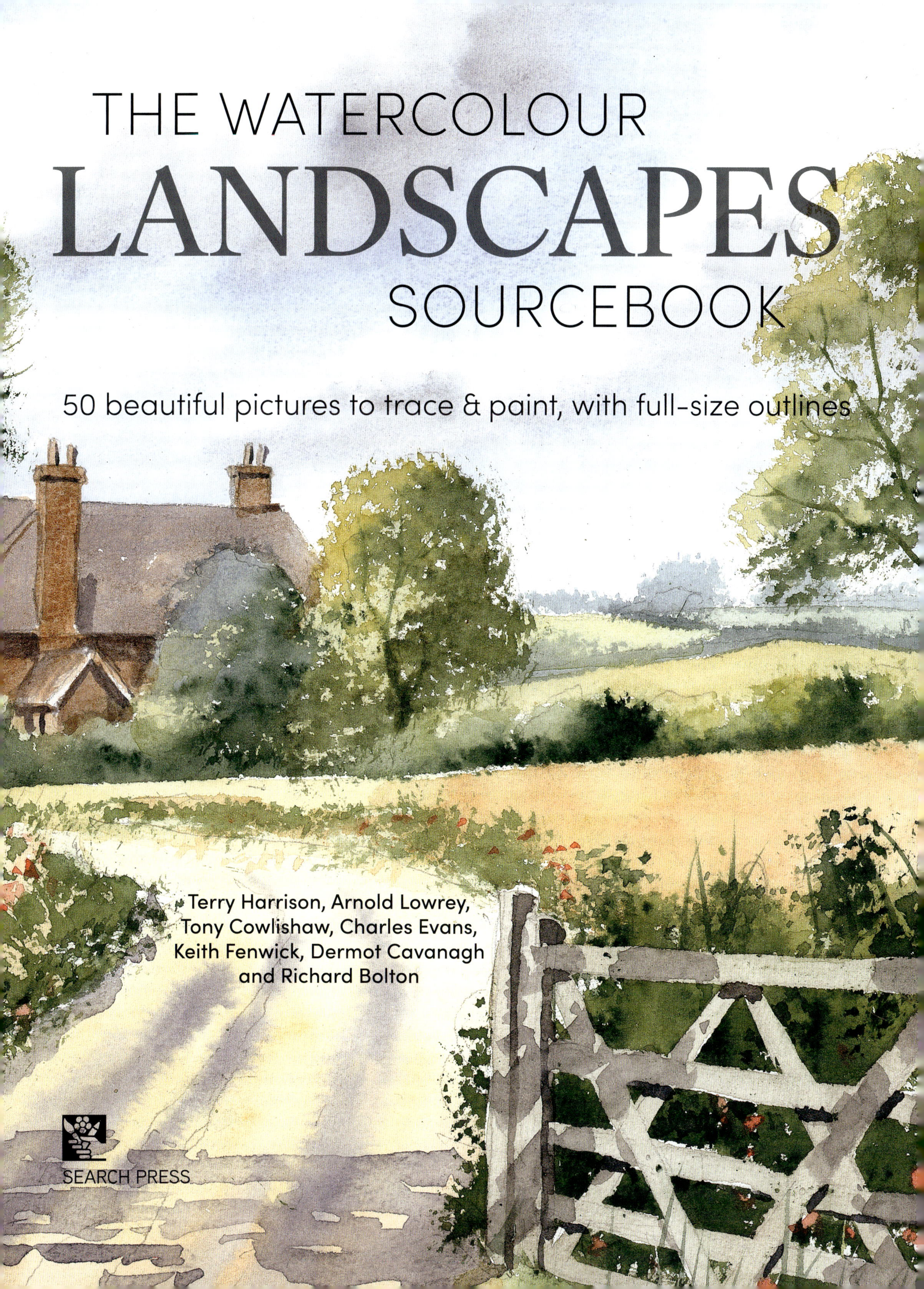

Terry Harrison, Arnold Lowrey,
Tony Cowlishaw, Charles Evans,
Keith Fenwick, Dermot Cavanagh
and Richard Bolton

SEARCH PRESS

Contents

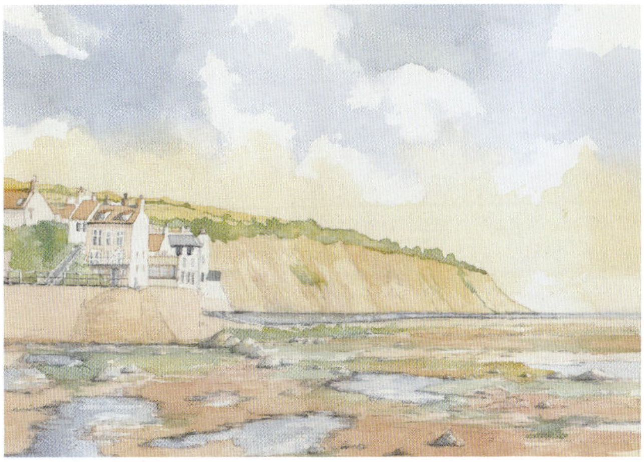

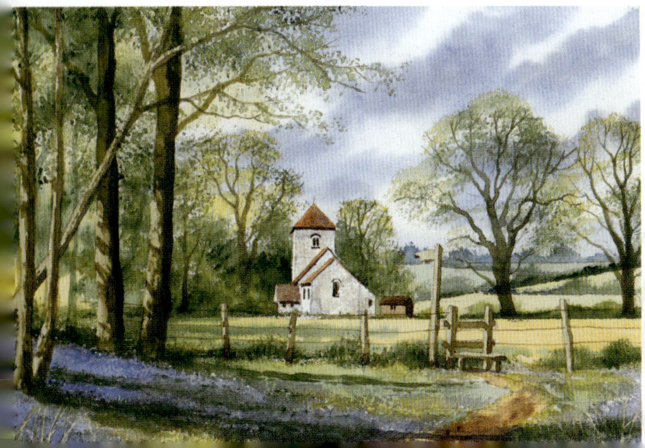

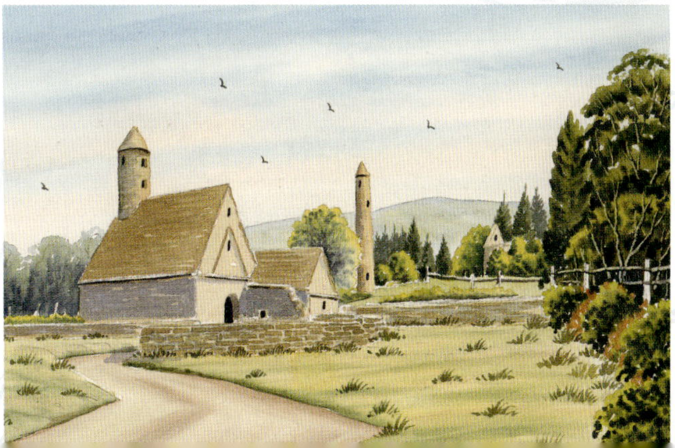

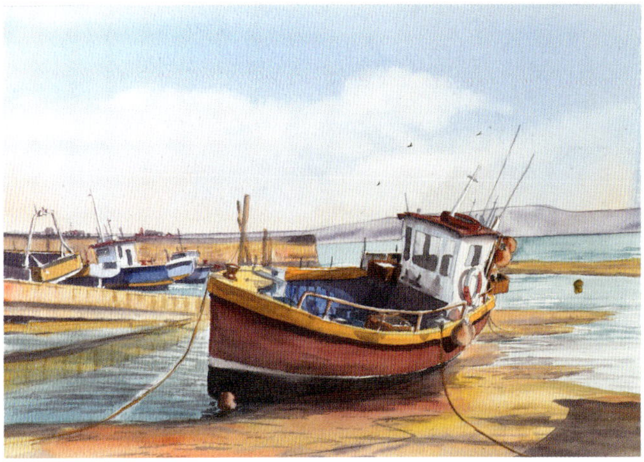

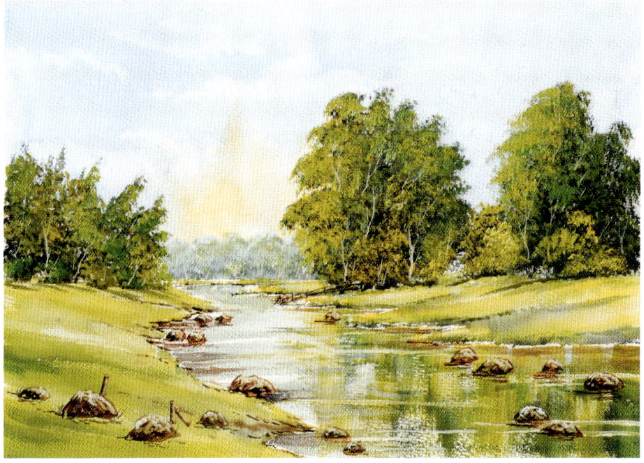

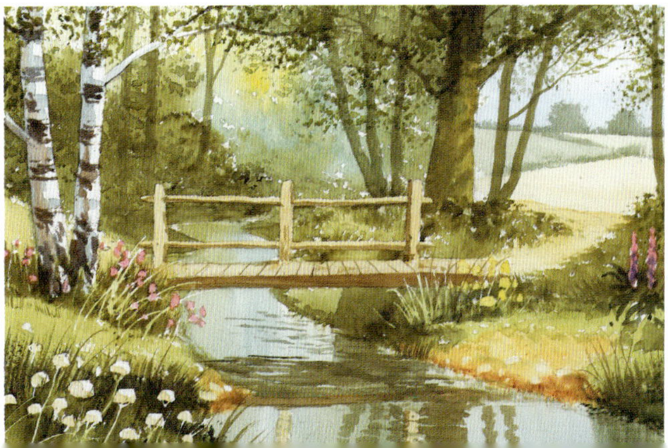

Introduction

In your hands you hold a huge range of project paintings that cover all aspects of the landscape – perhaps the quintessential subject for the watercolour artist. In these pages you'll find rolling hills, sunlit fields and dramatic mountains; along with rivers, streams and lakes, clear and stormy skies and more. The paintings feature subjects such as barns, farmhouses and harbours; flowers, trees and foliage; stone and brickwork; and light and shade.

People often say they would love to paint but they can't draw, and many amateur artists are let down by their drawing skills. There is also the problem of choosing the right subject to paint, and then there is the composition – it's enough to make you give up! Help is at hand in this book, as it contains outline drawings for each of the fifty landscape paintings. Follow the instructions on pages 8–9 on how to transfer the image on to watercolour paper, and you are ready to paint.

As this removes the first hurdle, the drawing, you will find yourself free to follow the easy step-by-step instructions to a successful painting. With success comes confidence, which leads to bigger and better things.

Through observation, self-confidence and practising time-tested techniques that actually work, learning to paint can be made easier, the frustration can be banished and painting can become a very rewarding activity. The guidance, hints and tips of seven master artists are contained in this book, so whatever style of landscape you seek to paint, you'll find something you love.

Whatever you choose, while you are using your watercolours to produce a painting to hang on your wall, you will also be absorbing the lessons and practising the techniques – and incorporating them in your own style of painting. Once you have gained confidence in using the paintings and outlines in this book, we hope you will be inspired to look for many more subjects in the world around you.

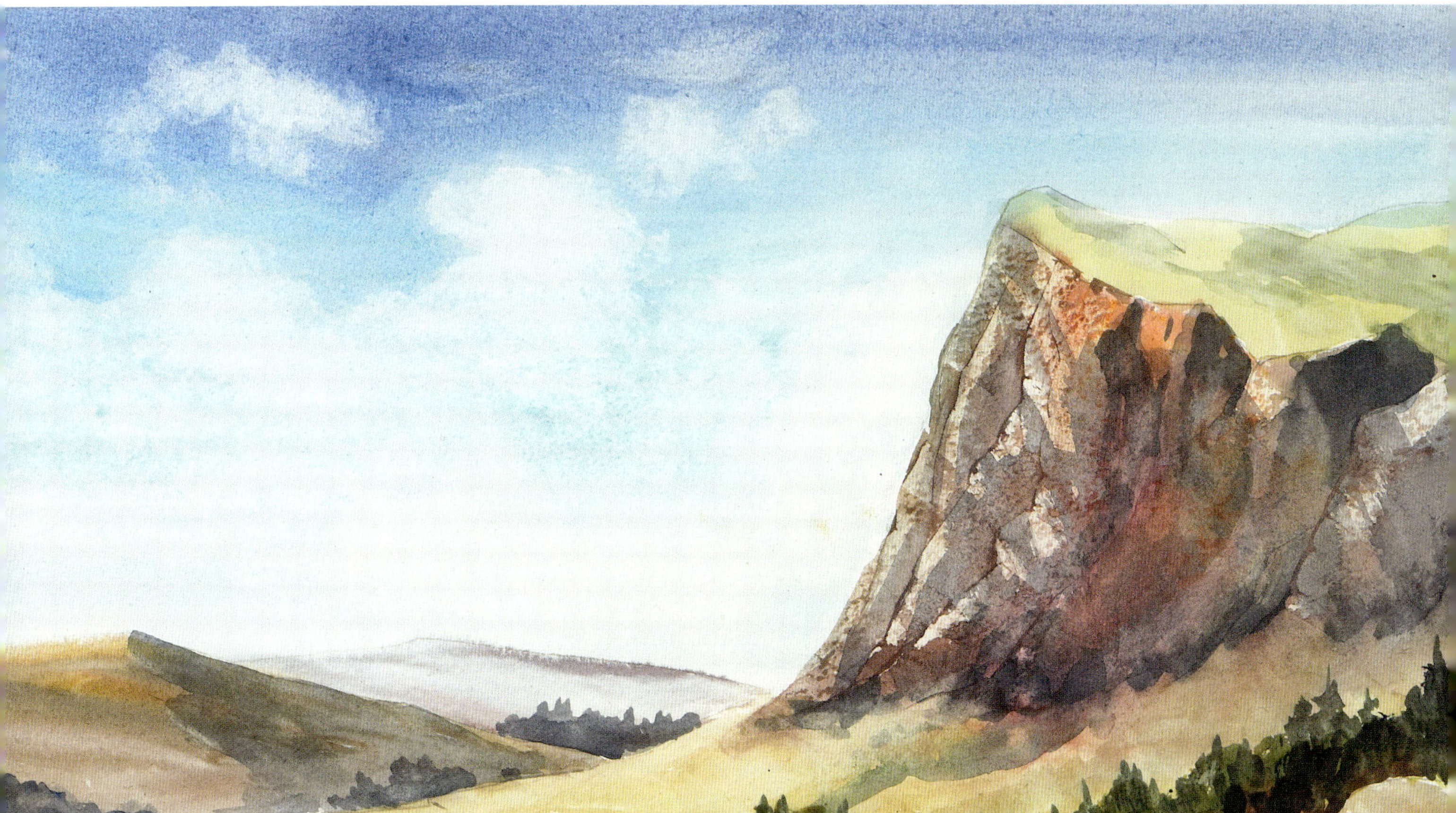

Water's Edge

by Arnold Lowrey

This painting also appears on page 41.

Transferring the image

You do not need to remove the outlines from the book to transfer them onto watercolour paper if you follow the methods shown below. You can also photocopy or scan the outlines, enlarge them to the size you want and then transfer them as shown.

Using tracedown paper

This is a readily available paper for transferring images, sometimes known as graphite paper, and is similar to the carbon paper that was used in the days of typewriters.

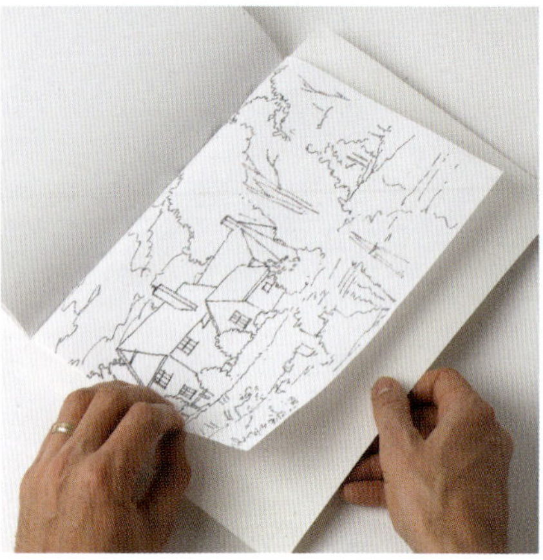

1 Slip your sheet of watercolour paper directly under the outline you want to use.

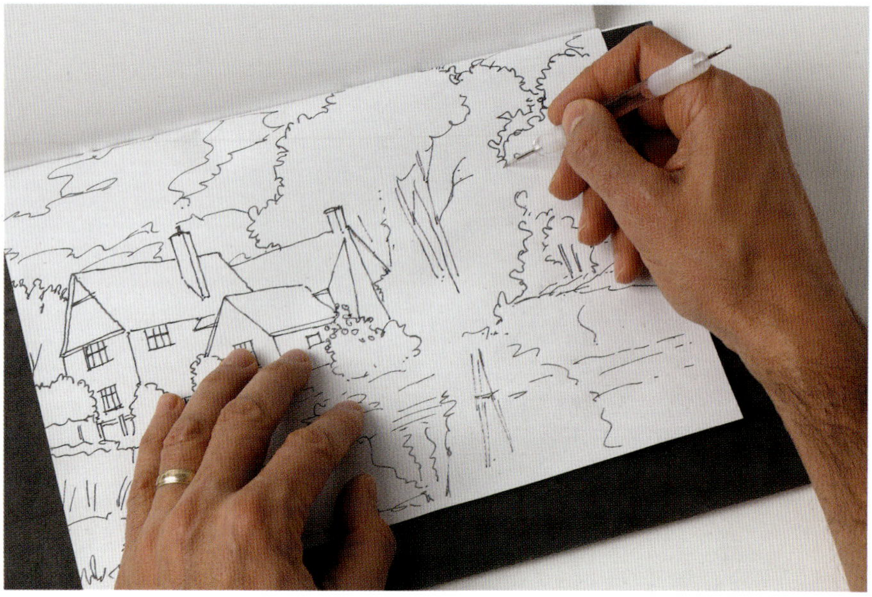

2 Slip a sheet of tracedown paper between the outline and the watercolour paper. Go over the lines using a burnisher.

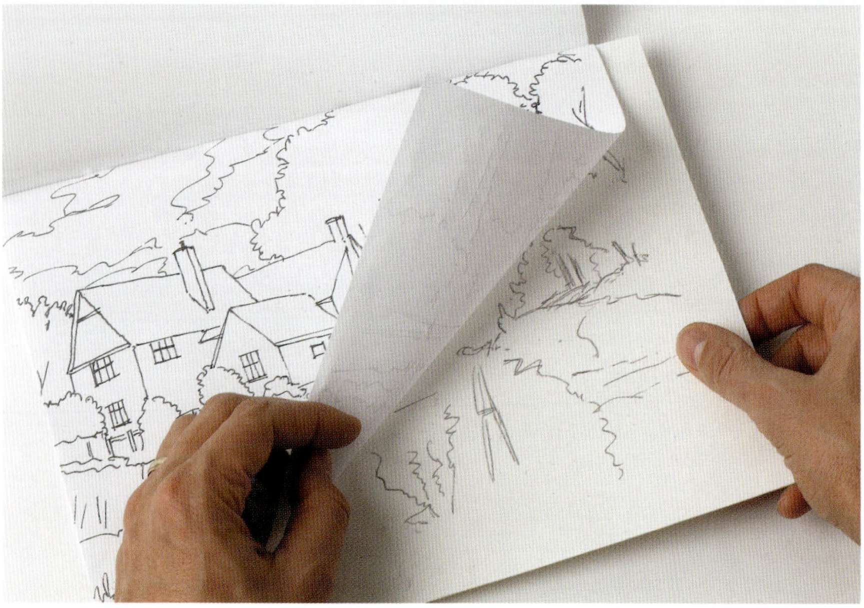

3 Remove the tracedown paper and lift up the outline to reveal the image transferred onto your watercolour paper, ready for you to begin painting.

Using pencil

You can transfer the outlines directly onto your watercolour paper from the pages at the end of this book, using a pencil and a burnisher. However, if you prefer not to work directly from this book, you can photocopy or scan the outline first, and transfer the outline from a copy in much the same way.

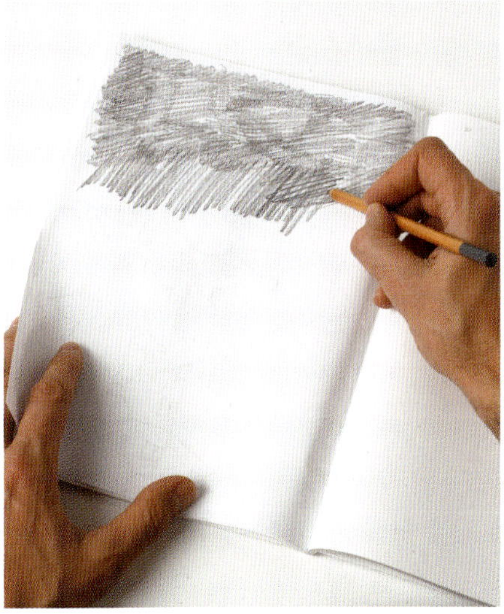

1 Scribble over the back of the outline with a soft pencil.

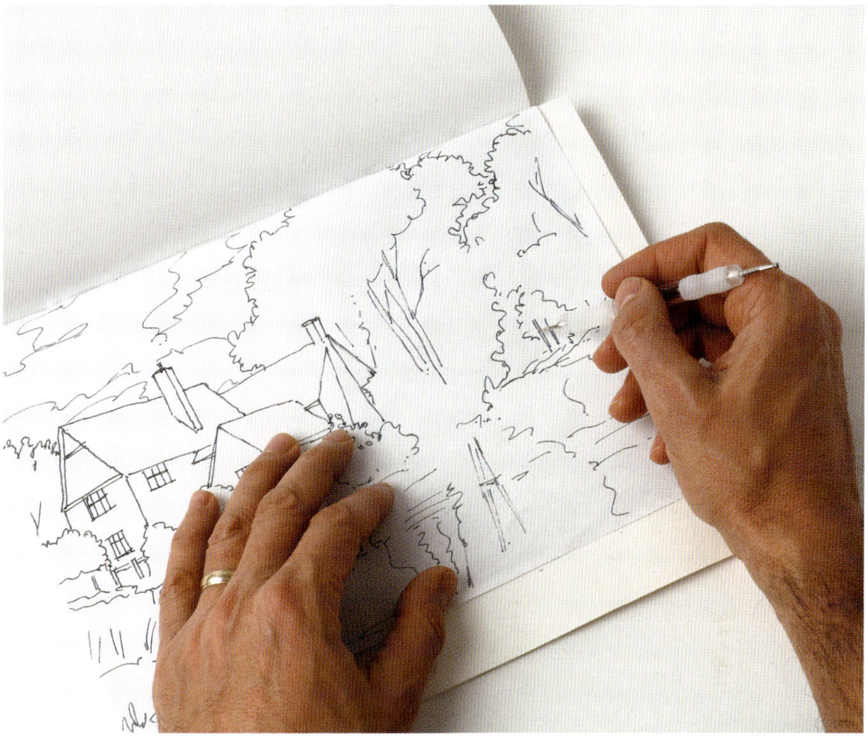

2 Turn the page so that you are looking at the image you want to transfer. Place your watercolour paper underneath the page. Go over the lines with a burnisher.

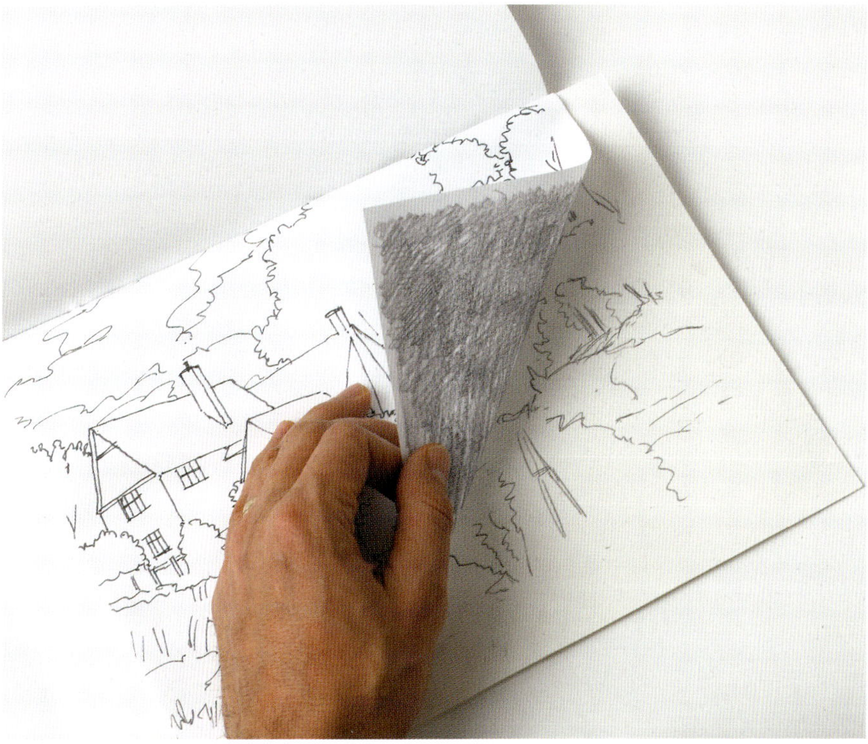

3 Lift the page to reveal the image transferred onto your watercolour paper. When you remove the watercolour paper, make sure you put a piece of scrap paper in between this outline and the next to avoid graphite from the back of the page transferring onto the next outline.

Using the outlines creatively

To get the most out of this book, you can use the outlines over and over again. Each project can be repainted in different seasons, as shown on these pages. You can also enlarge the images using a photocopier or scanner to the size you want.

You can even choose individual elements from different paintings and put them together to form a new composition – the church in *The Short Cut* (see page 25 and outline 2) can be replaced with the barn from *Open Gate* (see page 23 and outline 1), for instance. In this way you can create your own versions of the paintings.

Elements on the outlines like buildings, trees and boats are ideal for this purpose, but you can also try some freehand work by adding flowers, foliage, clouds and more. This is a great way to build your confidence and add some of your own personality to your paintings.

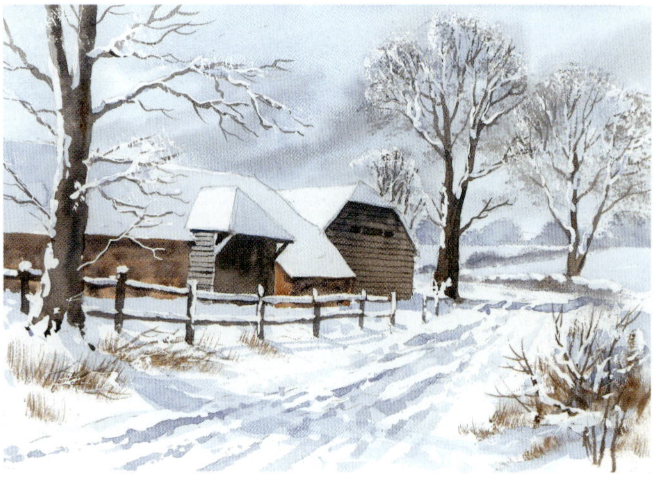

Summer Tracks

This painting uses outline 4 from Snow Tracks *(see above, and pages 28–29), but replaces the palette for a summery scheme. All the techniques you need are shown on the following pages, and the colours used are the same as in* The Open Gate *on page 22.*

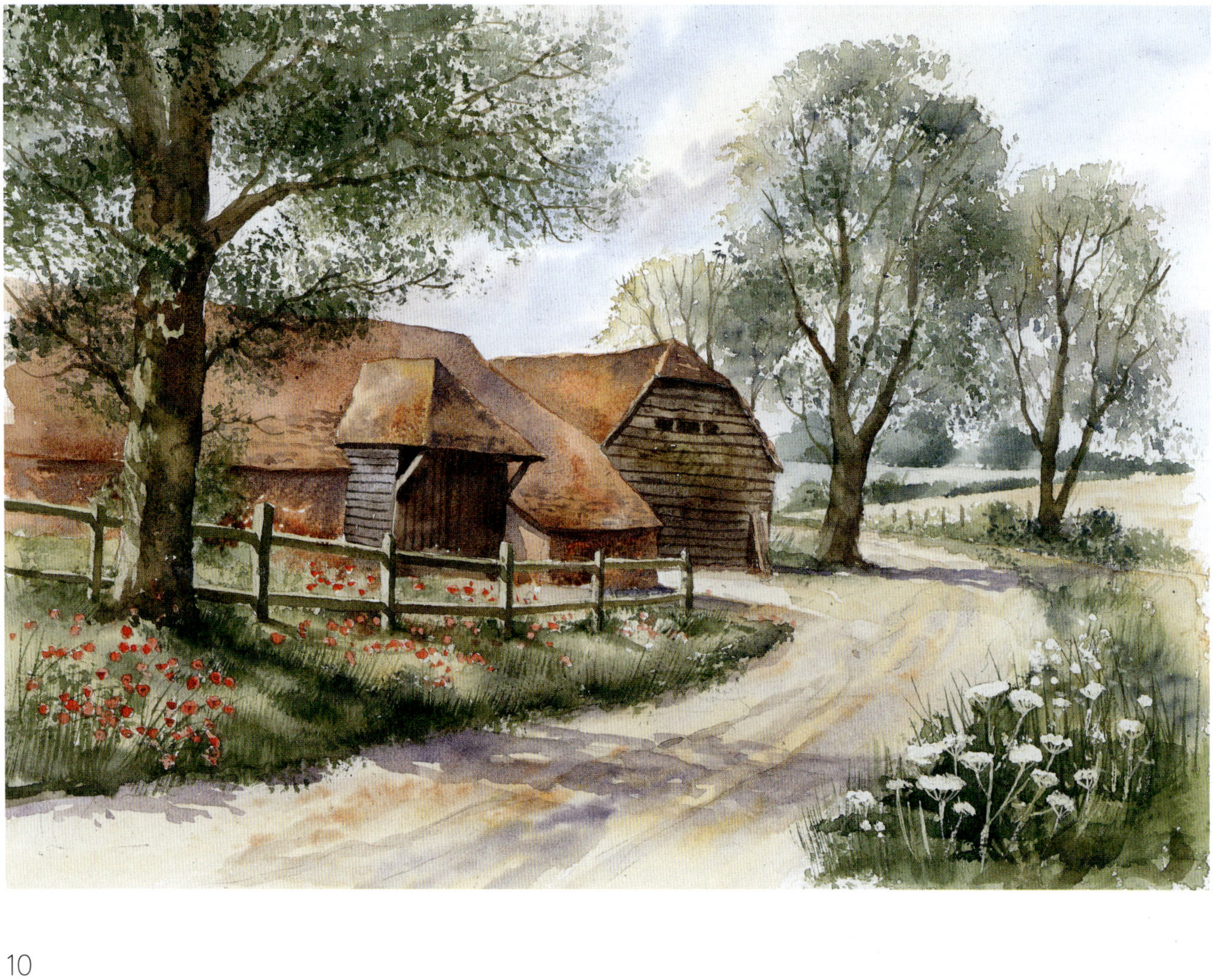

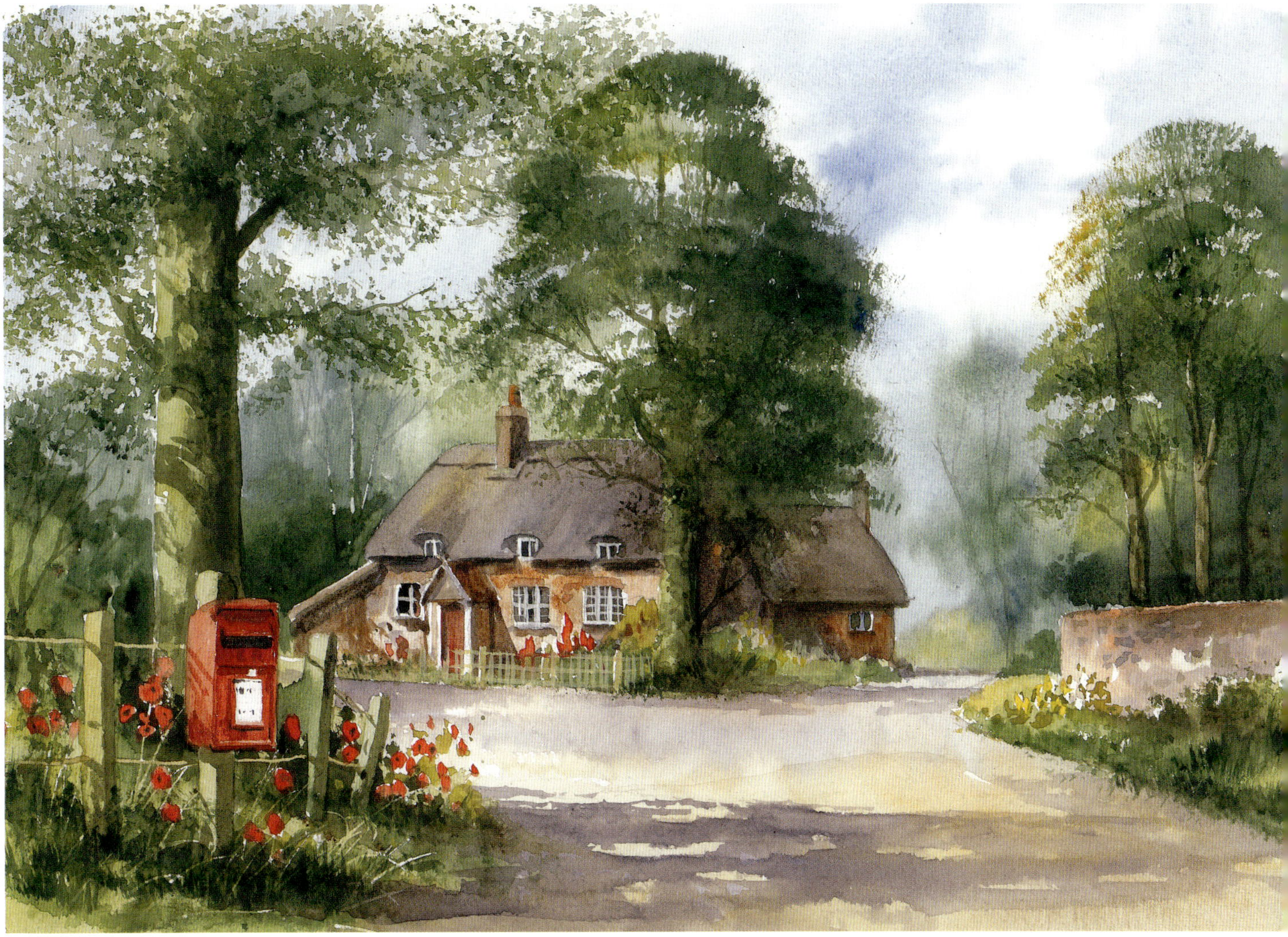

Summer Village

Here Village in the Snow *(see right; and pages 100–101, outline 35), has been revisited with a warmer scheme. Poppies and other splashes of red have been added as a complementary balance to the mainly green colour scheme.*

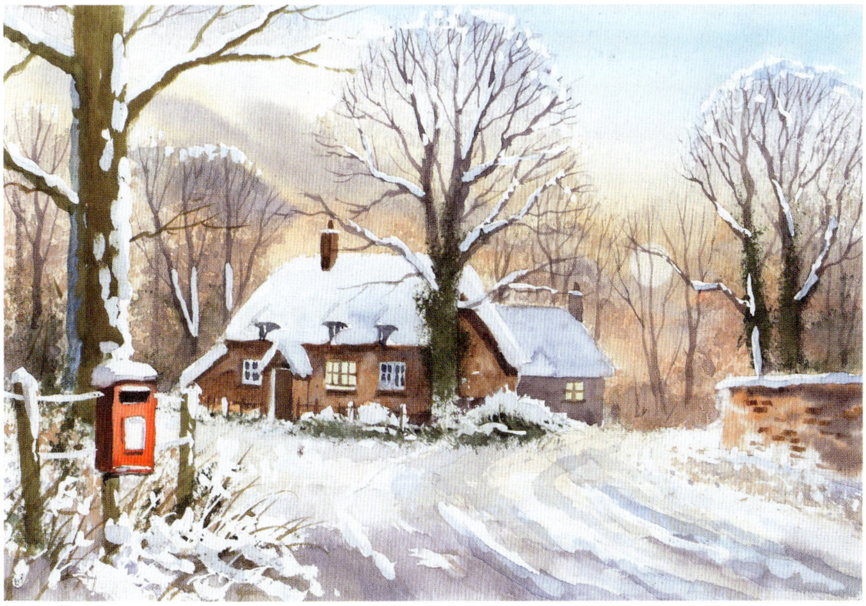

Techniques and effects

Wash techniques

Painting a large, flat area of colour is called applying a wash, and is fairly straightforward, but becomes more complicated as you add further washes and experiment with the possibilities that this technique opens up.

Start by mixing the colours in a palette. Make sure you have mixed enough colour before you start, because it will be difficult to mix more colour once painting has started.

Prop the edge of your board up a little, and with your largest brush, run a bead of paint along the top edge of the paper. Re-charge the brush and run it below the first line, so that the two lines run together. Continue down the paper in the same way until you reach the bottom.

The last line will leave a large bead of wash at the edge of the painting, which can be removed with the brush or with some paper tissue applied to the edge of the paper.

Flat wash and graded wash

A graded wash (bottom) is applied in the same way as a basic wash (top), only clear water is added instead of more paint. This dilutes the wash and creates a blending effect from colour to clear paper.

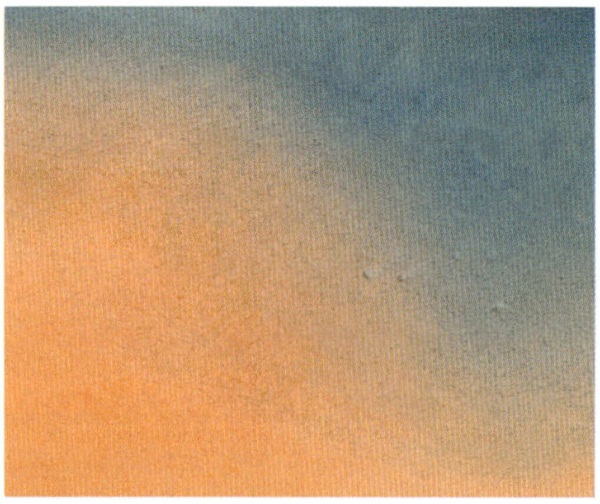

Mixed and variegated washes

Now you can see the possibilities of this technique. What if you mix two colours on the paper, or paint one wash over another? There is plenty of room for experimentation.

A variegated wash is similar, with different paints added in to a wet surface.

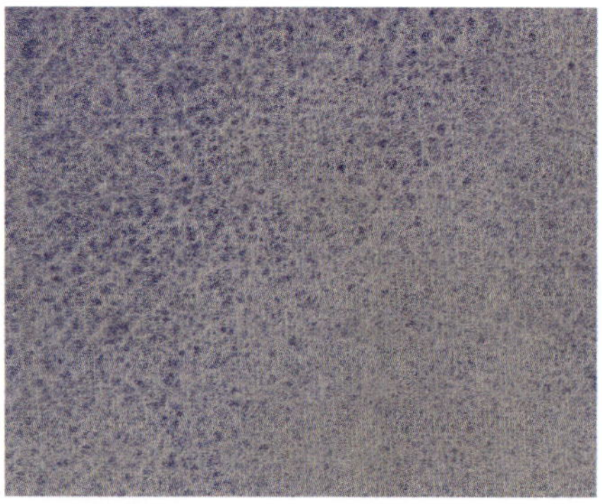

Granulation

Granular colours such as raw sienna, burnt sienna, burnt umber, cobalt blue and ultramarine blue tend to accentuate the texture of the paper as the particles fall into the hollows of the paper surface. This can create a useful effect.

Smooth finish with granulating paints

However, if you prefer a smoother finish, try drying the painting face down.

Wet into wet

Once you have experimented with wash techniques, it is only natural to wonder what will happen if a brush full of paint is placed on to the still-wet wash. This can be very exciting, as the new colour spreads out across the paper, gently mixing with the first colour. The board can be tilted to encourage the introduced colour to move this way and that to create whatever effect is desired. You can, however, come across one of the big risks of the wet into wet technique. The colours do not always blend evenly as expected, but sometimes form ridges or hard edges which can ruin a painting.

The cause of hard edges is uneven drying. A completed wash should dry evenly, so it is important to keep the board level during drying. However, if further brushfuls of paint are added during the drying process, then the area that has just received the paint will be a lot wetter, and as the painting dries, there will be pools of wet against the dried wash.

Factors such as different papers can affect the outcome, so hands-on experience is best for finding solutions.

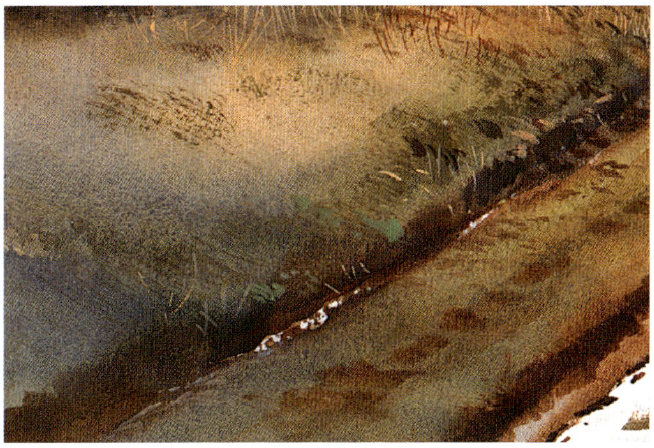

Wet into wet

This detail of Snow Thaw *(see page 128) shows a portion of the foreground. The bottom layer of grass shows how warm browns and blues have been applied with the wet into wet technique, giving a soft, evenly blended finish.*

Runbacks

'Cauliflowers' or runbacks in a wet into wet scene that has been incorrectly applied.

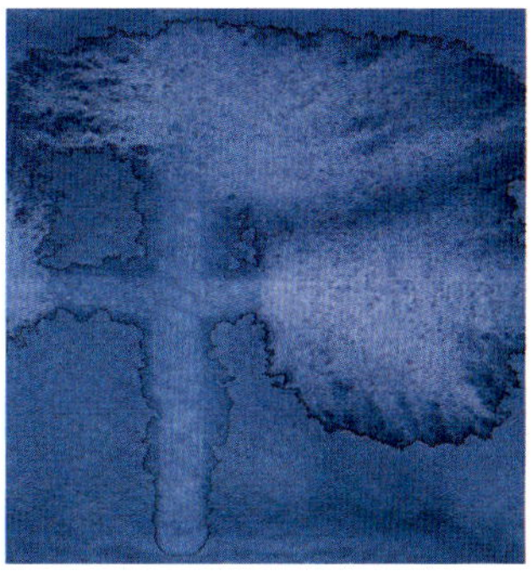

Wet into wet sky

Working into wet washes is idea for skies, enabling you to make soft clouds. Ultramarine blue has been painted into the wet surface of Naples yellow and a touch of alizarin crimson, to blend together softly on the paper.

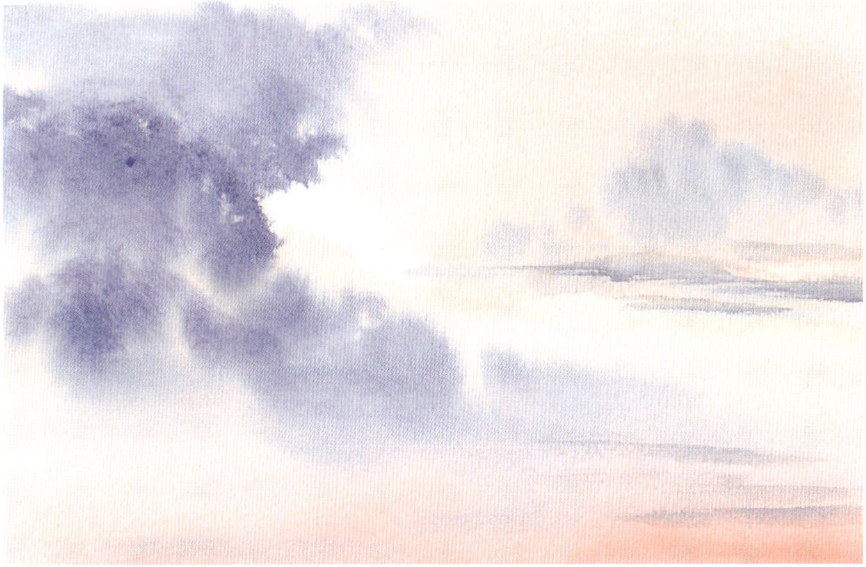

Dry brush

For dry brush work, we remove excess paint from the brush so that there is just enough left to make a mark on the paper. The brush can then be dragged and rubbed on the paper to impart some useful textural effects.

Getting the right amount of paint on the brush is tricky: too much and a heavy blob will be deposited on the paper, too little and no mark will be made. To get the wetness of the brush right, dab your brush against the edge of the palette and then touch a paper tissue to the edge of the hairs near the ferrule, to take away water without removing any paint.

The technique is useful for any area where texture is required: a brick wall, the ragged outline of trees or a ploughed field. It can be employed with a fine brush to do very detailed work, and with a large brush where the broken paint surface could give the speckle of light on an expanse of water. It works best on paper with a textured surface.

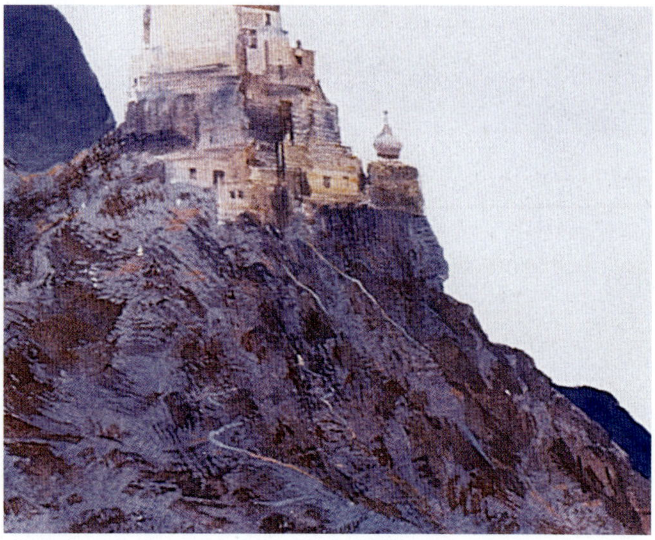

The mountains below Yumbulagang Monastery (see page 126) were painted using the dry brush technique to create the rocky texture.

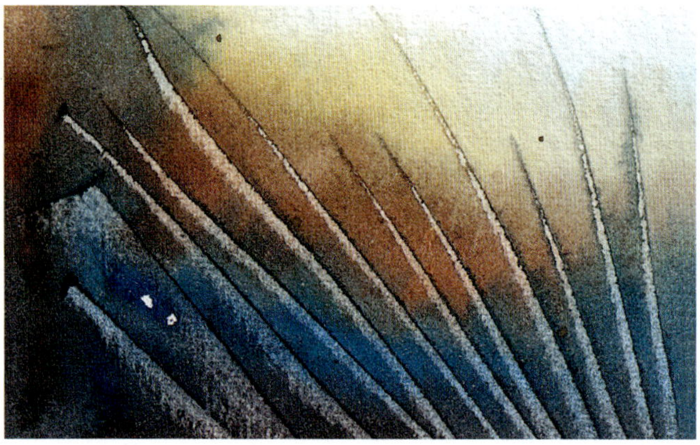

Scratching out and scraping

Paint can be scratched from the surface of a painting with a razor blade, craft knife or penknife. Wait until the paint is nearly dry – this is when it loses its shine. If scratched out too early, the marks on the paper will fill in with colour and dark lines will be produced instead of pale scratches. If the painting has dried too much, sweep a brushful of water on to the paper and it will become workable again.

Interesting textures can also be made by firmly scraping wet paint with the edge of a plastic card like a credit card, or a painting knife. The paint will be removed from the top of the paper but remain in the recesses, making great rocky or rough texures.

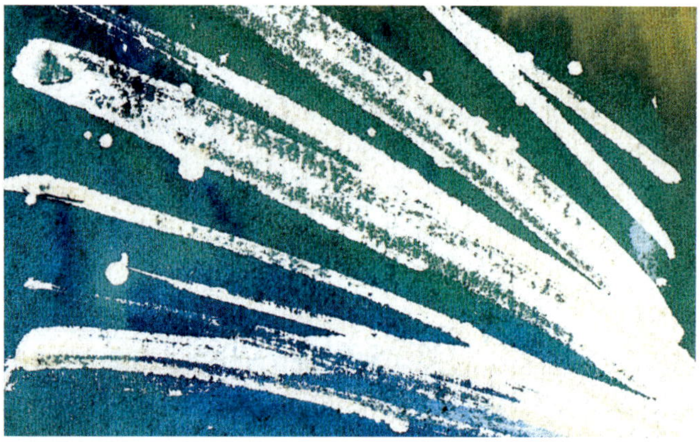

Using masking fluid

This liquid latex is brushed on to the paper and dries to a rubbery resist. When you want to remove it, it can be gently rubbed away with a finger or an eraser, revealing the layer underneath (in this case, clean white paper).

It is best to use an old brush to paint it on, as it tends to gum up brushes. You can protect the brush somewhat by wetting a bar of soap and running the brush through it before loading it with masking fluid. Clean the brush thoroughly after applying the masking fluid.

Wax resist

Candle wax can be rubbed on to the paper to form a resist. It is a rather haphazard technique, but I find the speckle of highlight it gives particularly useful for capturing the rugged texture of tree bark, and the roughness of stone walls.

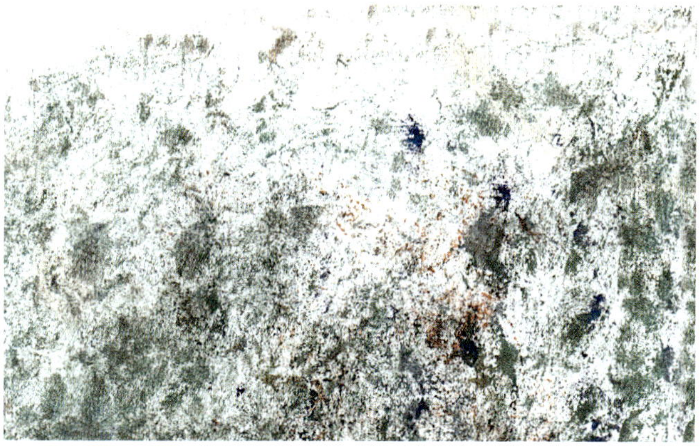

Dabbing

This is a technique for adding texture, and is particularly good for giving a soft, irregular outline to trees and foliage. After painting an area, dab it with a sponge, some screwed-up paper tissue or a piece of cloth.

Spattering

The effects of spattering can be very varied, depending on how it is done. The easiest way to achieve a fine spatter of paint is to tap the brush against a finger. Another way is to charge a bristle brush with paint and to drag your thumb across the bristles. Be sure to mask the work area, as paint spots will fly in all directions.

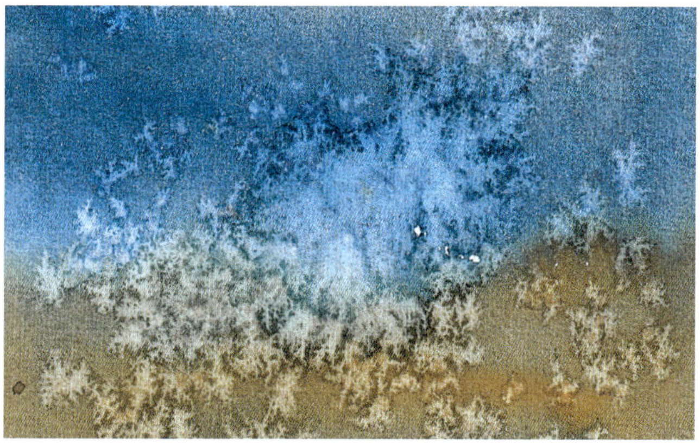

Salt

Normal table salt can be sprinkled into a mix of wet paint. As the salt dissolves, a pattern of spidery shapes appears on the paper. This is a rather unpredictable technique, but it can be very effective. Snow scenes are a popular choice of subject for this technique, but it is also useful in all kinds of areas, such as adding something a little livelier than a straightforward wash for the background.

Skies

The sky is an ever-present subject that changes from day to day and hour by hour. Its importance to a painting is fundamental, as it is often this that creates the atmosphere and makes a major contribution to the design of the composition. It is best to avoid drawing in the sky area, as lines can show up later, and with some papers, the use of an eraser can leave permanent marks that become evident when you lay a wash.

All the effects of wash painting and wet into wet play a big part in painting skies. It is an area in which you are not in complete control. Colours are brushed in and allowed to mix on the paper. The board is tilted to encourage movement, and you have to react quickly to these changes.

Hard edges are always a problem, and having a lot of water on the paper always creates risks, so try to remove some of the excess water by touching the edge of the painting with a paper towel or tissue.

Wet into wet sky

The base wash in the painting on the right was a mix of raw sienna with a touch of scarlet lake, merging into some Winsor blue. While the paper was still wet, ultramarine blue was brushed on to give the dark underside of the clouds.

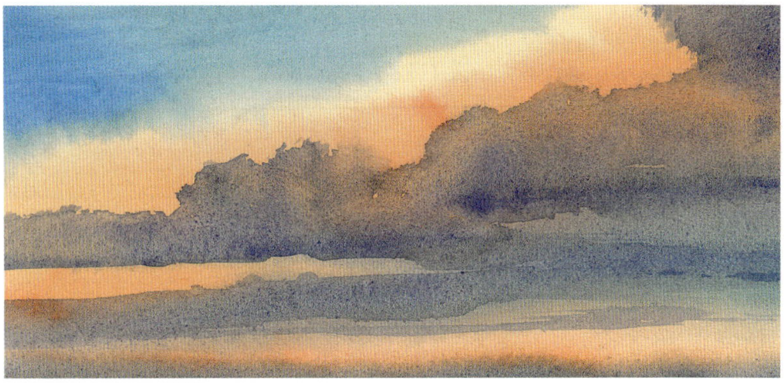

Split brush sky

This ragged-edged sky was created using a split brush technique. To get the hairs to splay out, dab the brush into the mixing tray, then dab it up and down on the paper to create a texture of foliage, or broken cloud. Rotate the brush continually in your hand, to avoid making a repetitive pattern. Avoid having too much paint on the brush, as this will produce large blots of paint. Needless to say, this is not a job for your finest sable, and it is best to reserve a brush specially for the task.

Wet into wet plus layers

This sky was created from a base wash of raw sienna and intense blue, followed by a little alizarin crimson and ultramarine blue, which were brushed on to the wet paper. When dry, the harder-edged clouds were added in alizarin crimson and ultramarine blue.

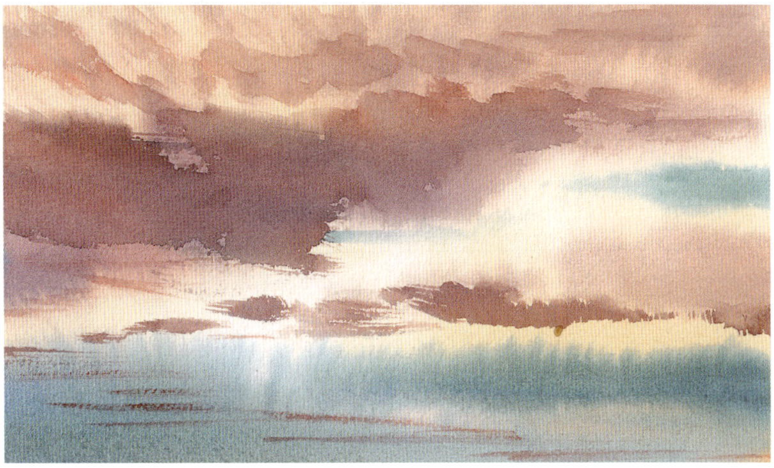

Water

Whether freshwater river, stream or lake, or coastal saltwater, areas of water in your painting are as changeable and varied as the sky. They are also ideally suited to watercolour – though just as with skies, they often require you to work loosely, surrender some control and trust in the paint to work its own magic.

Wet into wet for reflections

Water reflects whatever's above it. This is often the sky, but other shapes such as trees, hills and boats will also appear. Reflections show less contrast in tones than the object they reflect. If an object like a tree leans to the right of the painting, remember that the reflection will also lean to the right.

As this lake is so still, the reflections show more detail than you might expect; but never more than the object itself. The lake and reflections were painted with the same colours as the surroundings, but slightly diluted, and allowed to soften in while wet.

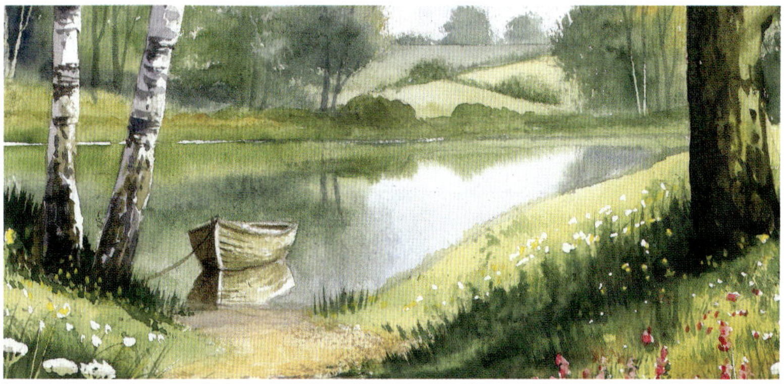

White water with body colour

Moving water crashing over rocks can seem chaotic and intimidating, but it flows in predictable places – look for rocks around which it is breaking to give you a starting point.

Foam and light-toned areas are important to suggest movement and sparkle. These can be retained with masking fluid applied beforehand or, as here, painted on afterwards with titanium white gouache or acrylic.

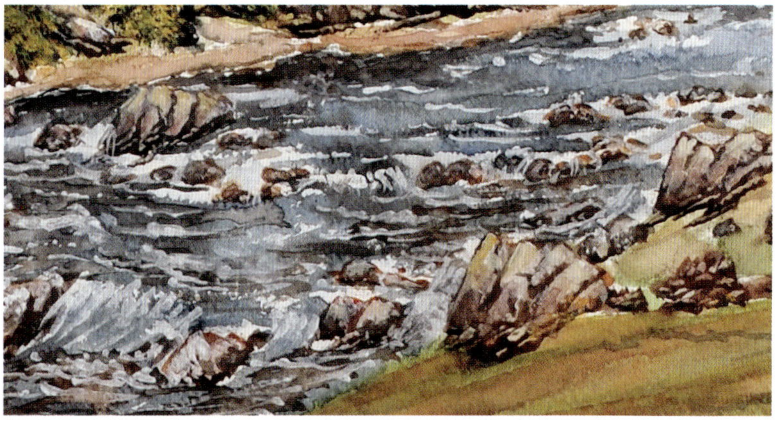

Dry brush for sparkle

The sense of light on water is a big part of the appeal of painting water, and the dry brush technique (see page 14) is a great way to ensure plenty of clean white paper is left showing.

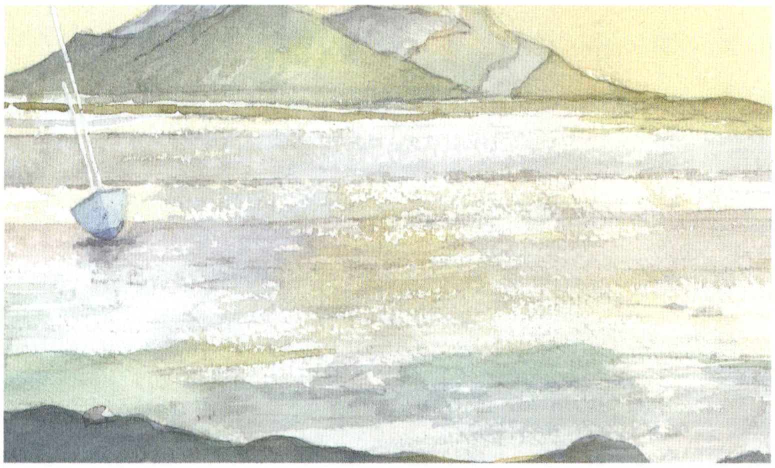

Trees and foliage

Trees are a major component in landscape painting, and are likely to feature in most of the scenes you wish to paint. A winter landscape of trees can be spectacular with all the branches and twigs exposed, and since there is no foliage, a lot more scenery is on show. This all changes in the summer as the landscape becomes draped in green. This is a taxing area for the watercolour painter: large areas of green can look lurid in a painting, so a good deal of sensitivity is required to make it work. Our preconceptions can also get in the way: we automatically think trees are green, and mix colours accordingly.

You will likely find you need to mix less green than you think you need – so if you are mixing viridian and Indian red for a dark shade of foliage, you need add only a little viridian. A few flecks of bright green added later as overpainting may be all that is needed.

It really pays to study previous masters of watercolour to see how they painted this challenging subject; every painter seems to have developed a characteristic style of his or her own.

There are many ways of approaching a subject, and using a variety of techniques, as shown on the opposite page, you can create a range of subtly different qualities.

The split brush technique is well illustrated in this painting, The Spreading Oak. *To form a ragged edge of foliage, the brush tip was splayed out into a number of points and then dabbed gently on to the paper to create the patchwork of leaves.*

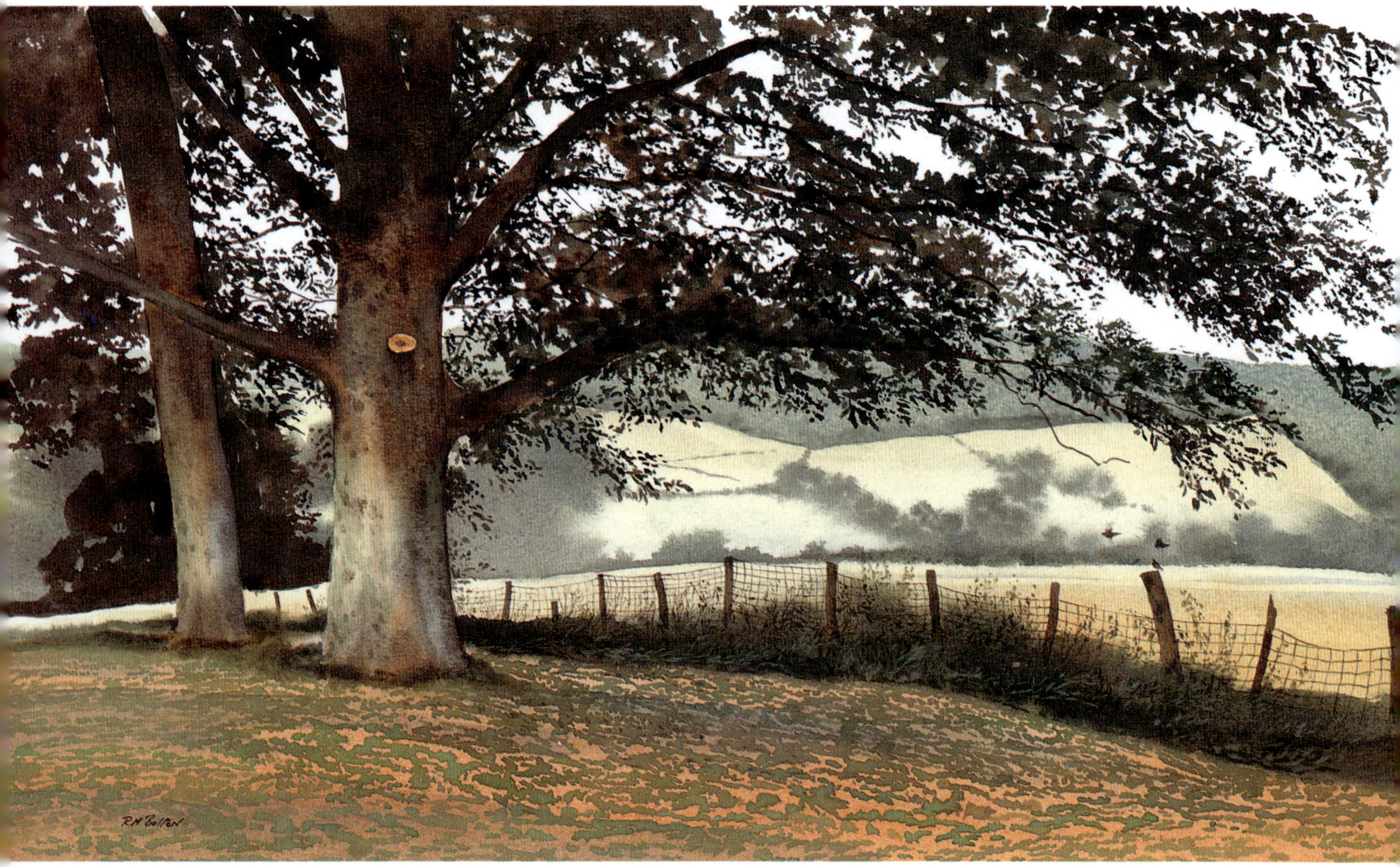

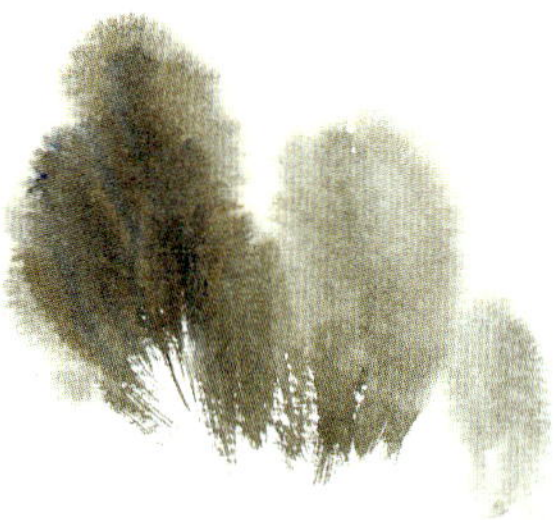

Wet into wet foliage

The wet into wet technique gives a soft, moody quality and works well in the distance and mid-ground. In the foreground, more work is needed to show the build-up of leaves and twigs.

Dry brush foliage

Dry brush is a very effective technique for foliage, and the texture of the paper can be used to give the necessary broken quality.

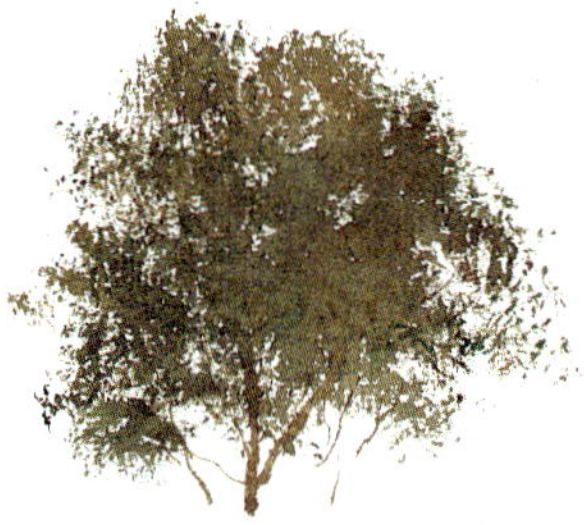

Split brush foliage

The hairs of the brush are splayed out and then dabbed up and down of the surface of the paper, giving a convincing dappled quality to the foliage. Rotate the brush continually in your hand, to avoid making a repetitive pattern, and avoid having too much paint on the brush.

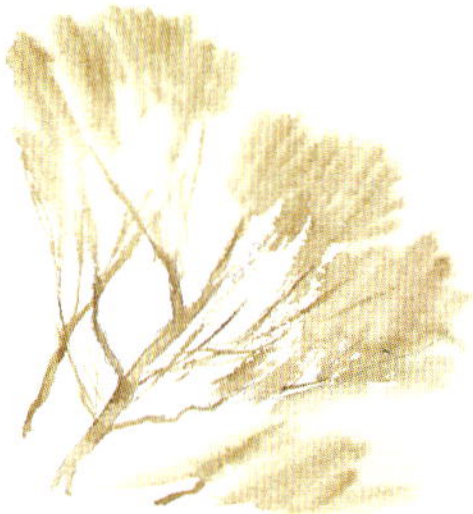

Wet into wet twigs

These twigs have been suggested by the wet into wet technique, which can be very effective.

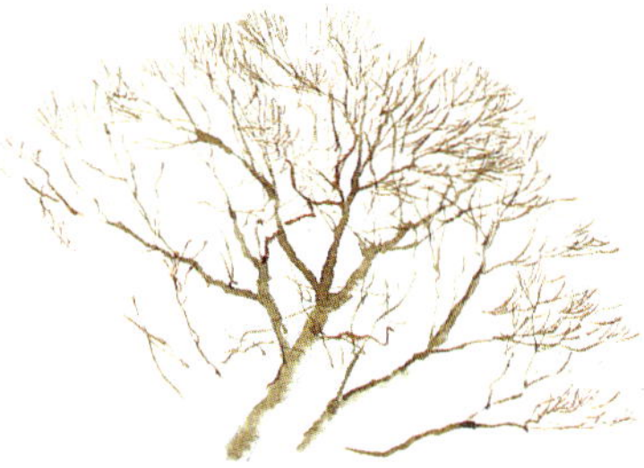

Twigs with a rigger

A very fine brush can be used to paint in all the detail of twigs. The rigger brush can be very useful in this area, and its long hairs are excellent for lots of sweeping, thin lines.

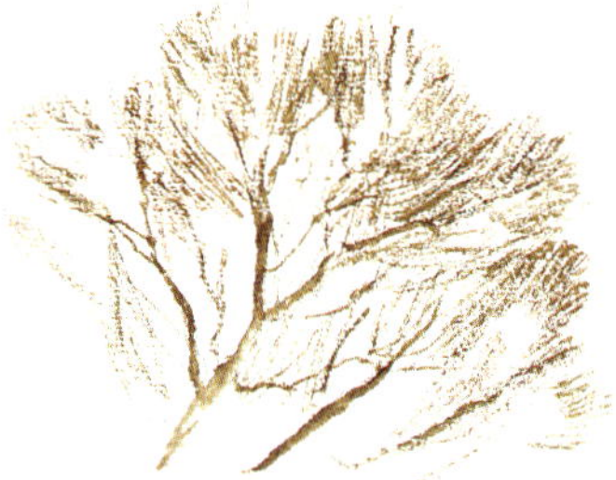

Dry brush twigs

A less time-consuming way to paint twigs is with the dry brush technique. You have to be sure that all excess paint has been removed from the brush before painting, as a mistake here could be costly.

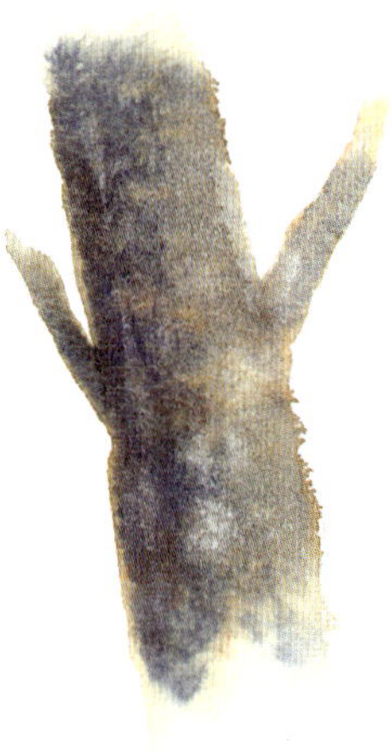

Wet into wet trunk

Colours have been dropped into the initial wash on this trunk wet into wet, to give a suitably mottled look.

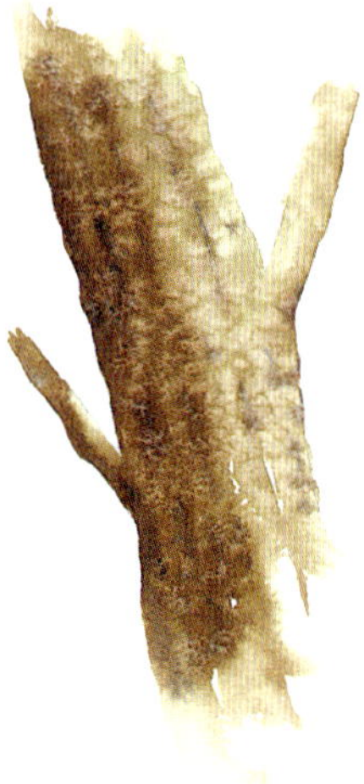

Salt on trunks

Create a textural quality by sprinkling salt on to wet paint. Here you can see the dappled effect this technique produces in a mix of sap green and burnt sienna.

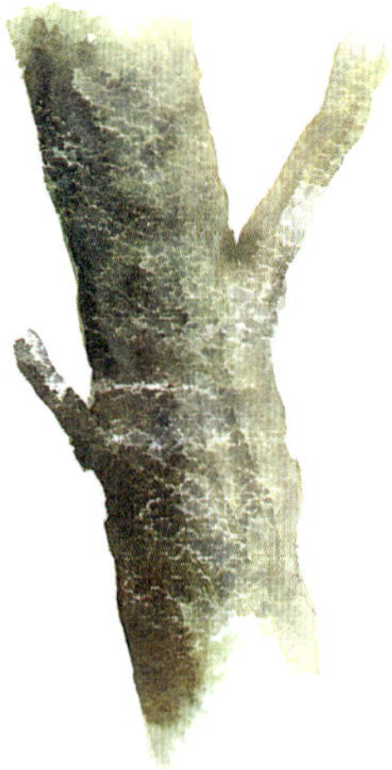

Wax resist for trunks

Candle wax works well to impart a textured look. Rub the candle on the paper before painting, and the wax works as a resist.

Country scenes

Terry Harrison

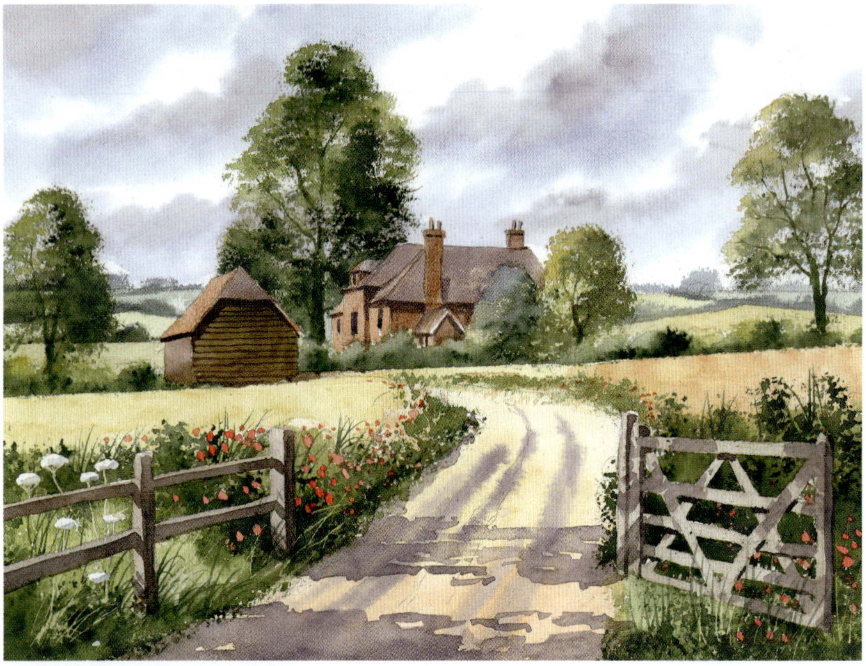

The Open Gate, page 22

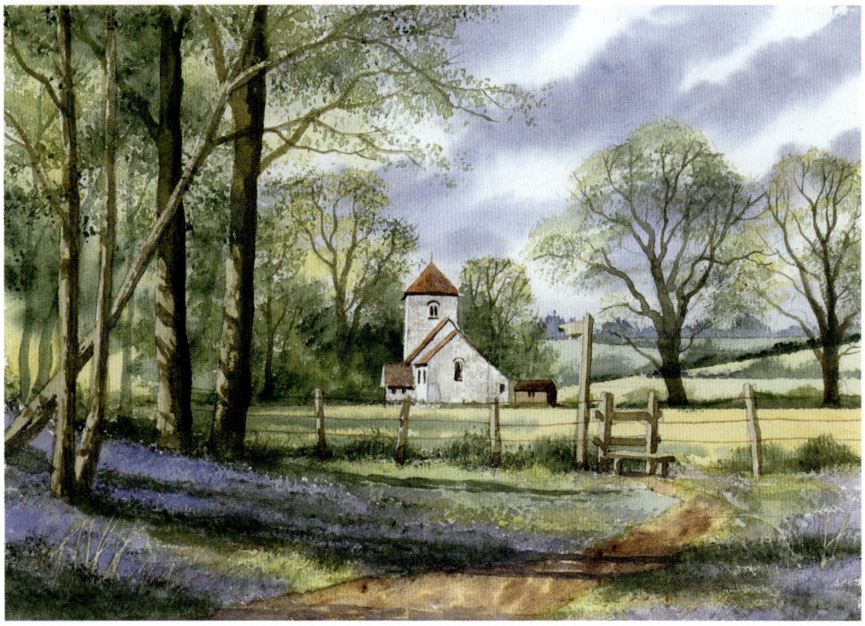

The Short Cut, page 24

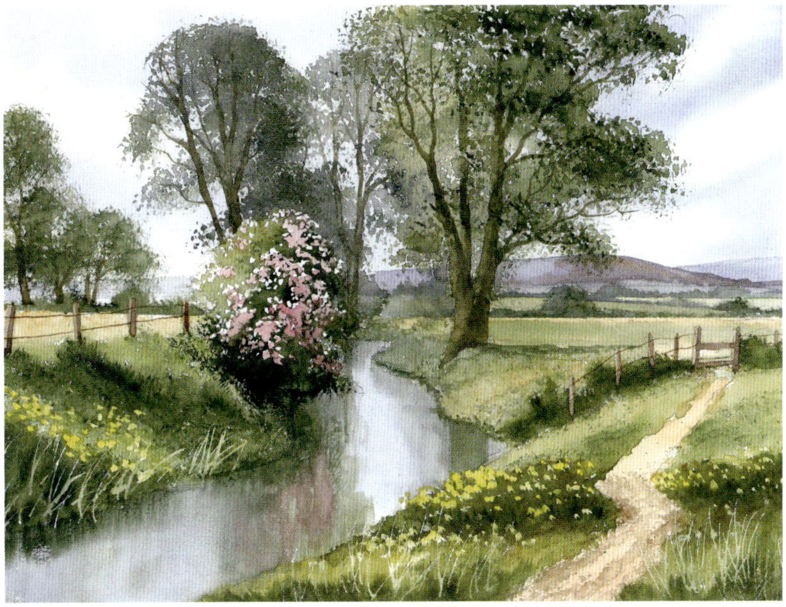

Blossom Meadow, page 26

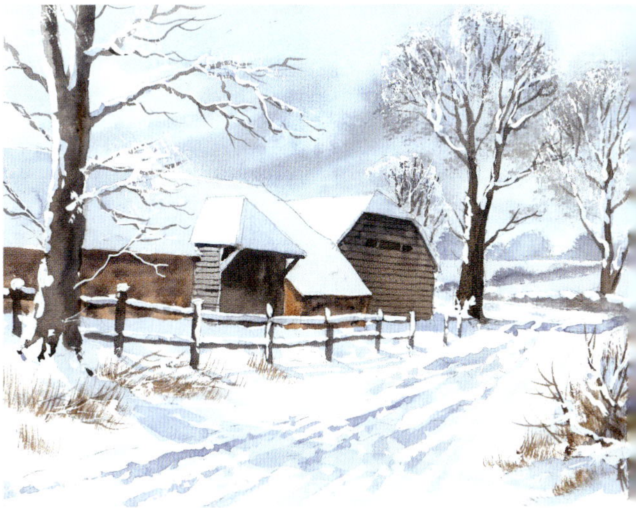

Snow Tracks, page 28

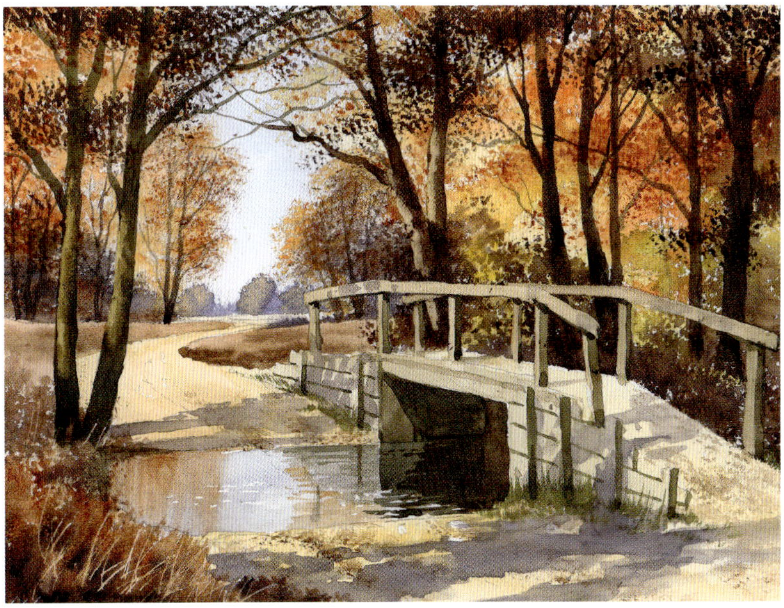

New Forest Bridge, page 30

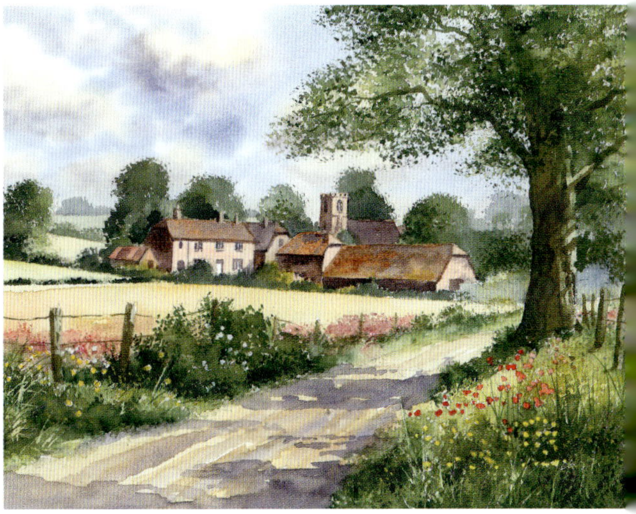

Over the Hedgerow, page 32

The Open Gate

If you are looking for a subject to fill the foreground and lead the viewer into a painting, an open gate is ideal. A stile is another way of inviting the viewer to venture further into a painting. This summer landscape gives you an opportunity to use a paper mask to protect the ground while you paint distant trees and hedgerows with a stippling technique: repeatedly tapping the surface with the brush to apply paint in loose shapes. When you lift away the paper mask, you'll find a nice clean line beneath the hedge (see page 26 for more). The trees in the middle distance frame the farmhouse and are painted using the golden leaf brush, a large brush with a mix of soft and stiff hairs.

Palette of colours

- French ultramarine
- Burnt umber
- Raw sienna
- Burnt sienna
- Shadow
- Midnight green
- Cobalt blue
- Country olive
- Sunlit green
- Cadmium red

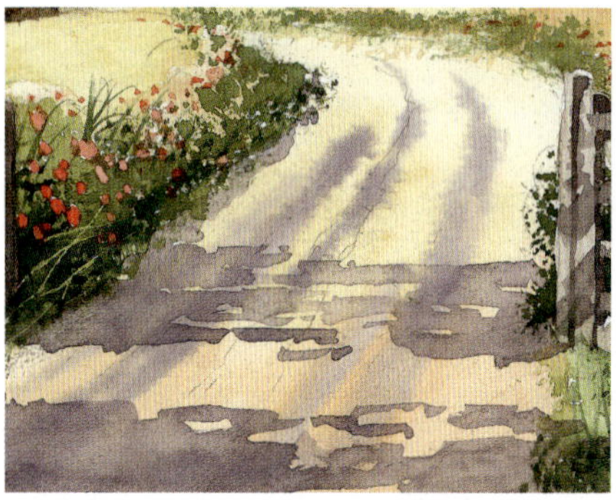

Having a road in the centre of the painting leads you towards the focal point, but it could divide the composition into two halves. To overcome this, place some shadows across the road at the bottom of the painting. This will link one side with the other and help to frame the painting.

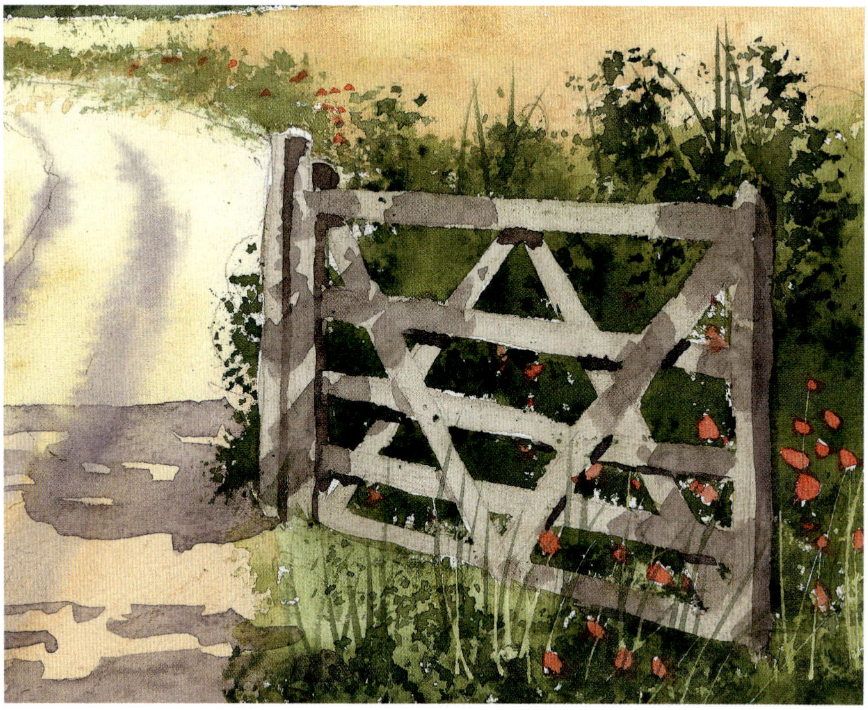

The woodwork of the fence and the gate in the foreground is masked with masking fluid, and the greens behind the fence and gate are painted very dark, so that when the masking fluid is removed, a strong contrast is created. The lighter detail stands out from the dark background.

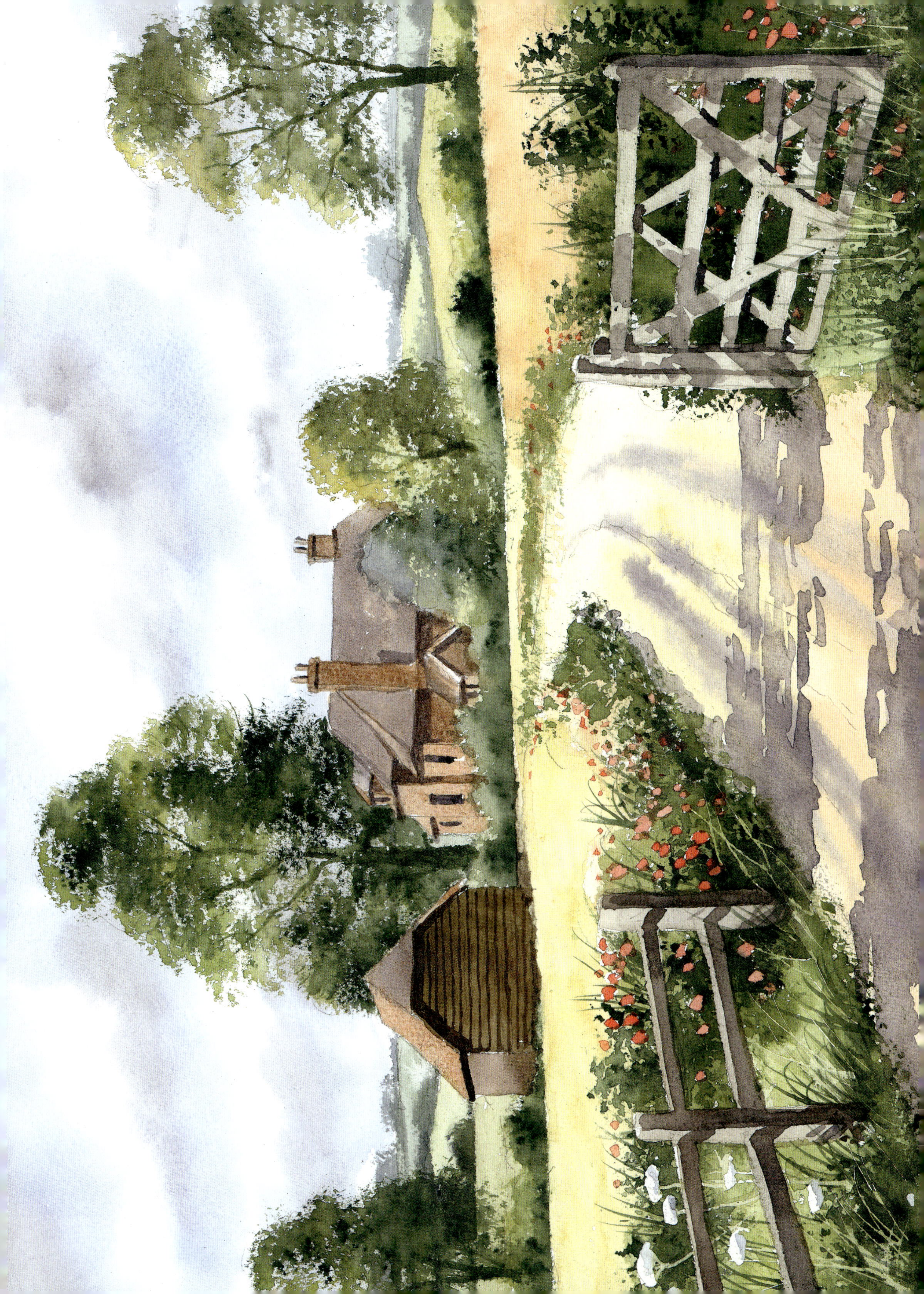

OUTLINE 2

The Short Cut

This is a very simple but effective composition. The church is the focal point and this is framed by the large trees in the foreground on the left, with the bluebells and shadows running horizontally along the bottom of the painting and the tree on the right completing the frame. The stile and signpost guide the viewer into the painting, and the footpath leads you through the stile and beyond. If you are in any doubt which way to go, just follow the signpost!

Palette of colours

- French ultramarine
- Burnt umber
- Raw sienna
- Sunlit green
- Midnight green
- Cobalt blue
- Country olive
- Permanent rose

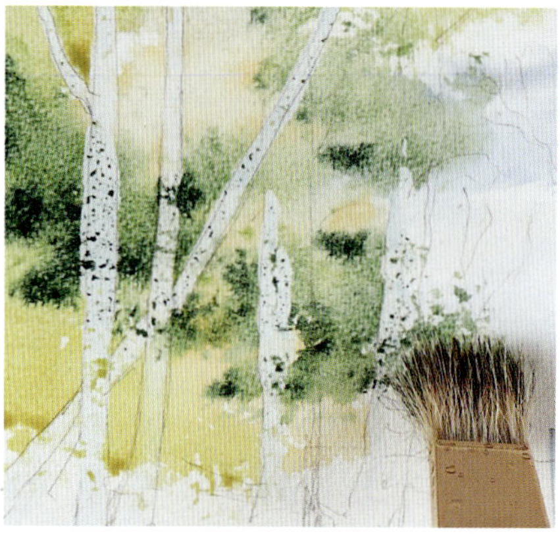

Applying masking fluid to the tree trunks before you apply the stippled colour helps to retain the light and shade and gives the impression of a bright, sunny spring day.

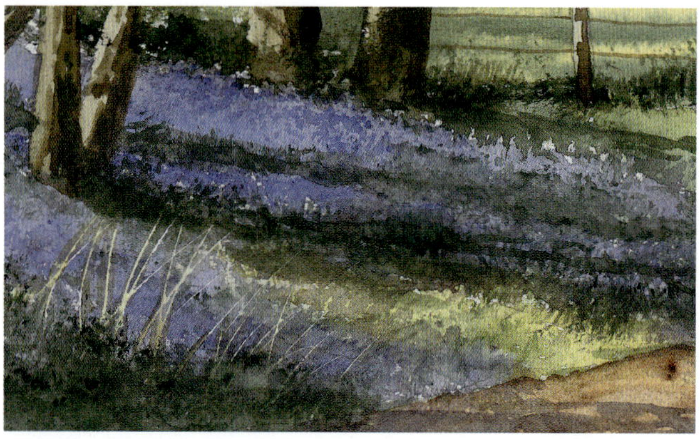

Contrast is important in this scene; particularly on the woodland floor. The bluebells are stippled on in layers, using light-toned mixes of cobalt blue and permanent rose. Once dry, darker midnight green is stippled on. The light grasses are masked out early on, and removed once the bluebells and greenery are established. You can then wash over the area with pale sunlit green.

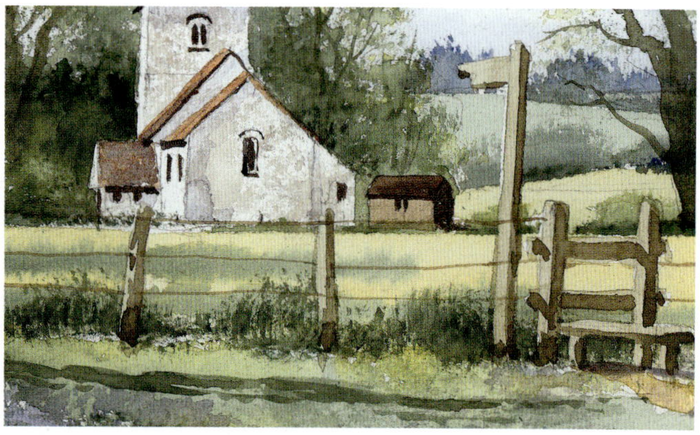

The fence posts, signpost and stile are painted with a pale mix of country olive and burnt umber – the lit parts of the foreground trees are painted with the same mix. Once dry, use a darker mix of country olive and burnt umber to add shade to the right-hand sides of the fenceposts, sign, stile and trees – you can use the same mix to add more branches, too.

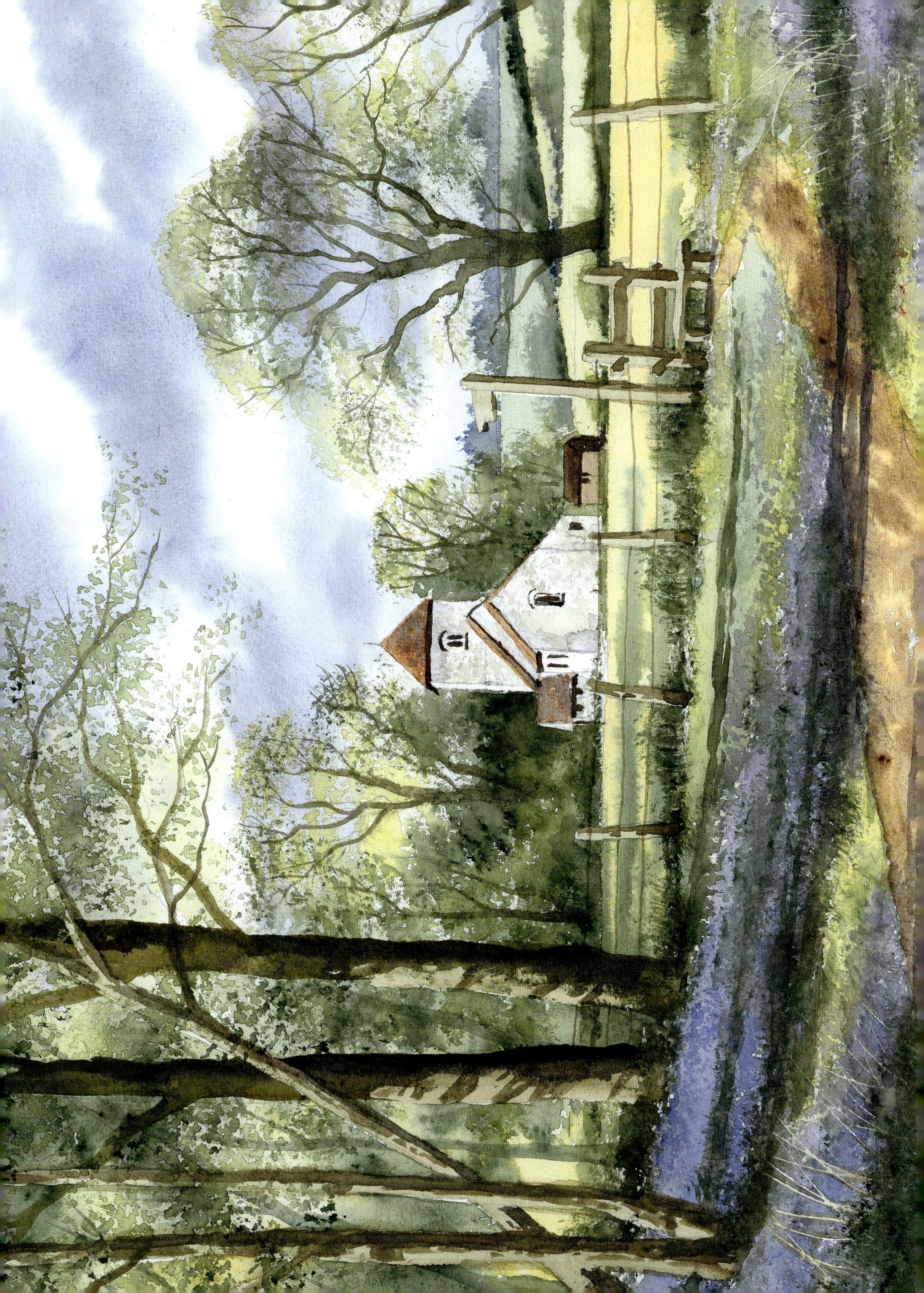

Blossom Meadow

This riverside footpath reminds me of many treks along riverbanks, looking for a subject to paint. Here, I was suddenly treated to a scene that has everything I look for in a painting. The tree in blossom is the focal point, and the lazy river leads you into the painting and the distant meadows with a glimpse of the faraway hills beyond.

This project gives you the opportunity to create distance in a painting with plenty of light bluey tones for the faraway trees and hedgerows, and the pale, soft shades of the hills on the horizon.

Palette of colours

- French ultramarine
- Raw sienna
- Burnt sienna
- Cobalt blue
- Midnight green
- Sunlit green
- Country olive
- Burnt umber
- Cadmium yellow
- Permanent rose

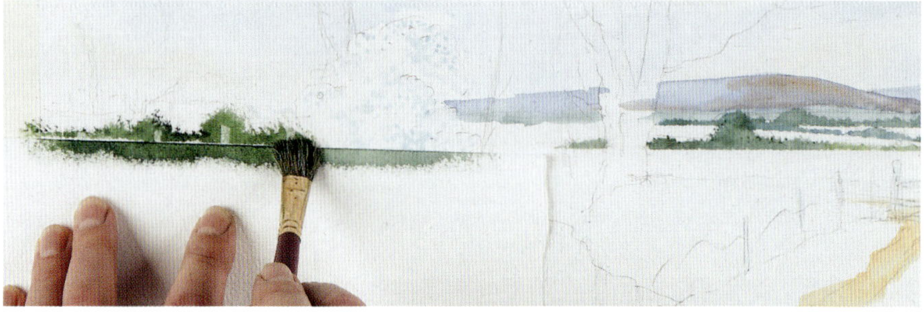

There are lots of different ways to mask your work and protect areas of the surface. As well as the masking fluid used on the blossom and foreground flowers and grasses, a clean sheet of paper can be used to mask the ground beneath hedgerows, as shown. Stipple over the top, and when the paper mask is removed, you'll find a clean line beneath.

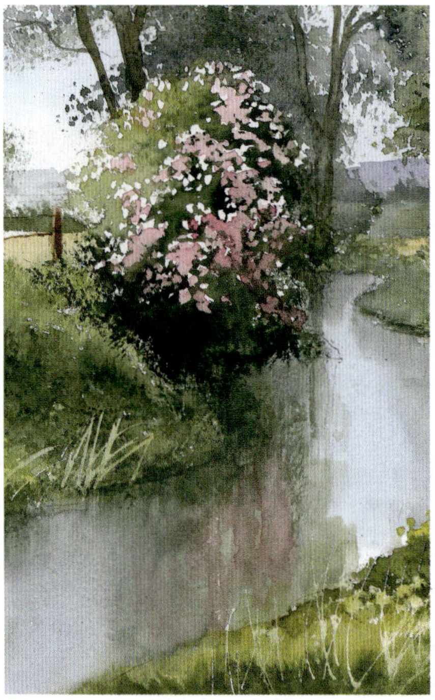

The blossoms need to be masked out at the start of the painting, and the tree painted around them. Once dry, the masking fluid can be removed, and the flowers added with permanent rose wet on dry. The river is painted with cobalt blue, and the reflection of the tree added with downward strokes of country olive. Touches of permanent rose are then added wet into wet.

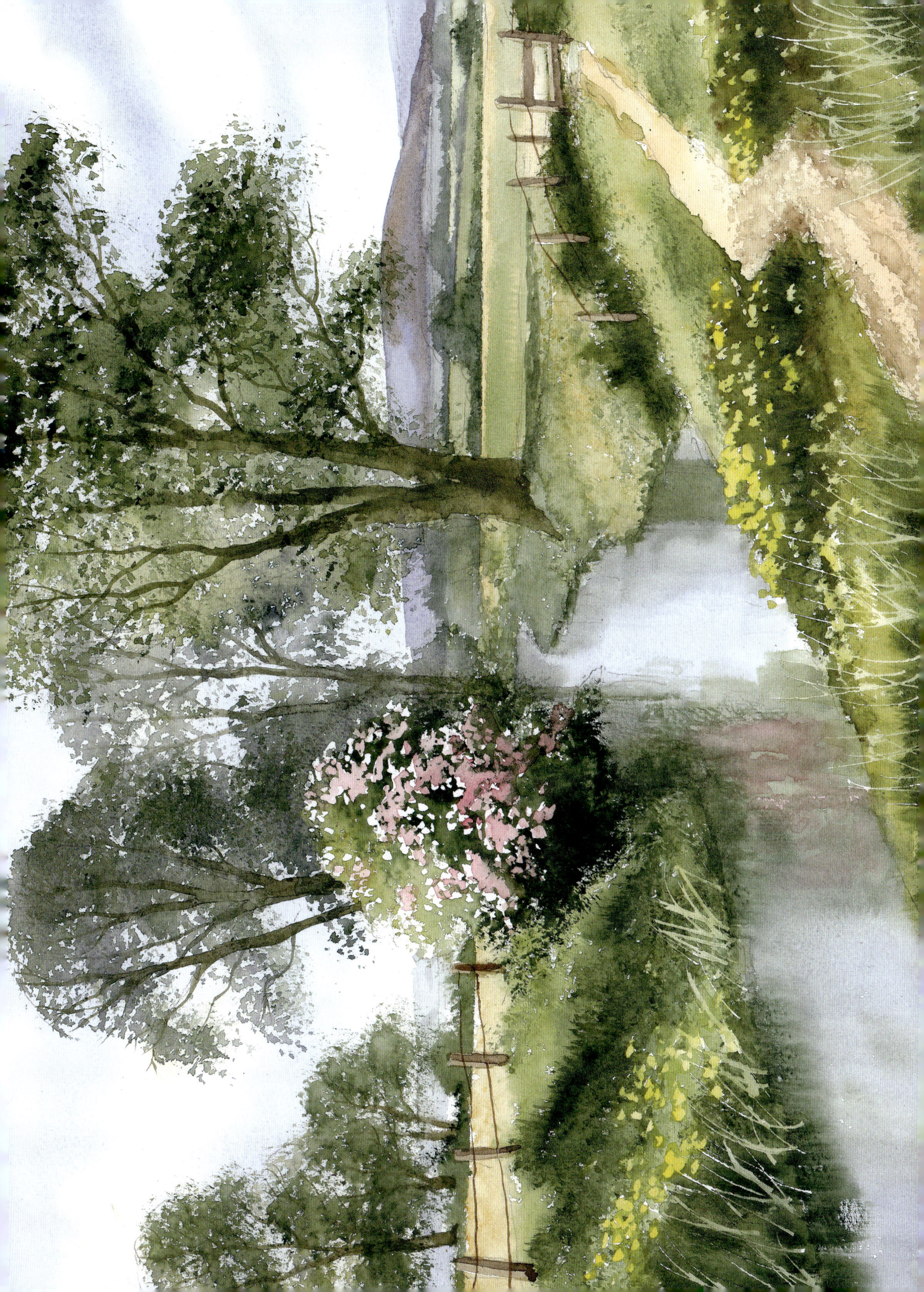

Snow Tracks

Masking fluid is a perfect medium to use when painting snow scenes, but care must be taken when applying it, as it dries very quickly and can ruin your brushes. Use a synthetic brush for masking fluid and run it over a bar of soap before loading it with masking fluid. This will protect the bristles from getting clogged. Rinse the brush thoroughly immediately after use.

If you fancy painting this scene as a summer landscape, as seen on page 10, you can use the colours and techniques used in the *Open Gate* project on page 22.

Palette of colours

- French ultramarine
- Burnt umber
- Burnt sienna
- Shadow
- Cobalt blue

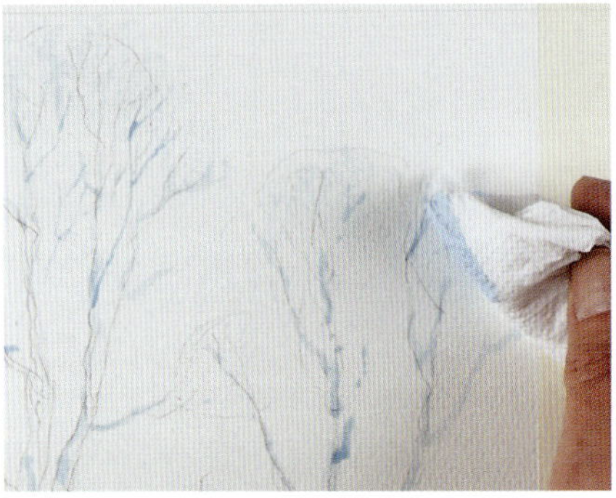

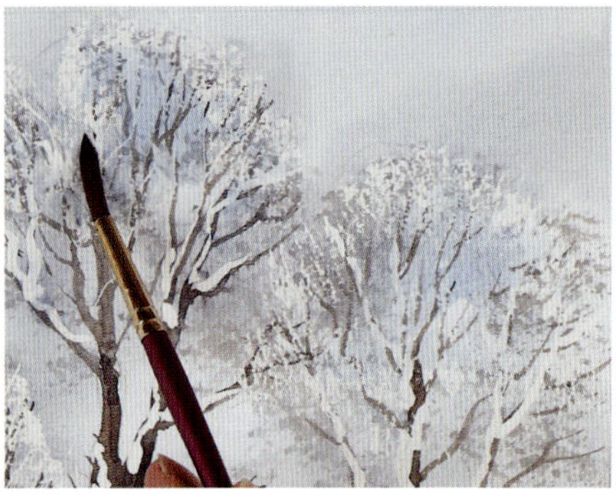

The dusting of snow on the trees is achieved by making a pad of kitchen paper, dipping it into some masking fluid, then very lightly tapping it over the trees. Practise this before starting the painting, and if it is not quite right on your first attempt, wait for it to dry, rub it off, then start again. You can then paint the sky with a wash of ultramarine and, once dry, lightly stipple winter foliage over the top using a fairly blue mix of ultramarine and burnt umber. At the end of the painting, remove the masking fluid, then paint a wash of cobalt blue over the snow, leaving white at the top.

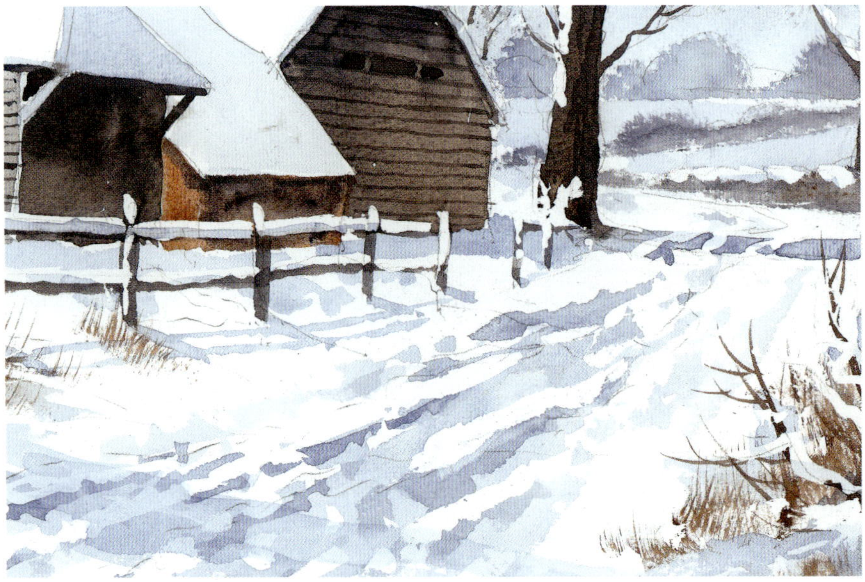

The contrast between the snow and buildings is what gives this painting such impact. The brightest white is the paper itself, while the snow shadows are pale mixes of cobalt blue with a touch of burnt sienna. A mix of ultramarine and burnt umber was used for the dark buildings.

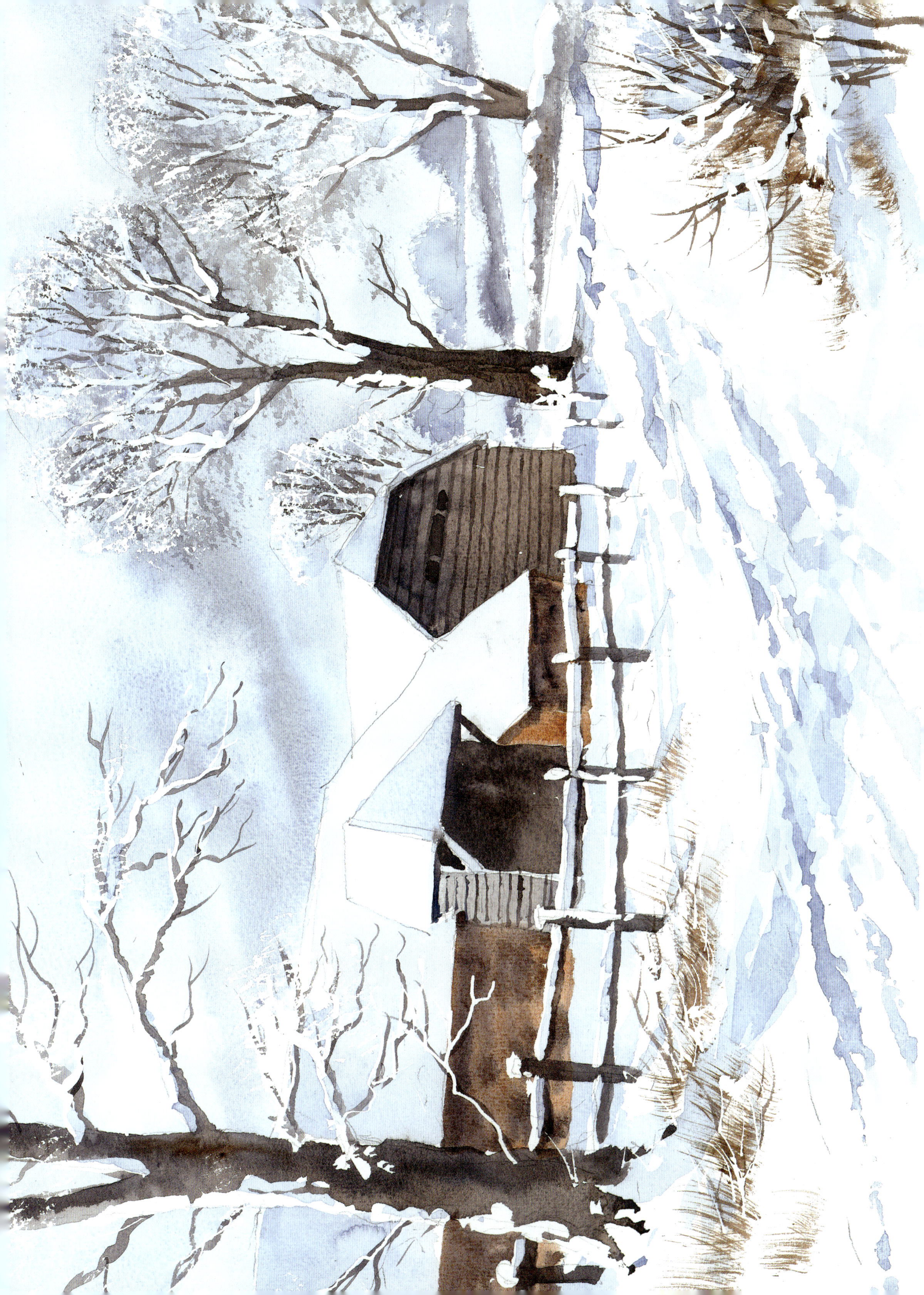

New Forest Bridge

Autumn in the New Forest, UK, is a magical time of year; the colours are amazing. This footbridge was in a part of the forest called Pig's Bush, which is an unfortunate name for such a beautiful location. The bridge has recently been replaced with a newer version, but the original is a much more appealing subject to paint.

This scene can easily be transformed into a summer landscape by using greens for the foliage: sunlit green replaces the gold colours, country olive replaces the reds, and midnight green is a substitute for the dark browns.

Palette of colours

- French ultramarine
- Cadmium yellow
- Raw sienna
- Cadmium red
- Cobalt blue
- Alizarin crimson
- Burnt sienna
- Sunlit green
- Burnt umber
- Country olive
- Shadow

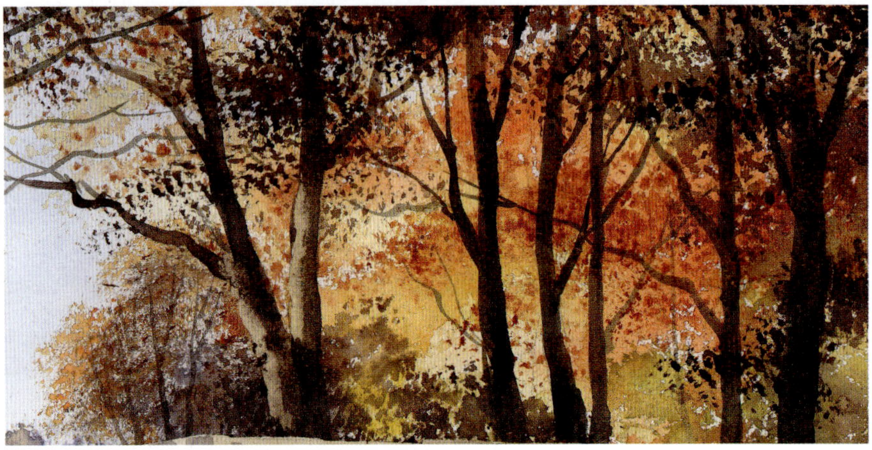

Most of the tree trunks are quite dark and are silhouetted against the golds and light reds of the foliage background. They are painted with a dark mix of ultramarine and burnt umber, with country olive added for areas in the light.

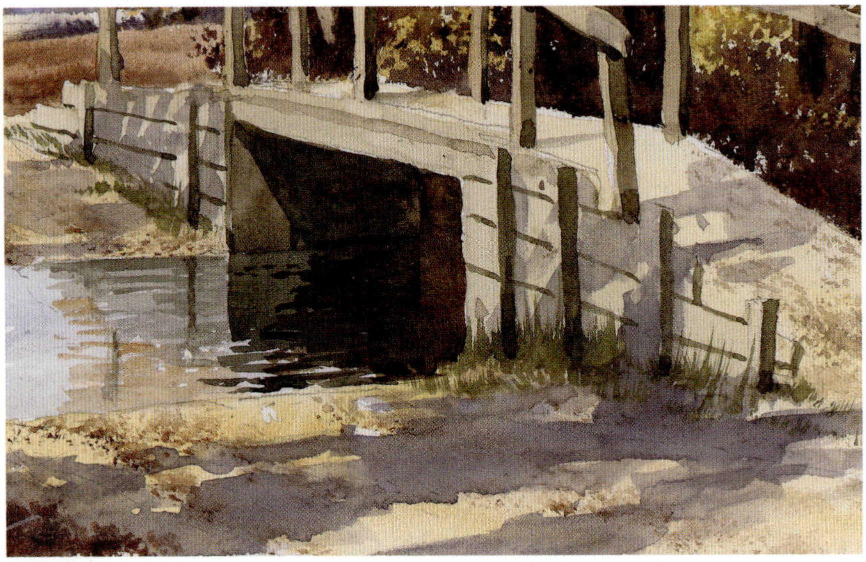

The shadow across the track at the bottom of the painting – painted, appropriately enough, with shadow – helps to frame the focal point of the bridge.

The water is painted with very pale ultramarine, while the reflection of the bridge is painted in two layers: firstly with an ultramarine, burnt umber and country olive mix, and secondly with a layer of burnt umber and ultramarine.

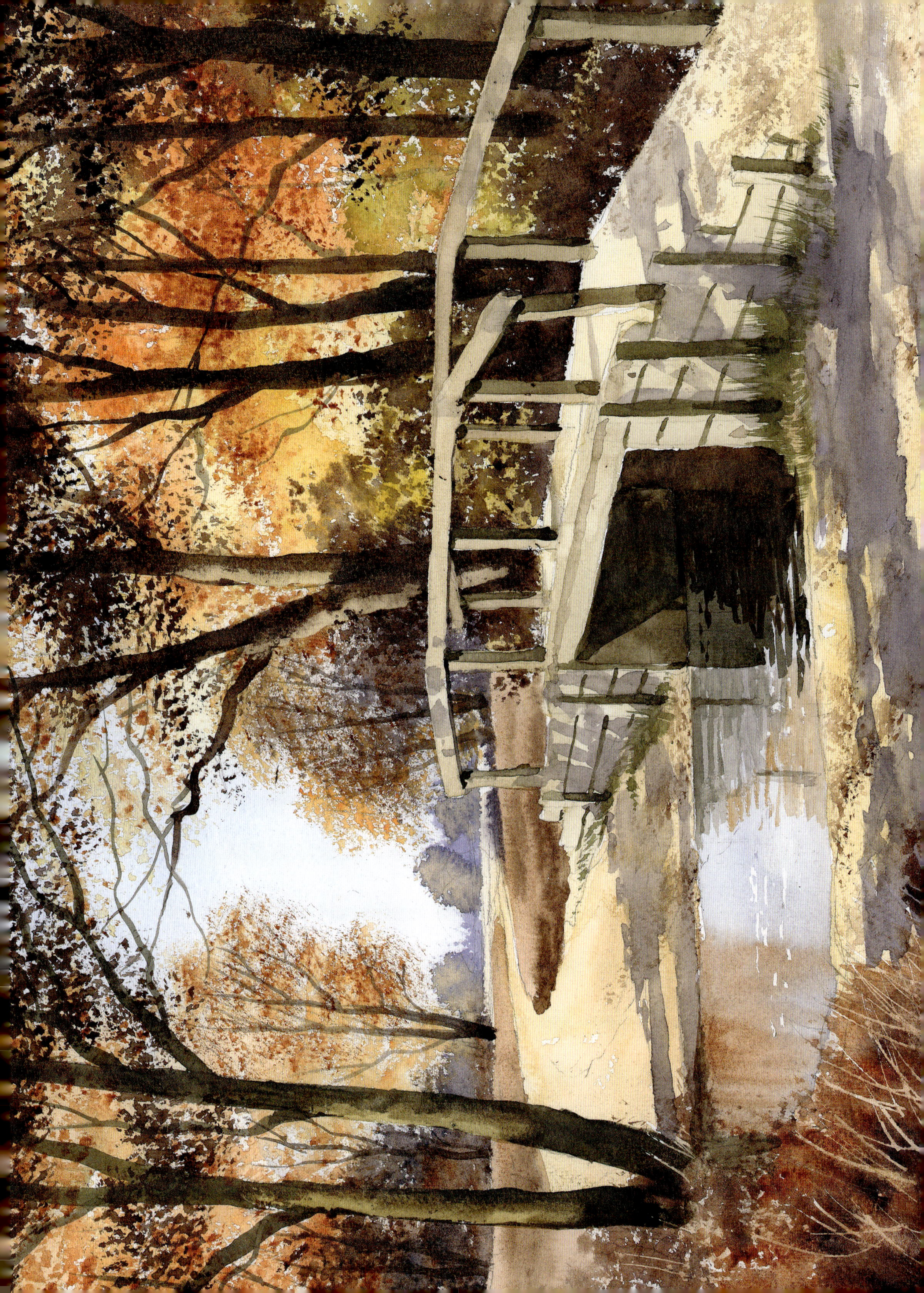

Over the Hedgerow

OUTLINE 6

This distant village scene with rustic buildings clustered around the church is framed by the overhanging tree and the shadow it casts over the road. Bathed in bright sunlight are a host of summer flowers that add colour and warmth to this fabulous country view.

Palette of colours

- French ultramarine
- Burnt umber
- Raw sienna
- Burnt sienna
- Shadow
- Midnight green
- Cobalt blue
- Country olive
- Sunlit green
- Cadmium red
- Cadmium yellow

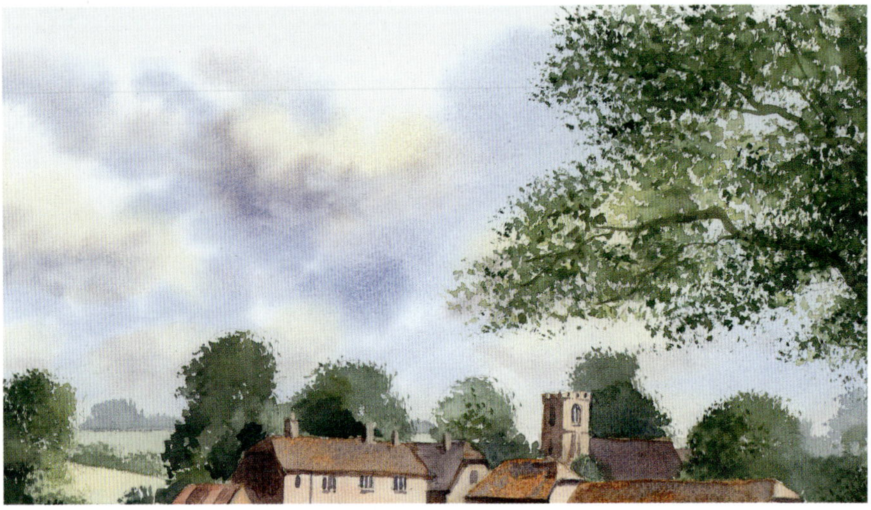

The sky was painted with pale French ultramarine, with a touch of burnt umber added for cloud shadows. A hint of raw sienna adds some warmth. Once dry, the foliage can be added with stippling, starting with country olive and with midnight green for the shaded areas.

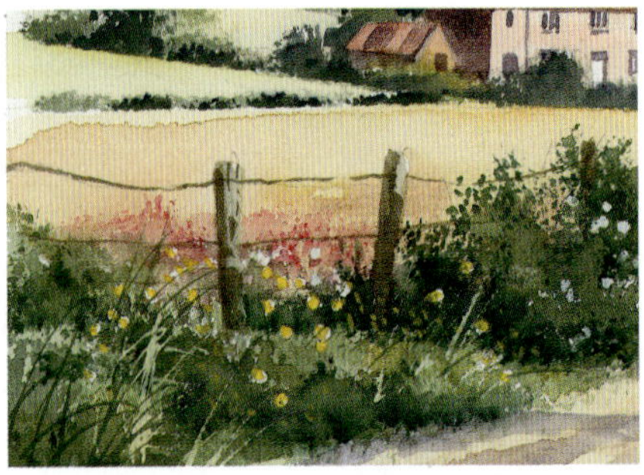

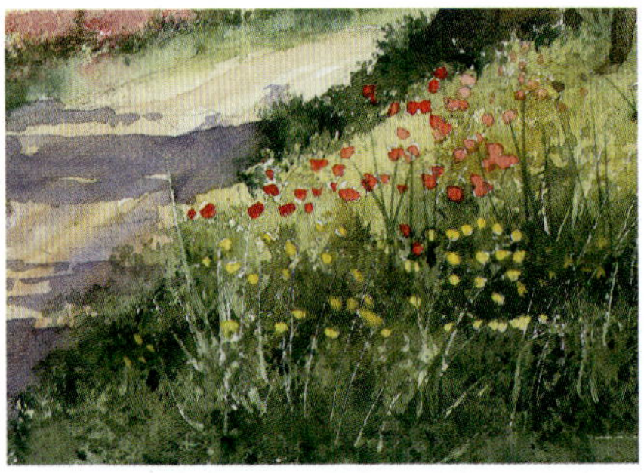

The flowers add a splash of warmth and colour to the scene. The distant poppies in the raw sienna field (above left) are painted wet into wet with cadmium red, while the foreground flowers are masked out and added near the end of the painting with cadmium red and cadmium yellow.

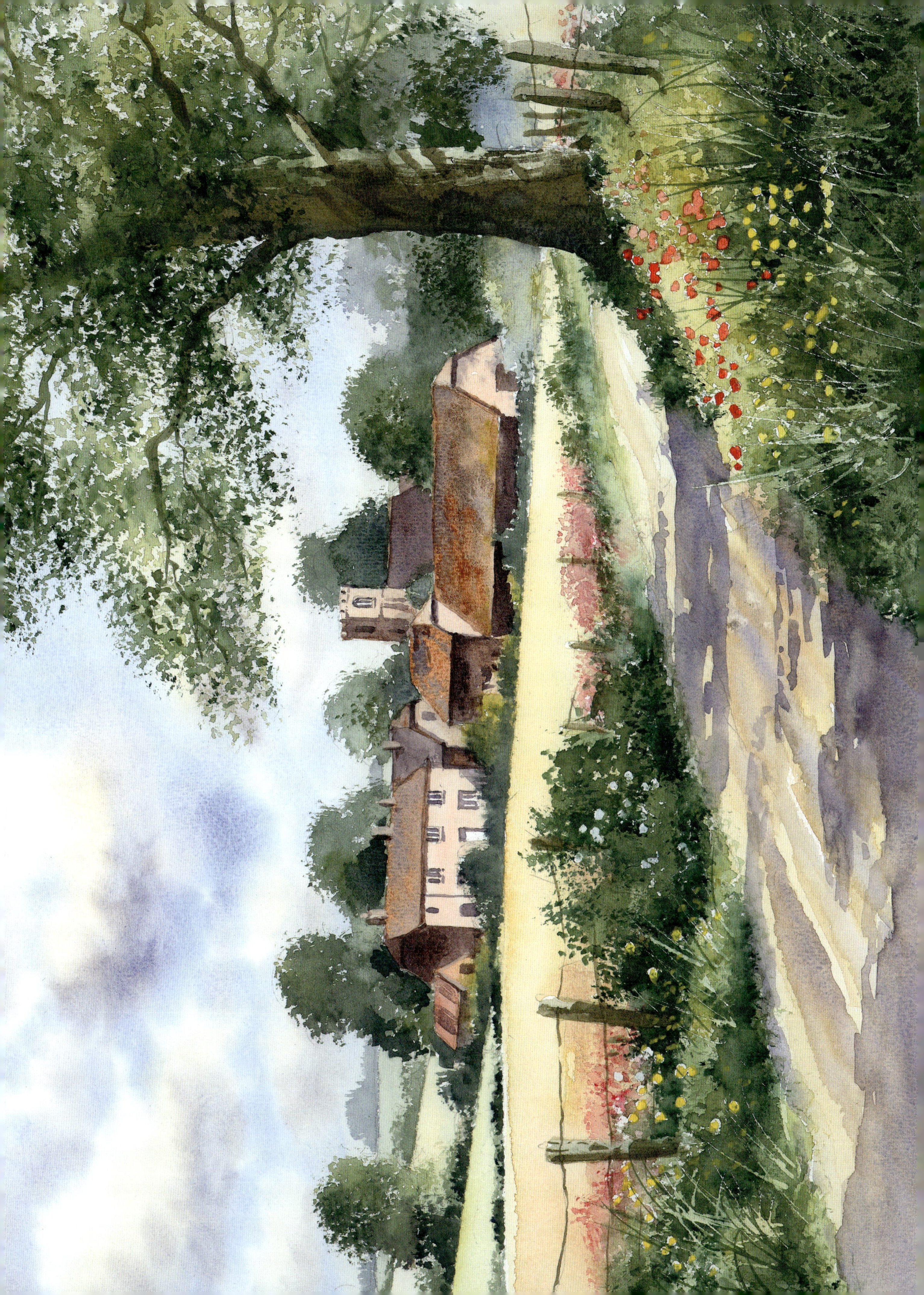

Hills and mountains

Arnold Lowrey

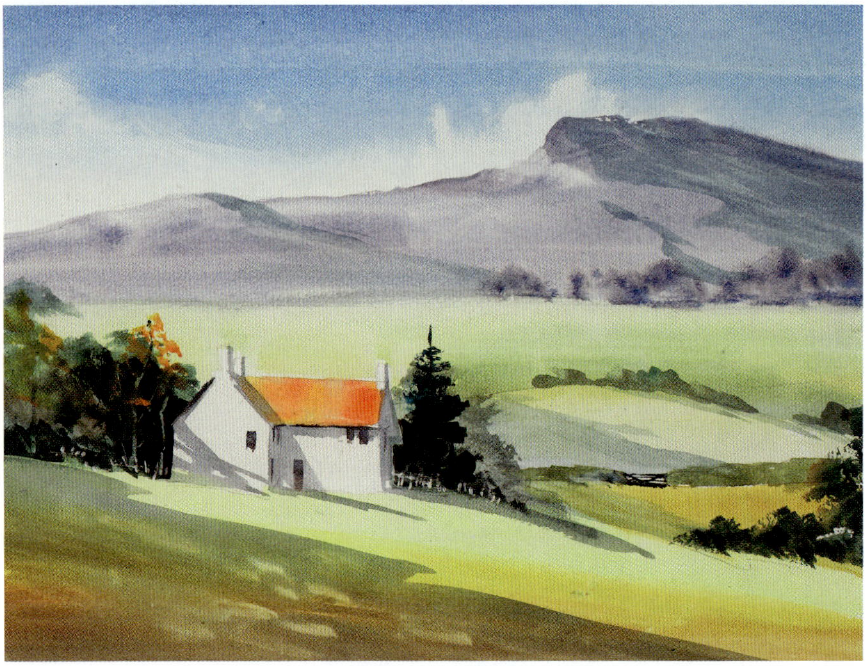

Distant Hills, page 36

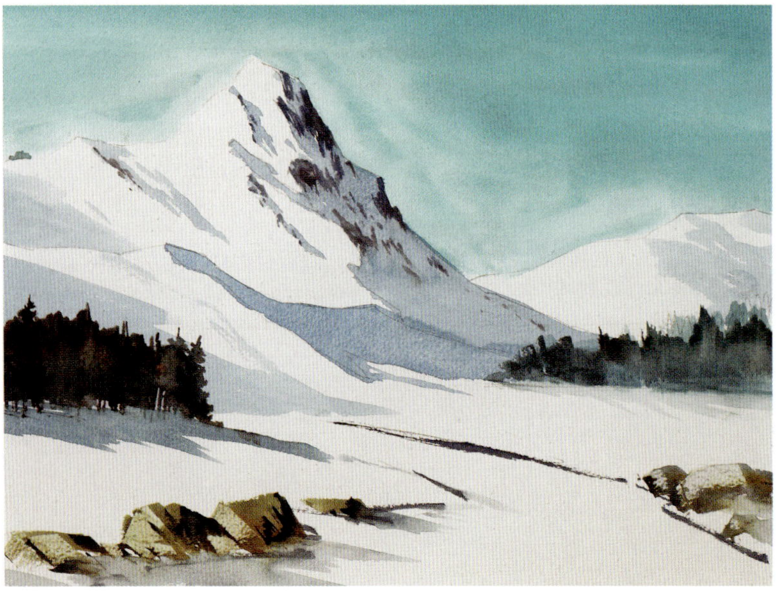

Alpine Scene, page 38

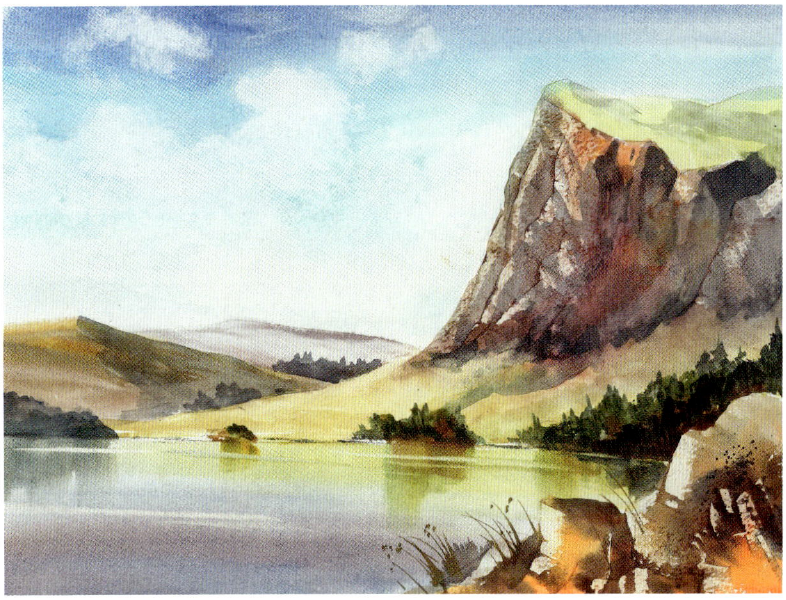

Water's Edge, page 40

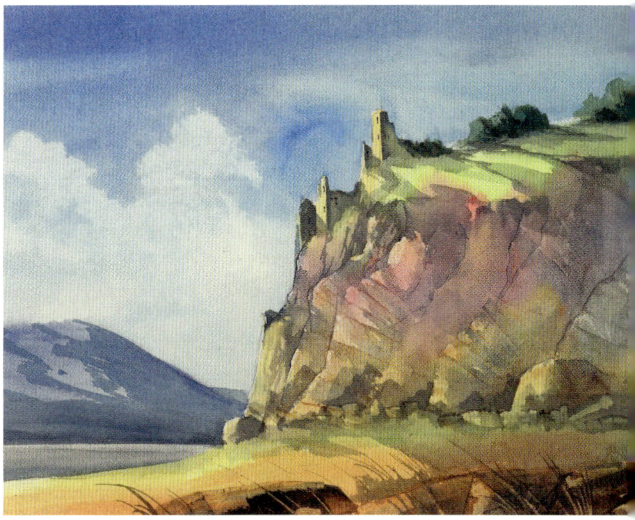

Castle on the Cliffs, page 42

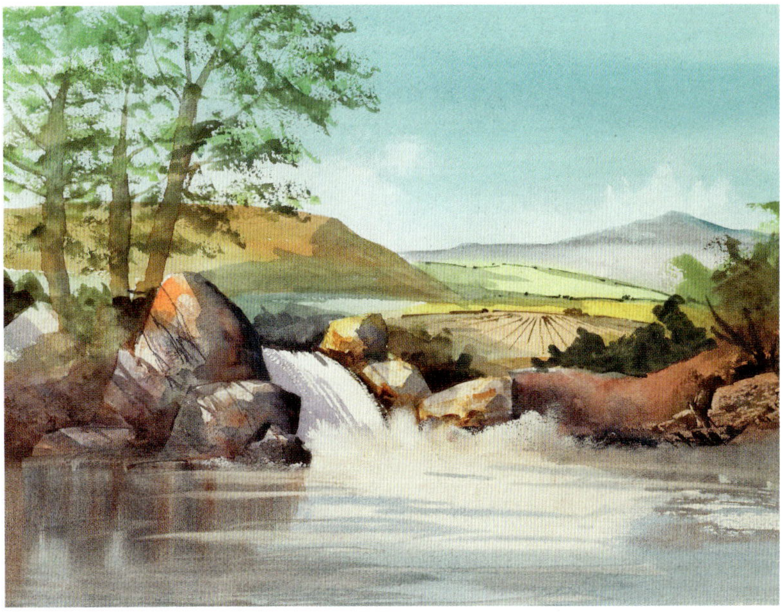

Mountain Stream, page 44

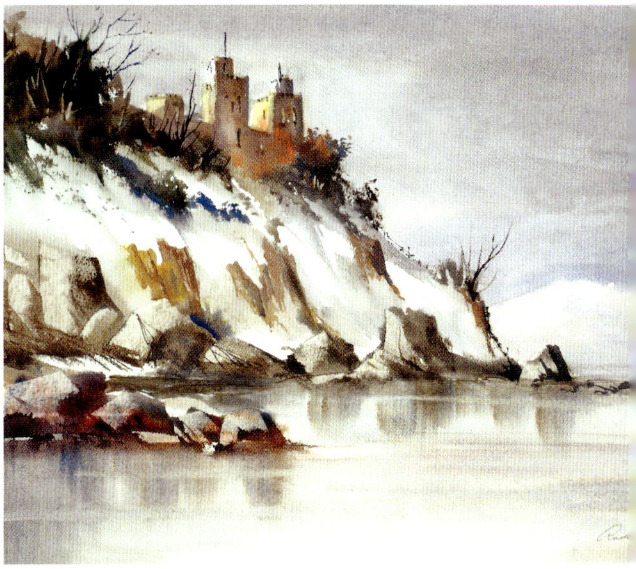

Castle, page 46

Distant Hills

OUTLINE 7

In this painting I have tried to portray a huge expanse of land with hills in the distance. The sunlight is coming from the left so I have painted the shadows accordingly, putting some dark trees against the house to make it appear more sunlit.

Palette of colours

- Cadmium scarlet
- Cobalt blue
- French ultramarine
- Cadmium lemon
- New gamboge
- Winsor blue (green shade)
- Burnt umber
- Burnt sienna
- Permanent rose
- Titanium white

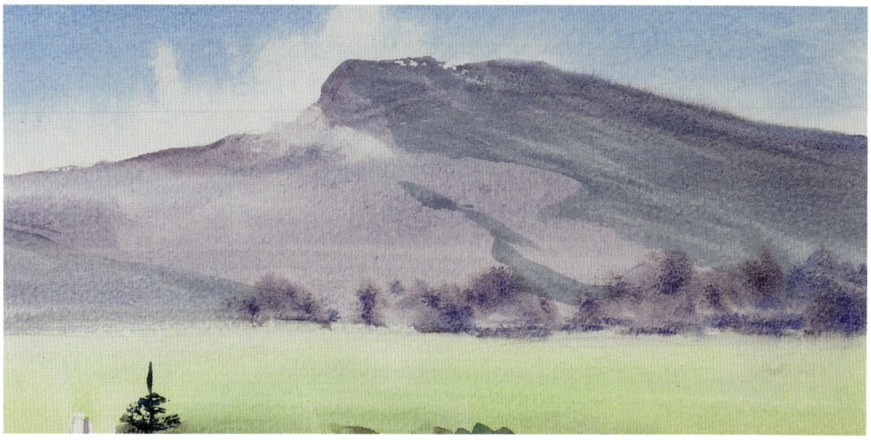

A 25mm (1in) flat brush can be used for the cobalt blue wash in the sky, and also to paint the distant hills with a mix of French ultramarine with a touch of cadmium scarlet. Lay in this blue mid-tone over the peak of the hill, blending it out to a paler tone towards its base. Using a stronger version of the same mix, put in the forest at the foot of the hill on the right. Use the side of the brush to paint in the shape of the forest rather than the individual trees.

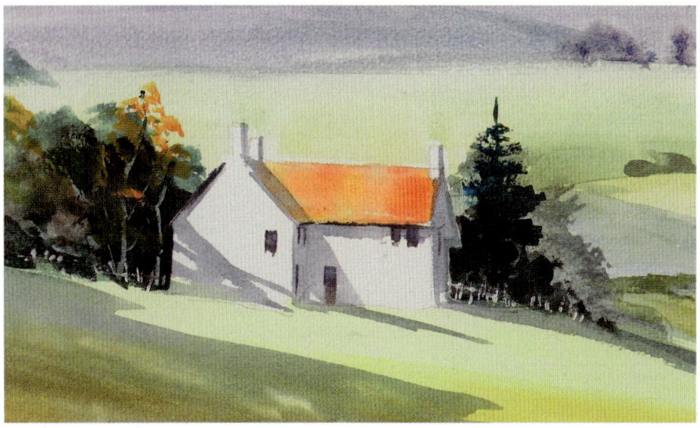

Placing the house in the foreground accentuates the scale of the landscape. The strength of tone and detail in the house and trees adds to the contrast with the pale, soft hills, making them seem further away.

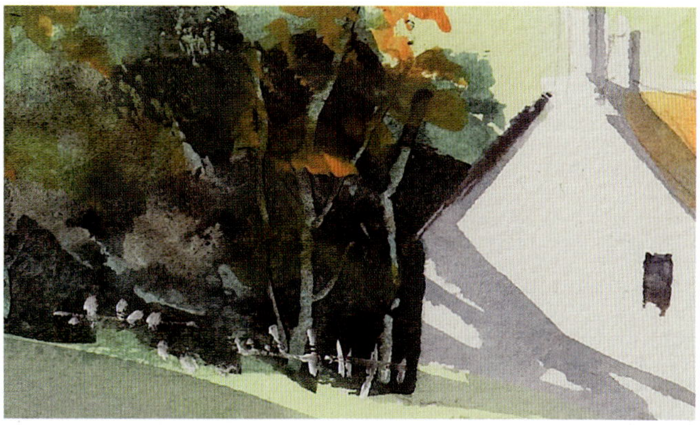

While the paint is still wet, you can use the end of a brush to scrape out the shapes of the tree trunks and branches.

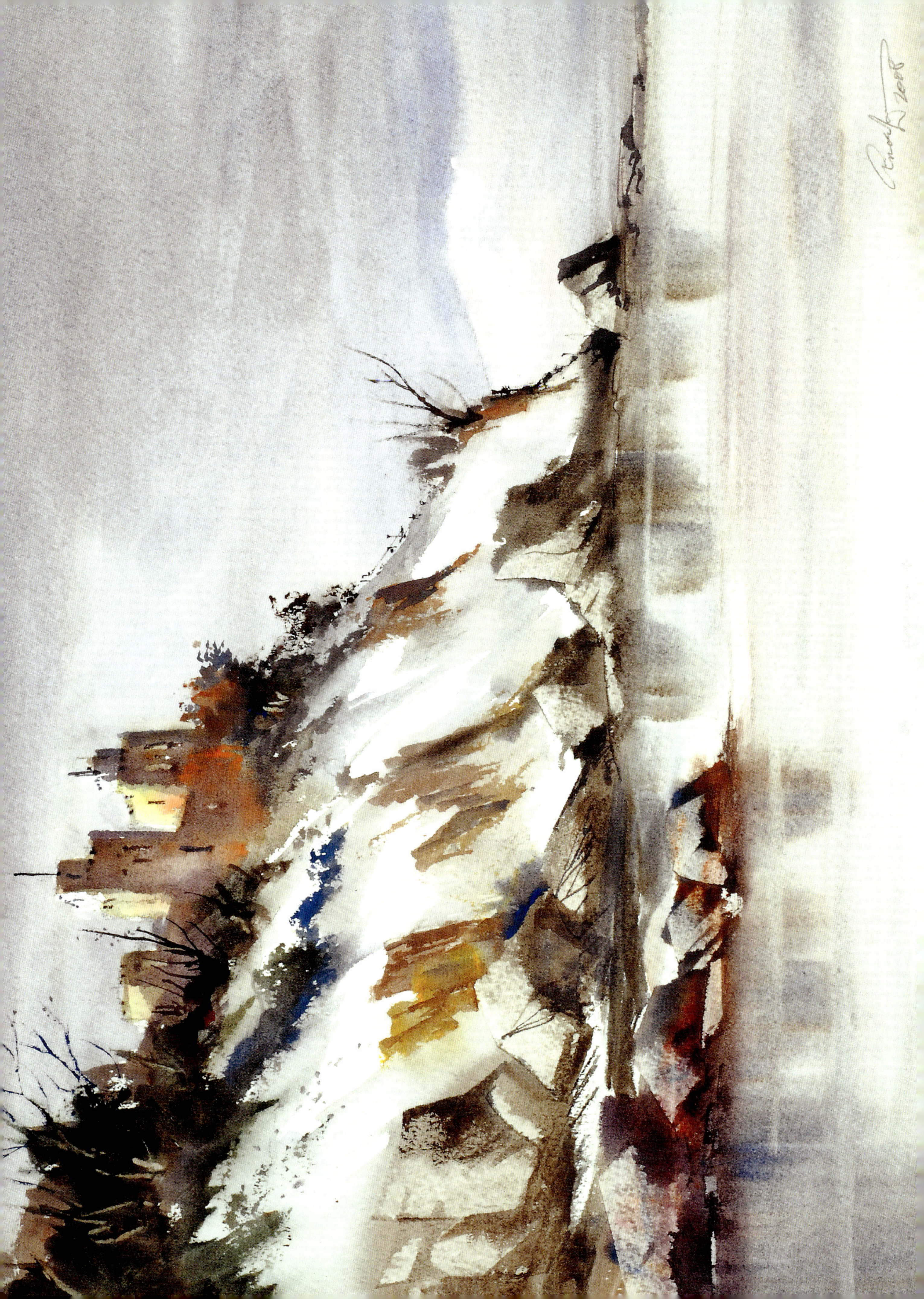

Coasts

Tony Cowlishaw

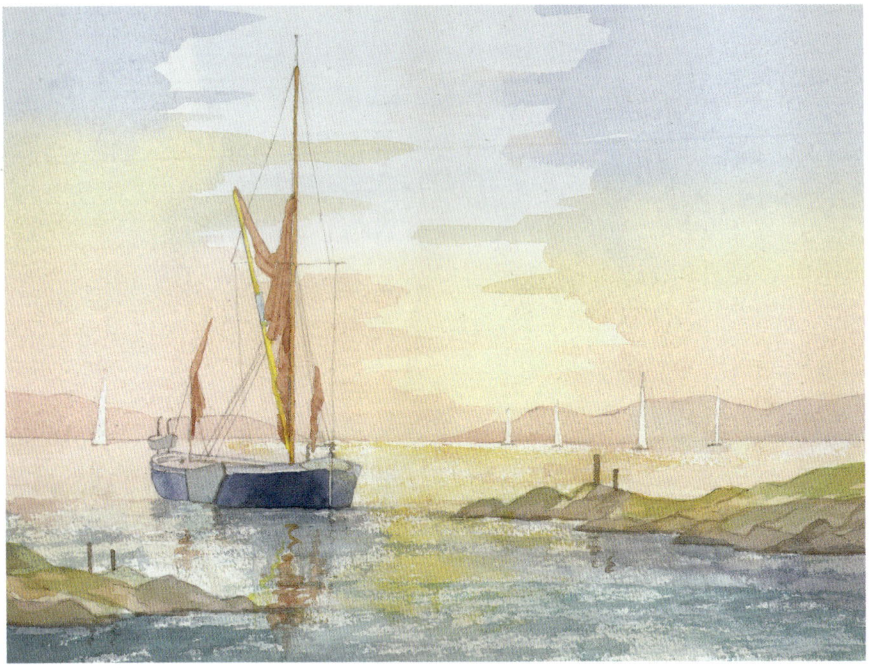

Barge in Creek, page 50

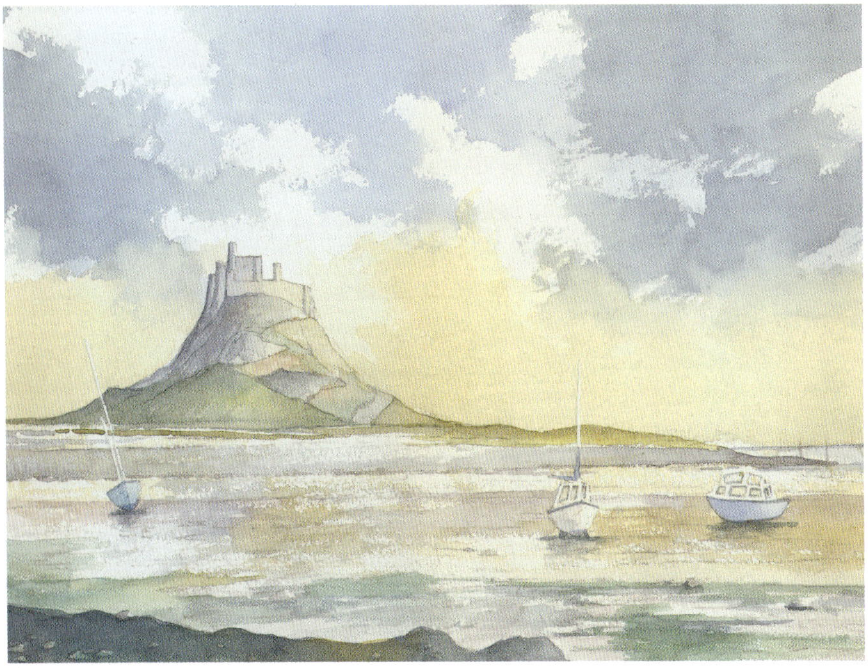

Lindisfarne Castle, page 52

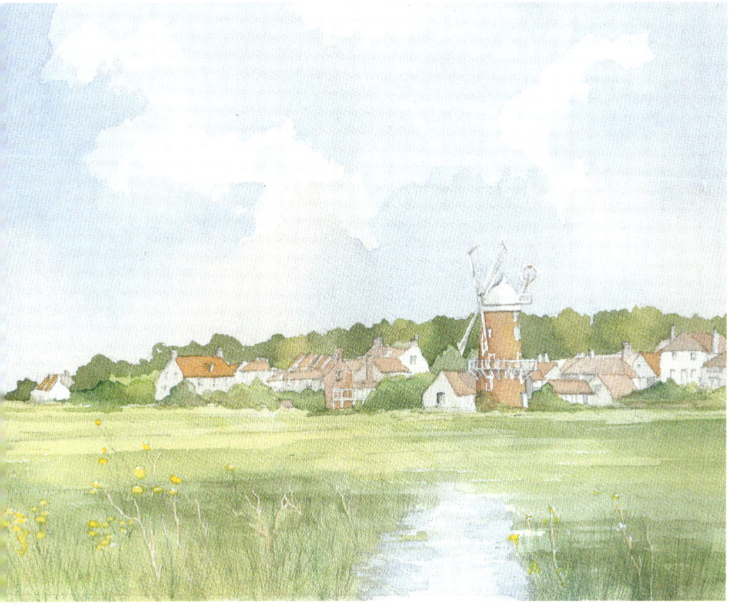

Marshland Windmill, page 54

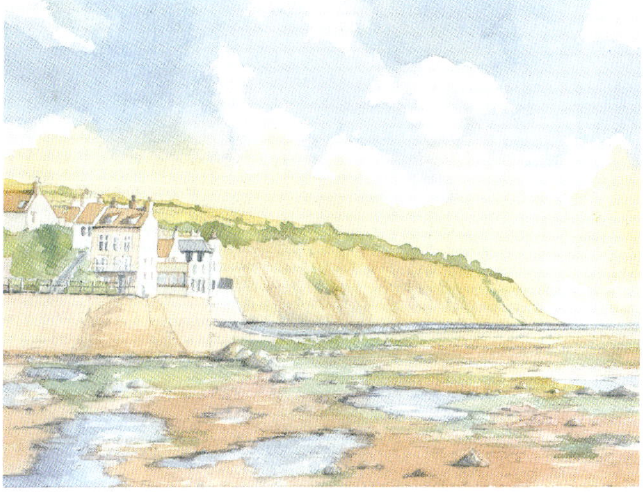

Coastal Cliffs, page 56

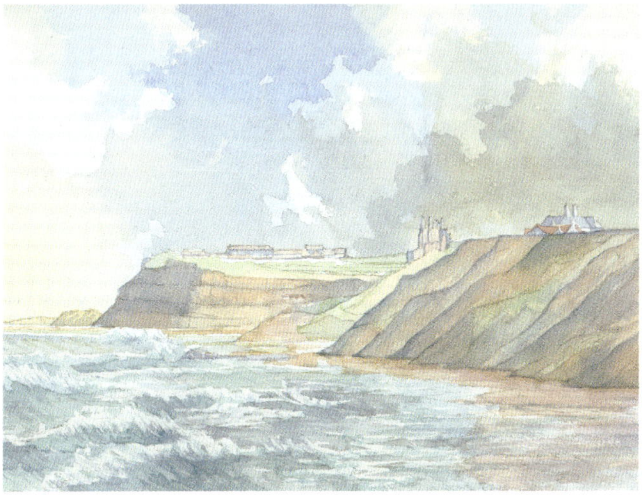

Stormy Coast, page 58

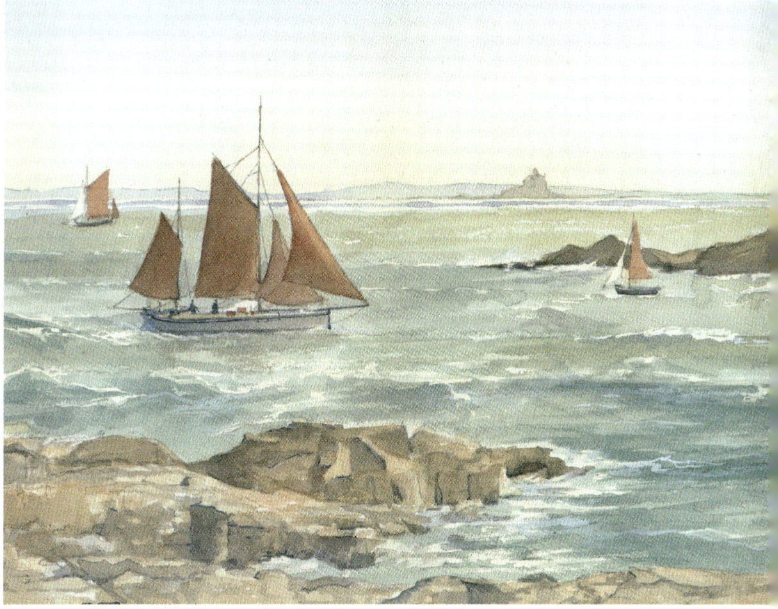

Towards Marazion, page 60

Barge in Creek

OUTLINE 13

This picture is of an old sailing barge in the evening light. I wanted to capture a dramatic evening sky with the corresponding atmospheric reflections in the water. I have included some pieces of land to the left and right in the foreground so that the eye travels towards the barge, which is positioned in the golden section.

Palette of colours

- Cobalt blue
- Raw sienna
- Payne's grey
- Indian red
- Alizarin crimson
- Viridian
- Cerulean blue
- Winsor yellow
- Ivory black

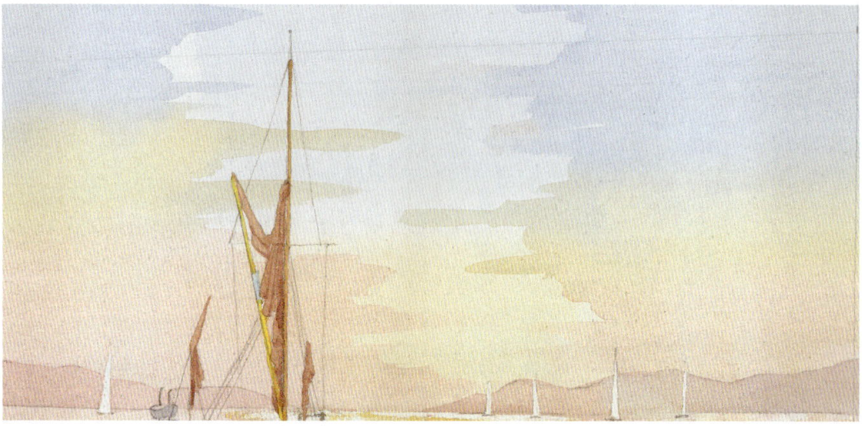

The sky is painted in a blended gradient from cobalt blue at the top, through to raw sienna lower down. Once dry, the clouds were painted with glazes of the same warm mix down to the horizon. Space is left in the glazes for the lighter first wash to show through.

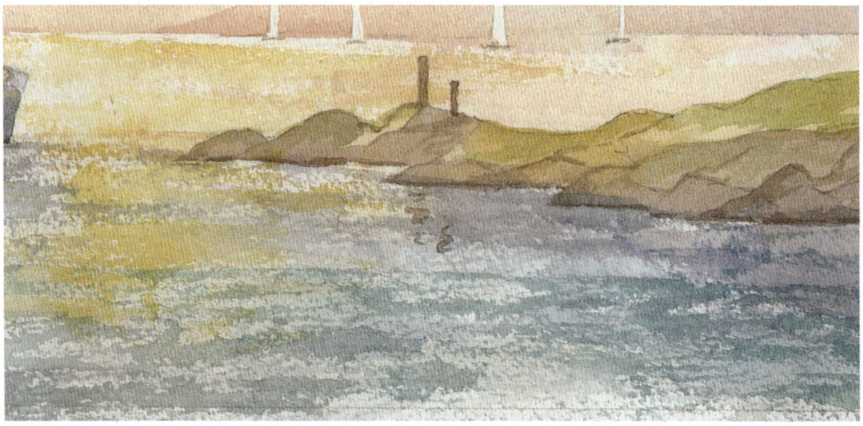

The water begins with a mix of Payne's grey with a little cobalt blue and alizarin crimson added. Use the side of a large brush to draw the mix lightly across the surface, turning the brush to release fresh paint.

Repeat the process with viridian, again drawing it lightly across the painting from the right to the centre. The darkest areas are placed with a third layer using a mix of viridian and Payne's grey.

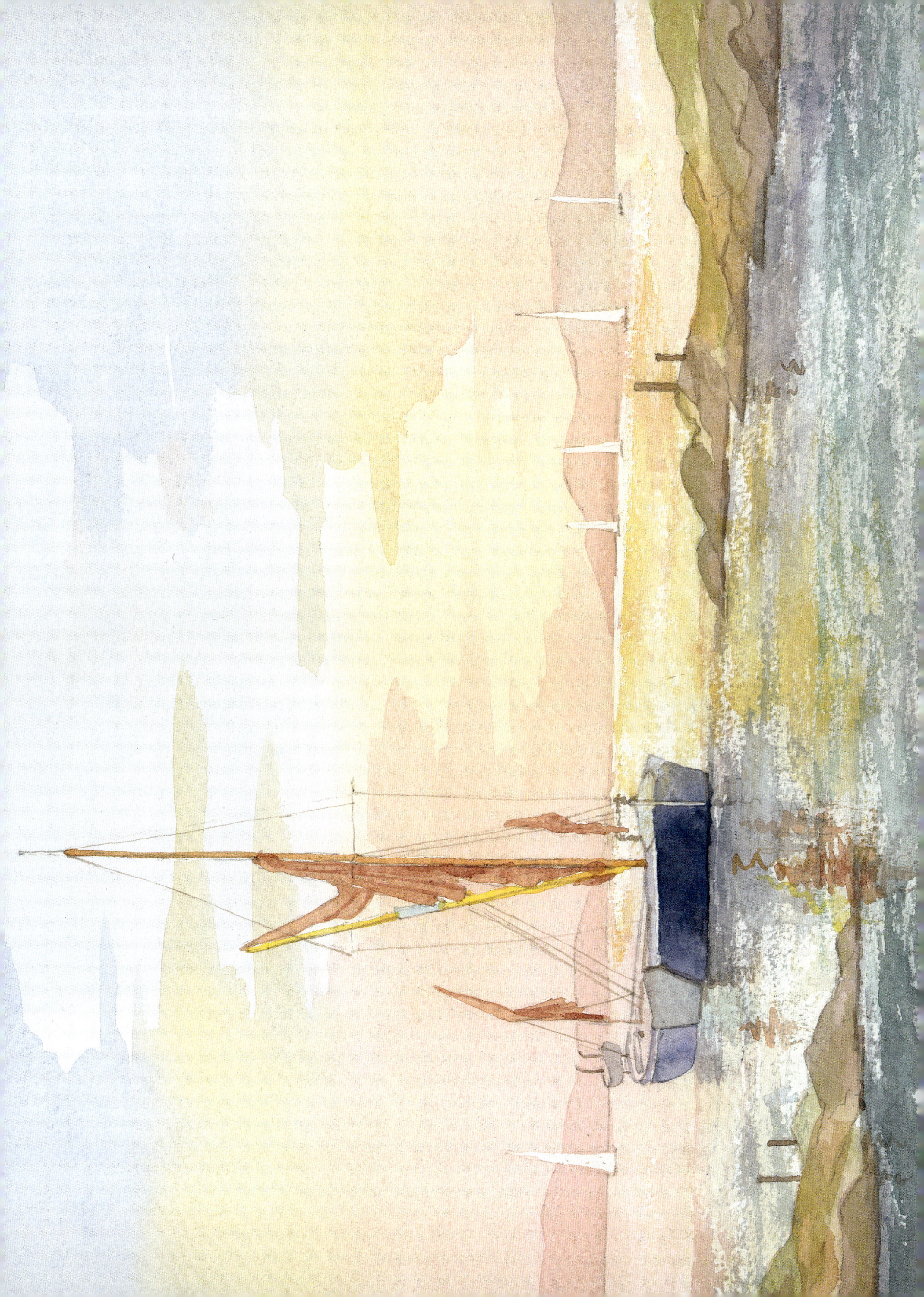

OUTLINE 14

Lindisfarne Castle

This dramatic castle provides a strong counterpoint to the sea and sky, creating a fantastic focal point. The painting is divided into various components: a dramatic sky, the castle, the water and the foreground; and each is important to the composition as a whole. Work through each section in turn to be sure of a cohesive finished painting.

Palette of colours

- Cobalt blue
- Raw sienna
- Payne's grey
- Winsor violet
- French ultramarine
- Winsor yellow
- Indian red
- Viridian
- Cerulean blue

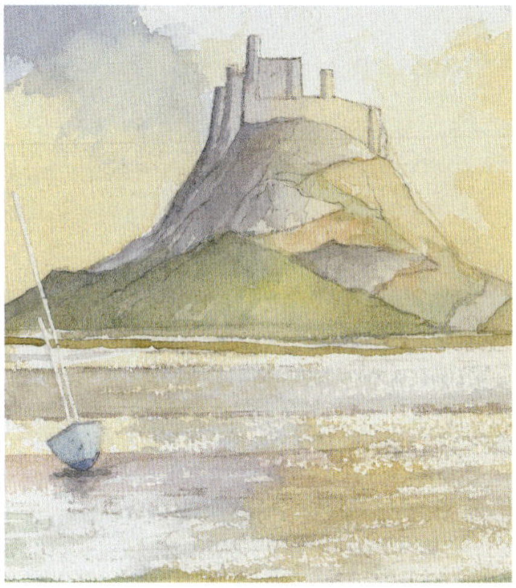

The water reflects the view, along with some small boats to add secondary points of interest. Use Payne's grey and Winsor violet for the castle shadow, and add cobalt blue to the mix for its reflection. The lighter side can be painted with raw sienna for both the hill and castle, and their reflections.

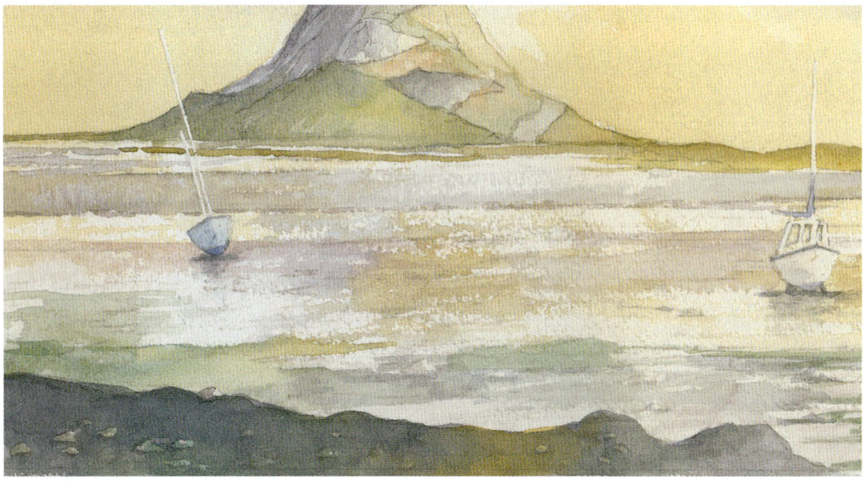

The foreground binds the whole painting together. Paint it using Payne's grey, with Winsor violet and raw sienna added wet into wet here and there to produce a variegated wash.

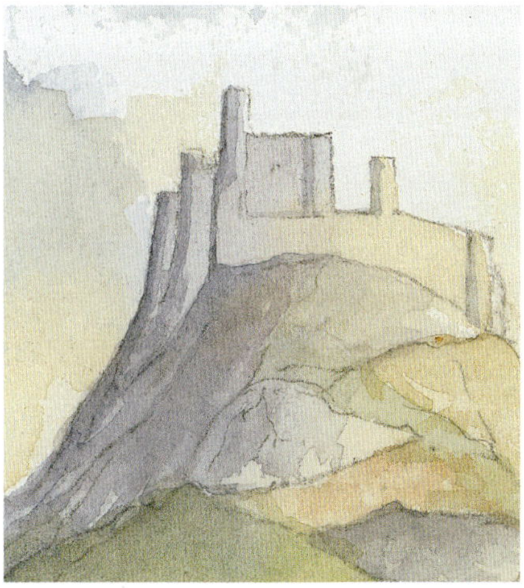

Add shadows to the castle wall with a mix of Payne's grey and cobalt blue, and midtones using a very dilute mix of Indian red and Payne's grey.

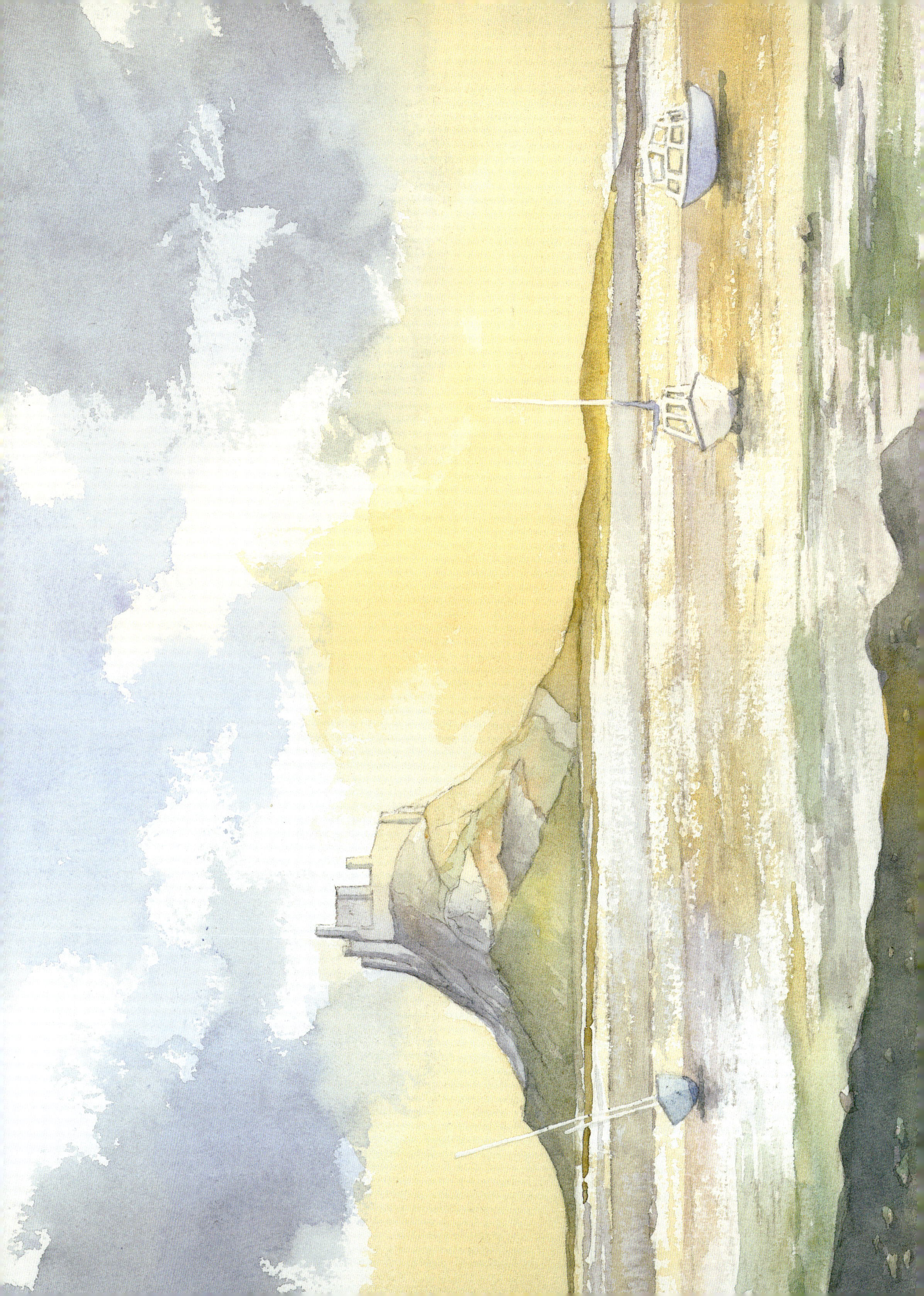

OUTLINE 15

Marshland Windmill

Coastlines often have many interesting areas for outdoor painting, even if the sea is not a major part of the composition. Cley Mill, which dominates the skyline for miles around the UK's Norfolk coast, is a perfect example. This viewpoint is taken from a path which runs between the mill and the sea.

Palette of colours

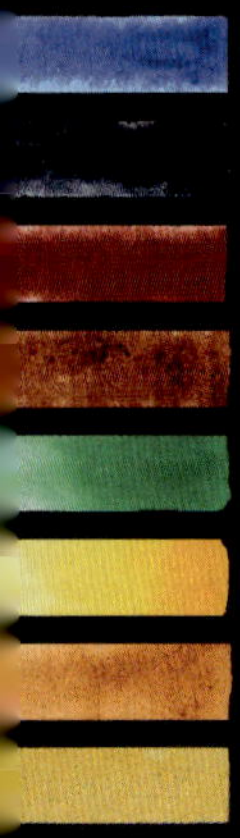

- Cobalt blue
- Payne's grey
- Indian red
- Burnt umber
- Viridian
- Winsor yellow
- Raw sienna
- Cadmium yellow

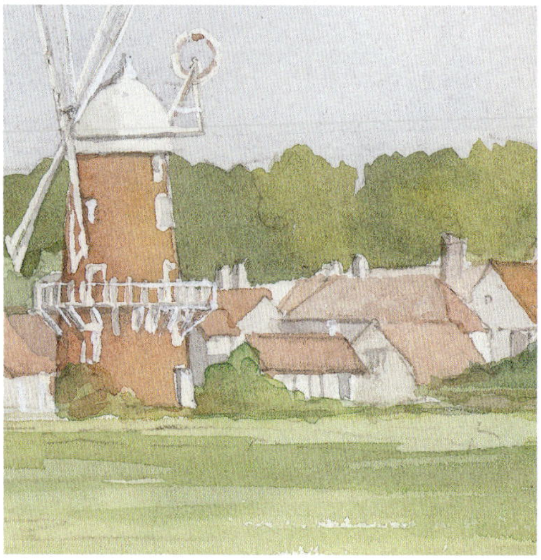

The mill is painted with a wash of Indian red and a little raw sienna for the shaded side and raw sienna in the light on the right-hand side.

The surrounding buildings are painted with slightly more dilute versions of the same mixes, along with touches of cadmium yellow and Payne's grey for variety.

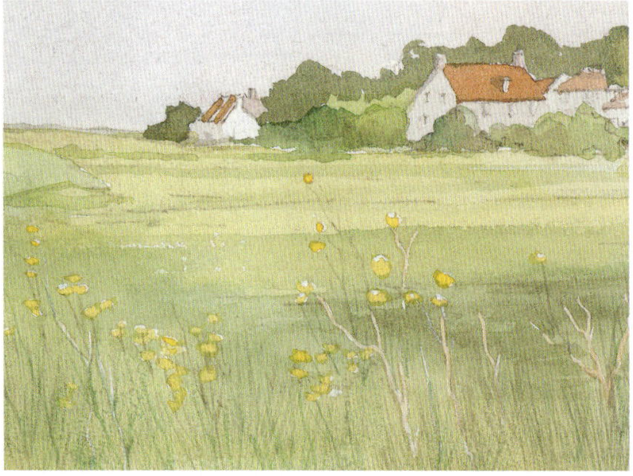

The flowers are painted with Winsor yellow and cadmium yellow – this mix is strong enough to stand out against the sunlit greens of the grass, which is painted by laying in a wash of Winsor yellow, then adding a mix of burnt umber, viridian and Winsor yellow for a bright, variegated finish.

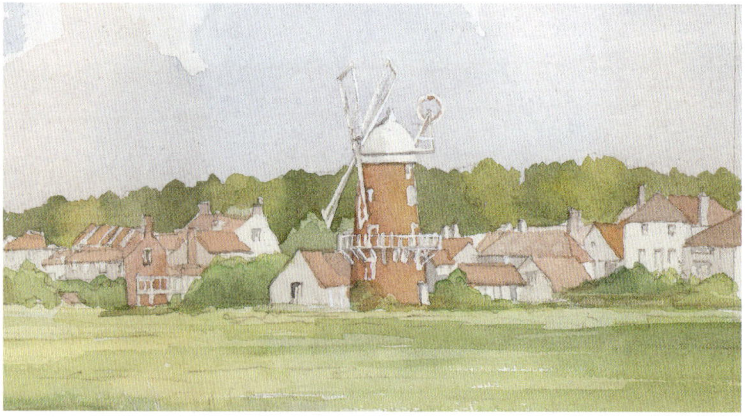

The background foliage is painted before the windmill and houses; but it needs enough impact to provides contrast and complements with the reds of the buildings. The green used for it is a dark green mix of burnt umber and viridian, with touches of Winsor yellow.

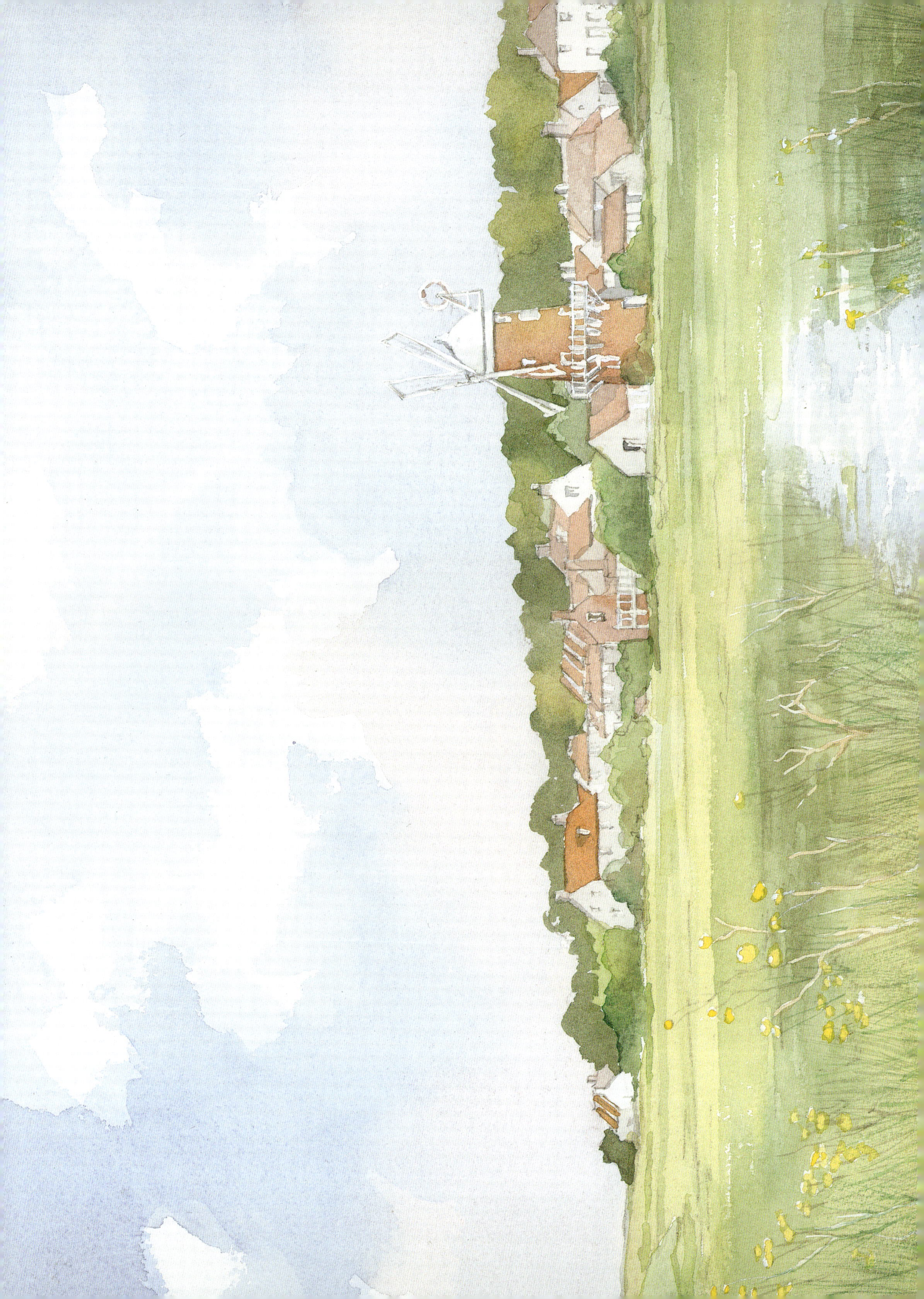

Coastal Cliffs

OUTLINE 16

Robin Hood's Bay, in the UK, lies between steep sandstone cliffs. This view is from the beach, looking inland. The central cliff captures the whole atmosphere of the village.

Palette of colours

- Cobalt blue
- Raw sienna
- Winsor yellow
- Indian red
- Burnt umber
- Viridian
- Payne's grey
- Cadmium red
- Cadmium yellow
- Winsor green

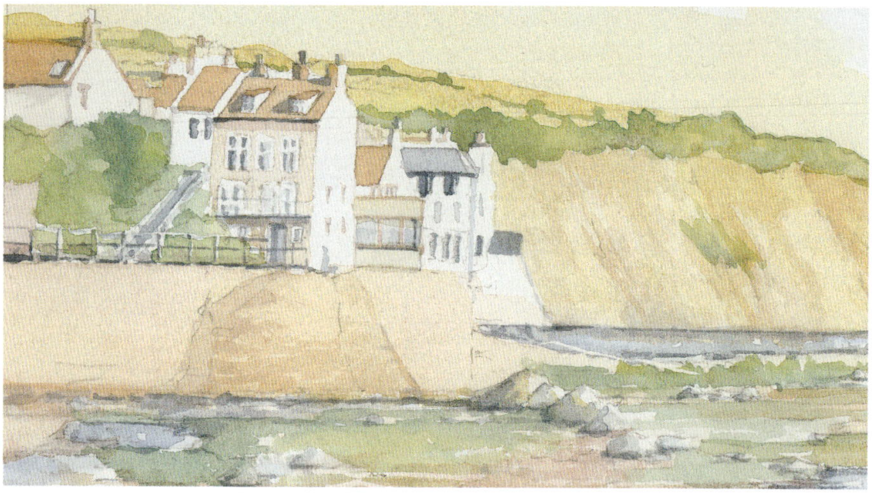

Apply masking fluid to selected rocks and reflections in the rock pools in the foreground, the window frames in the midground, and the right-hand sides of some of the buildings. The light is coming from the right, so masking fluid should be on this side of objects to preserve the highlights.

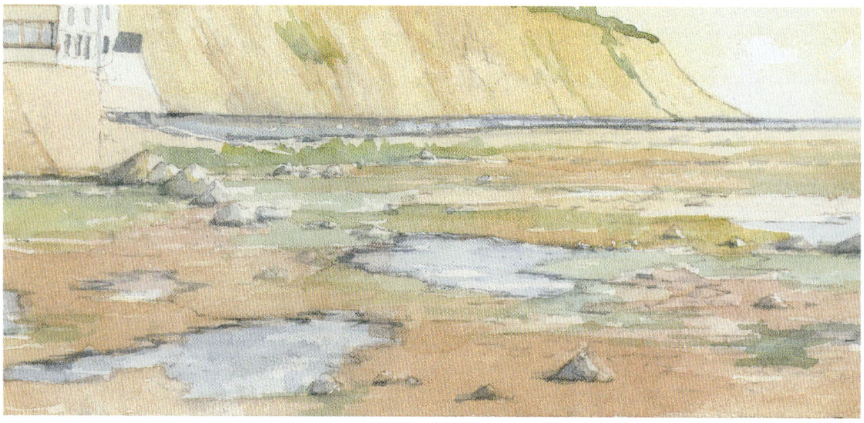

The pools of water are painted with cobalt blue. Those in the midground are reflecting the sky, so add raw sienna wet into wet. Paint the background sea with a darker mix of Payne's grey and cobalt blue.

The sandy area is raw sienna and Indian red, warmer towards the bottom of the painting, while the patches of seaweed are a burnt umber and viridian mix, varied with Winsor yellow.

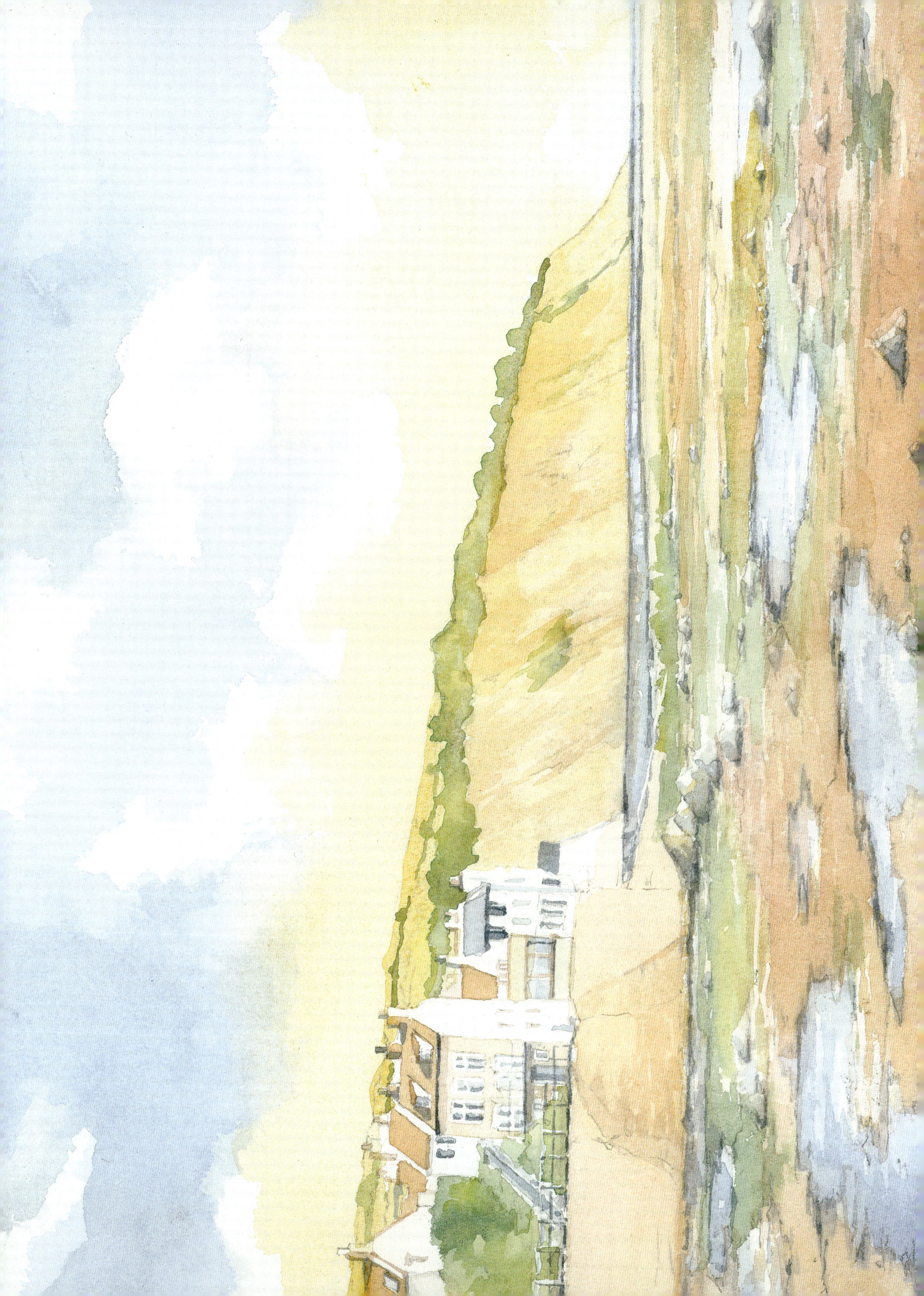

17

OUTLINE

Stormy Coast

This is a dramatic painting of a storm over a small coastal town. The viewpoint looks towards the derelict abbey and includes the town below. The high waves emphasize the atmosphere within the painting.

Palette of colours

- Cobalt blue
- Raw sienna
- Ivory black
- Payne's grey
- Indian red
- Viridian
- Winsor yellow
- Winsor violet

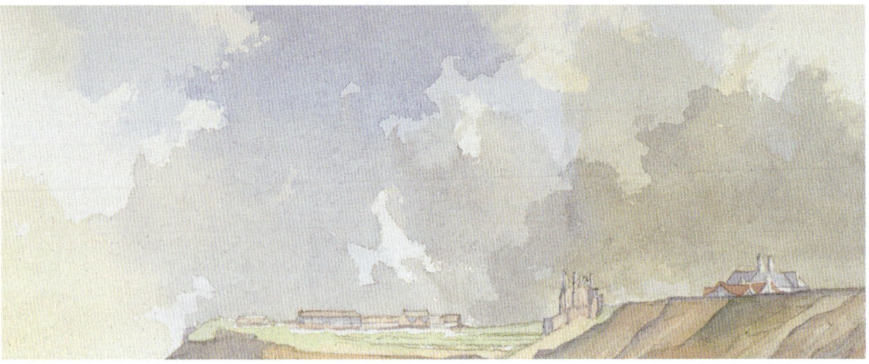

The storm cloud is moody, but not too dark in tone. Establish the sky with cobalt blue, leaving gaps for clouds, then build up the storm cloud with cobalt blue and Payne's grey. Add a tiny touch of ivory black at the horizon. On the right and left of the painting, work raw sienna into the sky wet into wet.

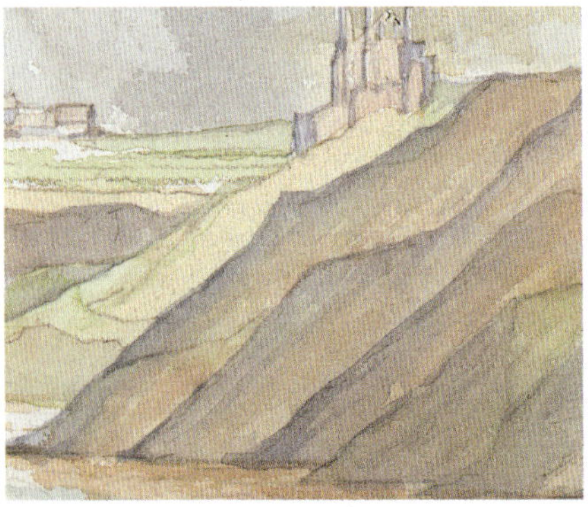

Paint the warm cliffs using raw sienna, dropping in touches of Indian red and a green mix of viridian and Winsor yellow.

Once dry, add the shadows in fine lines with a mix of Winsor violet, Payne's grey and cobalt blue; then bring in the warm mix wet into wet to blend it out. Work each section in turn.

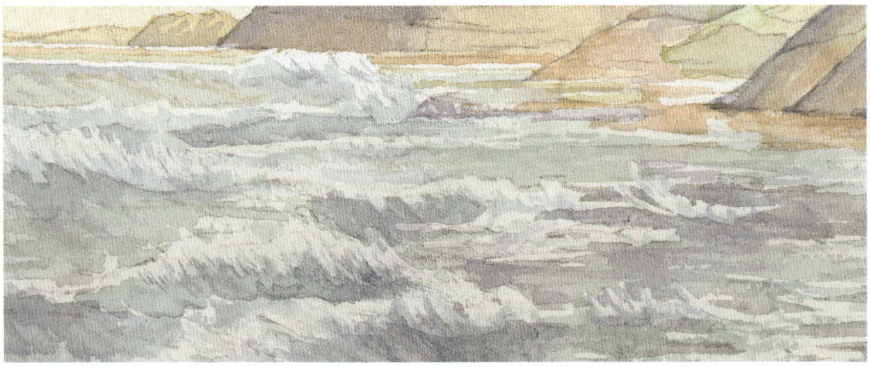

The waves add a lot of drama to the painting. Keep the foam on top white with masking fluid. Start from the horizon by laying a mix of cobalt blue, with a little raw sienna and Payne's grey. Add viridian and more raw sienna as you advance to the midground, and swap to a mix of cobalt blue and Payne's grey in the foreground.

Once dry, shade the cresting waves in turn with a mix of cobalt blue and Payne's grey by drawing a fine line under the foam and quickly drawing it down diagonally using your finger. Once dry, remove the masking fluid to reveal the fresh clean paper.

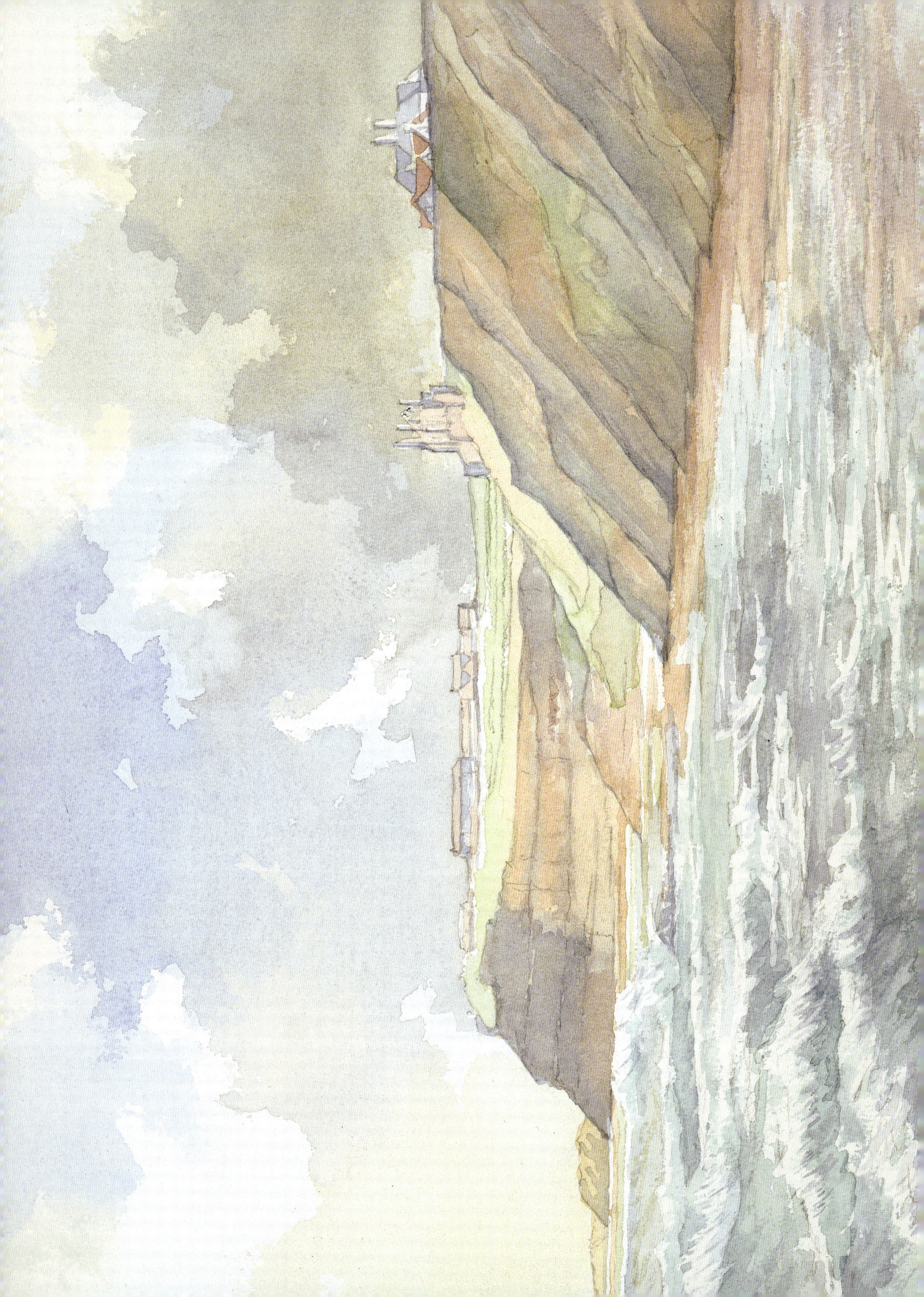

OUTLINE 18

Towards Marazion

The distant form of St Michael's Mount, in Cornwall, UK, is the focal point of this painting.

Palette of colours

- Cobalt blue
- Raw sienna
- Payne's grey
- Winsor yellow
- French ultramarine
- Indian red
- Viridian
- Winsor violet

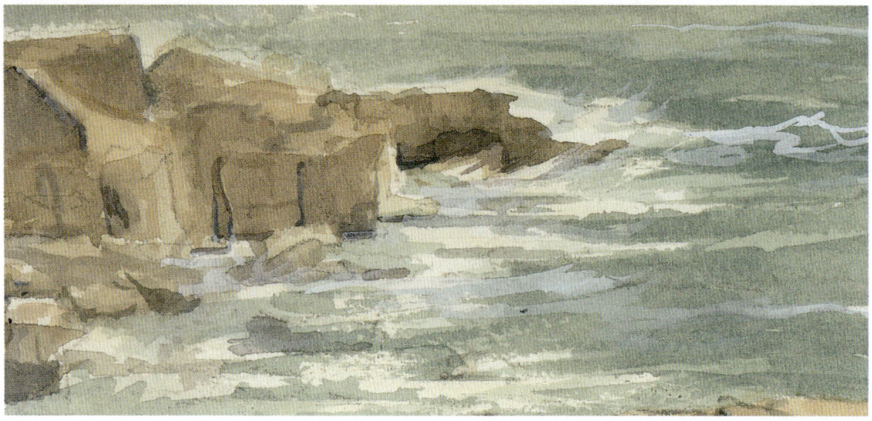

Keep the sparkle on the water bright by applying masking fluid to the wave formation. Use viridian, Payne's grey and cobalt blue to make delicate shades of blue-green mixes to define the colours of the sea.

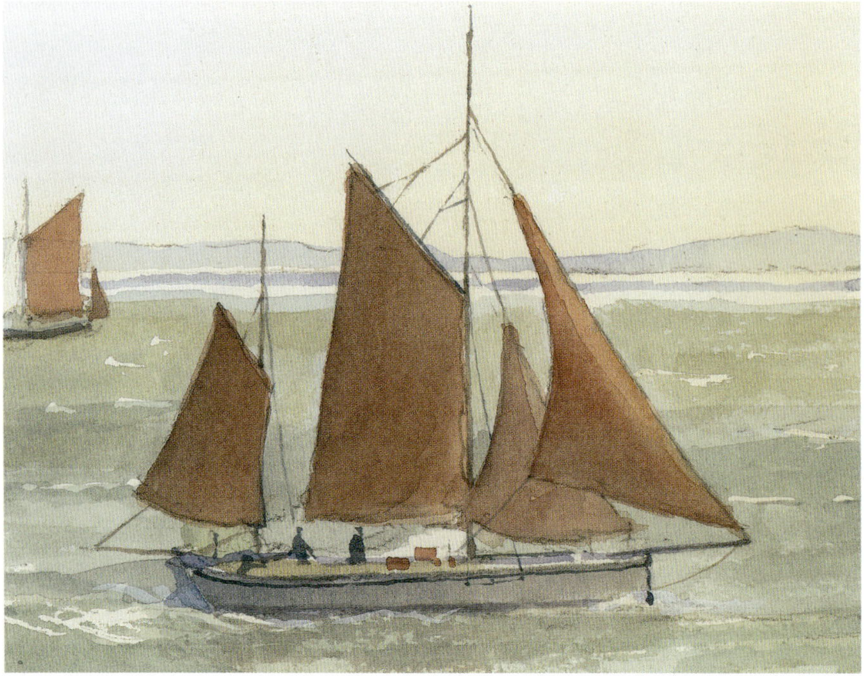

Use a mix of raw sienna and Indian red for the basis of the sails. Once dry, add Payne's grey to the mix and shade the left-hand sides, as the light is coming from the right-hand side.

Paint the hull with a mix of French ultramarine, Payne's grey and a little raw sienna.

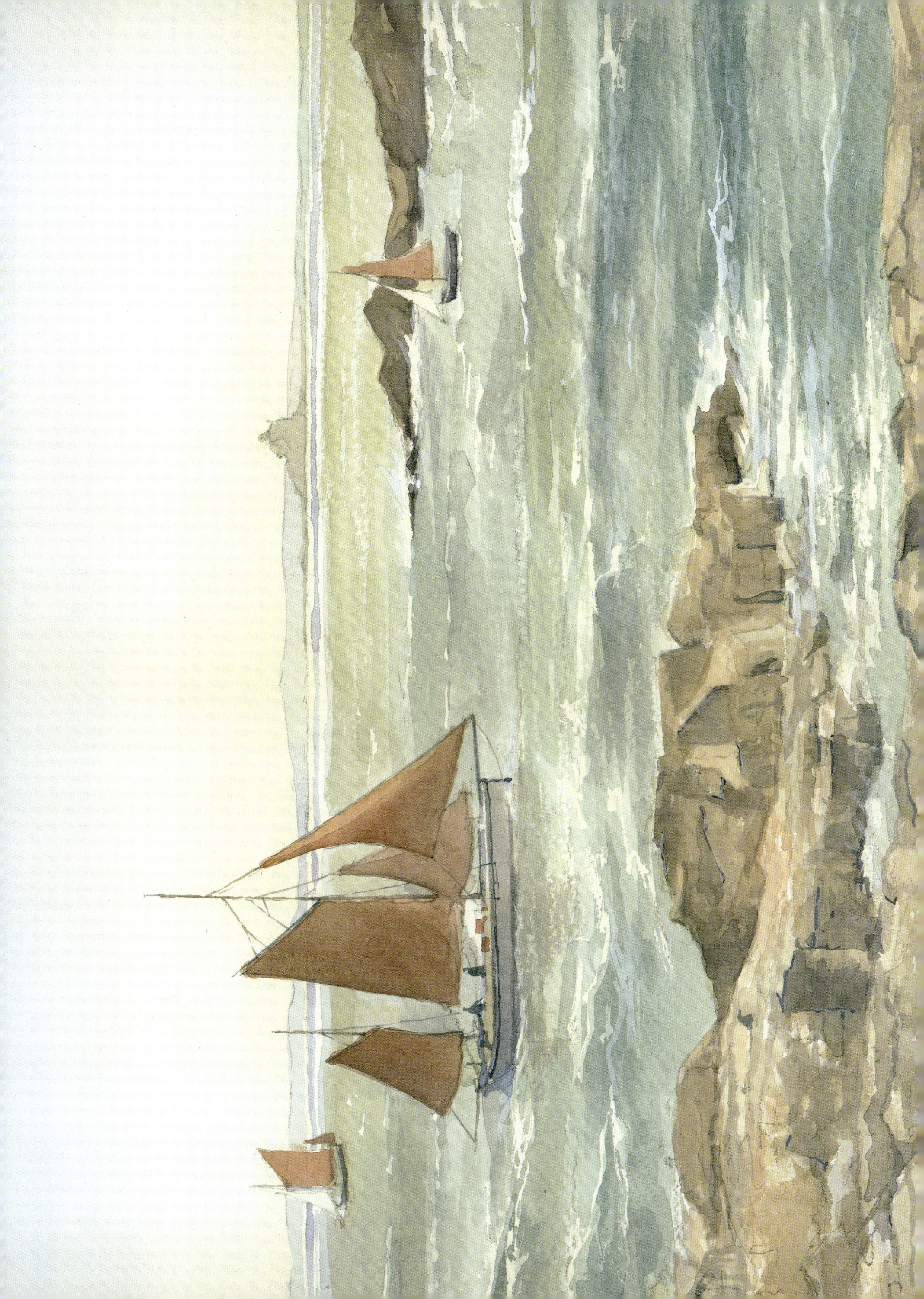

Irish landscapes

Dermot Cavanagh

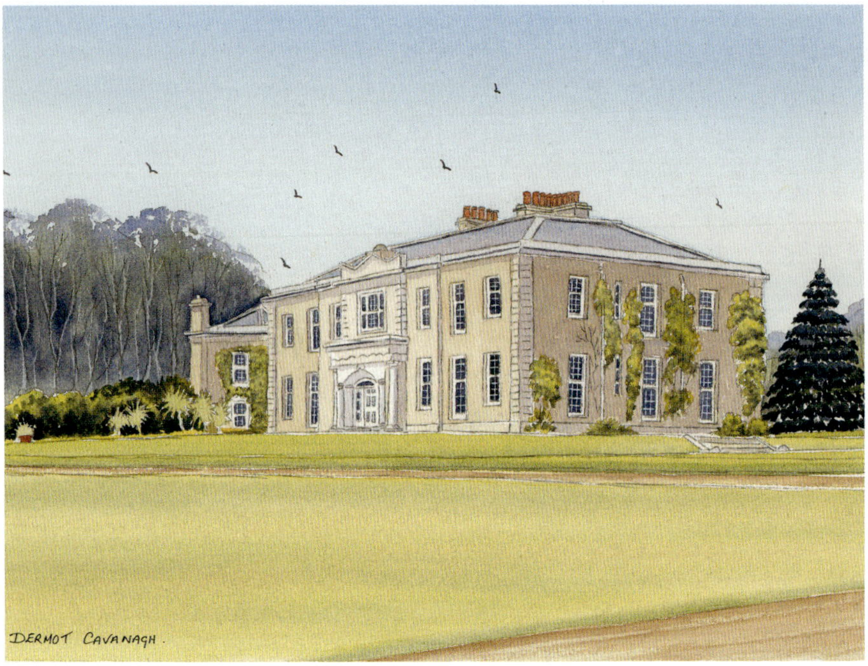

The Argory, page 64

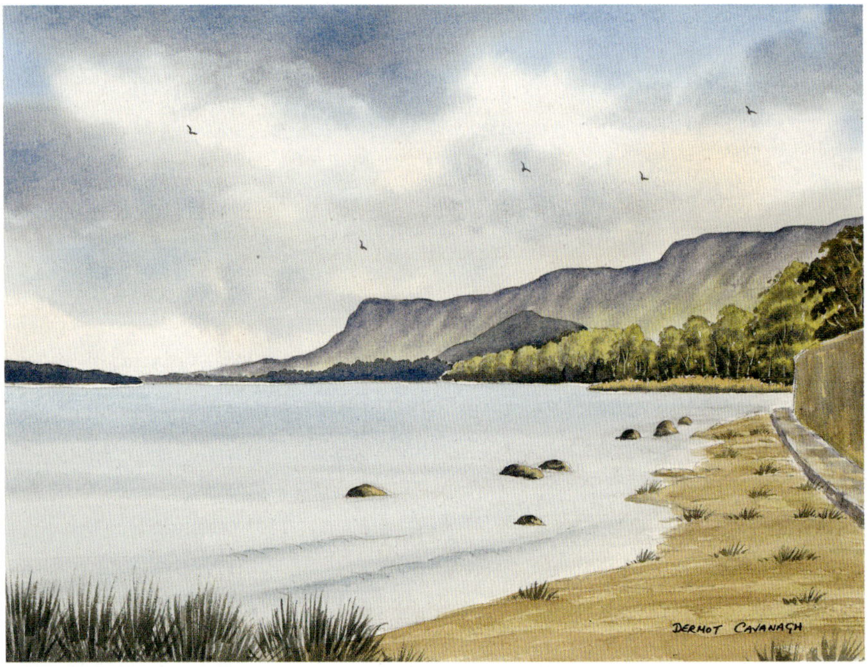

Glencar Lake, page 66

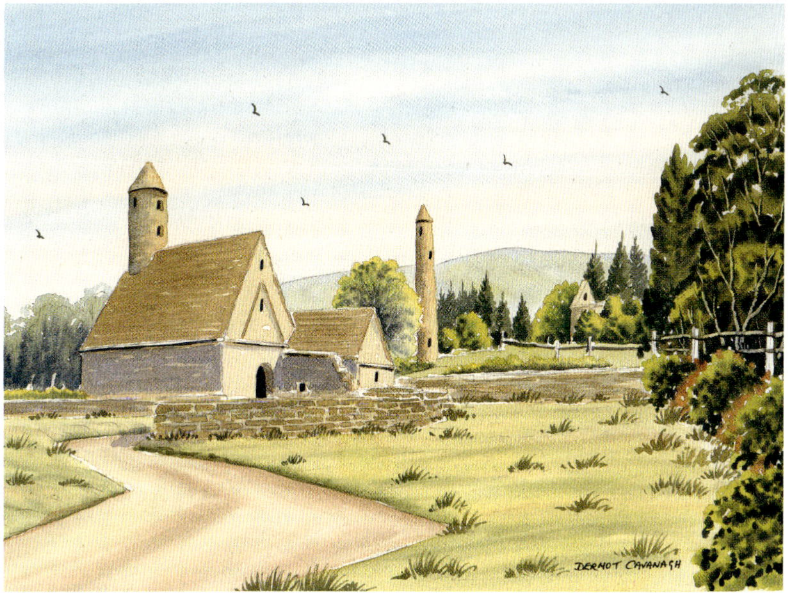

Glendalough, page 68

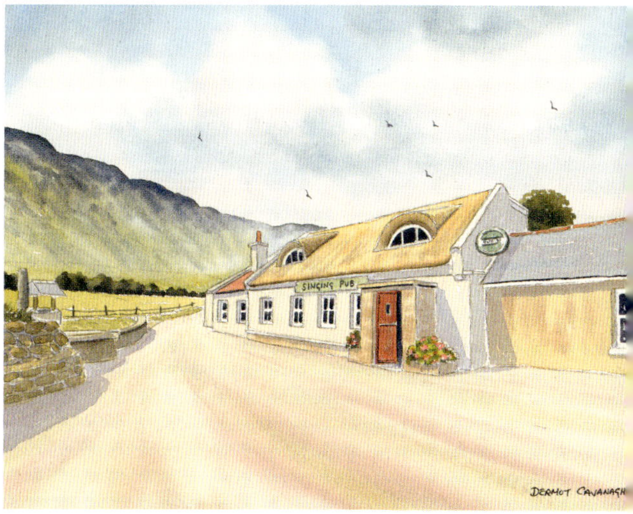

The Singing Pub, page 70

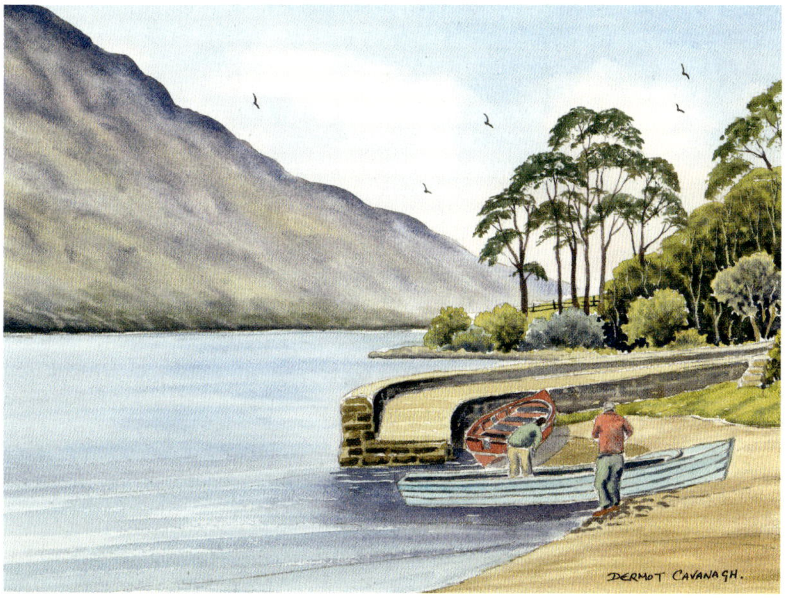

Doo Lough, page 72

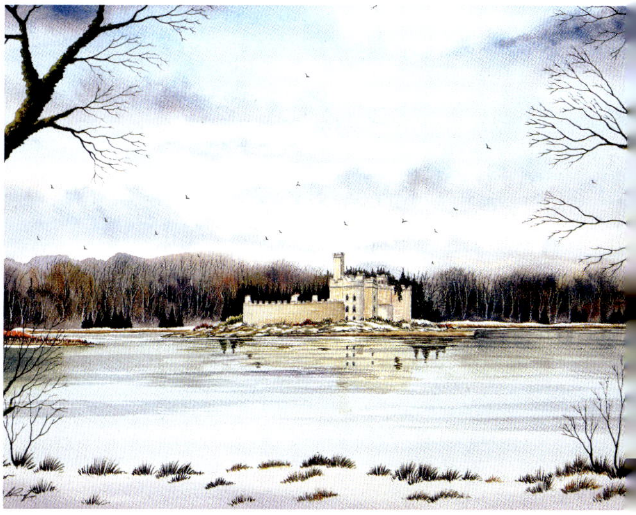

Castle Island, page 74

19

OUTLINE

The Argory

Built in the 1820s, the Argory is an Irish gentry house offering sweeping vistas over the River Blackwater, scenic woodland and a courtyard and barns. I have a studio in the octagon room of the west wing. For this exercise I painted the front and east-facing façade of the house, treating a complicated scene very simply. The sunlit house front creates an effective contrast with the shadows on the east-facing walls. The house is nicely framed by the dark trees to either side.

Palette of colours

- Winsor blue (red shade)
- Cerulean blue
- Winsor yellow
- Cobalt turquoise (light)
- French ultramarine
- Light red
- Alizarin crimson
- Raw sienna
- Dioxazine violet
- Winsor red
- Neutral tint
- Titanium white

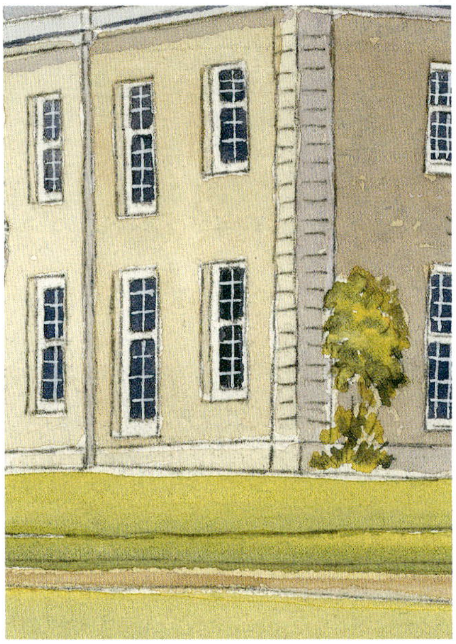

The walls of the house are painted with a wash of raw sienna, cerulean blue and Winsor red. Keep mixing this in the palette as the colour will granulate.

Paint in small sections, starting with the main façade, then outwards from there. The downpipes and creepers divide the wall into sections, which helps.

Once dry, use a strong shadow mix of French ultramarine, with tiny bits of light red and Winsor red for the areas in shadow.

The same shadow mix used on the wall (see above) is strengthened to block in the windows and door as well as to add shadows under the eaves and the lead flashing.

The window frames and details can then be re-established with titanium white and a rigger brush.

Use a mix of two brushfuls of water with cerulean blue and alizarin crimson for the roof; and light red for the chimney pots.

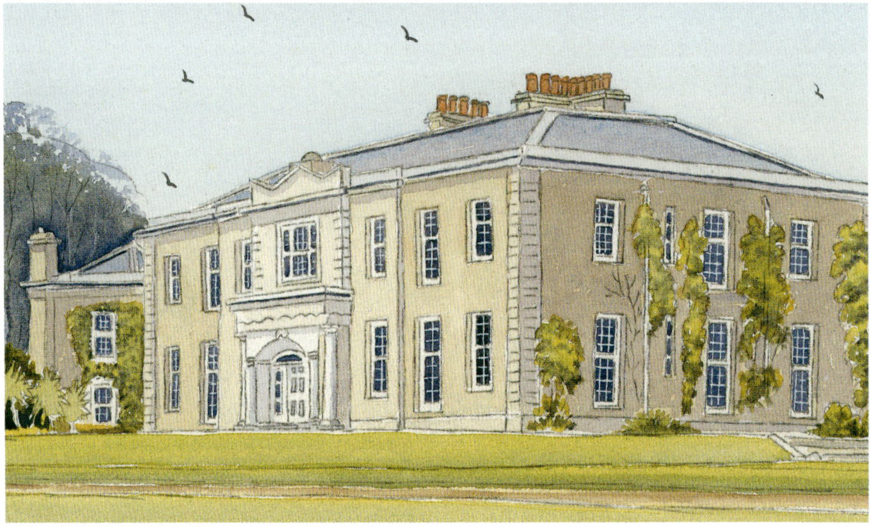

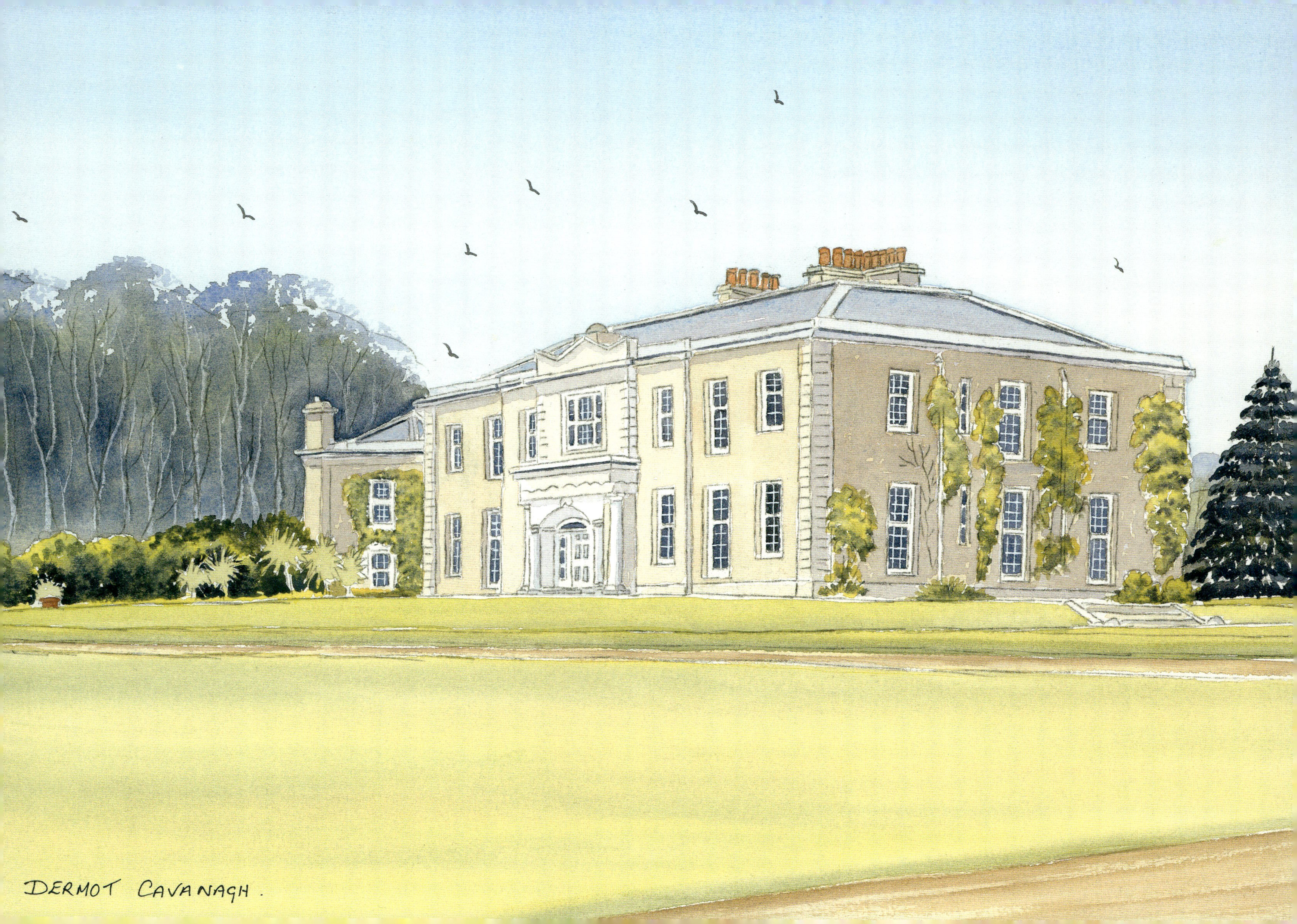
DERMOT CAVANAGH.

Glencar Lake

This lovely lough is in a deep valley north of Sligo town and just south-east of Benbulbin mountain. From this viewpoint, looking west along the lough from a nearby road, the scene is a perfect composition for a painting. The horizon is slightly below half-way down and the bulk of the mountain is off-centre and to the right. The right-hand foreground leads you in, and the dark grass gives balance to the left-hand side. The lough shore, the wall in the bottom left, the line of green trees in the middle distance and the mountain all create linear perspective, with the lines sloping away as they recede.

Palette of colours

- Winsor blue (red shade)
- Cerulean blue
- Light red
- Neutral tint
- Raw sienna
- Winsor yellow
- French ultramarine

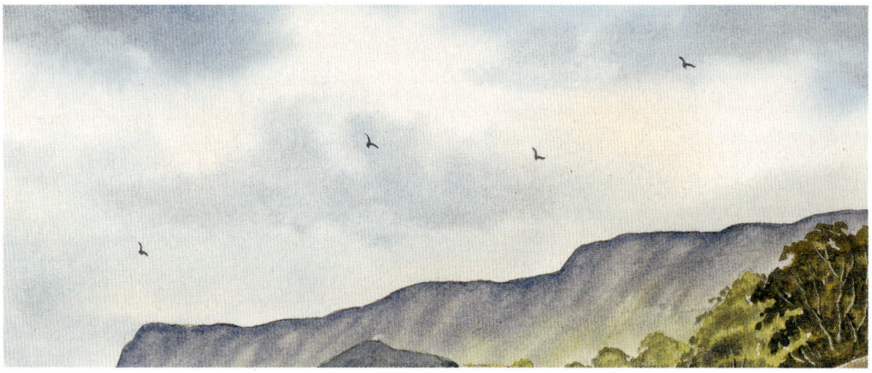

Wet the paper from the top down to the waterline, then bleed in a mix made from three brushfuls of water with light red, creating blustery shapes. Paint the sky in from the top left-hand corner with a mix of four brushfuls of water with Winsor blue and cerulean blue. Leave white space for cloud shapes, then use what is left on the brush to create an underbelly for the clouds. Scrub the brush dry vigorously on kitchen paper, then blend and diffuse the colours while the washes are wet. Finally, add darker clouds with a mix of two brushfuls of water with cerulean blue and neutral tint. Make them smaller at the bottom to create perspective.

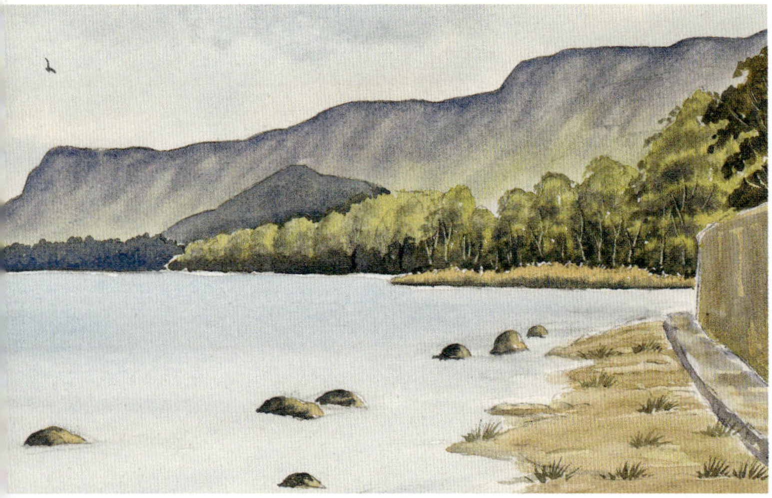

For the distant trees, use a mix of two brushfuls of water with French ultramarine, a little Winsor yellow and a tiny bit of light red. The blue distance creates aerial perspective, strengthening the sense of distance.

For the sunlit area of trees you'll need three mixes: three brushfuls of water with Winsor yellow and a little Winsor blue; two brushfuls with lots of Winsor yellow, lots of French ultramarine and a little light red to make a dark green; and two brushfuls with French ultramarine and light red for the darkest tones.

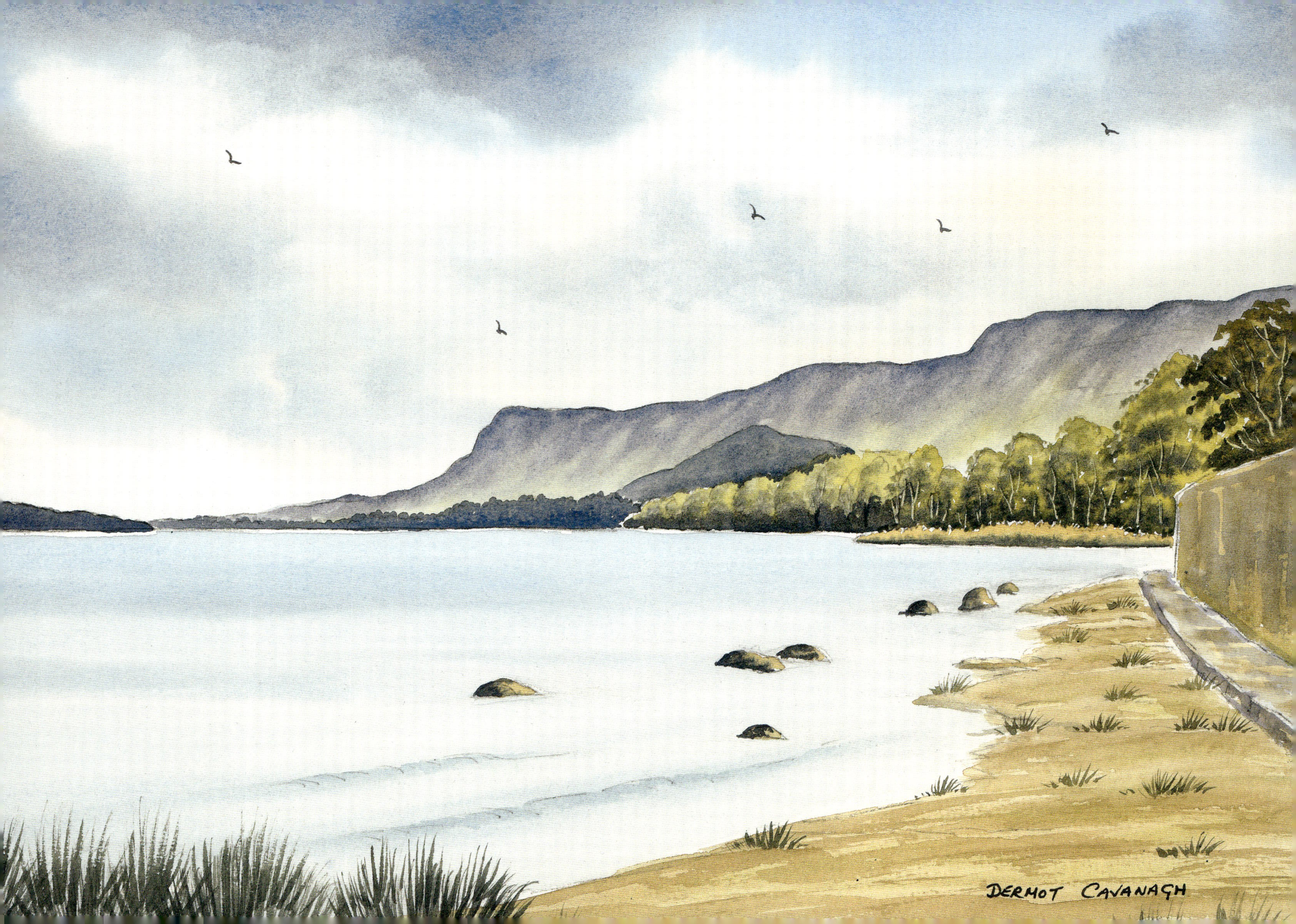
DERMOT CAVANAGH

OUTLINE 21

Glendalough

Glendalough's spectacular scenery and rich history make it one of the most visited places in Ireland. Located in the Wicklow Mountains, it was a monastic settlement founded in the sixth century by the hermit monk, St Kevin. My surname, Cavanagh, originates from there; it is an anglicization of the Gaelic Mac Caomhánach 'son of Caomhán' (or follower of Kevin).

Palette of colours

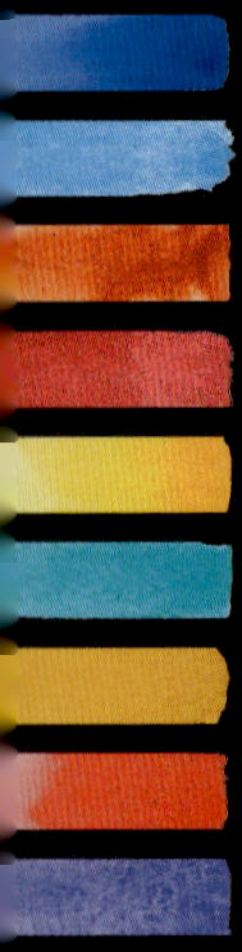

- Winsor blue (red shade)
- Cerulean blue
- Light red
- Alizarin crimson
- Winsor yellow
- Cobalt turquoise (light)
- Raw sienna
- Winsor red
- French ultramarine

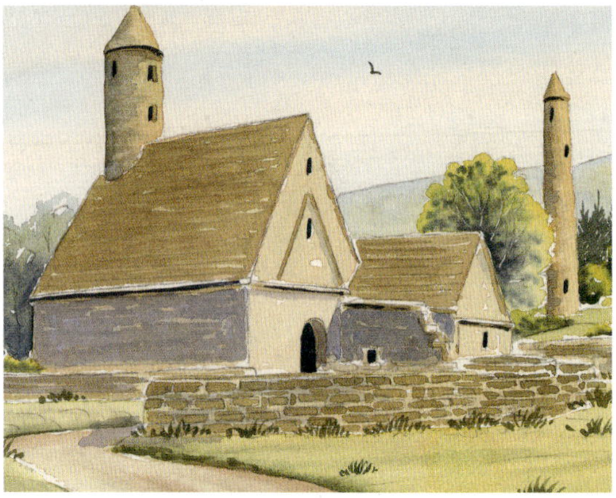

The only building material shown is dry stone, with no windows, doors, roof tiles or eaves to add interest. To create form and drama in the buildings, I placed the sun high and to the right, which produces very dark interior shadows.

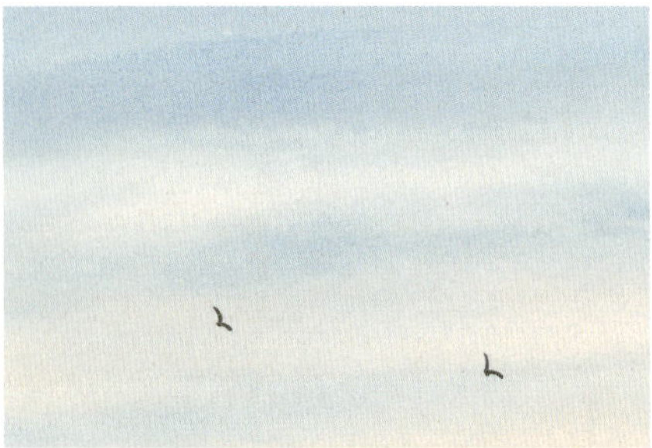

I kept the sky very simple, so as not to compete with the busy foreground. The mixes were four brushfuls of water with Winsor blue and cerulean blue; and three brushfuls of water with light red and alizarin crimson. Wet the paper evenly, cutting round the roofs, then streak the second wash across lower down the sky.

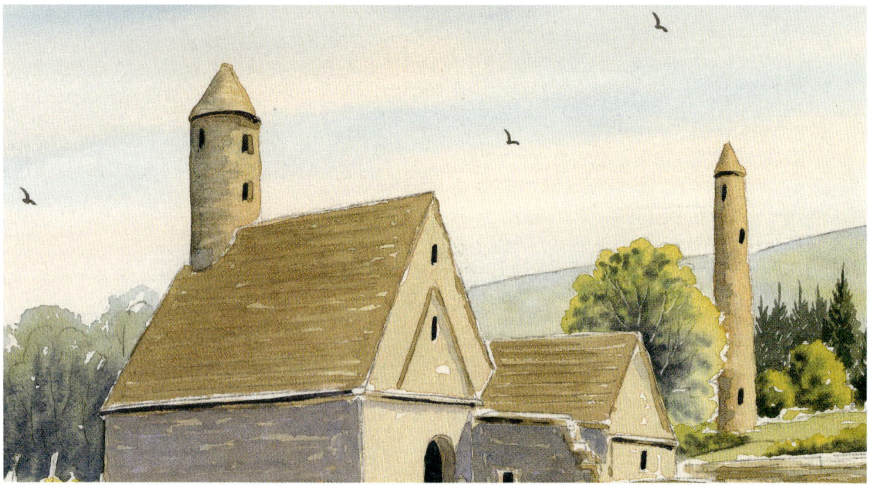

Two mixes form the basis for the stonework: three brushfuls of water, raw sienna and a little cerulean blue; a thicker mix of two brushfuls with raw sienna, Winsor red and cerulean blue. Start with the roof, blocking in the shape with the first wash, then bleed in the second in random marks. Once dry, the roof is darkened with a mix of raw sienna, Winsor red and cerulean blue.

Move on to the walls and towers, adding French ultramarine wet into wet for shadows on the walls. Details are added with a very dark mix of French ultramarine and light red.

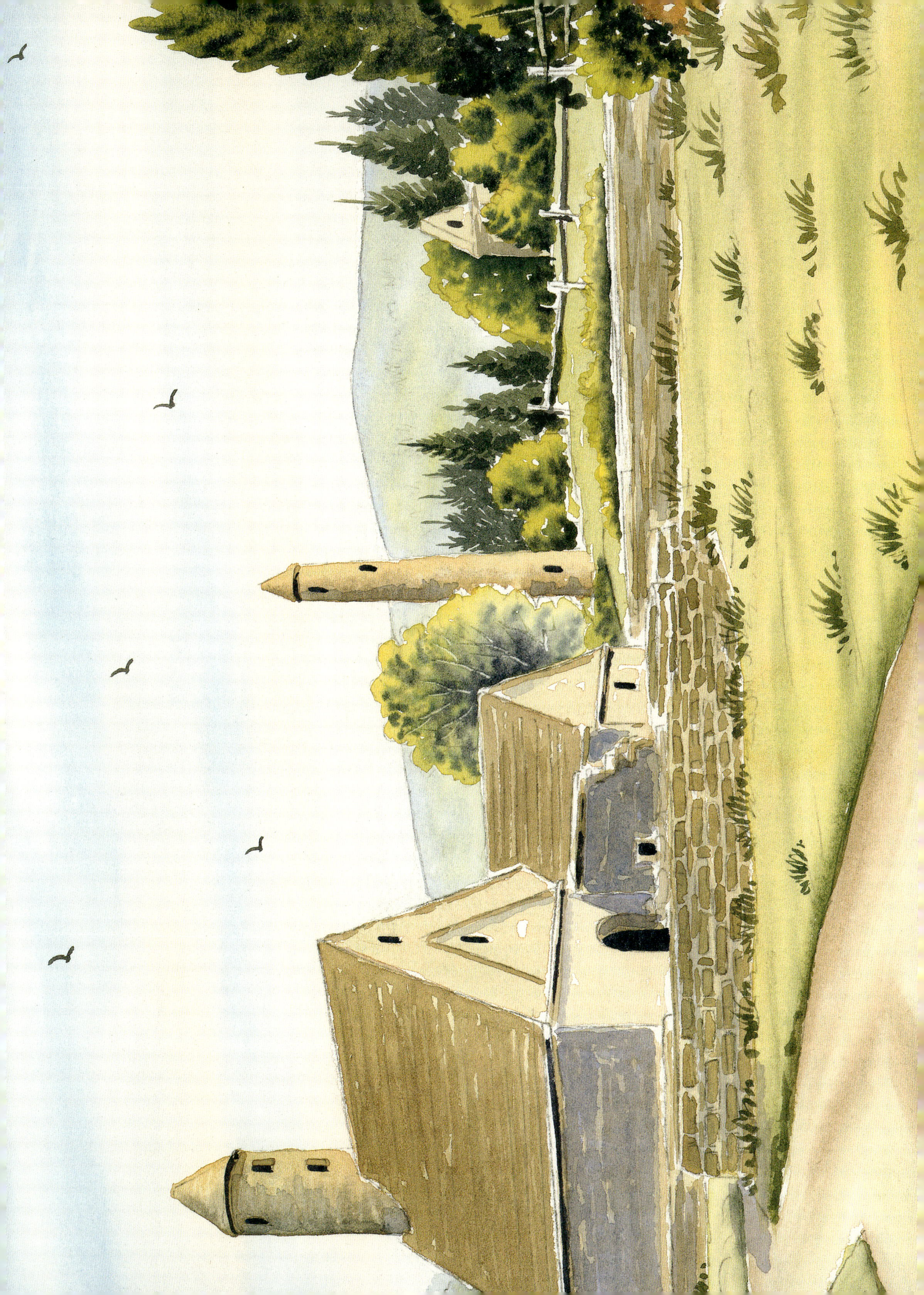

The Singing Pub

22

OUTLINE

The Singing Pub is one of Ireland's great music pubs, situated along the mountain road around the Atlantic Drive on the Rosguill Peninsula. Rosguill has a wealth of painting locations and a few excellent thirst-quenching pubs when you need a break. I feel a song coming on – anyone for a pint?

Palette of colours

- Winsor yellow
- Raw sienna
- Light red
- French ultramarine
- Cerulean blue
- Winsor blue (red shade)
- Burnt sienna
- Neutral tint
- Alizarin crimson
- Cobalt turquoise (light)
- Winsor red
- Dioxazine violet

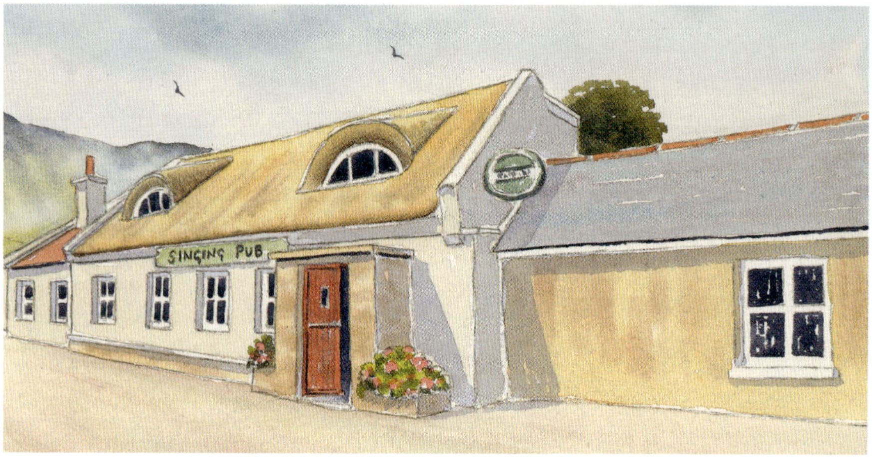

What I like about the painting is the warm, welcoming atmosphere it portrays, which contrasts well with the shadows, especially the darkness of the window panes. Some people think the windows should reflect the sky colour, but this is only the case with much larger windows.

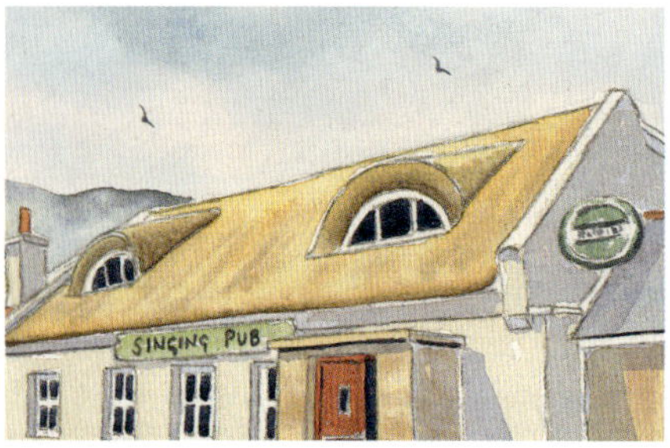

Paint the thatched roof with three brushfuls of water with Winsor yellow and raw sienna; and raw sienna and light red. Add shadows with light red and French ultramarine.

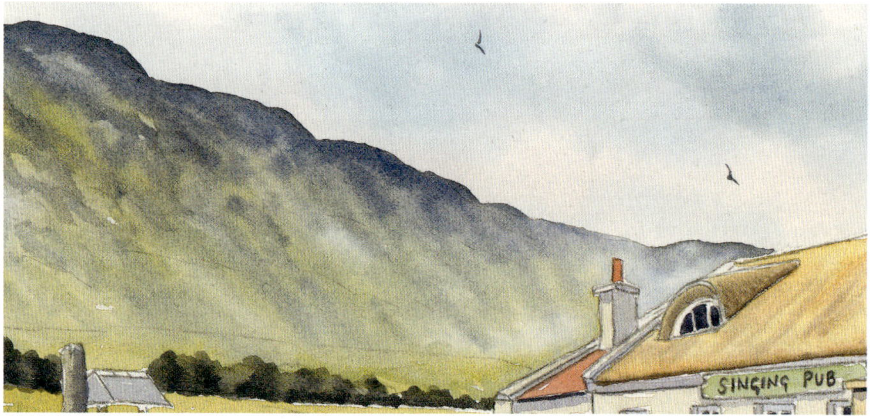

Wet the mountains with water but not right to the top edge. Use three brushfuls of water with French ultramarine and a little light red to define the shape of the mountains, then bleed in two brushfuls with Winsor yellow and a touch of French ultramarine from two-thirds of the way up, cutting round the well. Define the profile of the mountains with two brushfuls of French ultramarine and light red, then pull legs down for ruts and crevices. Squeeze the brush dry and nip it into a paddle shape, then use it to smooth and manipulate the colours.

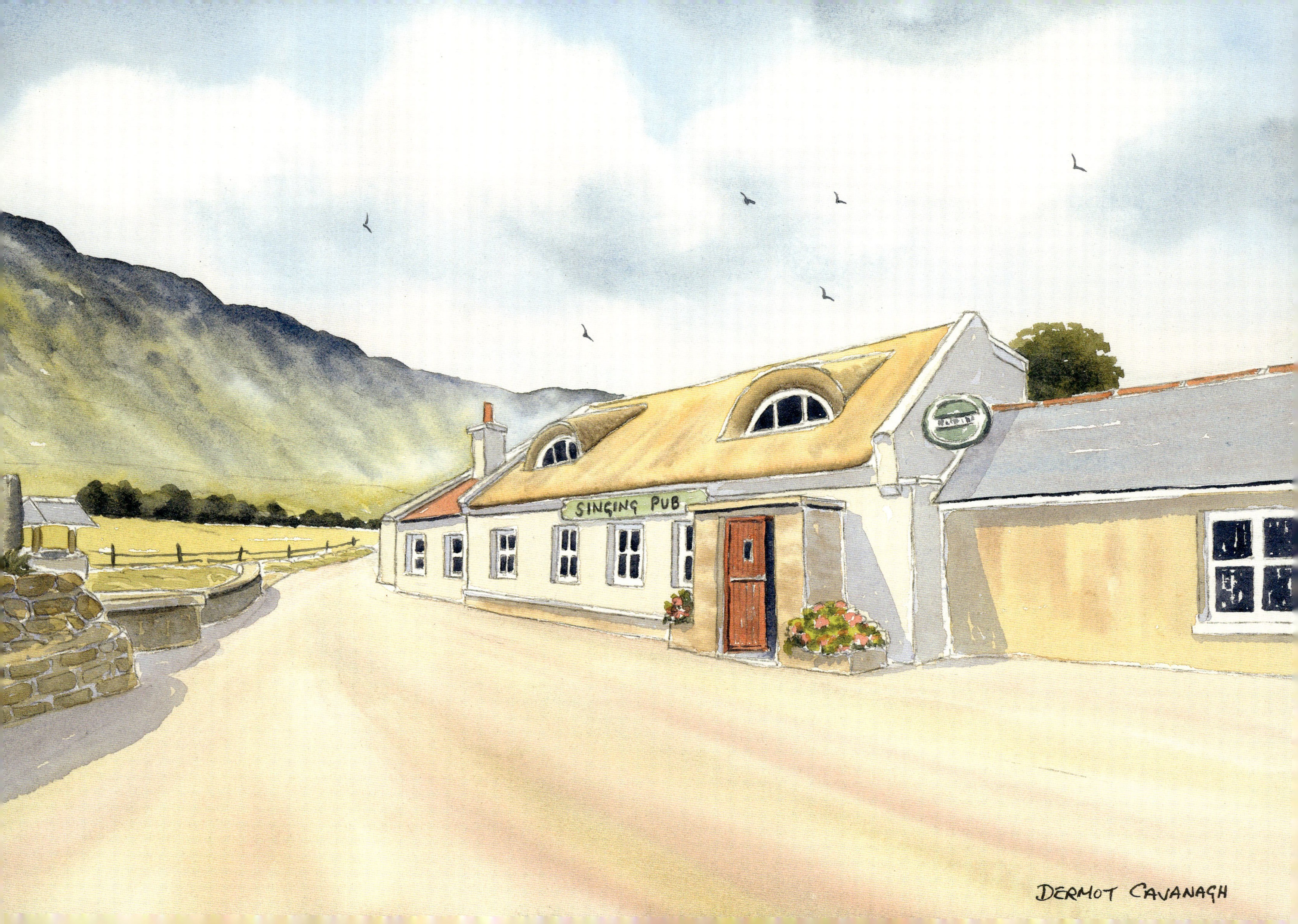
SINGING PUB
DERMOT CAVANAGH

Doo Lough

OUTLINE 23

In the heart of Connemara, between the town of Louisburgh and Delphi Lodge, in a wild and unspoilt valley of extraordinary beauty lies the deep and formidable Doo Lough (Black Lake). Overlooked by the tallest mountains in Connemara, the lakes and rivers of the Delphi Valley are famous for their salmon and sea trout fishing. I do hope you enjoy it.

Palette of colours

- Winsor blue (red shade)
- Cerulean blue
- Alizarin crimson
- Raw sienna
- Neutral tint
- Winsor yellow
- Cobalt turquoise (light)
- Light red
- French ultramarine
- Burnt sienna
- Winsor red

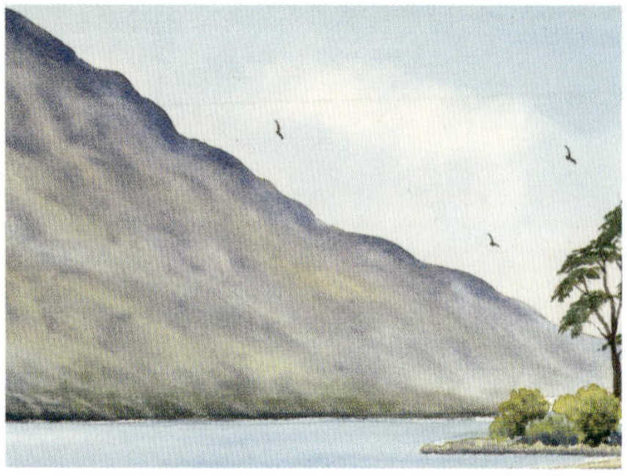

The mountain is painted with four washes: four brushfuls of water with French ultramarine and a little light red; three brushfuls with Winsor yellow and French ultramarine; the same with alizarin crimson and cerulean blue; and two brushfuls with French ultramarine and light red.

Emphasize the texture using a dry flat brush, to pull the marks in little arcs, following the direction of the land.

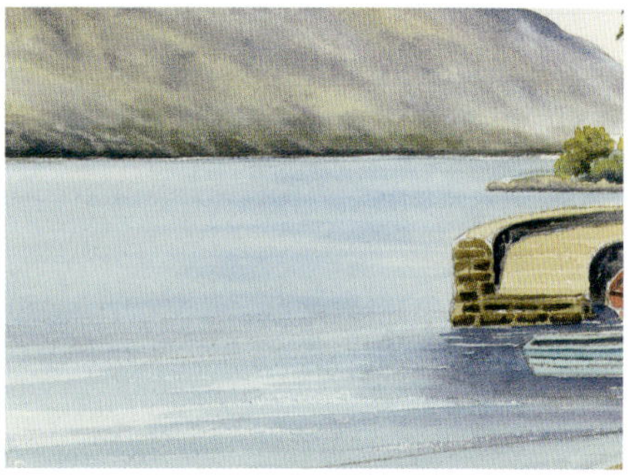

Paint the lough with a dilute wash of Winsor blue with a tiny bit of cerulean blue. Brush clean water on to the paper, then brush in the wash with horizontal lines, using the flat edge of the brush.

Add more Winsor blue for strength in darker areas.

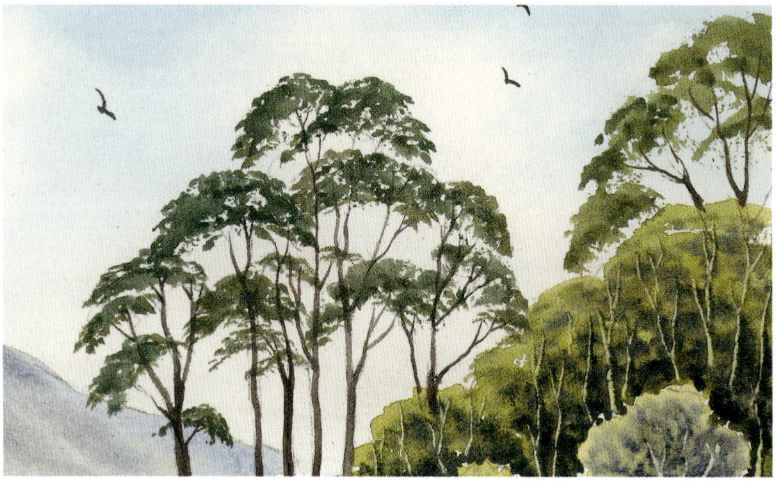

Mix burnt sienna and neutral tint, then use a rigger to paint the silhouetted trunks of the background trees, painting up from the bottom and tapering the strokes to indicate the natural thinning of branches and twigs. Paint the foliage with a no. 8 brush in a flat hold with a mix of raw sienna and Winsor blue, then modify and shape the blocks of foliage with the point of the brush. Paint the foliage of the trees on the far right with a mix of Winsor yellow, French ultramarine and a little light red.

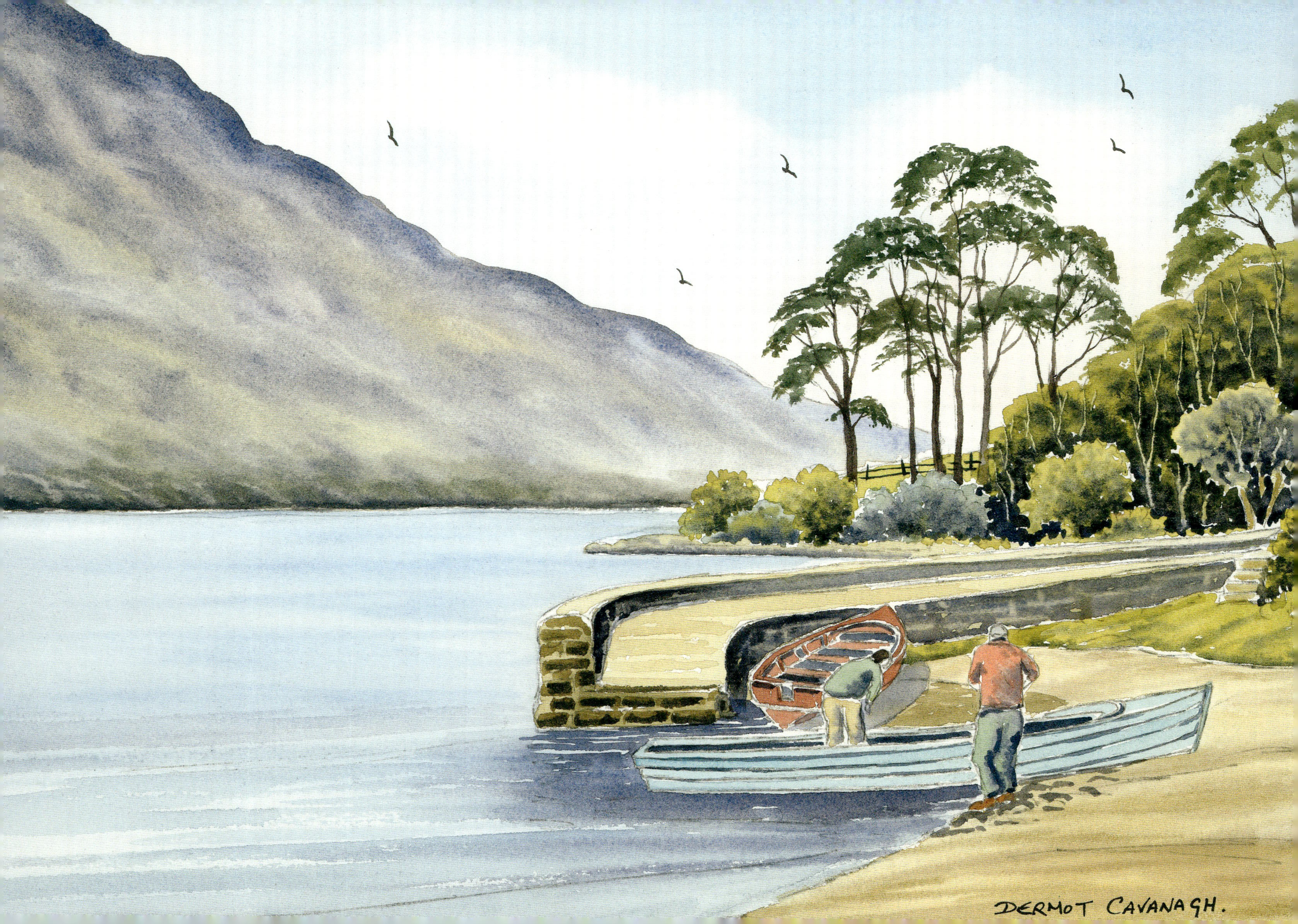
DERMOT CAVANAGH.

Castle Island

OUTLINE 24

Castle Island is in Lough Key, County Roscommon and is part of the Shannon–Erne Waterway, a navigable canal linking the River Shannon in the Republic of Ireland with the River Erne in Northern Ireland. This simple but effective painting captures the mystic atmosphere of the place.

Palette of colours

- Winsor blue (red shade)
- Cerulean blue
- Alizarin crimson
- Raw sienna
- Neutral tint
- Winsor yellow
- Cobalt turquoise (light)
- Light red
- French ultramarine
- Burnt sienna
- Winsor red

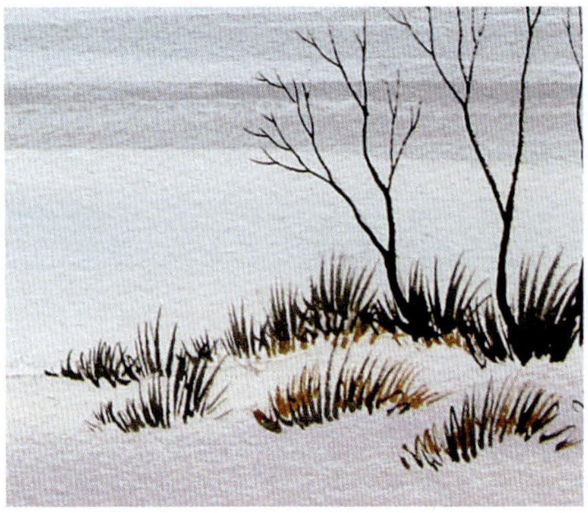

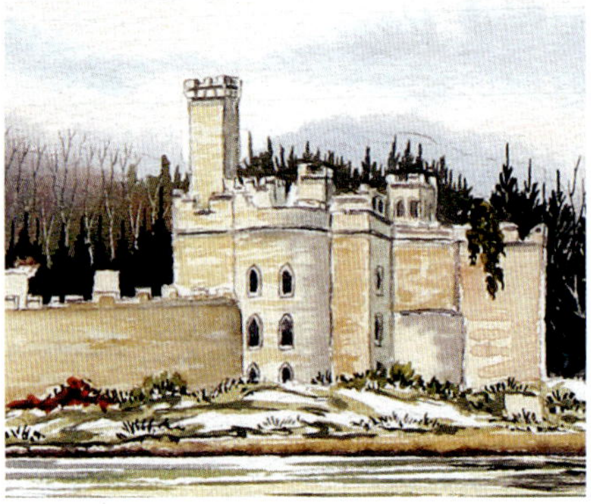

It is clearly a cold day, but the painting has plenty of warmth. To create this I used a very dilute mixture of light red and alizarin crimson in the lower half of the sky, the foreground water and snow washes (above left). I used warm washes of raw sienna and burnt sienna and light red on the castle walls (above right).

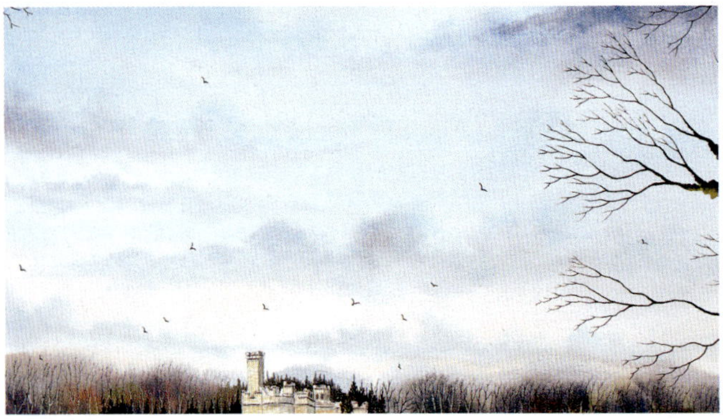

The warmth is all contrasted by the cool bluish washes. The pale blue in the sky is a dilute wash of cerulean and Winsor blue while the clouds are a slightly stronger mixture of cerulean blue and a little neutral tint bled in and blended while the sky was still wet.

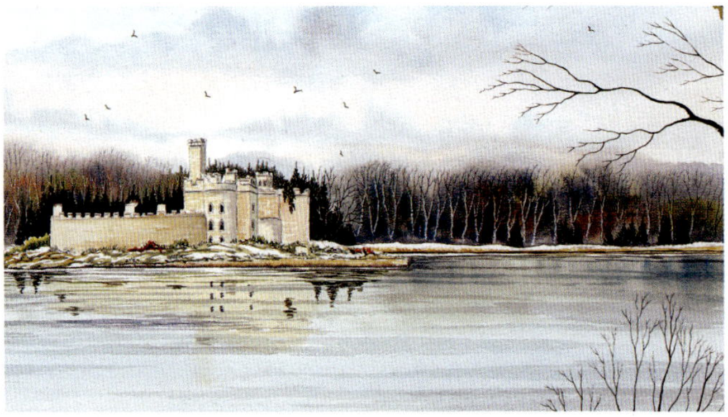

The green and rusty red washes I bled into the background trees also add warmth. The background trees were painted with varying strength washes of French ultramarine and a little light red, painted wet into wet. The sunlit tree trunks were scratched out with a penknife just before the washes dried.

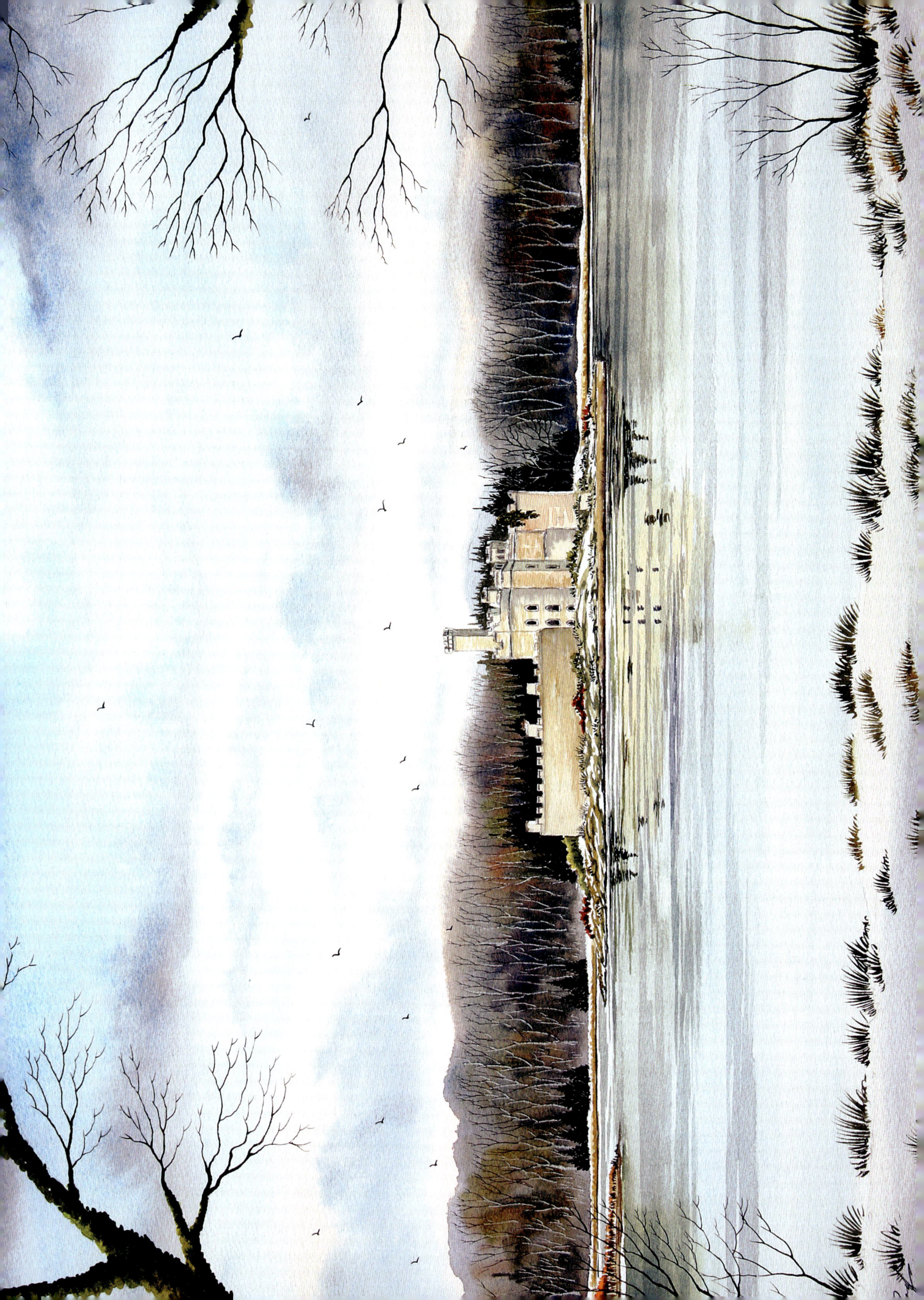

Boats and harbours

Charles Evans

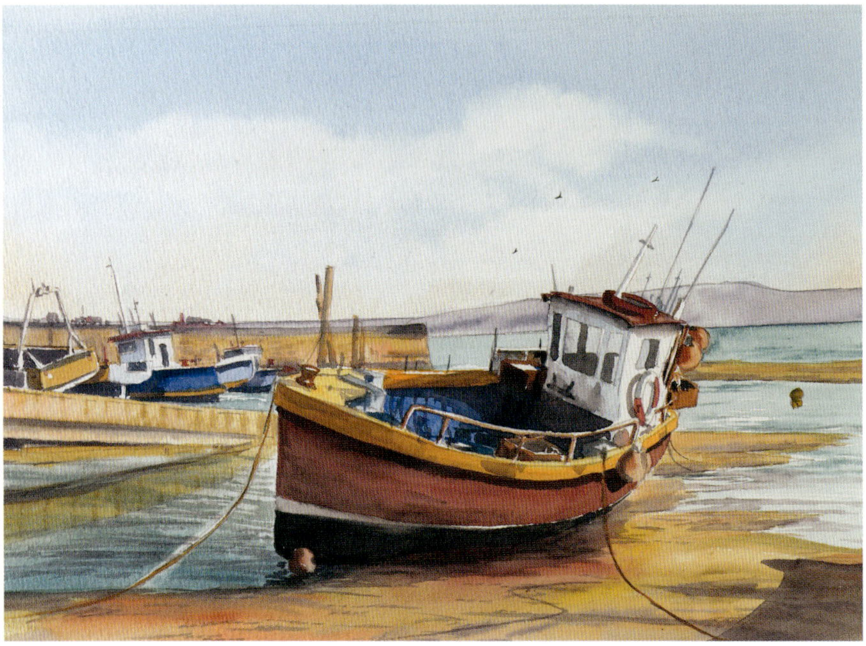

Newquay, page 78

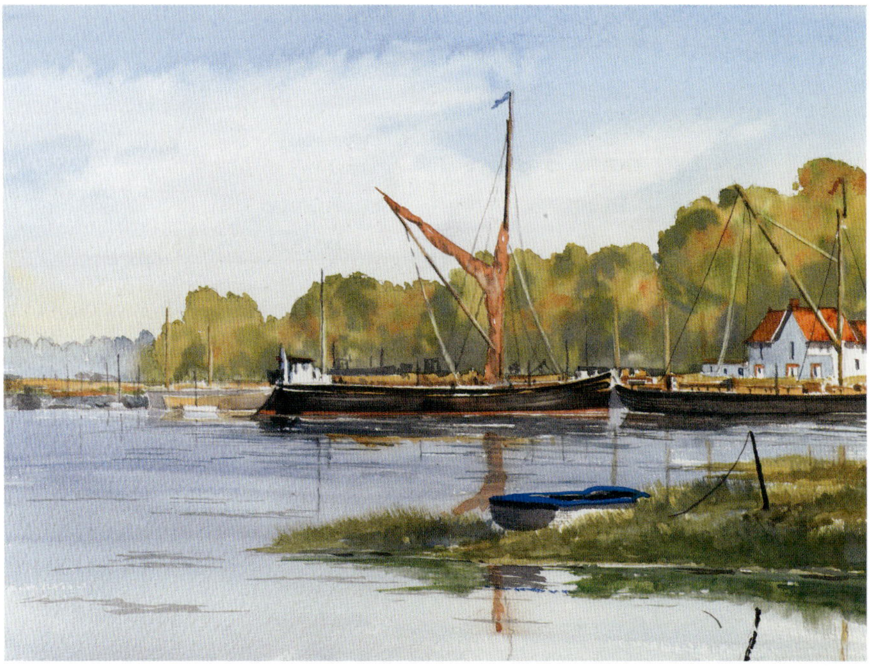

Pin Mill, page 80

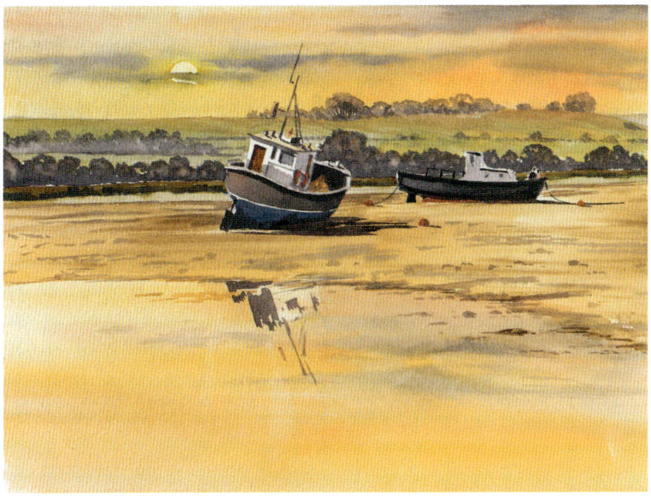

Alnmouth Estuary, page 82

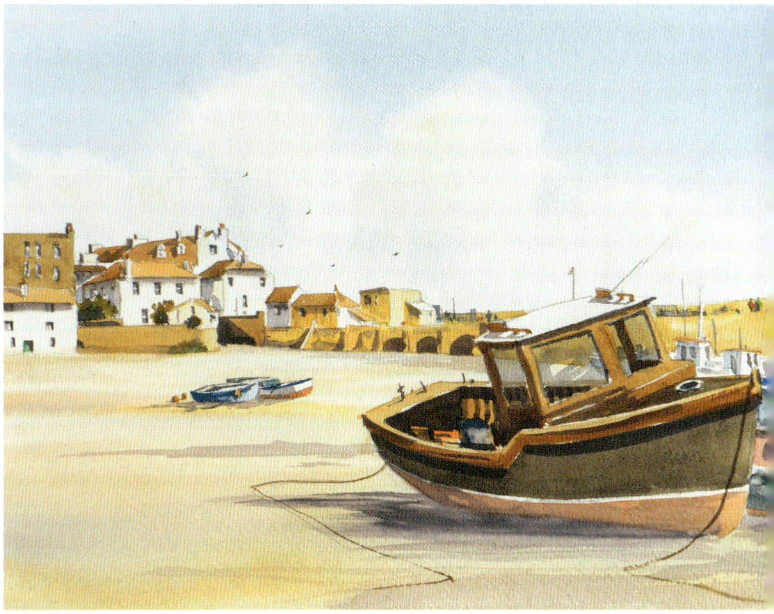

St Ives, page 84

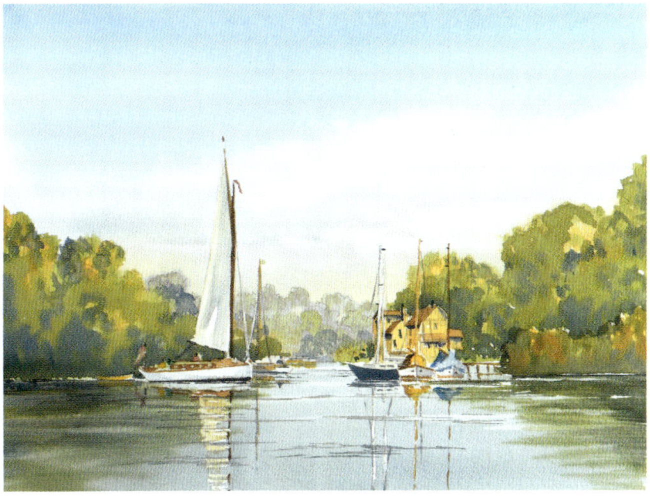

Norfolk Wherry, page 86

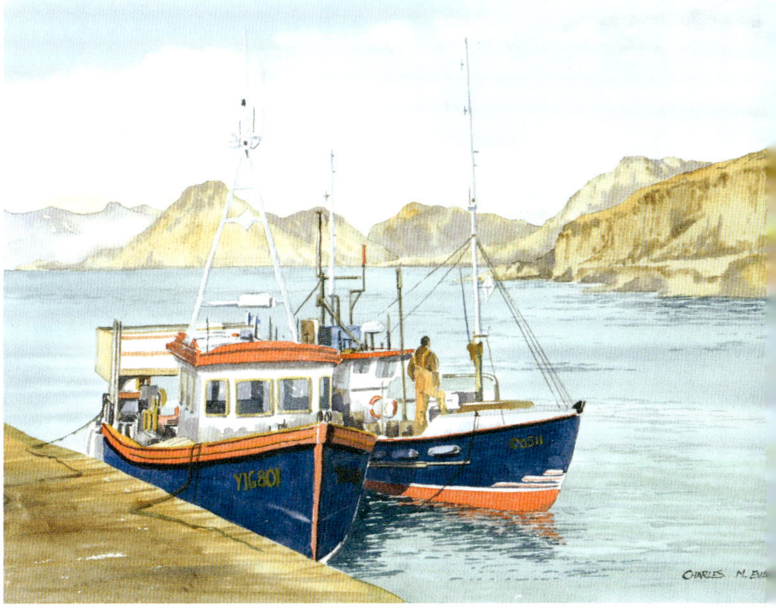

Scottish Fishing Boats, page 88

Newquay

OUTLINE 25

This is a strong painting, with an overall warm feel owing to the colours used in the mixes. You will notice that I use the same blue in the sea as I do in the sky and this is a handy rule of thumb that will make sure the colours in your paintings look natural.

Palette of colours

- Yellow ochre
- Alizarin crimson
- Cobalt blue
- Hooker's green
- Raw umber
- Light red
- Burnt sienna
- Cadmium red
- French ultramarine

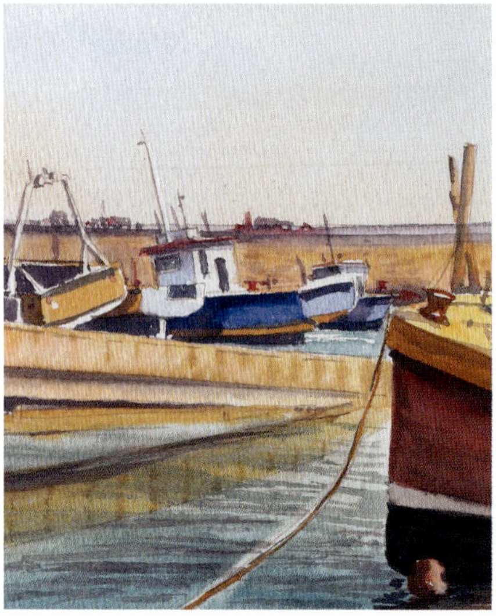

Cobalt blue is the common colour for the sea and sky. In the sky, it is blended into light red near the horizon; while in the water it is mixed with Hooker's green.

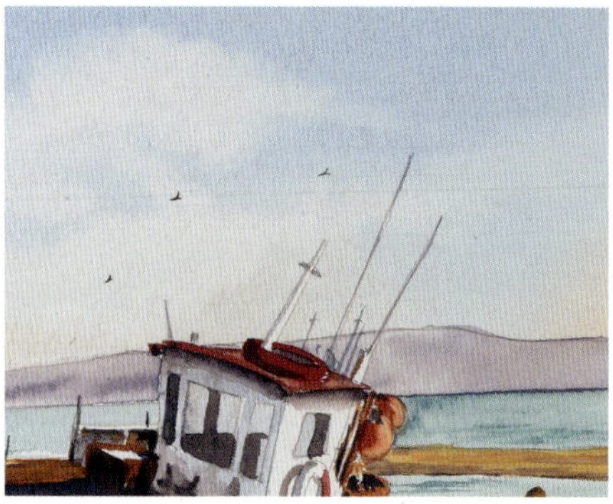

Mix cobalt blue with a touch of alizarin crimson, and use a 20mm (¾in) flat brush to paint in the background hills. Use the corner of the brush to paint around the corners of the boats and other sharp angles. Adding detail brings areas forward, and we want to avoid this in the background. Lifting out highlights, by using a dry brush to draw wet paint out of an area, adds interest without making the area advance.

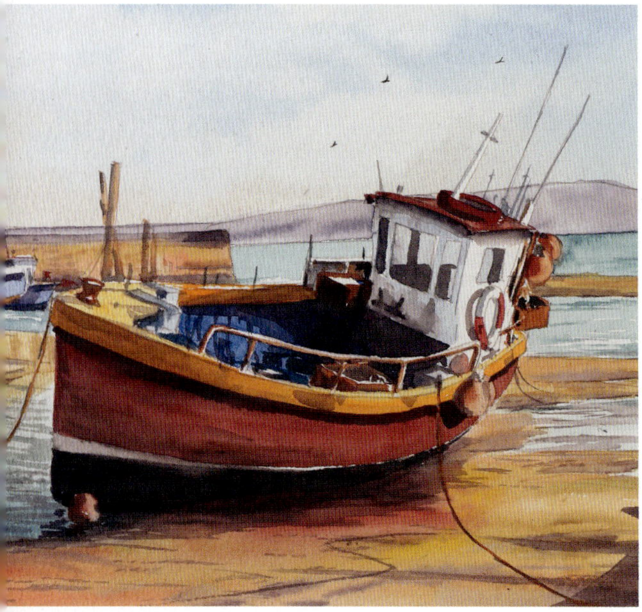

The windows are cobalt blue with a touch of burnt sienna, the inside of the boat pure cobalt blue – work carefully around the railings. Strengthen with a second wash once the first is dry. Then add raw umber to the blue to paint the boxes at the back. Use yellow ochre to paint the gunwale, lifting out areas in direct sunlight. The main hull is cadmium red; the bottom a very dark mix of French ultramarine and burnt sienna.

You can add shading and detail to the interior of the cabin and the buoys with cobalt blue, then add a touch of alizarin crimson and paint the aerials.

Use a shadow mix of burnt sienna, cobalt blue and alizarin crimson to paint the box at the front and the inside of the boat, softening the tone with a damp brush. Once dry, make a stronger shadow mix by adding more burnt sienna and use it to strengthen the shading across the whole boat.

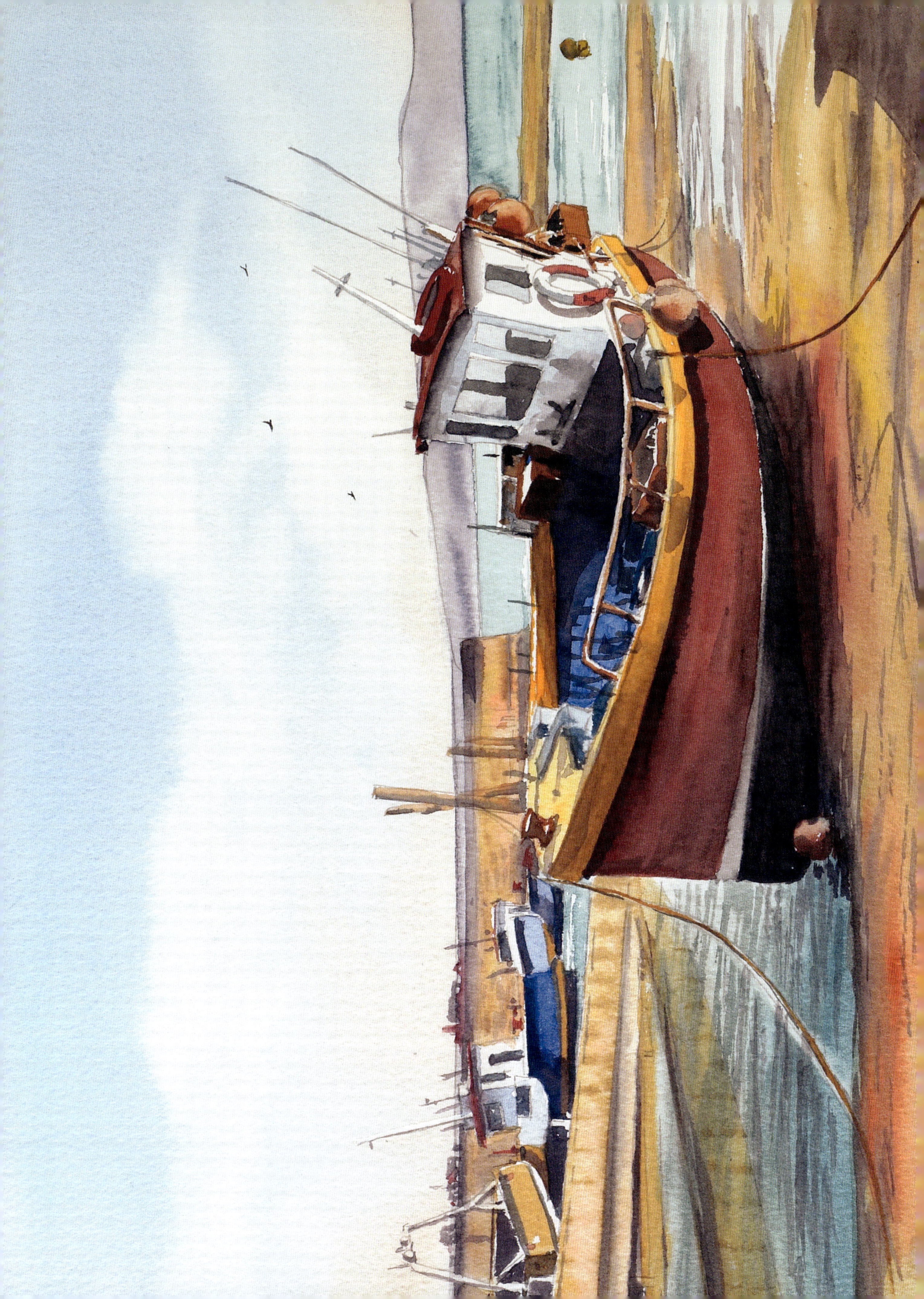

OUTLINE 26

Pin Mill

Pin Mill is one of my favourite Suffolk locations. The old boats that often moor here mean that it is always a timeless scene.

Palette of colours

- Yellow ochre
- Alizarin crimson
- Cobalt blue
- Hooker's green
- Raw umber
- Light red
- French ultramarine
- Burnt sienna

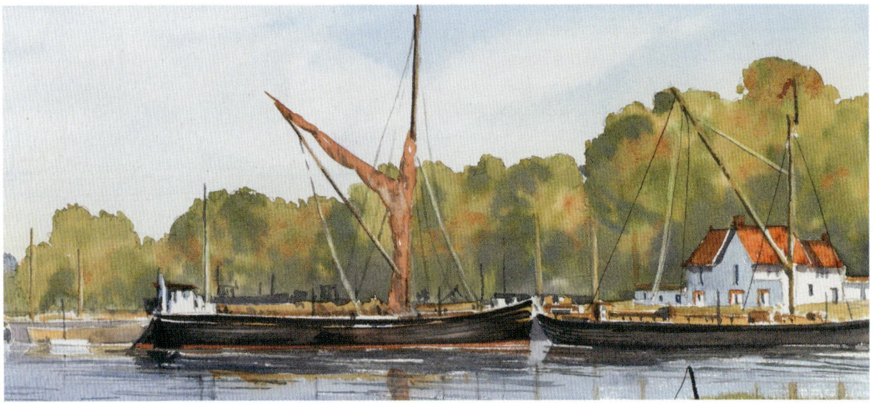

Paint the treeline with yellow ochre at the top, then add a mix of yellow ochre and Hooker's green wet into wet. Next, make a mix of Hooker's green and burnt sienna and drop it in along the lower parts of the trees. To complete this area, add touches of pure burnt sienna to add texture as shown.

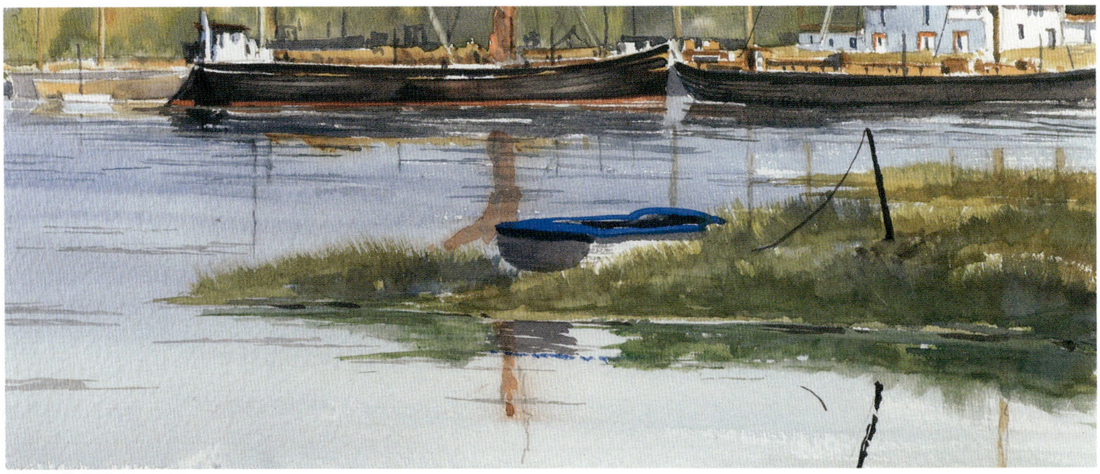

Make a very dilute wash of cobalt blue with a touch of light red. With quick, light strokes of the 20mm (¾in) flat brush, paint the river, leaving white patches showing through. Use a light touch and quick movements to avoid muddying and spoiling the picture – no pressure!

Use a stronger mix to add ripples and wavelets with the side of the 20mm (¾in) flat brush. Make them dark where the boats meet the water.

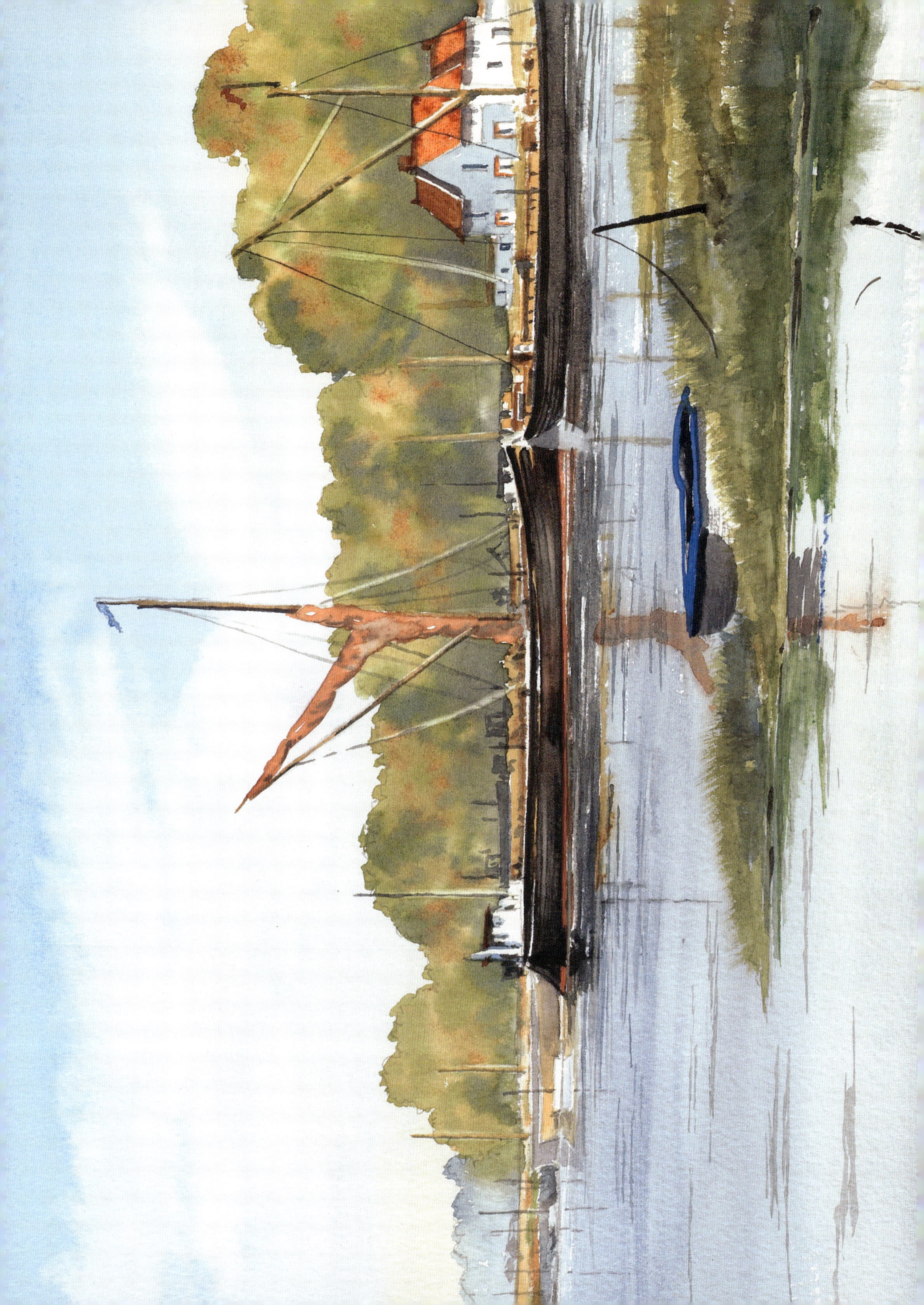

Alnmouth Estuary

OUTLINE 27

There are a lot of strong colours used in this painting, but do not worry, it will look fantastic once you are finished. Trust me, I'm an artist!

Palette of colours

- Yellow ochre
- Cadmium yellow
- Cobalt blue
- Light red
- Hooker's green
- Raw umber
- French ultramarine
- Burnt sienna
- Alizarin crimson
- Cadmium red

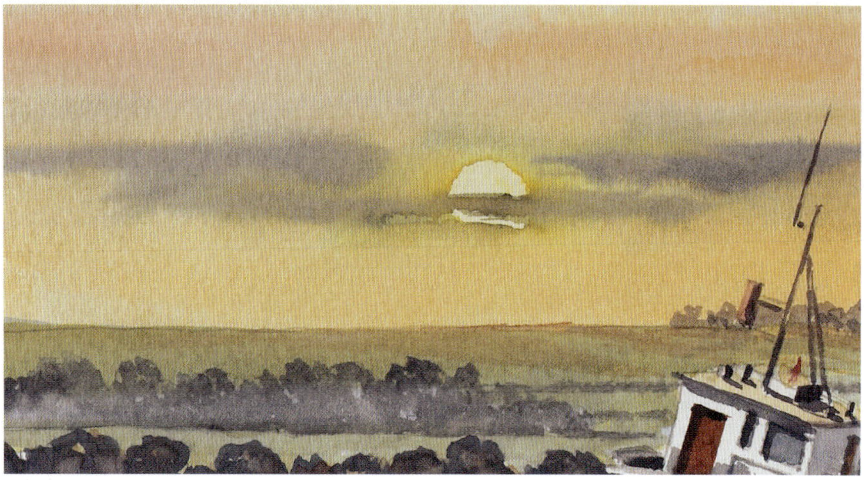

Wet the sky using the 38mm (1½in) flat brush, and drop in yellow ochre. Add light red wet into wet to vary the colour. Add a patch of cadmium yellow into the sky, then twist kitchen roll into the centre to lift out a circle for the sun.

Still working wet into wet, make a cobalt blue and light red mix, and use the 20mm (¾in) flat brush to add clouds. Remember to take the clouds in front of the lifted-out sun. Even the great Turner forgot to do this once!

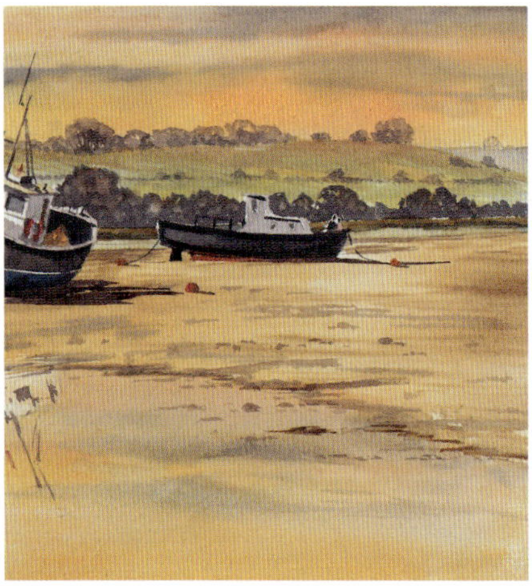

The sky and water are painted with the same colours, and are best painted at the same time.

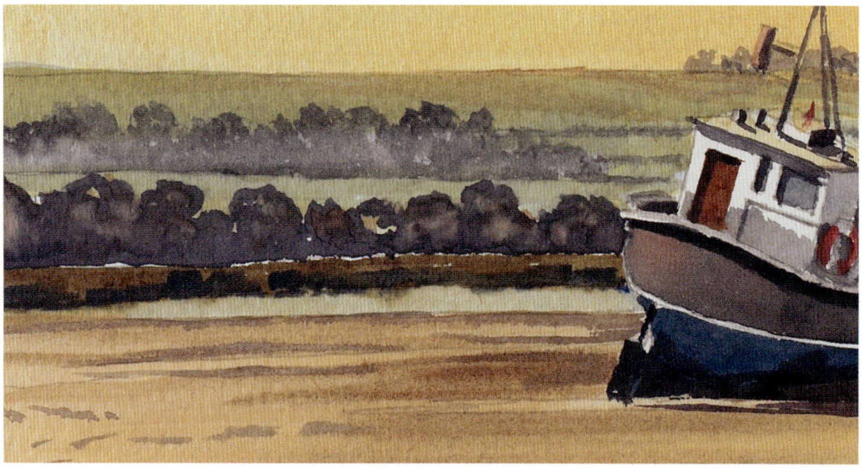

Paint the midground hedgerows with a dilute mix of cobalt blue and light red, and strengthen the mix for dark areas further forward. For the foreground bushes, add burnt sienna to the mix.

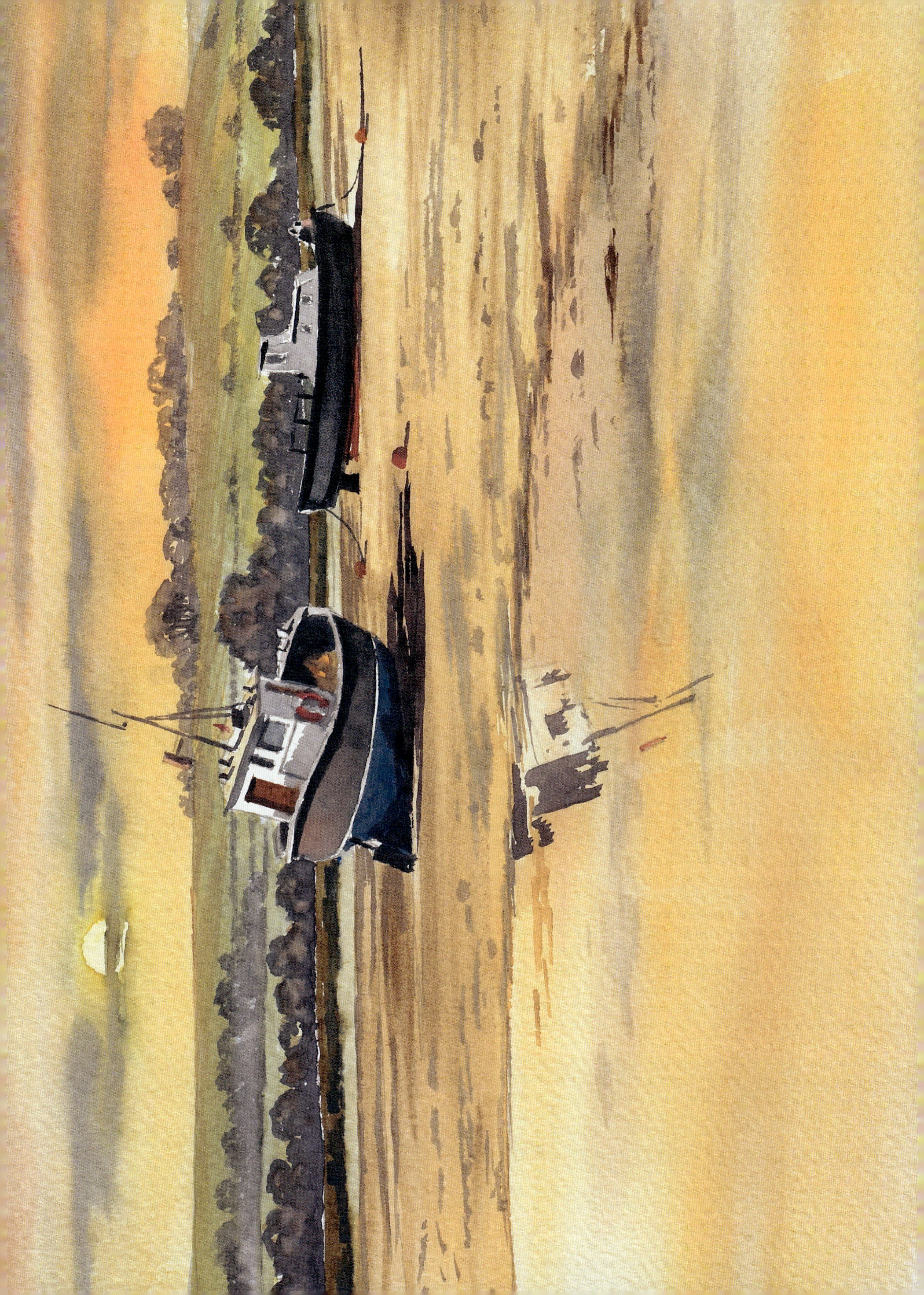

St Ives

OUTLINE 28

St Ives, in Cornwall, UK, is a very popular holiday destination for millions of people, and you can easily see why. In this painting, a lovely jumble of buildings complements the boats beautifully.

Palette of colours

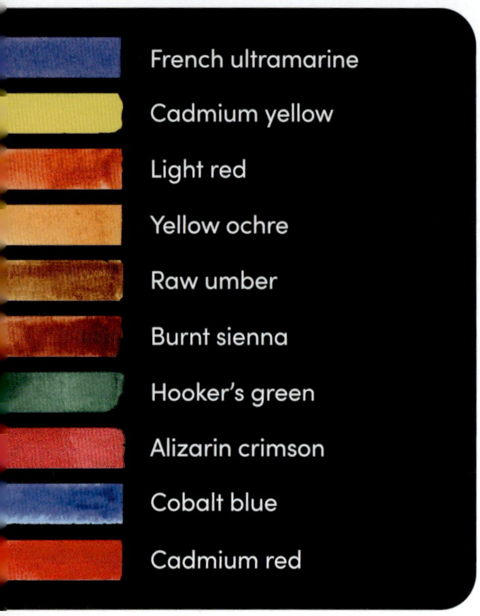

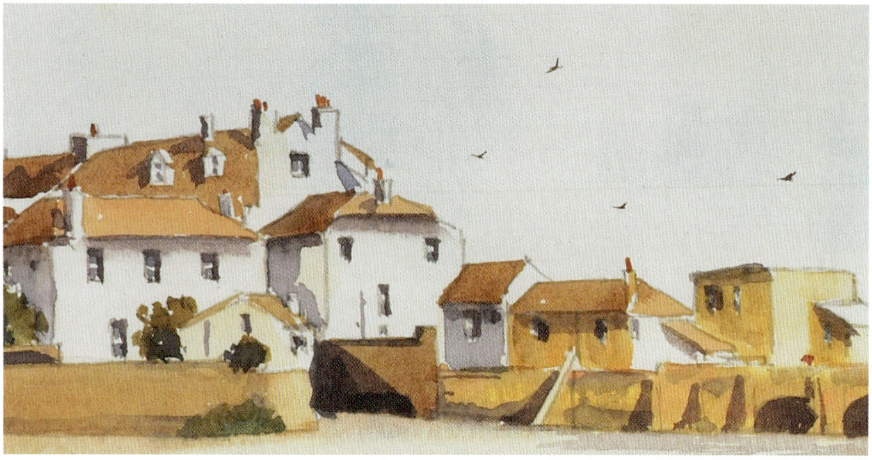

Vary the rooftops by using burnt sienna and raw umber, alone or in varying combinations. Be careful to leave a tiny sliver of dry white paper between each section of rooftop to avoid them bleeding together, and to keep them crisp.

Use mixes of yellow ochre and raw umber, or raw umber and burnt sienna, for some of the buildings, varying the amount of water you add to alter the tone.

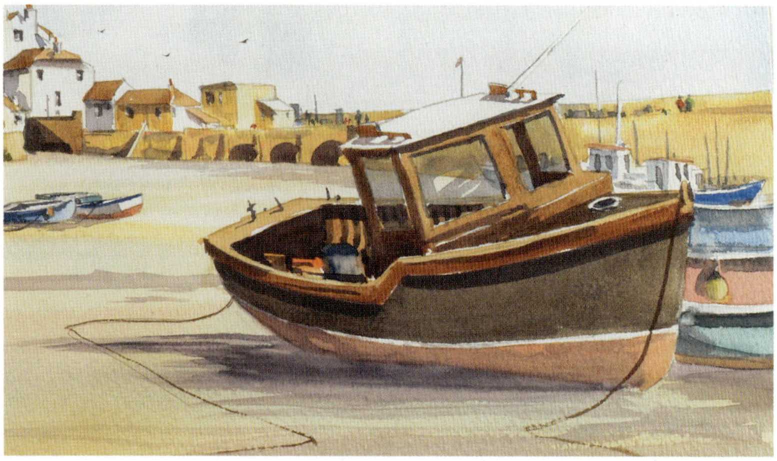

Use a mix of raw umber and burnt sienna to block in the main areas of the cabin and gunwale, diluting it for lighter areas, and light red for the bottom of the hull. Use a mix of French ultramarine and burnt sienna for the hull and front deck.

A shadow mix of French ultramarine, alizarin crimson and burnt sienna is really versatile – you can use it to add shading and cast shadows to both the buildings and the boat.

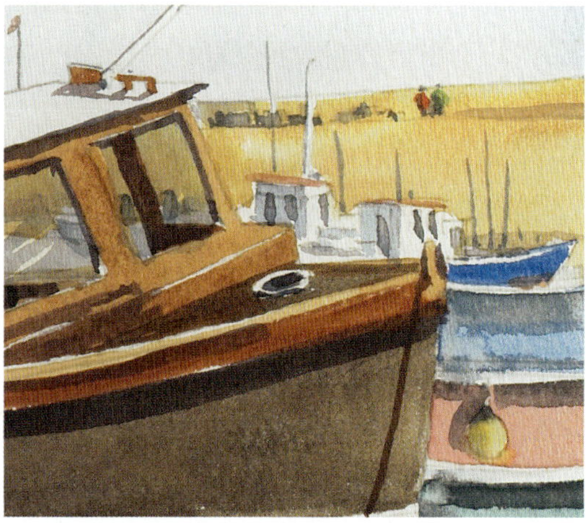

Add the masts, mooring ropes and seagulls at the end of the painting using a rigger brush and a black mix of French ultramarine and burnt sienna. These final details really help to finish the picture.

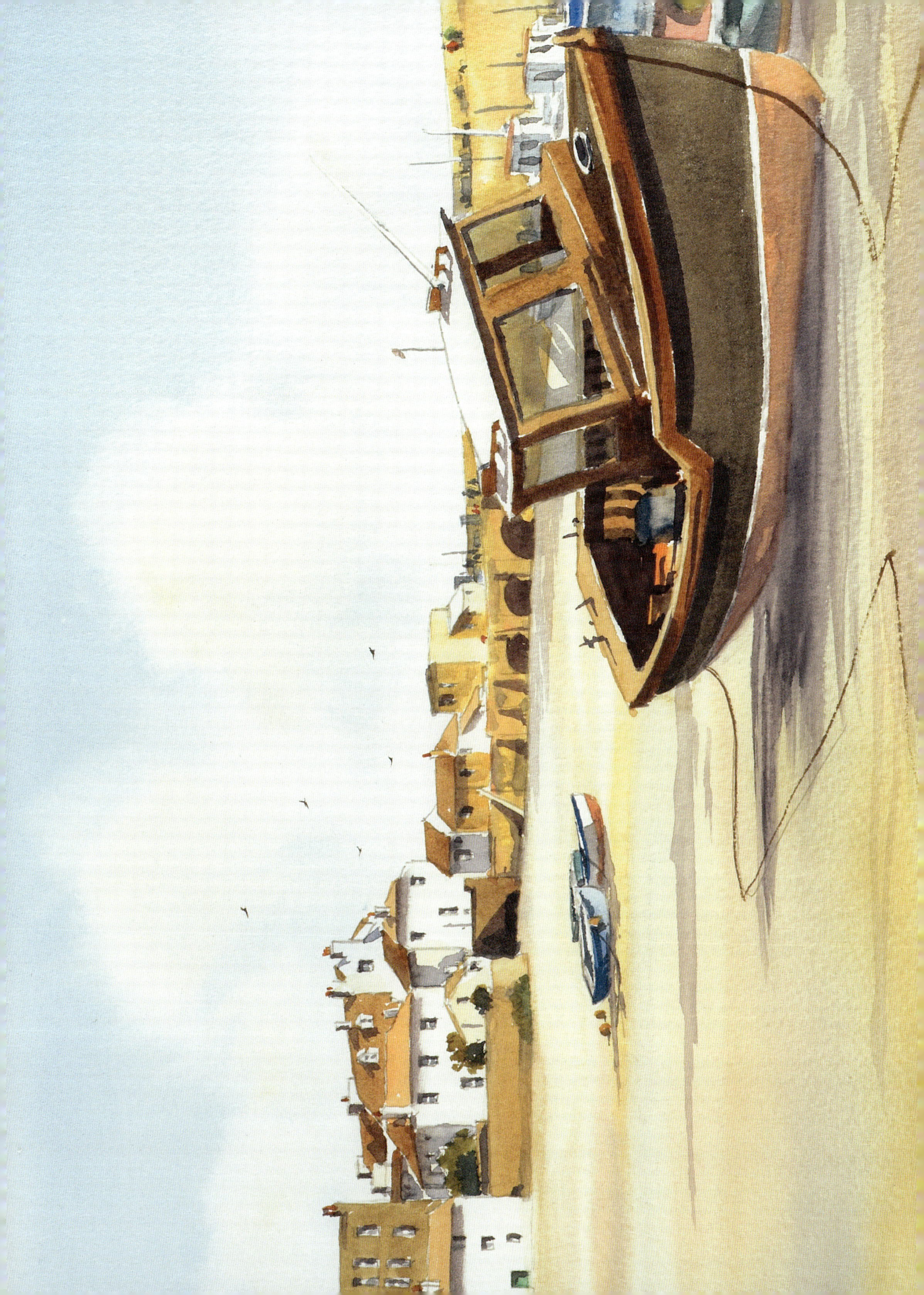

Norfolk Wherry

OUTLINE 29

The wherry – a traditional boat for carrying cargo or passengers across canals – in this picture is actually called *White Moth*. I spent a fabulous week running a painting holiday on board her: enchanting!

Palette of colours

- Yellow ochre
- French ultramarine
- Alizarin crimson
- Light red
- Hooker's green
- Burnt sienna
- Raw umber
- Cadmium red
- Cadmium yellow

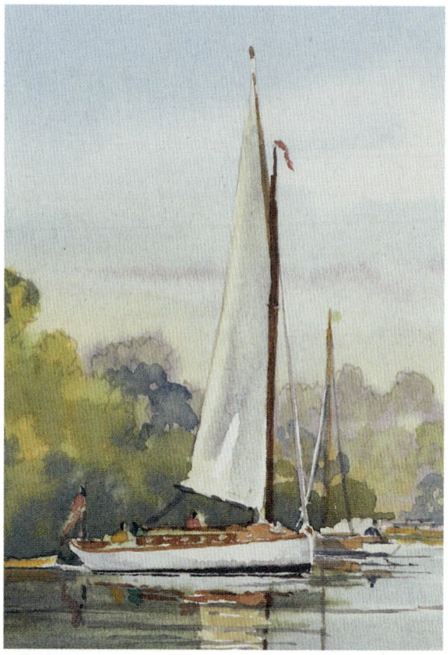

The main wherry is protected with masking fluid to keep it clean while the sky, trees and water are painted around it. Once removed, paint the mast with a mix of raw umber and burnt sienna. Shade this with a black mix of French ultramarine and burnt sienna down the left-hand side.

Paint the pennant with cadmium red, then paint the top of the boat with a mix of raw umber and burnt sienna, working carefully round the portholes.

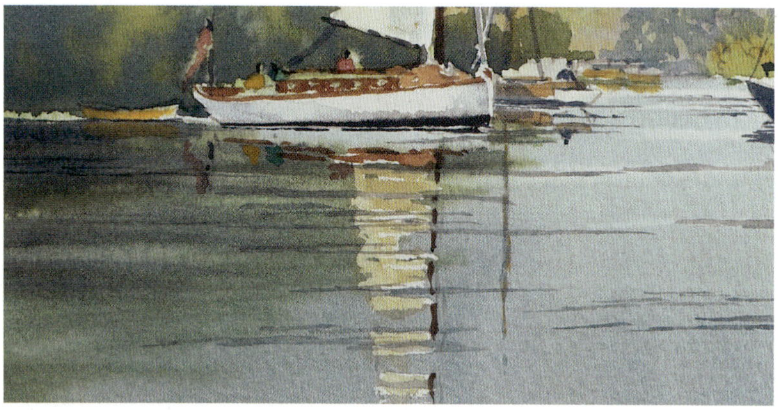

Use the black mix to paint the bottom of the hull and the broken reflection, then paint the figures and their reflections with cadmium red, cadmium yellow, Hooker's green and the black mix (French ultramarine and burnt sienna) for details.

Use a mix of yellow ochre and raw umber with a touch of French ultramarine to paint the sail and the reflection. Leave a touch of white to signify a crease. Add shading to the boat with dilute French ultramarine, softening the shading with the tip of a clean wet brush.

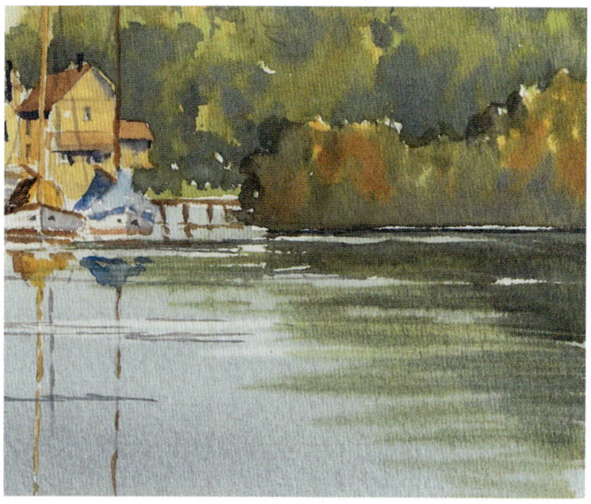

Use the 38mm (1½in) flat brush to wet the river. Mix Hooker's green with burnt sienna, and use the edge of the brush in a broken zigzag motion to paint reflections of the trees on both sides as shown.

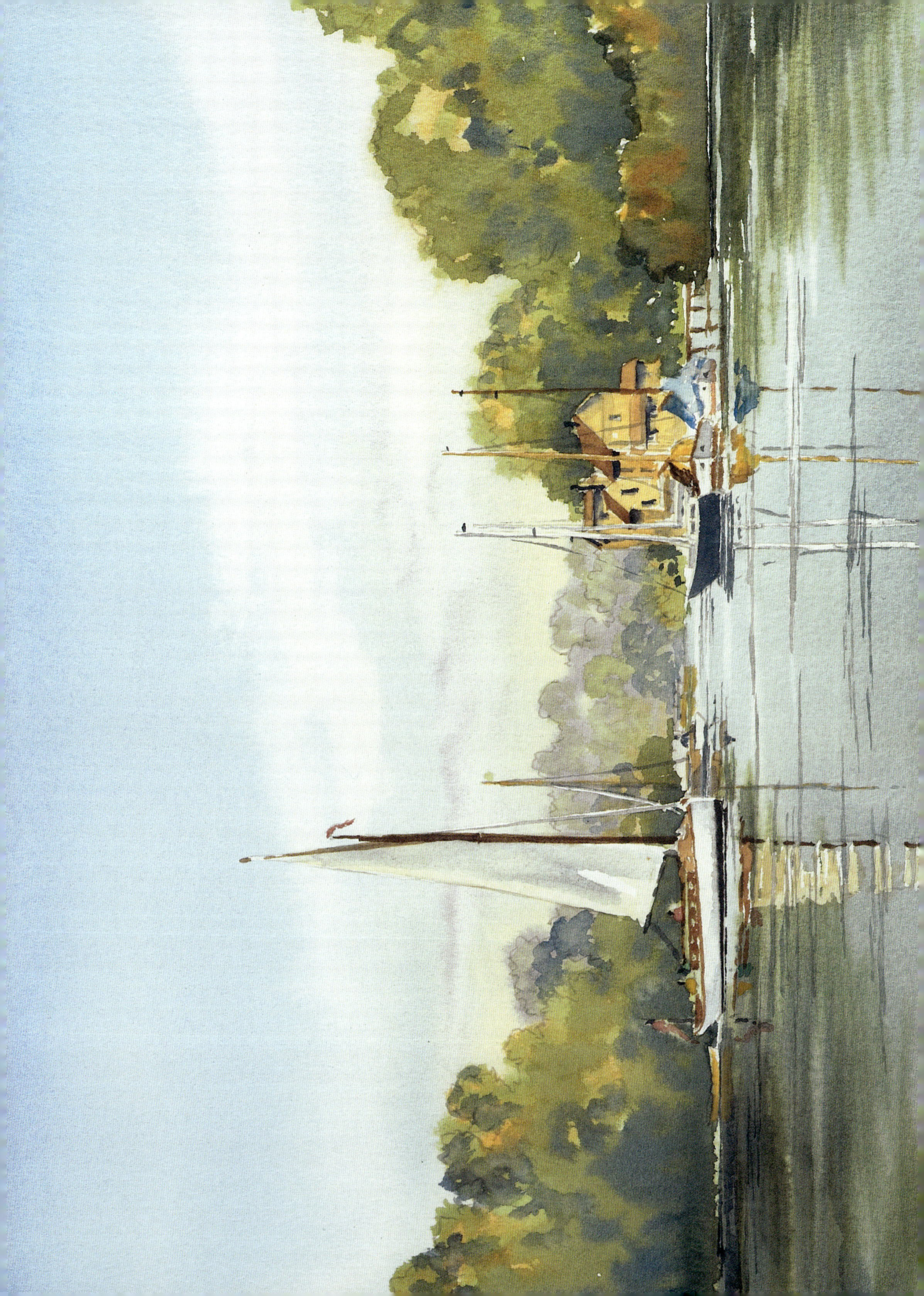

OUTLINE 30

Scottish Fishing Boats

My theory in life is that everyone should have a go at painting, as I believe it is the biggest stress-buster around. When you concentrate your mind on painting it takes over from everything else in the day. It's a real breath of fresh air – and that sense of freshness is what we tackle here.

Palette of colours

- Yellow ochre
- Cobalt blue
- Raw umber
- Alizarin crimson
- Light red
- Burnt sienna
- Cadmium red
- French ultramarine

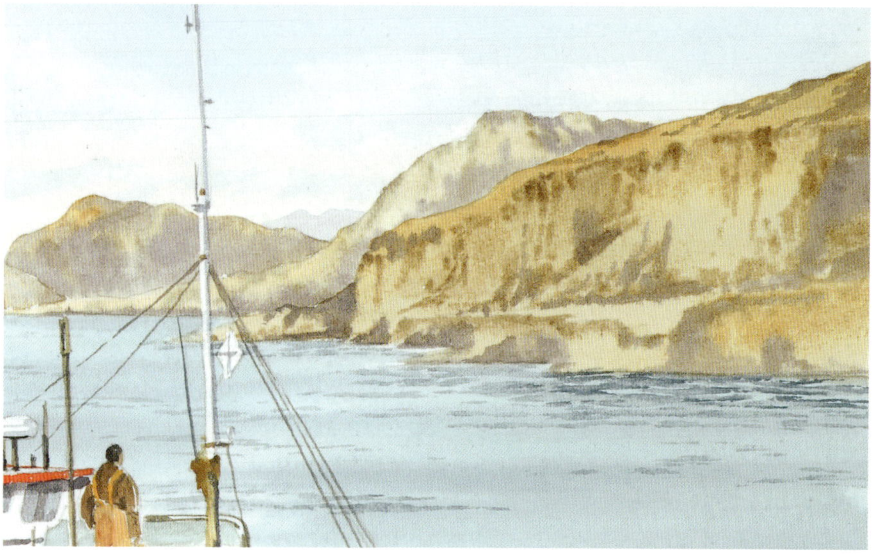

The rocky land mass can be painted with yellow ochre and raw umber; with shadows added afterwards using a mix of cobalt blue, alizarin crimson and burnt sienna. Avoid adding too many details, particularly further back. Dilute your mixes with water for more distant mountains to create a sense of distance.

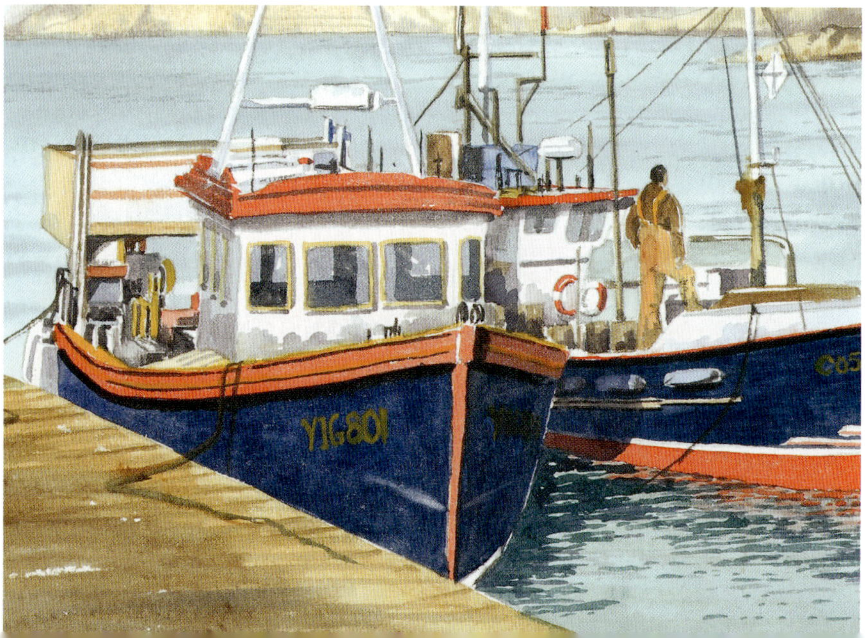

Bold, bright colours are the order of the day here, with cadmium red and French ultramarine used for the boats. Keeping the white areas clean will give the most contrast and impact.

The crew can wear what you like – burnt sienna and yellow ochre are good earthy colours to try.

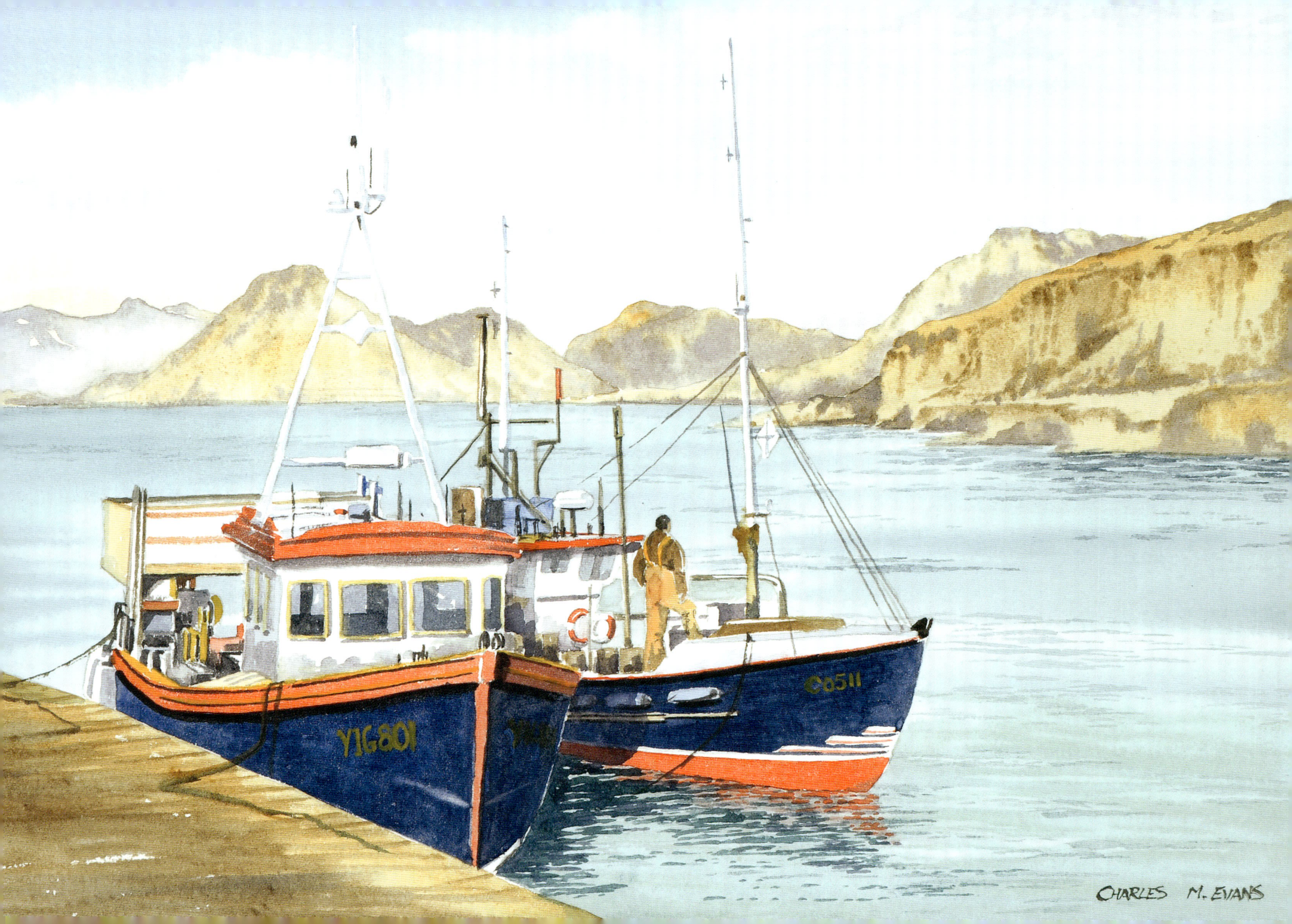
YIG801
CO511
CHARLES M. EVANS

Rustic scenes

Terry Harrison

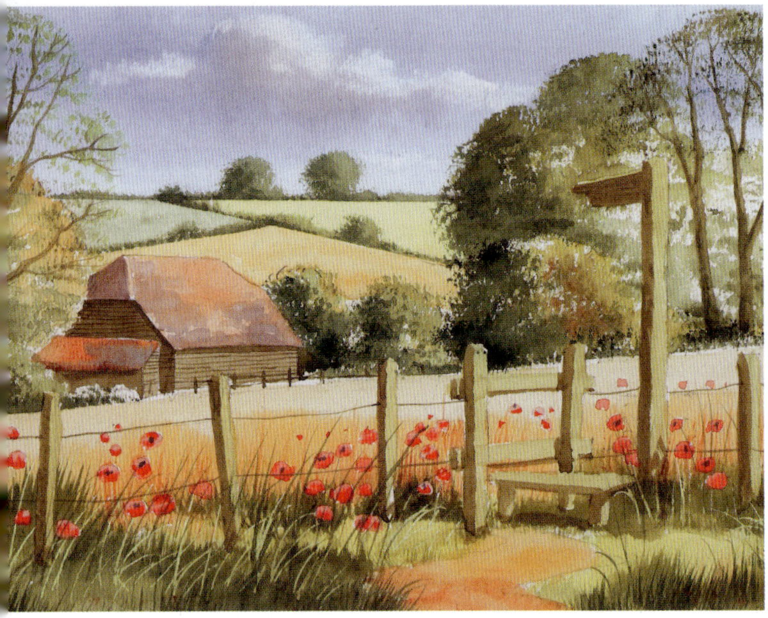

Poppy Field, page 92

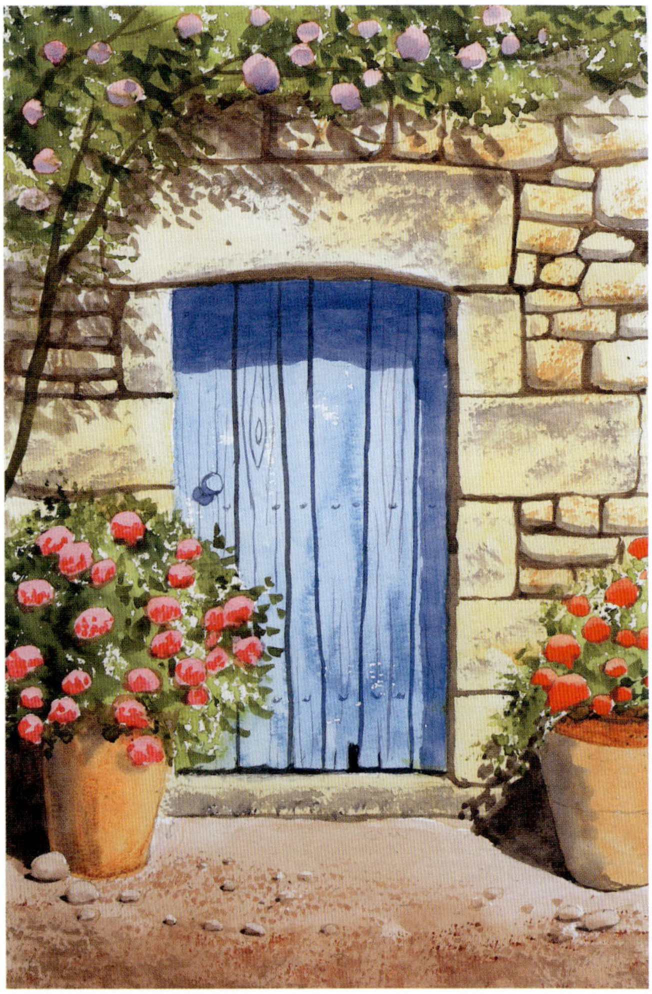

Doorway, page 94

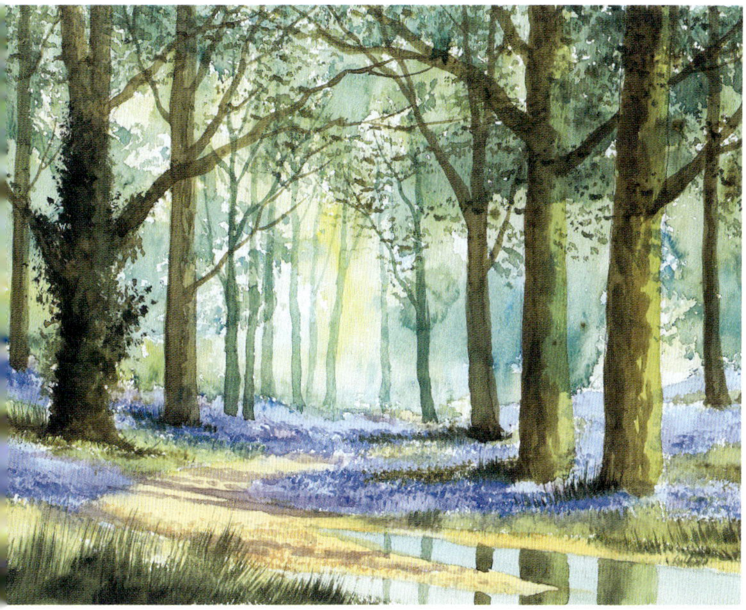

Bluebell Woods, page 96

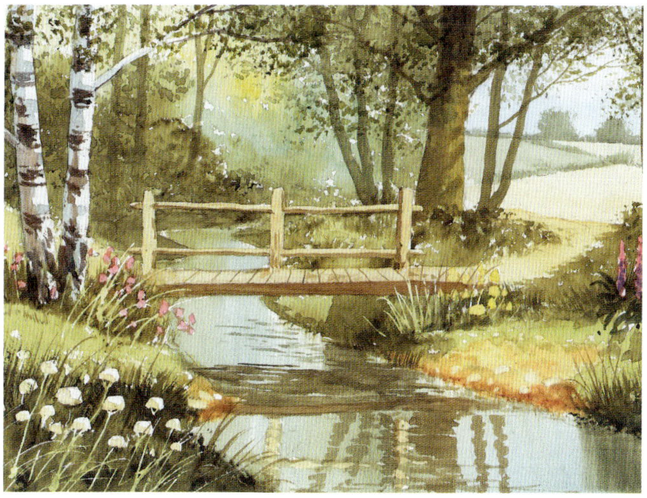

Footbridge in the Woods, page 98

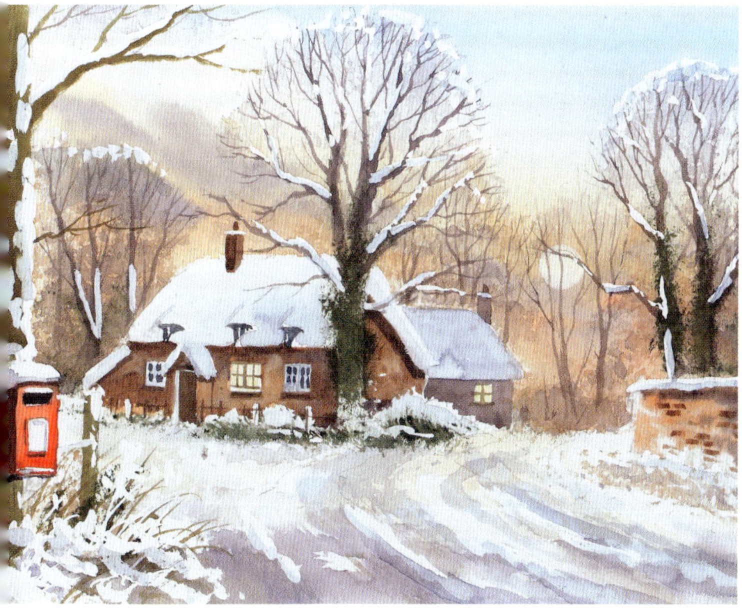

Village in the Snow, page 100

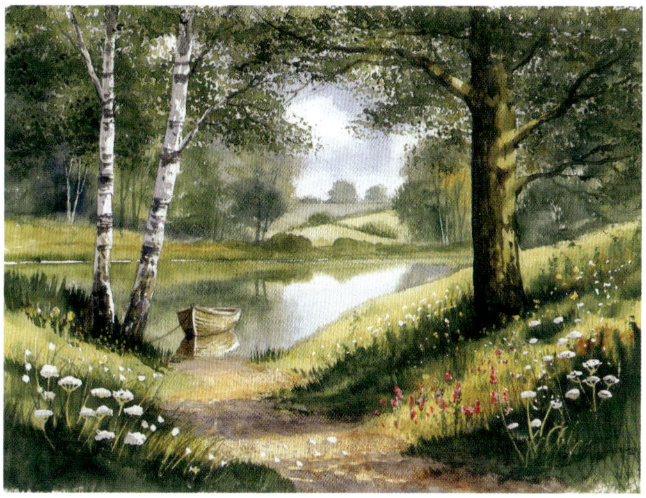

Lakeside Flowers, page 102

OUTLINE 31

Poppy Field

This is a typical Terry Harrison scene. The subject matter is so paintable, with soft, rolling countryside, a patchwork of fields and a splash of bright colour in the foreground, framed by one of my favourite subjects, a footpath, stile and signpost.

Palette of colours

- French ultramarine
- Cadmium yellow
- Raw sienna
- Cadmium red
- Cobalt blue
- Alizarin crimson
- Burnt sienna
- Sunlit green
- Burnt umber
- Country olive
- Shadow

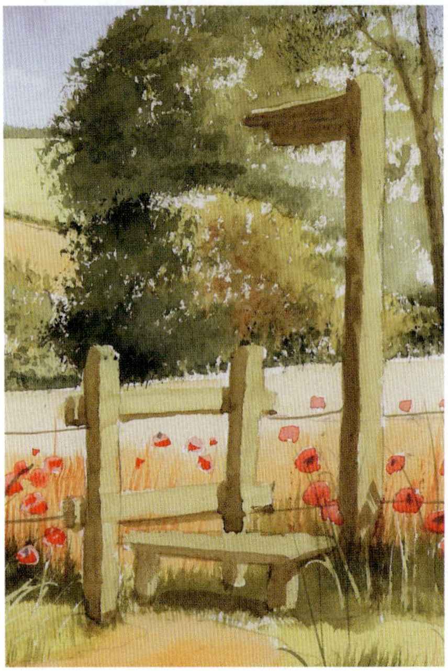

Mask out the fence and stile and paint the background; once the paint is dry you can remove the masking fluid with a clean finger. Paint all the woodwork with a thin wash of raw sienna and sunlit green; and use country olive and burnt umber to paint the shaded side of the woodwork along with the shadows cast by the posts on the horizontals of the stile.

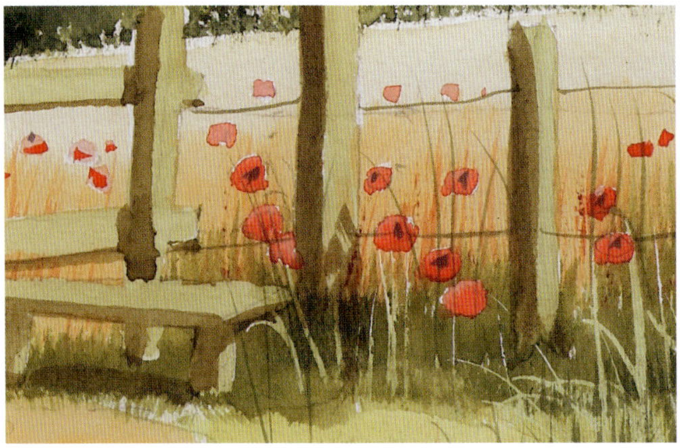

Mask the poppies at the start; and remove them along with the rest of the masking fluid on the fences. Paint the poppies by applying a light wash of cadmium red, then dropping in a deeper mix of the same colour wet in wet. Flick up tall grasses among the poppies with a rigger brush and country olive; then add the poppy centres using the colour shadow.

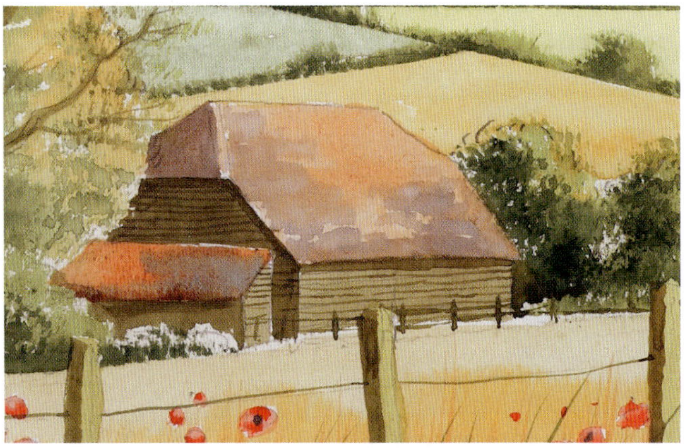

Paint the roof of the barn using a thin wash of burnt sienna. Drop in shadow colour wet into wet to suggest roof tiles. Paint the lean-to roof with stronger burnt sienna and drop in a touch of French ultramarine. This colour granulates, giving a textural result. Use a mix of burnt umber and country olive for the walls; stronger in the shadow. Once dry, paint the shadow under the roof and the weatherboarding with fine lines of the same darker mix.

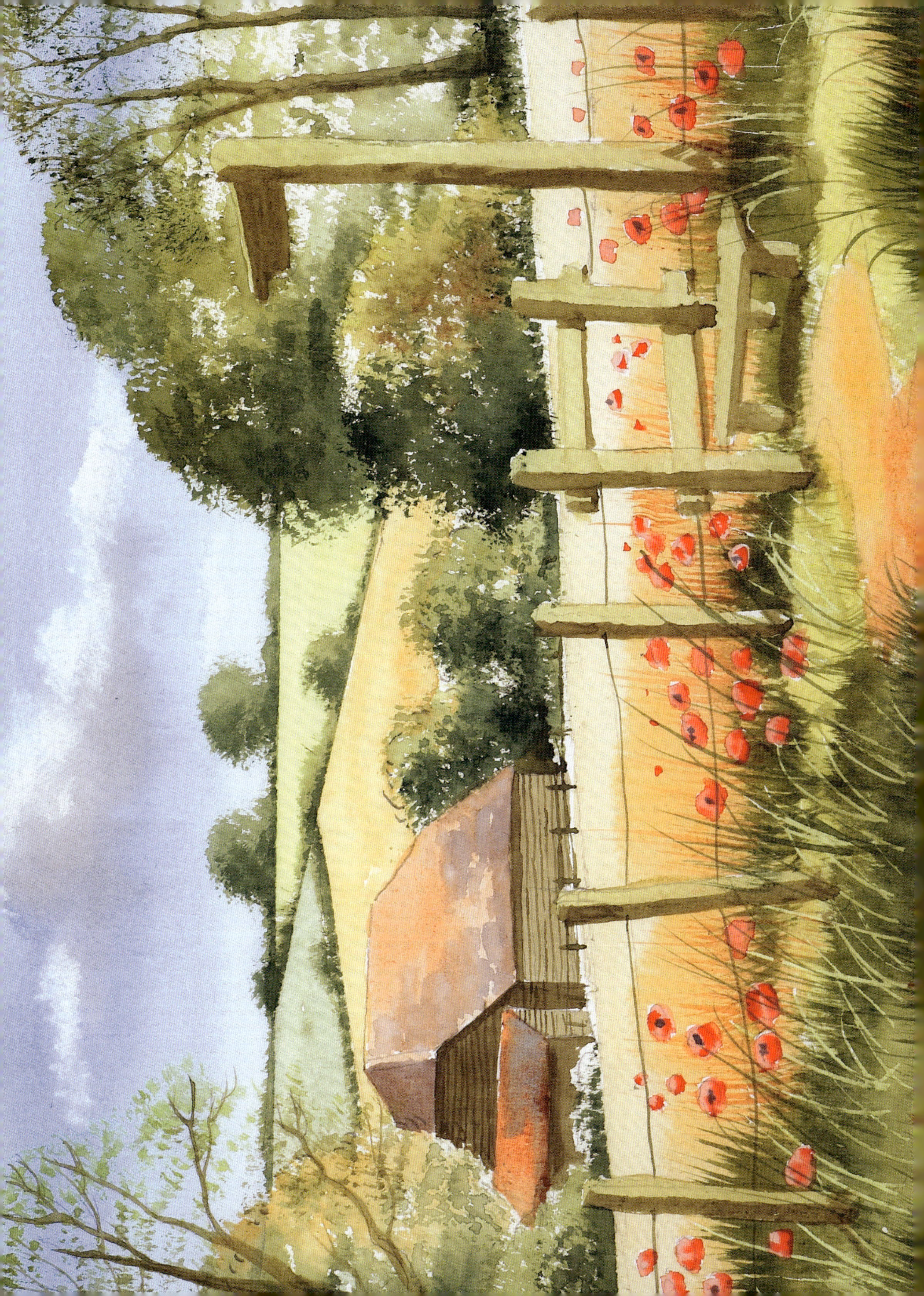

Doorway

The beauty of this subject is in the vibrant colours and warm sunlight, reminiscent of hot summer days or a favourite holiday. This is a simple scene with a strong, bright feel about it.

Palette of colours

- Raw sienna
- Burnt sienna
- Burnt umber
- Shadow
- Sunlit green
- Country olive
- Midnight green
- Cobalt blue
- French ultramarine
- Permanent rose
- Cadmium red

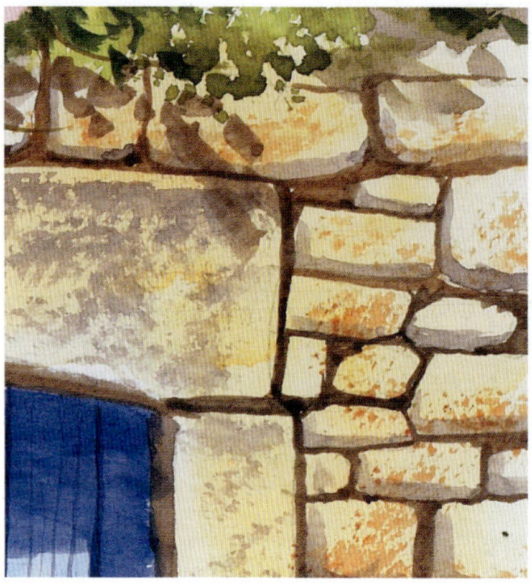

The stonework is painted over a base of pale raw sienna with a warm mix (raw sienna and a touch of burnt sienna) stippled in while wet to create a mottled effect.

Paint the outlines of the stones with a mix of burnt sienna and shadow, and stipple on shadow here and there. Use shadows to shade the undersides and left-hand sides of the stones.

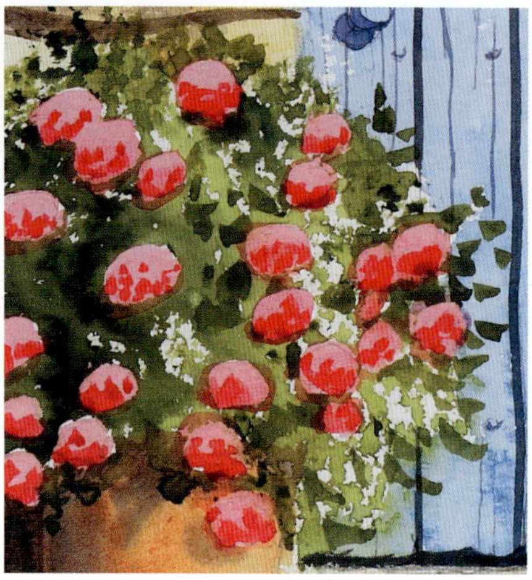

Mask out the pink flowers, and paint the greenery using stippling, with sunlit green in the light and midnight green in the shadow. The flowers themselves are painted with a light wash of permanent rose, then shaded with stronger permanent rose. The red flowers are painted in the same way, using cadmium red instead.

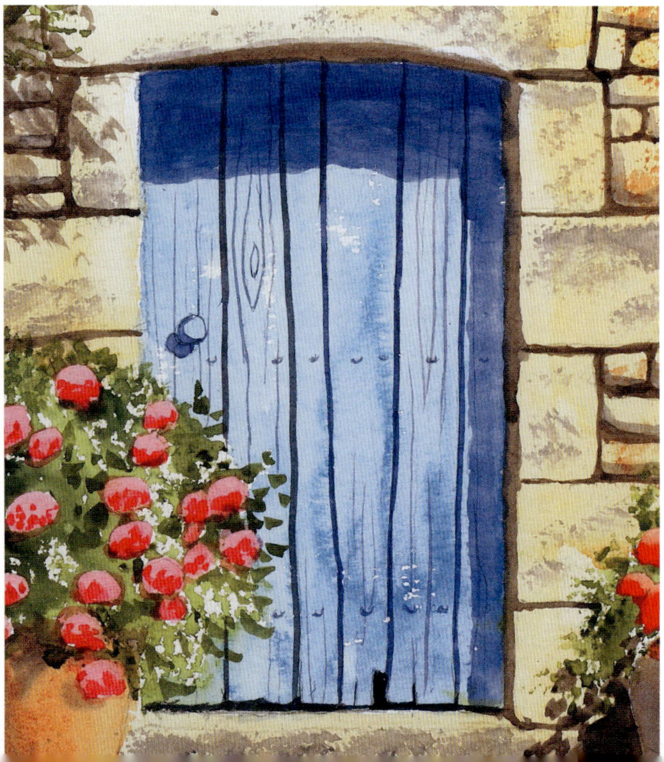

The door starts with a pale wash of cobalt blue. The panels are picked out with a mix of shadow and cobalt blue, while the woodgrain, rivets and handle are picked out with shadow on its own.

The darkest details at the bottom are a mix of ultramarine and burnt umber, while the cast shadow at the top is the mix of shadow of cobalt blue.

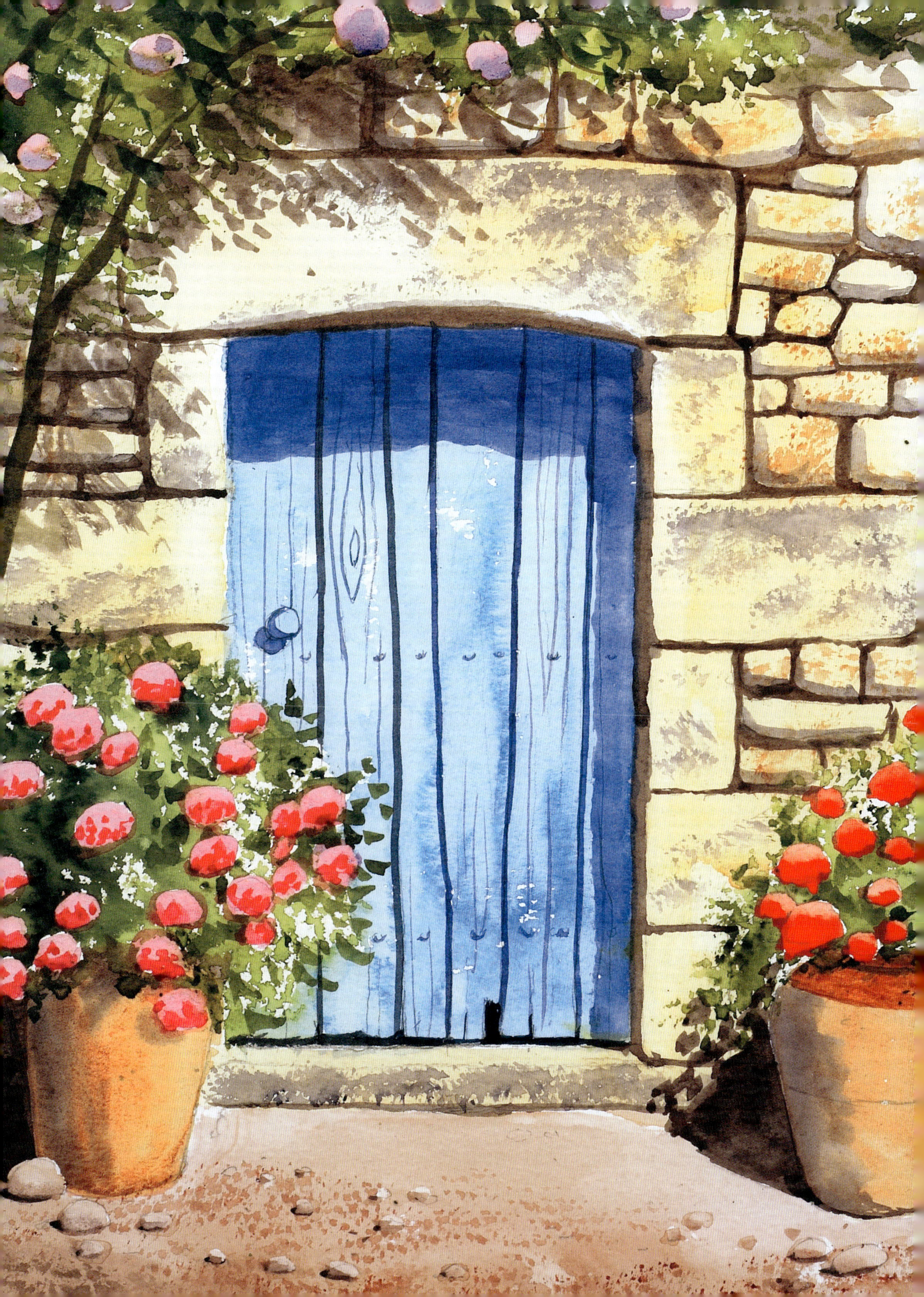

OUTLINE 33

Bluebell Woods

Bluebell woods have a mystique about them, which makes them so appealing to paint. Bluebells bloom for such a short period of time, but our memories of a walk in a bluebell wood remain for a lifetime. To capture that mood is a bonus for an artist. I hope this demonstration will bring back happy memories.

Palette of colours

- Cobalt blue
- Cadmium yellow
- Sunlit green
- Midnight green
- Permanent rose
- Country olive
- Raw sienna
- Burnt umber
- Burnt sienna
- Shadow

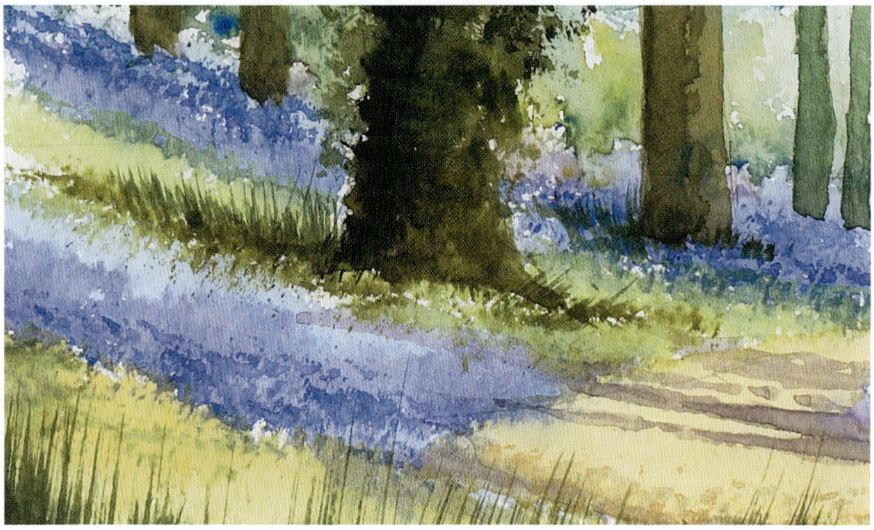

The bluebells themselves are painted with a mix of permanent rose and cobalt blue. This is stippled on from the back, and strengthened as you advance towards the foreground. By the time you reach the bottom of the painting, you can go back with the stronger mix and add shadows and detail wet into wet.

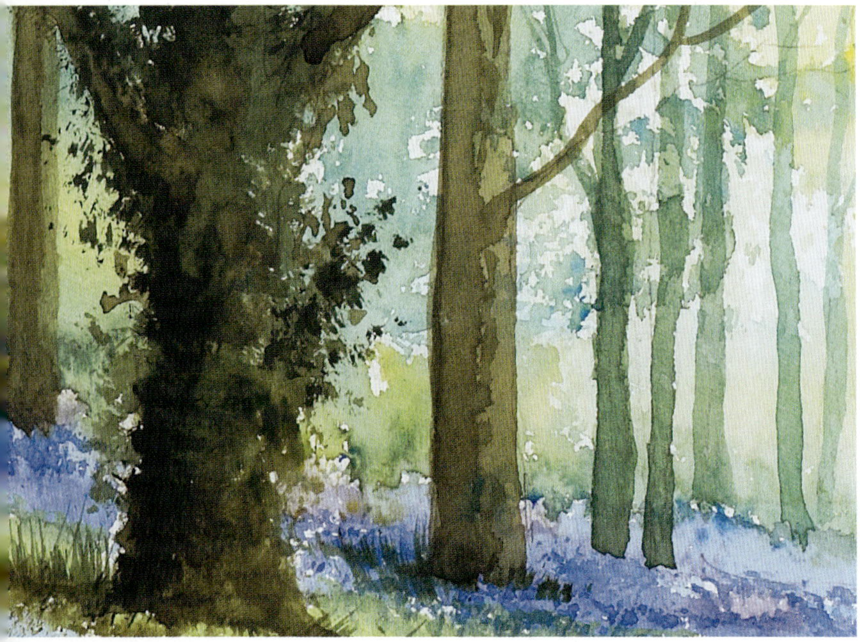

While the bluebells are important, the rest of the wood supports them. The background is all painted with stippling, using cobalt blue, cadmium yellow and then a mix of sunlit green and cobalt blue.

To create a sense of distance, the background trees are painted with little detail, using a pale mix of cobalt blue and sunlit green. The midground trees are a mix of country olive and burnt umber, and shaded with a darker mix of the same colours. The closest trees are a mix of country olive and burnt umber, and have ivy detailing in a darker version of the same mix.

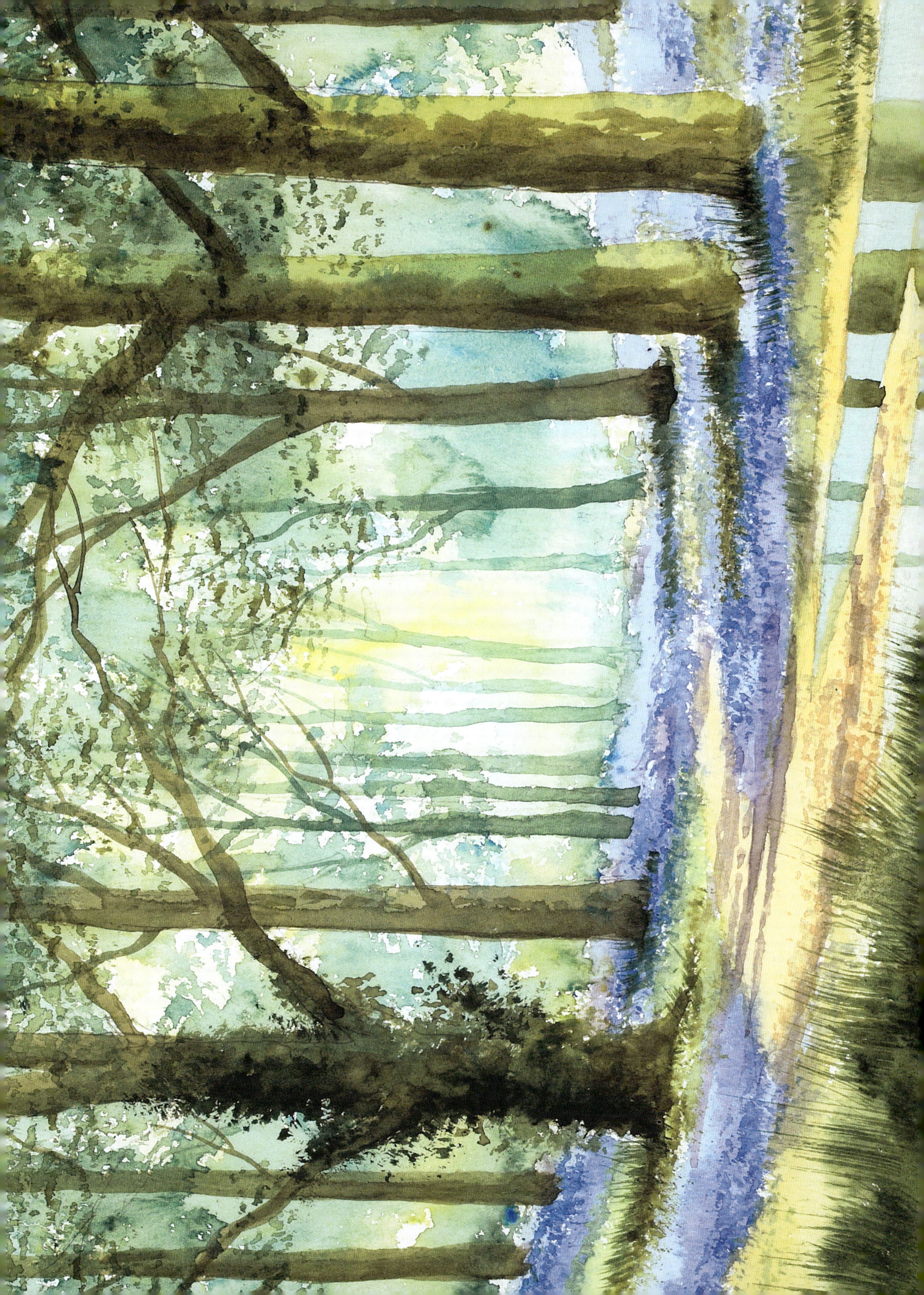

Footbridge in the Woods

This subject captures the moment when, while out walking in the woods, you happen on a tranquil scene, interrupted only by the sound of birds and rippling water. Then you whip out your paints and dash off a masterpiece! Seriously, this scene has a strong focal point and the composition leads you through the picture and off into the distance.

Palette of colours

- Cobalt blue
- Midnight green
- Sunlit green
- Raw sienna
- Cadmium yellow
- Country olive
- Burnt sienna
- Burnt umber
- French ultramarine
- Permanent rose
- Yellow ochre

The path leading to the footbridge is raw sienna, to which burnt umber is added for the bridge itself. Once dry, add shading and detail with a mix of burnt umber and country olive.

The handrail on the bridge is painted separately, later on, and is left masked-out while you paint the bridge. That allows you to paint the river in one go, using cobalt blue and country olive, with more country olive added for the greener areas.

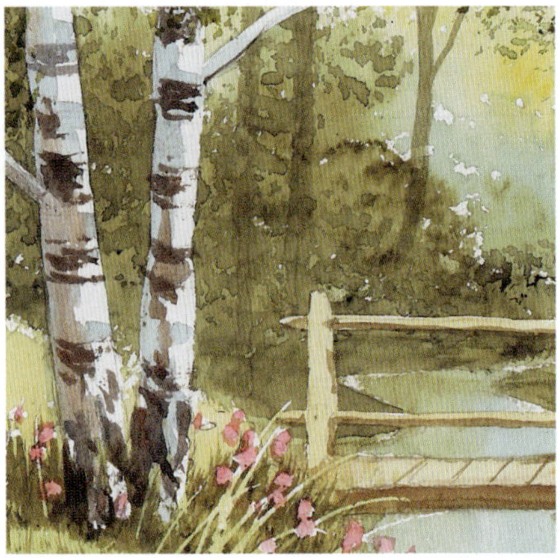

Masking fluid also makes the silver birches easy. Paint the left-hand side with a mix of cobalt blue and burnt umber, using horizontal brush strokes to suggest the patchy bark. While wet, add burnt umber for darker areas. Allow these to dry, then use a rigger brush to add the ragged markings with a mix of French ultramarine and burnt umber, using the dry brush technique.

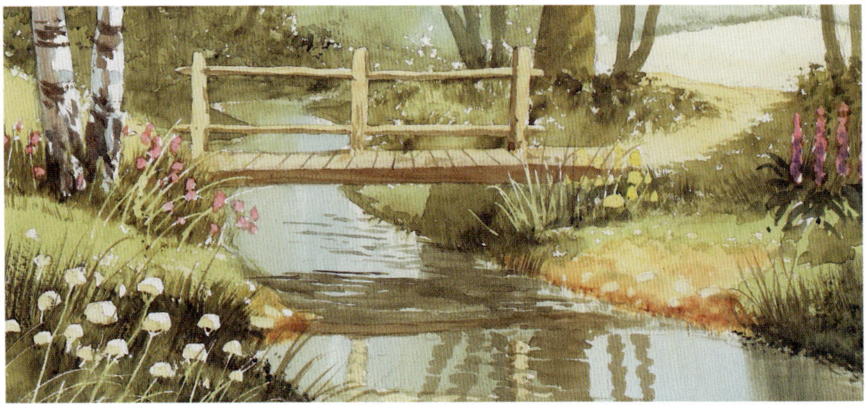

Foreground flowers add a pop of colour. The foxgloves and other pink flowers are added with permanent rose followed by a mix of cobalt blue and permanent rose. The white flowers are painted with a thin mix of yellow ochre, leaving plenty of white paper. The yellow flowers are cadmium yellow.

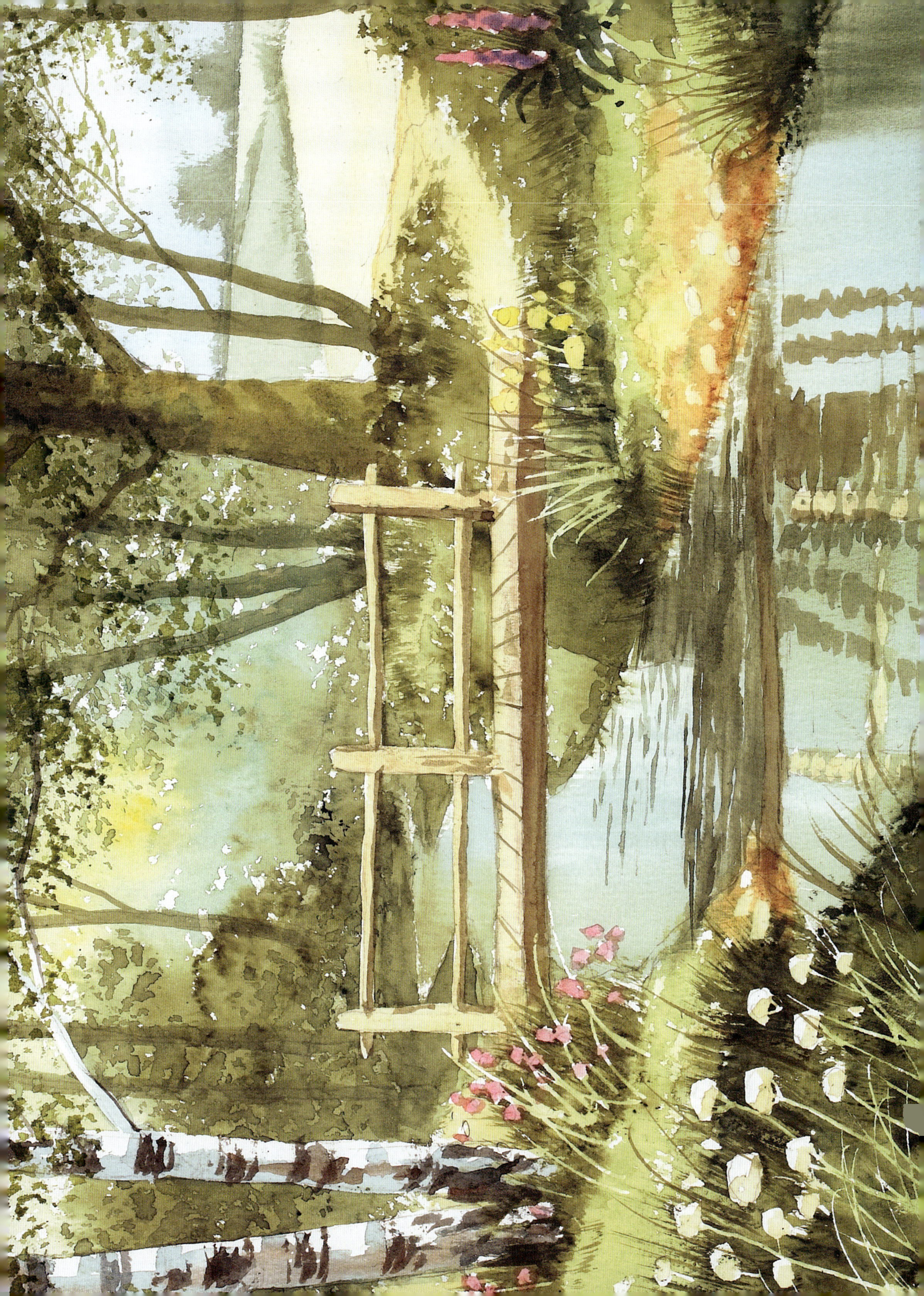

OUTLINE 35

Village in the Snow

I have chosen to paint this snow scene at sunset. The reason for this is that I am not a fan of cold, moody paintings. I much prefer warm, friendly and inviting subjects.

Palette of colours

- Cadmium yellow
- Permanent rose
- Cadmium red
- Cobalt blue
- Shadow
- Alizarin crimson
- Burnt sienna
- Burnt umber
- French ultramarine
- Midnight green
- Hooker's green
- Country olive

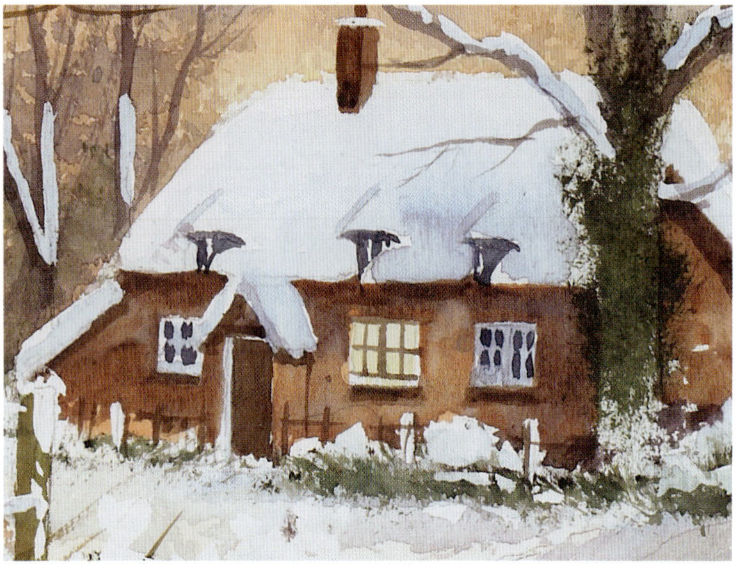

A light at the window adds a sense of life, preventing the cottage from looking abandoned. Note that the details on the light window are dark; while the details on the dark window are light. It's the contrast in tone, rather than the colours, that is key.

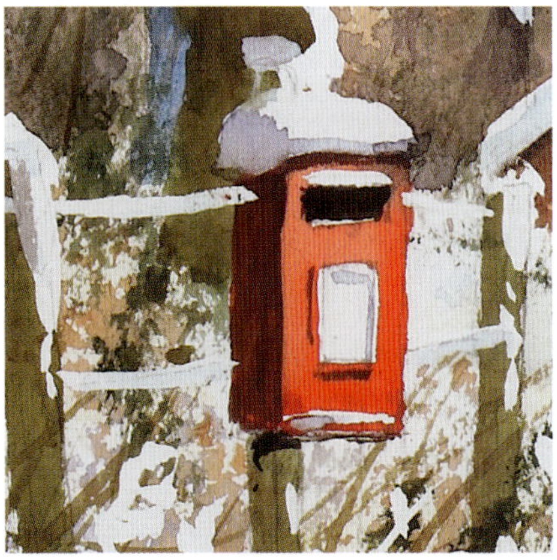

The post box adds a splash of strong colour in the foreground, emphasizing the warm colour range of the scene.

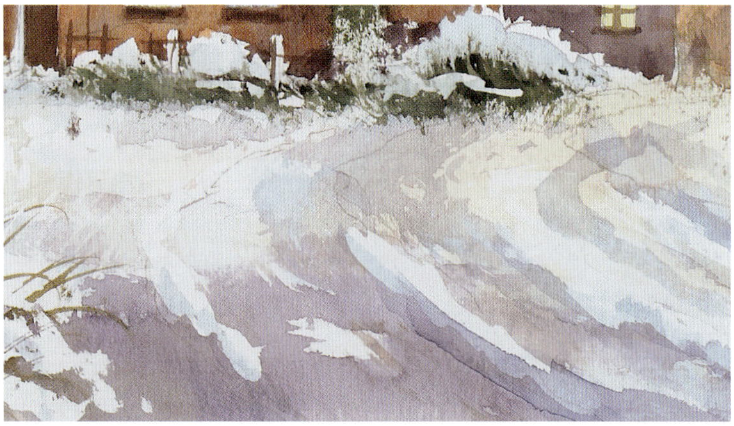

Barely any of the foreground snow is actually white paper – most of it is shadow, or a mix of permanent rose and cadmium yellow.

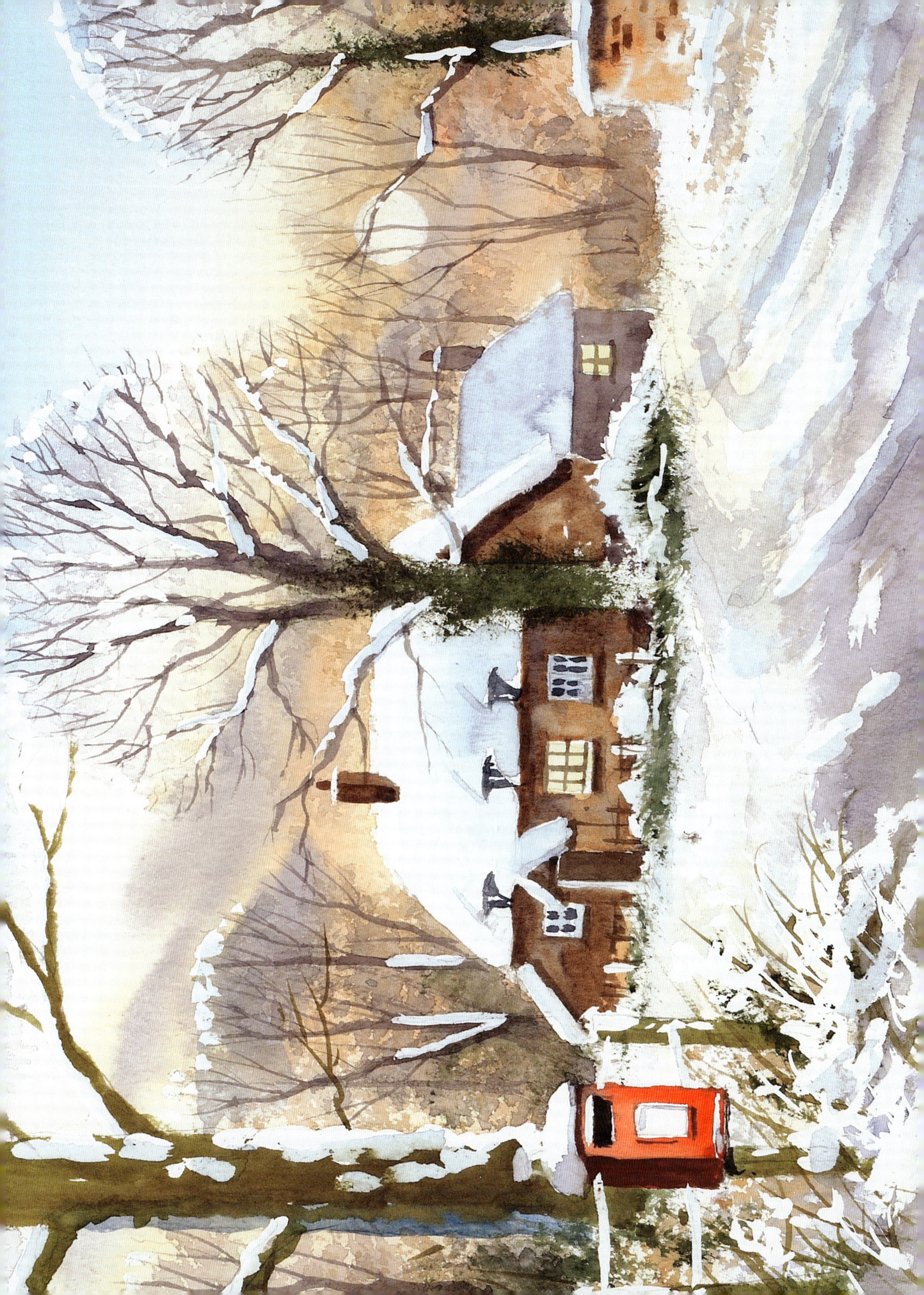

OUTLINE 36

Lakeside Flowers

The footpath in this scene leads the eye invitingly towards the lake and the boat. The flowers add a dash of colour and interest to the foreground, and tall trees with over-arching foliage frame the scene. You could experiment with different colour schemes from the one I have chosen.

Palette of colours.

- Cadmium yellow
- Sunlit green
- Midnight green
- Permanent rose
- Country olive
- Raw sienna
- Burnt umber
- Burnt sienna
- Shadow
- Alizarin crimson
- Cobalt blue

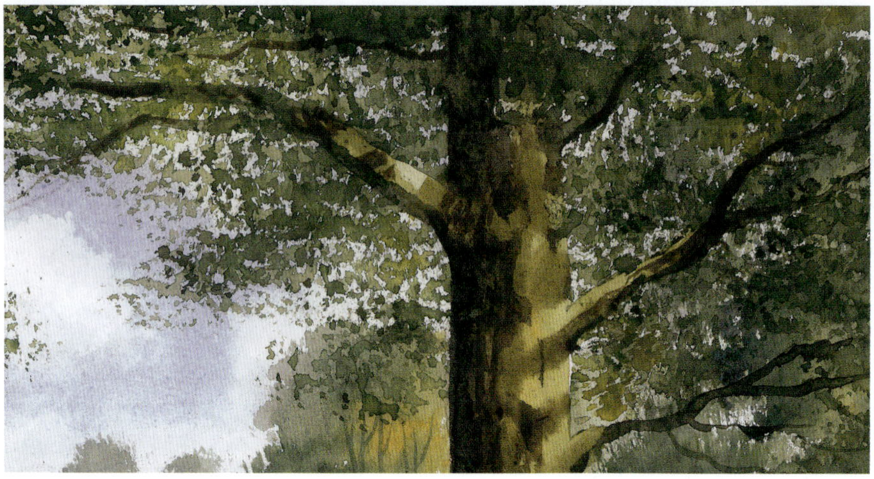

The dense foliage is produced with lots of overlapping layers of stippling, made using a large 50mm (2in) brush. The layers start with pale country olive, over which is added another stronger, nearly dry layer of country olive. The trees and branches are added now using a mix of raw sienna and sunlit green, and shaded and textured with burnt umber and country olive. A final layer of country olive is then stippled over the area.

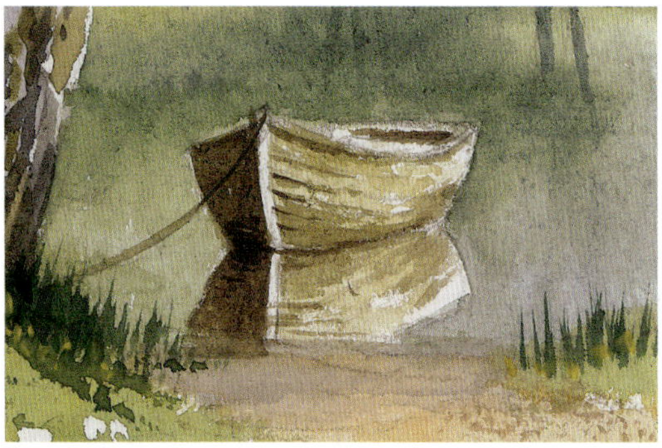

The boat is painted with a pale mix of country olive with a little burnt umber – more of which is added for the shadows and details. Paint the reflection at the same time, using slightly paler versions of the mixes.

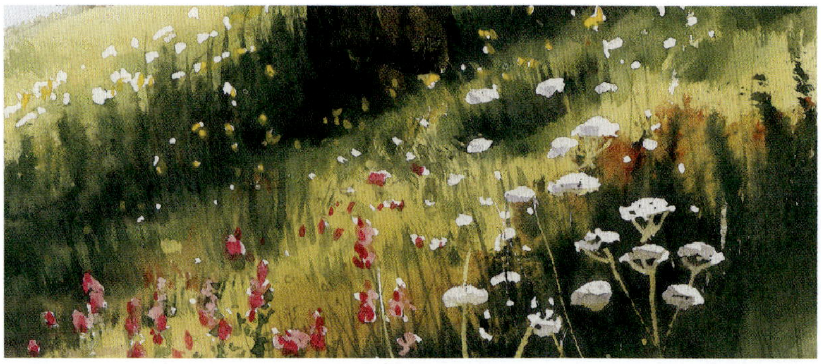

The foreground flowers are picked out with pure colours – I've used cadmium yellow and permanent rose, as well as leaving some white (shaded with pale sunlit green), but why not pick some of your own favourite flower colours, instead?

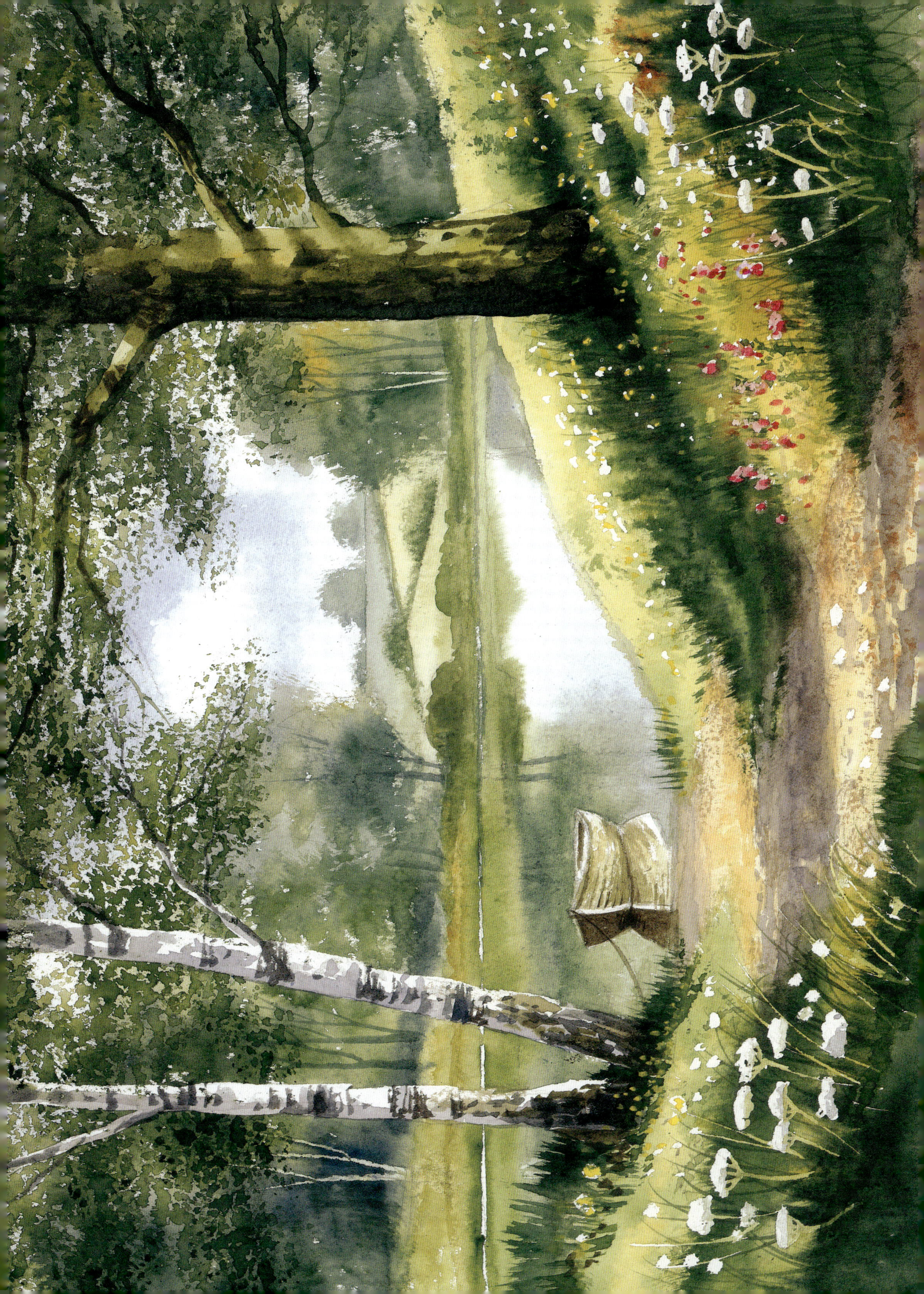

Rivers and streams

Keith Fenwick

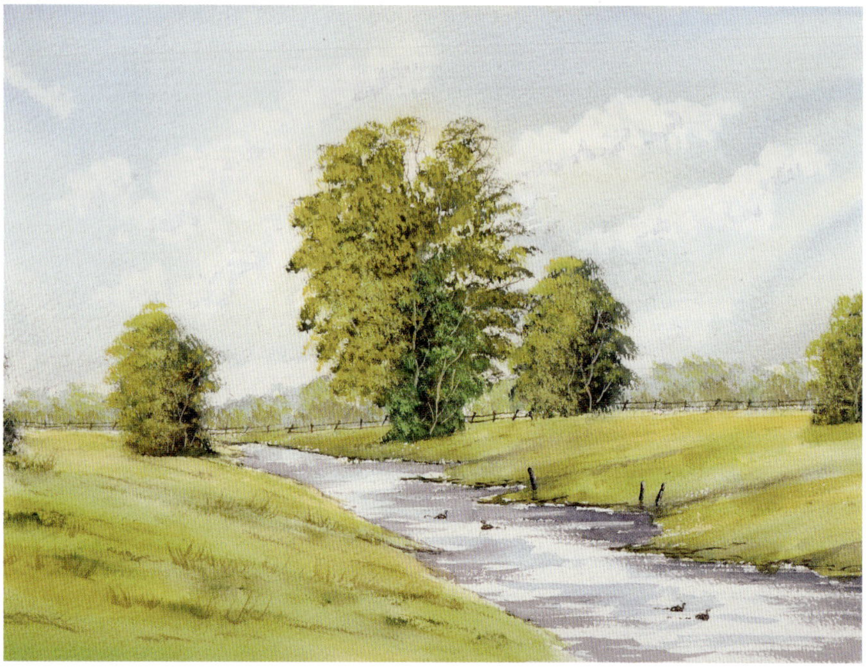

New Forest Stream, page 106

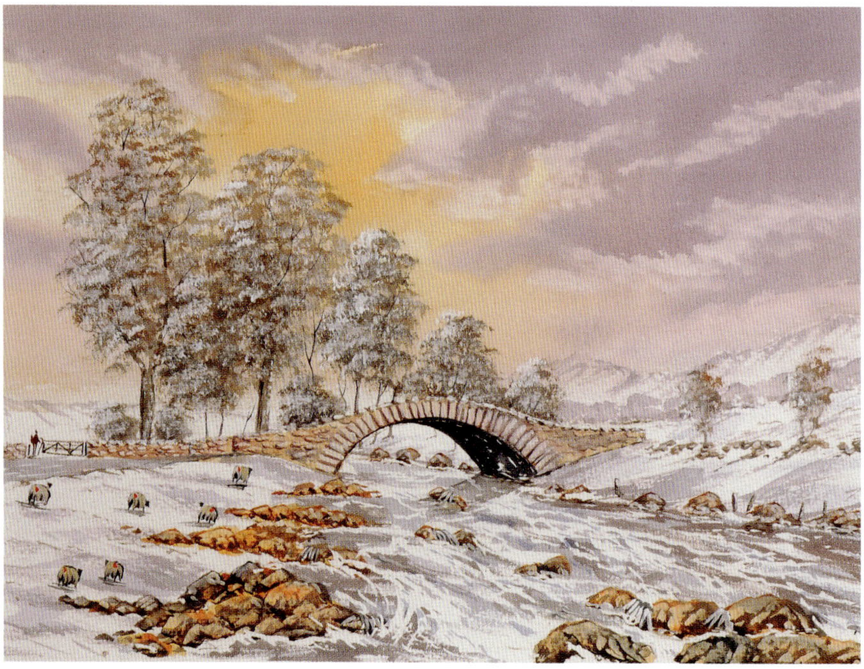

Bridge Over Stream, page 108

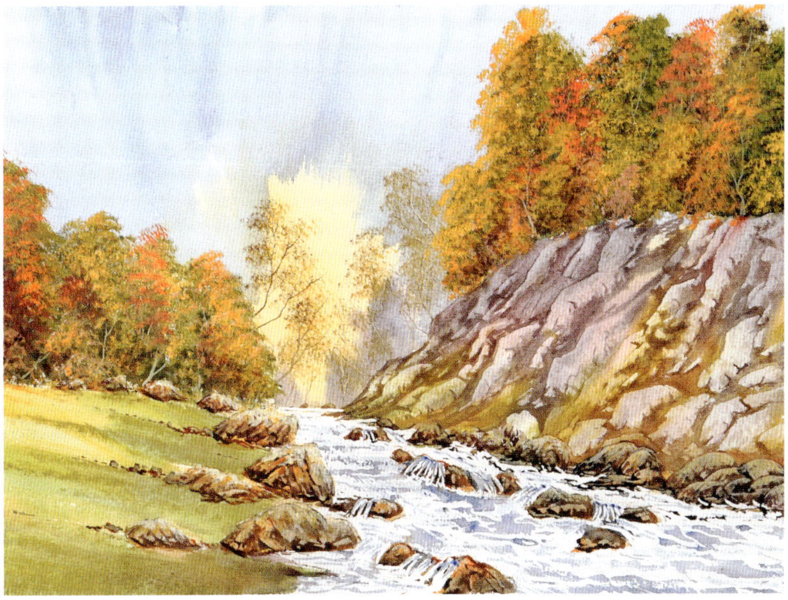

Welsh Gorge, page 110

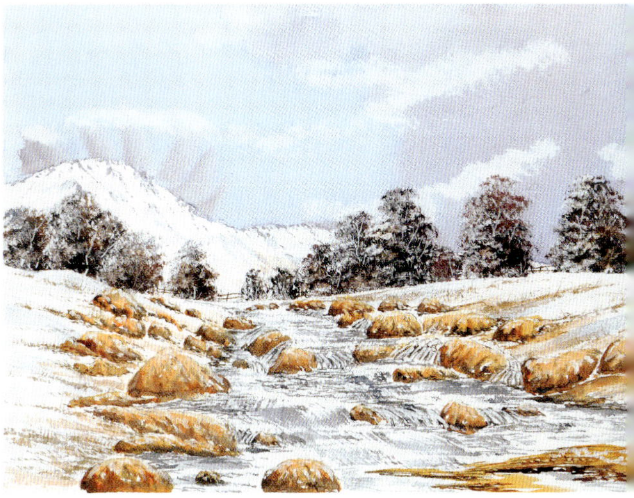

River Esk, page 112

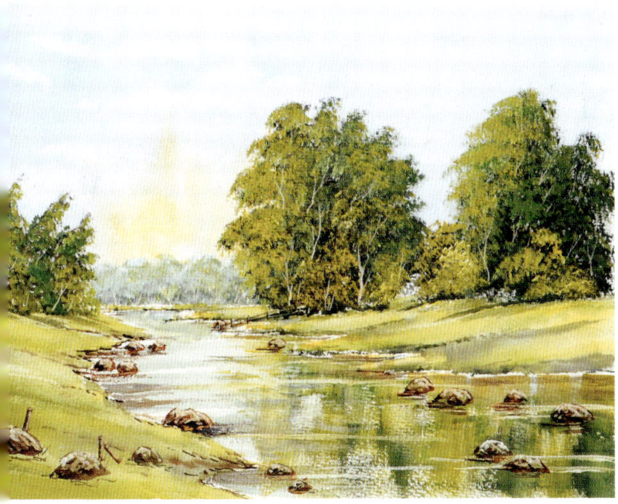

River Wear, page 114

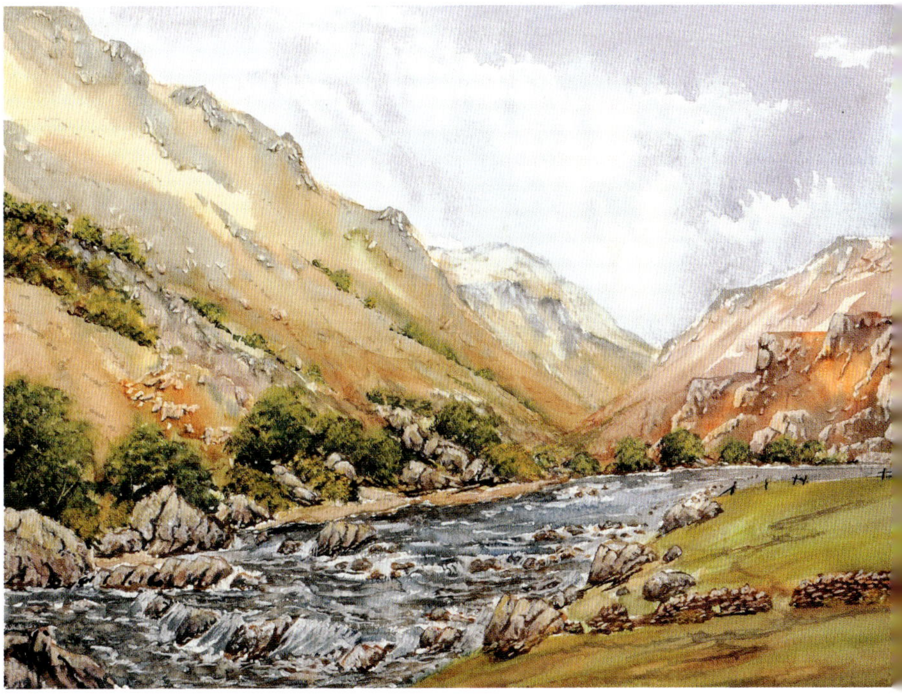

Rocks and Running Water, page 116

New Forest Stream

This is a simple stream flowing through the fields. It has no clearly defined riverbanks and the subject matter makes a simple but attractive composition. Note how the inclusion of a few posts and the addition of a little bird life improves the composition.

Palette of colours

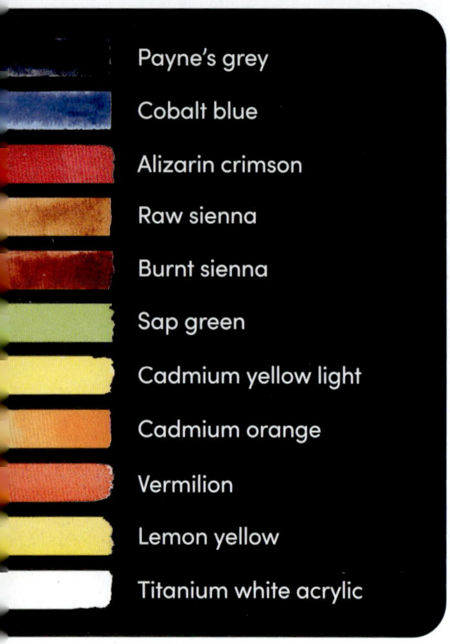

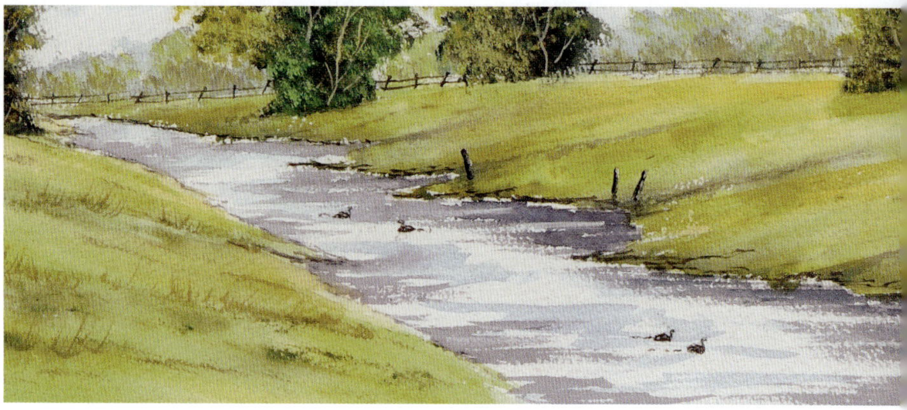

Paint in the stream using horizontal strokes of cobalt blue: light in tone in the background and darker towards the foreground. Allow to dry thoroughly. Add Payne's grey and a touch of alizarin crimson to the cobalt blue to add depth to the river, working inwards from the bank. Finally, add more Payne's grey and some burnt sienna to the mix and define the waterline along the banks with dots and dashes.

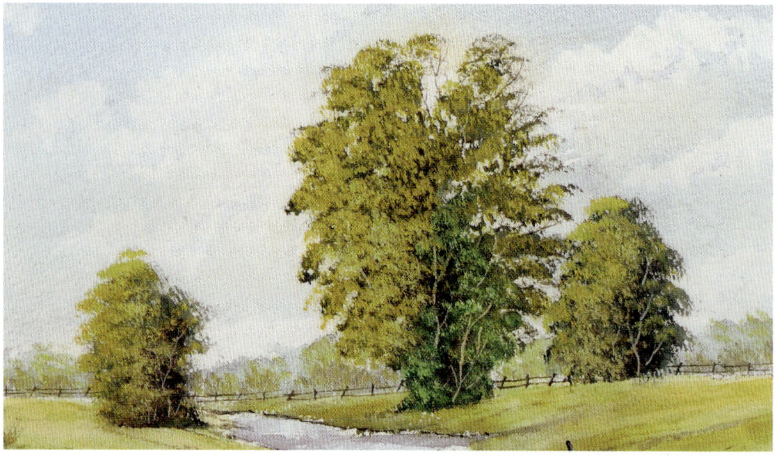

Stipple to create the tree foliage, using a mix of cadmium yellow light, sap green and a touch of titanium white acrylic, to work over a dark base of Payne's grey, sap green and burnt sienna. Once dry, build up highlights with more cadmium yellow light added to the mix.

You can add ivy to the central tree with a mix of sap green, a little cadmium yellow light and a touch of titanium white acrylic.

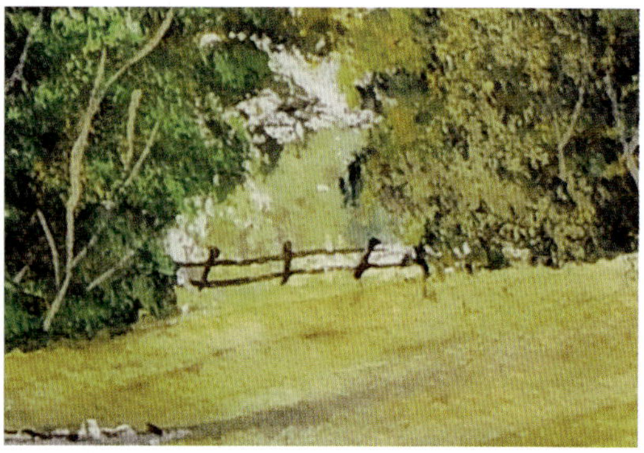

Mix Payne's grey and burnt sienna, and use a fine rigger to paint in the fence.

It is important when painting fences that we do not paint them square. The distance between the fenceposts should be approximately twice the height of the fence.

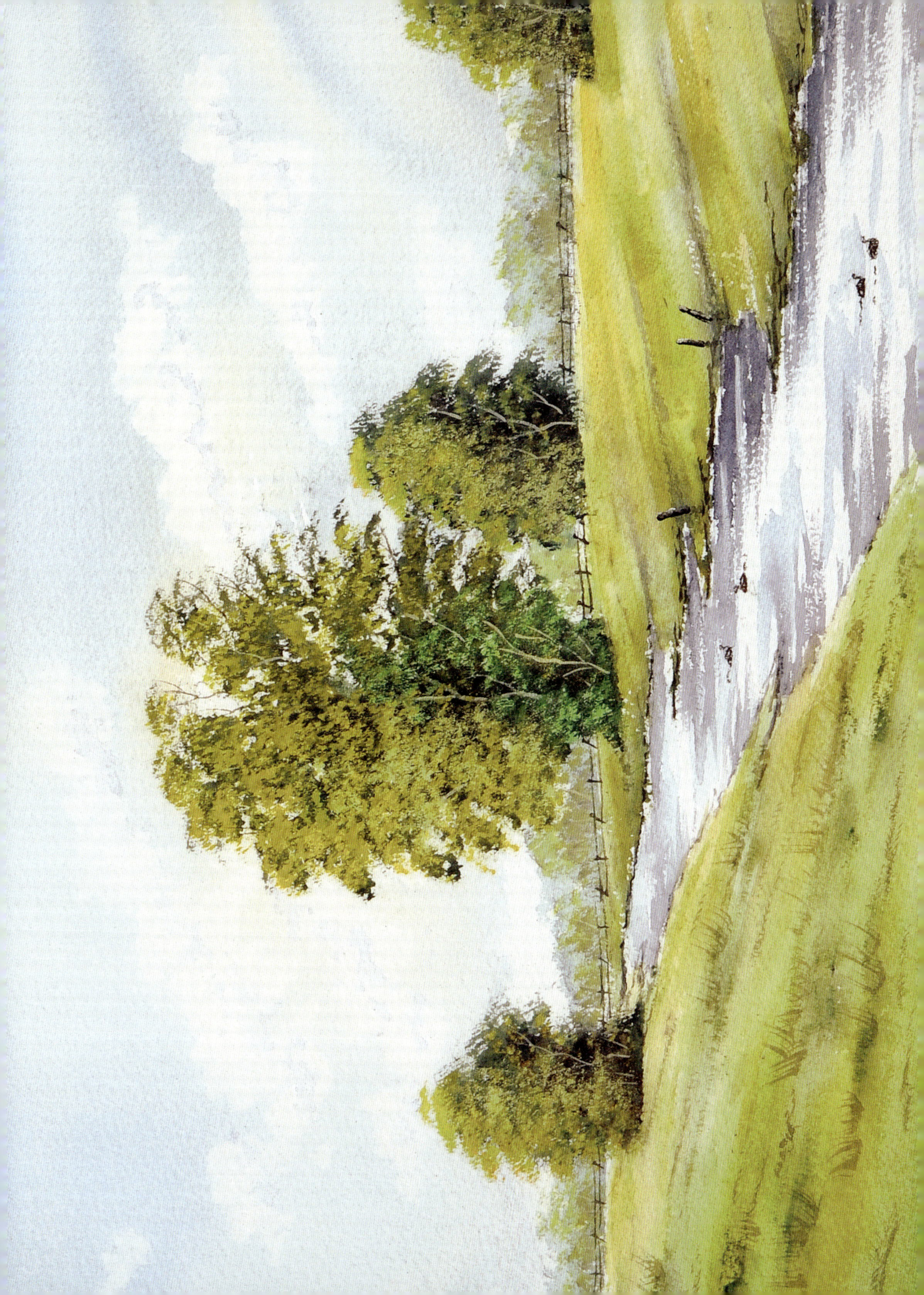

OUTLINE 38

Bridge Over Stream

This is one of my favourite scenes to paint. Here it is painted as a winter scene, with a colourful evening sky to contrast with the snow-covered distant mountains and foreground. Take the opportunity to practise painting fast-flowing water. I have included a few Lakeland sheep to add interest.

Palette of colours

- Payne's grey
- Alizarin crimson
- Raw sienna
- Burnt sienna
- Cobalt blue
- Titanium white acrylic

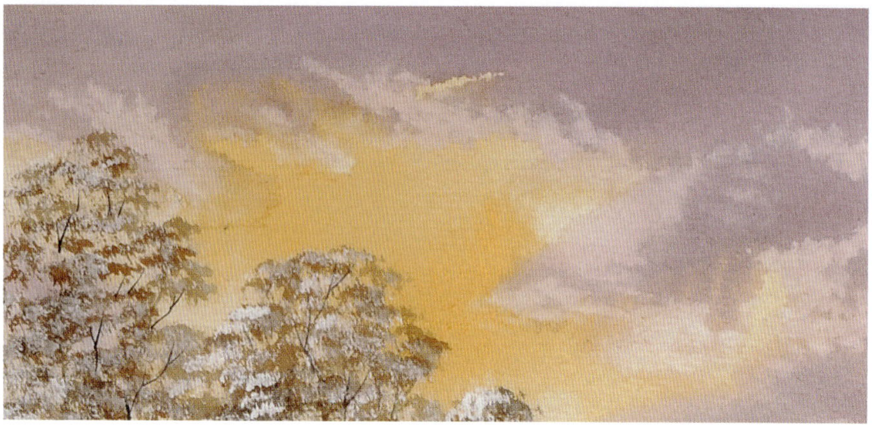

The dramatic sky is achieved by applying a raw sienna wash across the sky, then adding a dilute mix of Payne's grey and alizarin crimson wet-into-wet for the darker clouds, leaving an area in the centre clean so the raw sienna shows through.

While the paint remains damp, use a clean paper tissue to lift out clouds. Turn the tissue so that it is always clean and dry when you touch the paper.

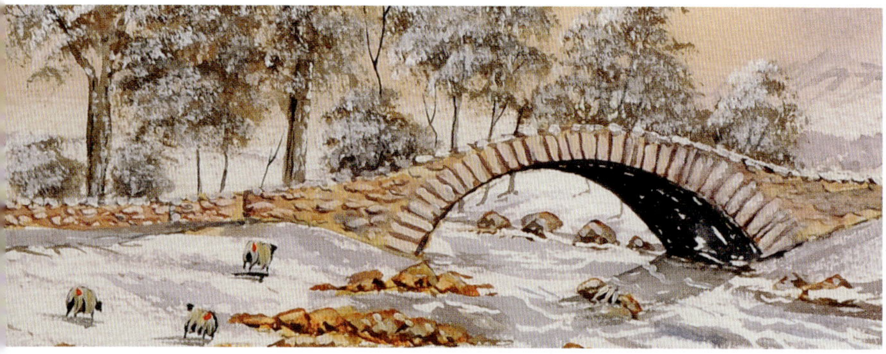

The stone wall and bridge start with a raw sienna wash, to which touches of burnt sienna and a purple mix of alizarin crimson and cobalt blue are added wet-into-wet. The structure of the bridge is then created by gently scraping out shapes to suggest stonework.

Once dry, add shadows with deep purple mix of Payne's grey and alizarin crimson, and highlights with a mix of titanium white acrylic and raw sienna.

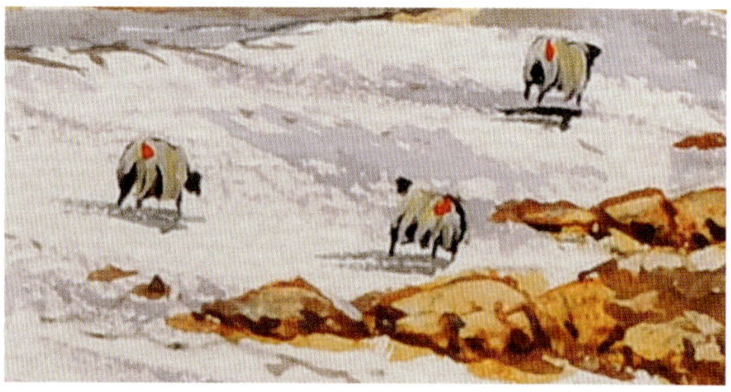

For the sheep, mix Payne's grey and burnt sienna and paint horseshoe shapes with a rigger. Add small triangles on the left or right for the heads – make sure they're attached to the bodies, or the sheep get very upset!

Using titanium white acrylic paint the fleeces, then shade underneath with a little Payne's grey. Allow to dry, then highlight with a raw sienna and titanium white mix before adding a tiny red dot of alizarin crimson to each.

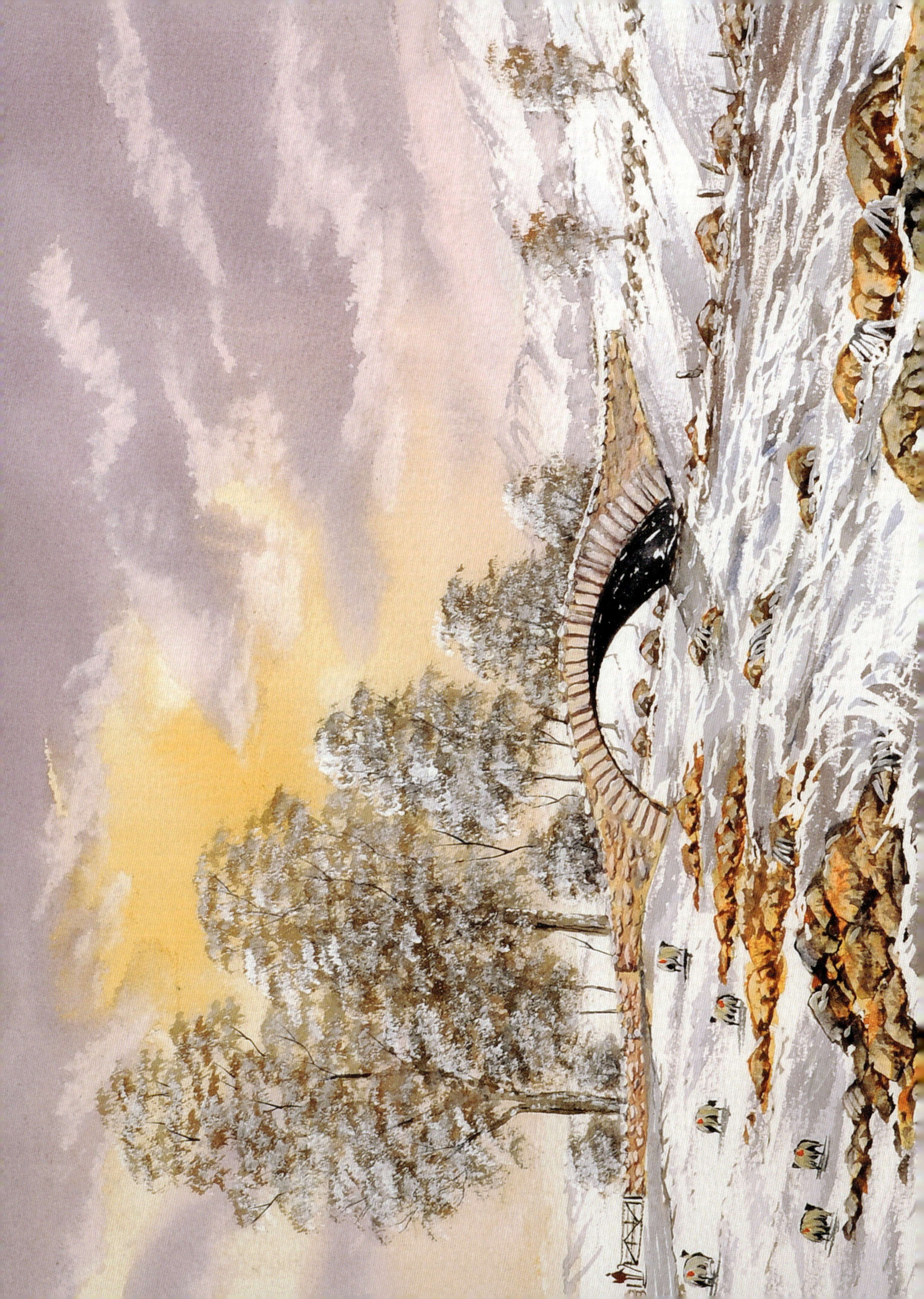

Welsh Gorge

Gorges like this are common in the Welsh landscape. The rugged rocky embankment and fast-flowing water over the rocks make for a great composition. This painting provides an opportunity to experiment with colour mixing for the autumn foliage.

Palette of colours

- Payne's grey
- Cobalt blue
- Alizarin crimson
- Raw sienna
- Burnt sienna
- Cadmium yellow light
- Lemon yellow
- Cadmium orange
- Sap green
- Vermilion
- Titanium white acrylic

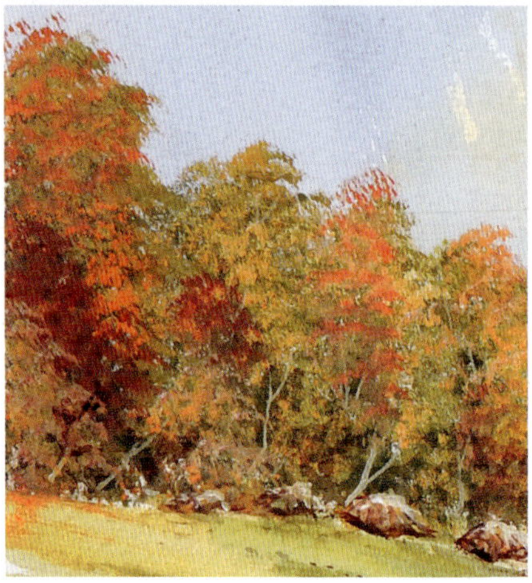

Paint in the background of the trees with stippling, using a mix of Payne's grey and sap green. While the paint is wet, scratch in a few marks to suggest trunks and large branches.

Allow to dry thoroughly, then use cadmium yellow light and cadmium orange to gently stipple on foliage with a light touch. Add sap green, vermilion and lemon yellow to your colours to complete the underpainting on the trees.

Once dry, create highlights by adding a little titanium white acrylic to your mixes and repeating the stippling process.

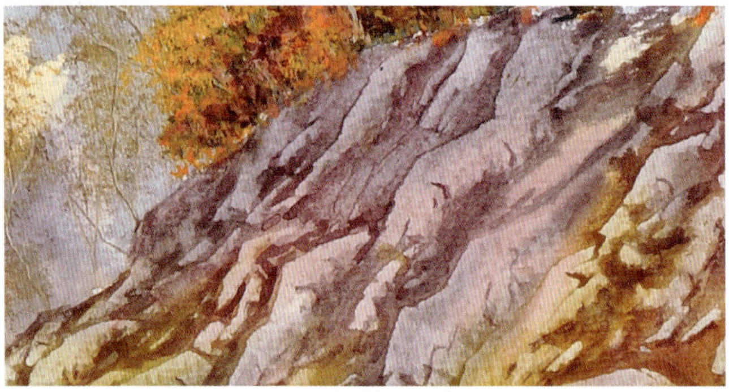

The rock structures of the gorge are made by scraping with a painting knife. Angle the knife as you reach ground level to create the impression of the sloping angle of the cliff. It might help to think of the process as buttering your bread!

The paint used here is a raw sienna wash with a purple mix of alizarin crimson and cobalt blue added wet into wet. Develop this variegated wash with Payne's grey, lemon yellow and sap green.

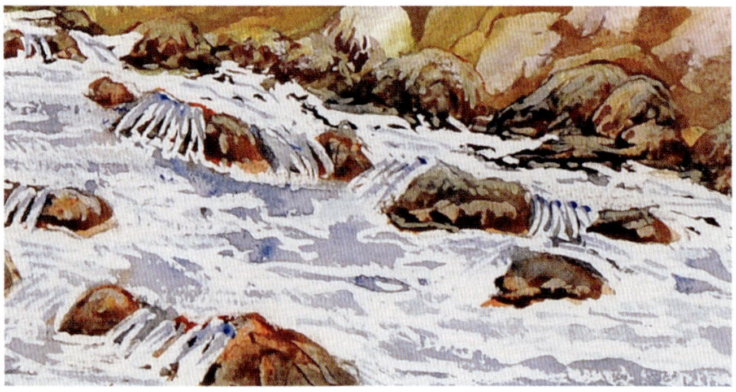

The rocks in the water are painted in the same way as those in the gorge. For the water itself, dance across the stream with a large brush and cobalt blue, creating a dash-and-dot effect, then add Payne's grey to the blue and go over aspects of the water again.

Allow the paint to dry completely, then switch to a rigger brush to add touches of a darker mix of Payne's grey and cobalt blue between the rocks.

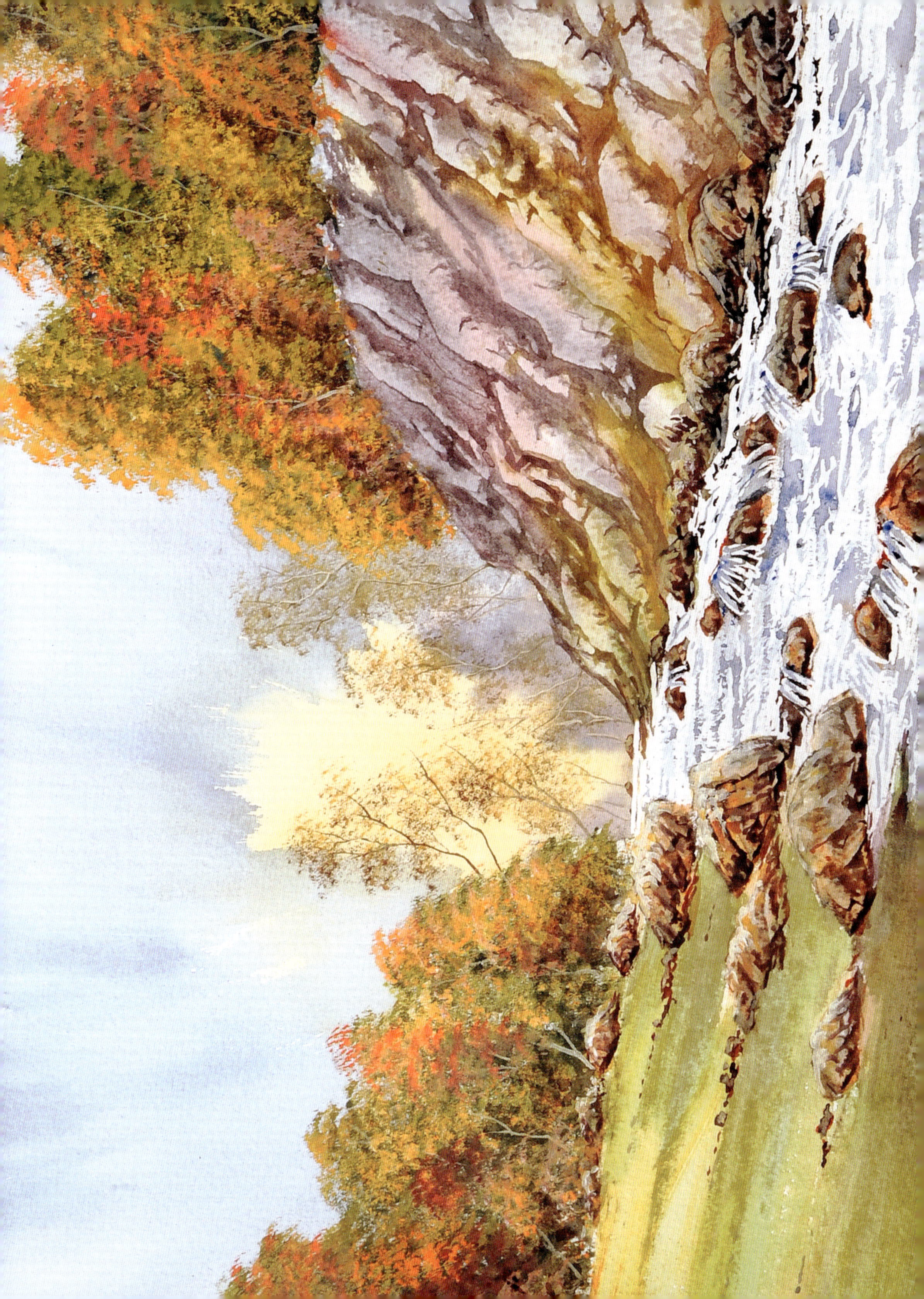

OUTLINE 40

River Esk

A pleasing winter scene providing the opportunity to capture snow-covered mountains. There are lots of rocks in the painting – note the variety of shapes and sizes and how the water runs between them.

Palette of colours

- Payne's grey
- Cobalt blue
- Alizarin crimson
- Raw sienna
- Burnt sienna
- Titanium white acrylic

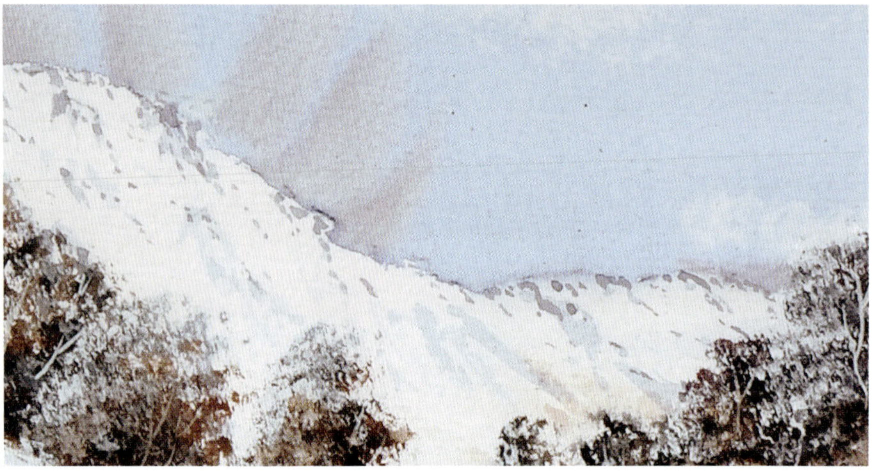

Less is more, so do not overdo the snow-capped mountains. Paint in the shadows on the clean paper using dilute cobalt blue. Dab the paint on with the tip, then draw it out into broken dots and dashes with the side of the brush. Work around the top of the mountain with a darker mix created by adding a little Payne's grey to the mix.

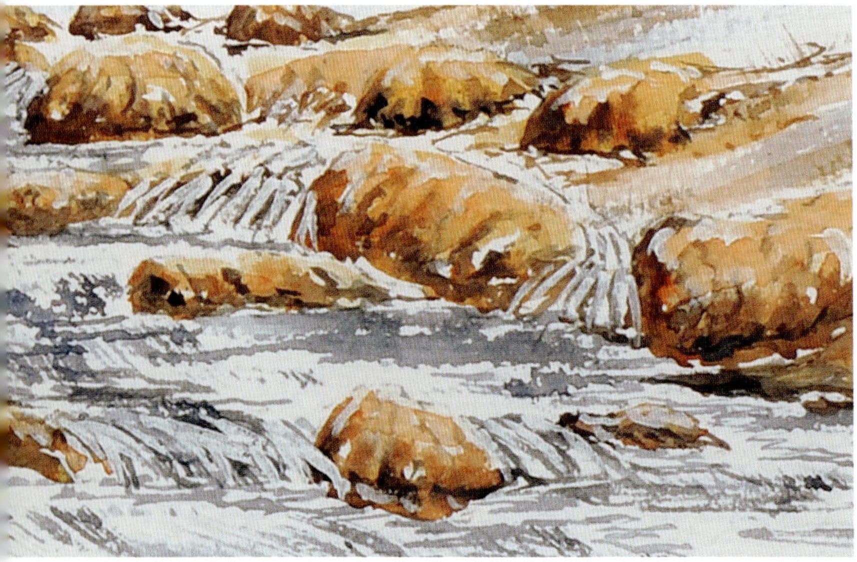

Paint the rocks with raw sienna and add burnt sienna at the base. Once dry, add depth to the rocks with a mix of Payne's grey and alizarin crimson applied to the bases.

For the water, apply a mix of cobalt blue and Payne's grey, using light touches to leave some of the white paper showing through. Work from the distance to the foreground.

Work a deeper mix of the colour into the areas closer to the banks and create horizontal ripples in the water with the same mix. Highlight once dry with titanium white acrylic.

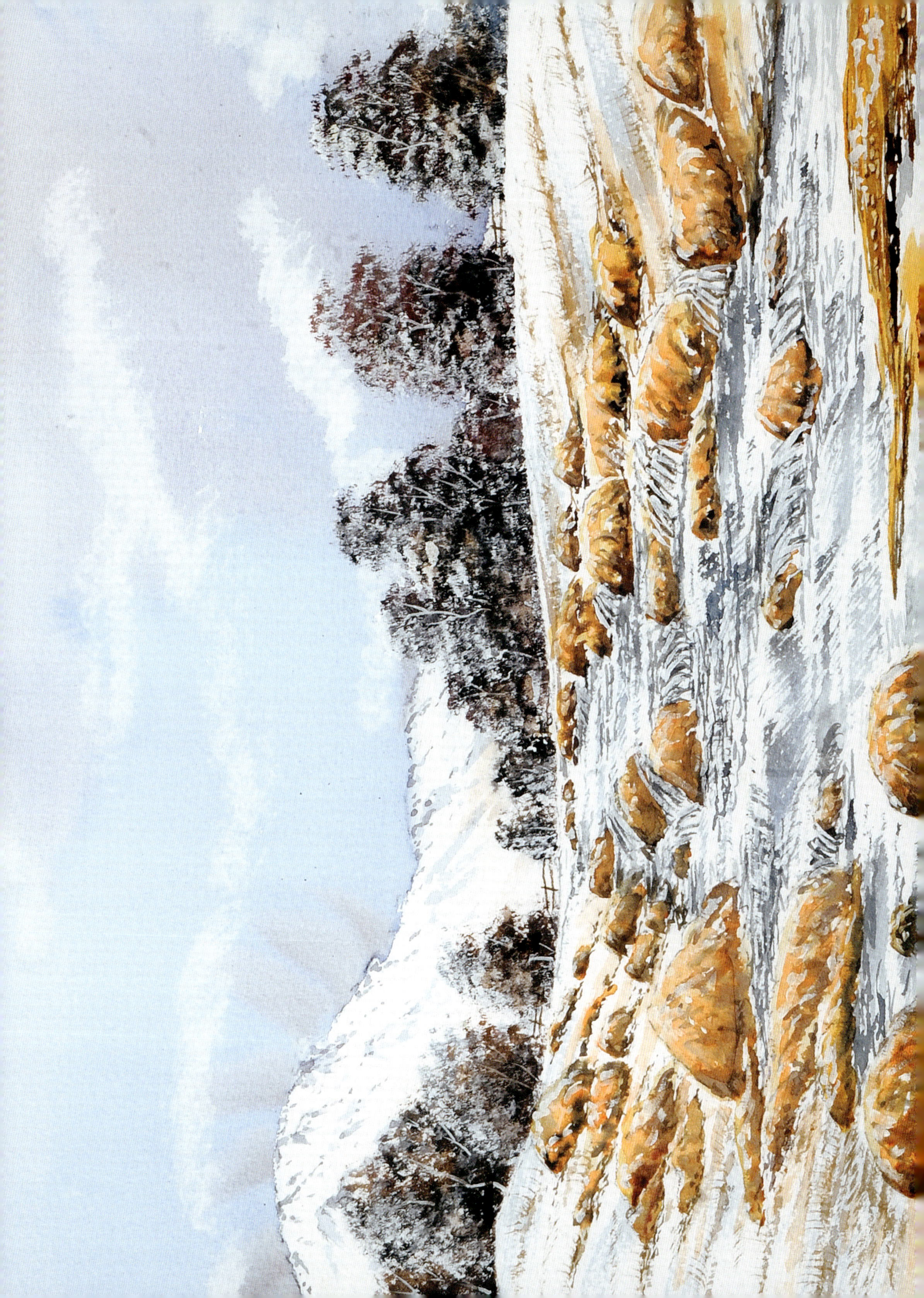

41

OUTLINE

River Wear

A calm and pleasing composition, providing an opportunity to practise mixing the wide range of greens in this landscape. The reflections are subtle and enhance the painting, while a simply painted fence improves the overall effect.

Palette of colours

- Payne's grey
- Cobalt blue
- Alizarin crimson
- Raw sienna
- Burnt sienna
- Sap green
- Cadmium yellow light
- Titanium white acrylic

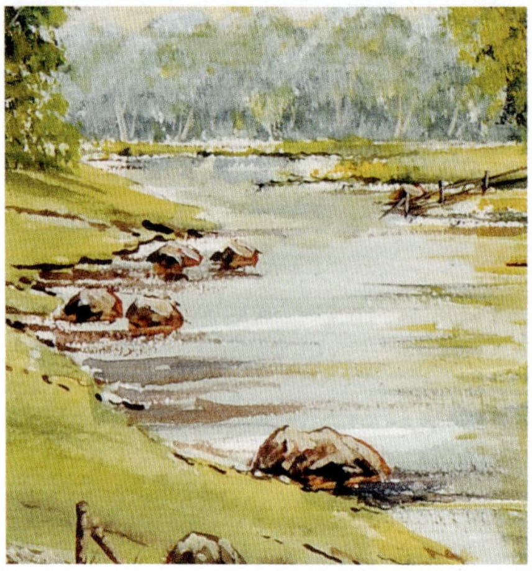

Paint the whole river in one go. Make a dilute mix of cobalt blue with a hint of sap green and use the size 14 round to lay in the water with quick horizontal strokes.

Once dry, add a little more dilute cobalt blue to the mix to add a subtle reflection of the trees at the horizon.

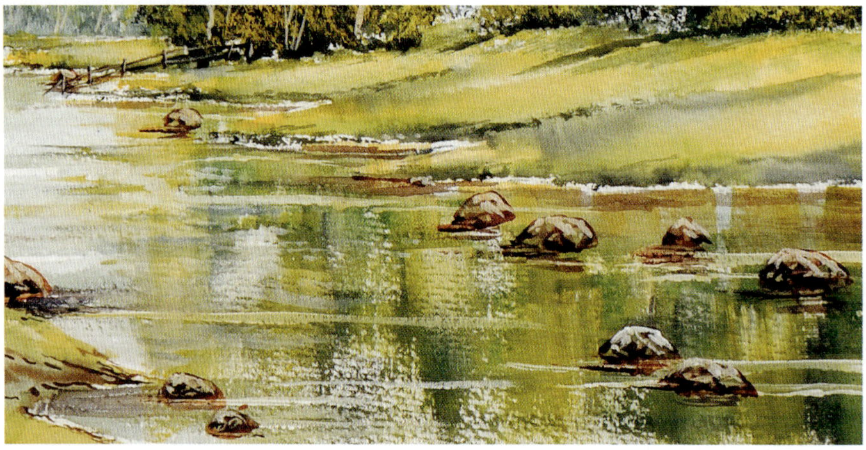

The foreground reflections need to reflect the trees. Hold a large flat brush nearly flat against the paper and draw down mixes made from sap green, cadmium yellow light and raw sienna. Add vertical strokes of a sap green with Payne's grey mix to create the darkness reflected from the trees.

Use a mix of cadmium yellow light and titanium white acrylic to add vertical strokes to represent reflections of the light areas in the trees. Turn the brush on its side and draw the wet paint horizontally with smooth lines.

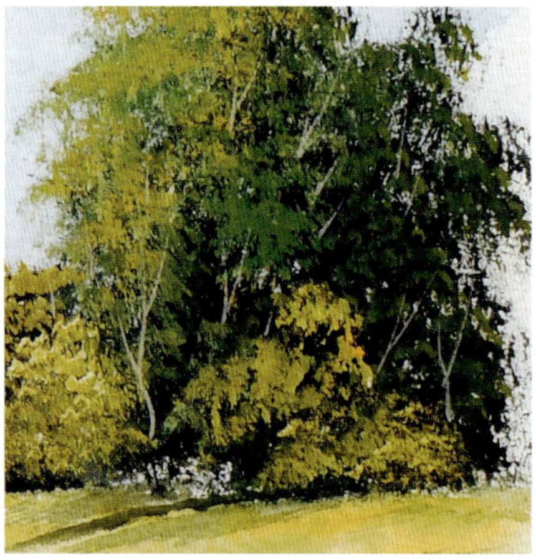

Notice the depth of shadow in the trees – this is very important for realism.

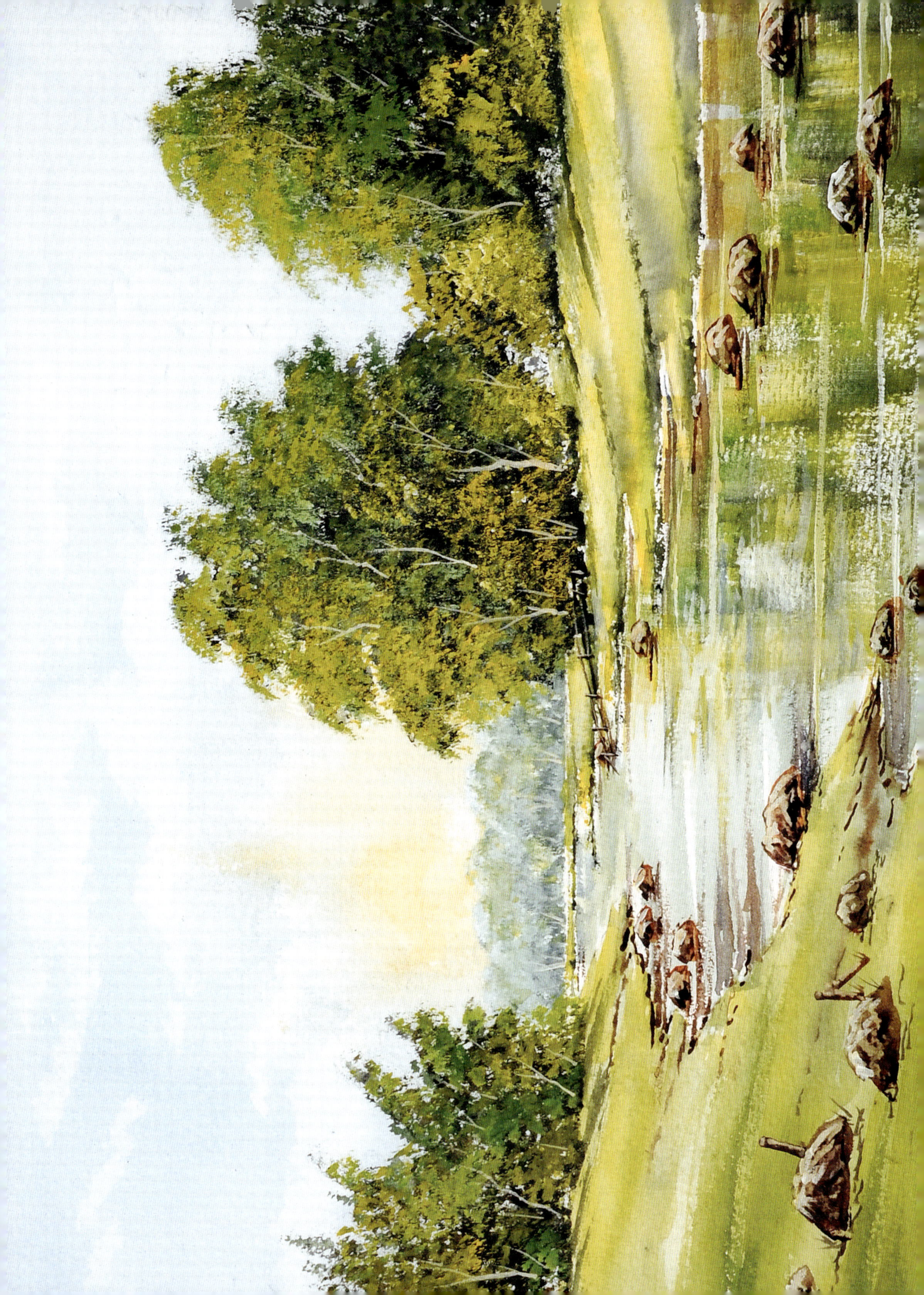

OUTLINE 42

Rocks and Running Water

As an artist, I feel a part of nature when I sit alongside a river, stream or mountain beck attempting to capture the atmosphere and mood of the landscape in paint. I'm in heaven listening to the sound of running water and if I'm quiet, I may even enjoy the company of the local dipper, heron or duck.

Palette of colours

- Payne's grey
- Alizarin crimson
- Raw sienna
- Burnt sienna
- Cobalt blue
- Sap green
- Cadmium yellow light
- Cadmium orange
- Vermilion
- Lemon yellow

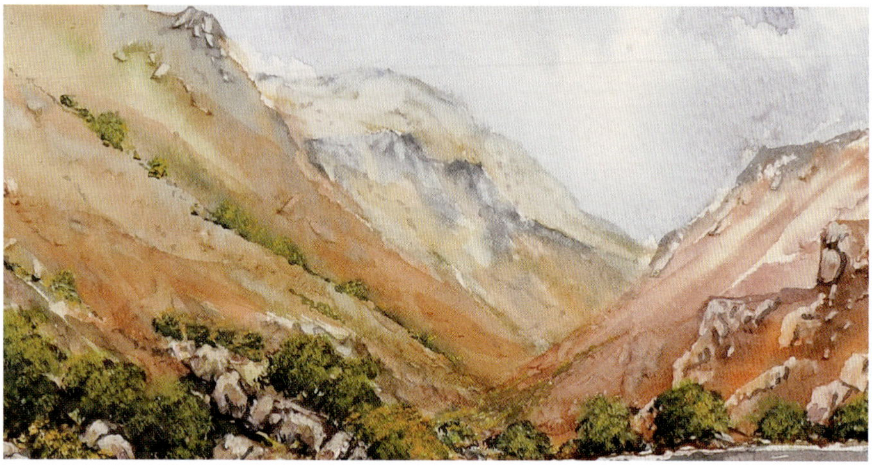

Note the range of subtle colours in the mountains, painted wet into wet. Use the minimum number of brush strokes to avoid colour mixing on the paper, and hold a tissue in your other hand to remove surplus paint from your brush, as required.

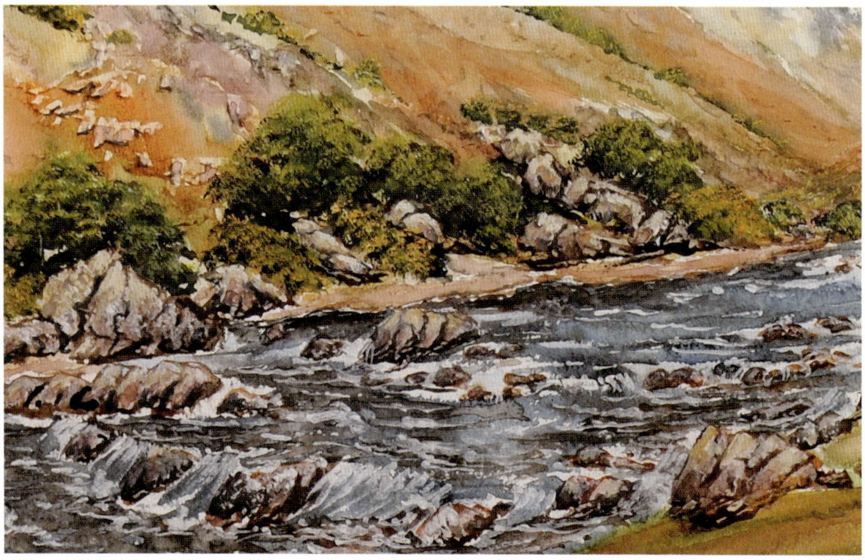

The fast-flowing river leads the eye into the distant mountains. On the outline, I have sketched in foliage, scree and indications of water flow patterns but it is not expected that you follow these suggestions exactly.

The amount of detail you paint is your choice, and I want you to have fun and enjoy yourself, not worry about small details.

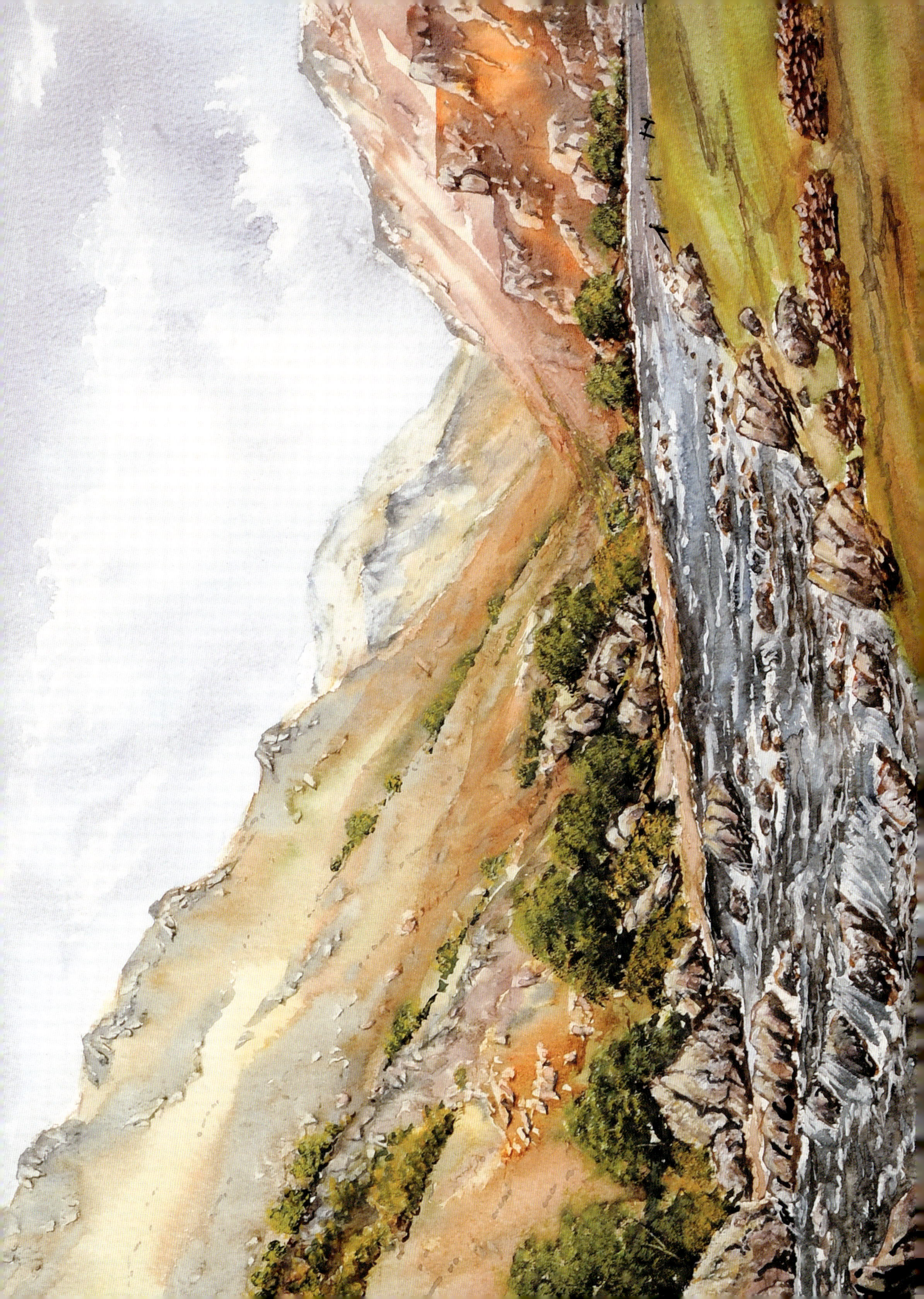

Atmospheric scenes

Richard Bolton

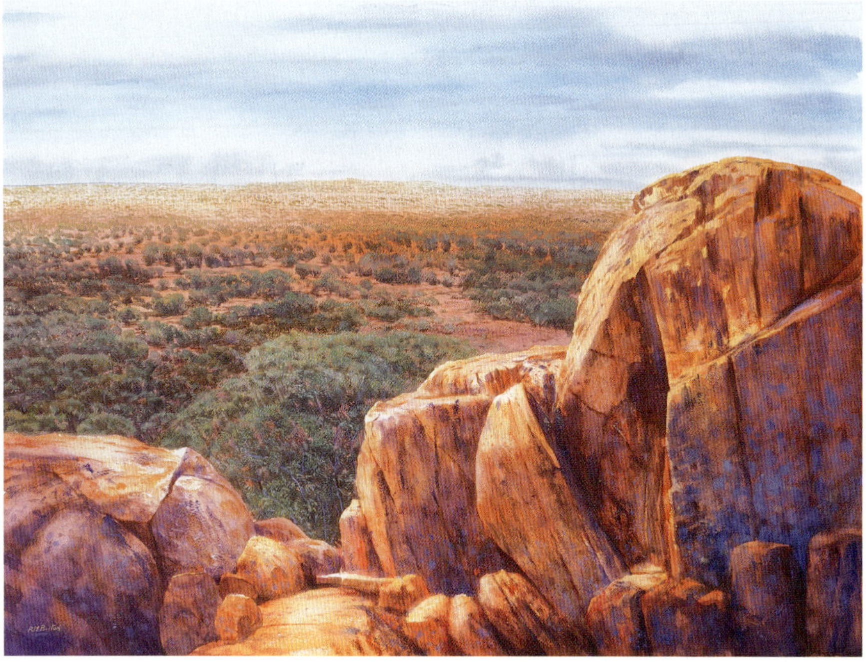

Undara Landscape, page 120

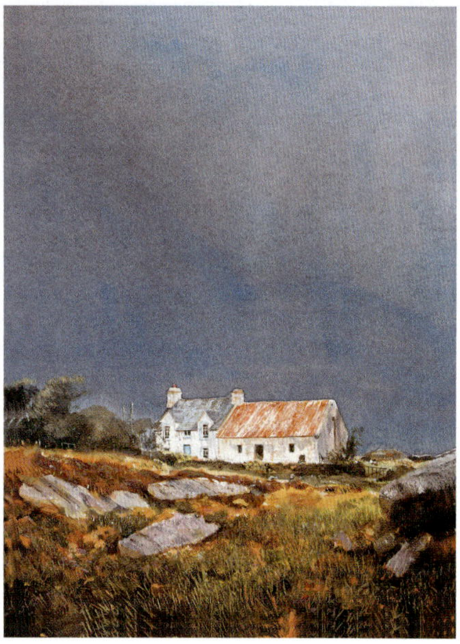

Farmhouse, page 122

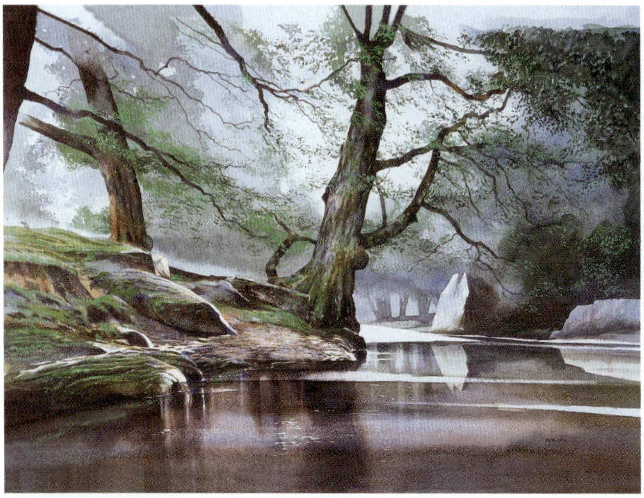

Reflections in the River Wye, page 124

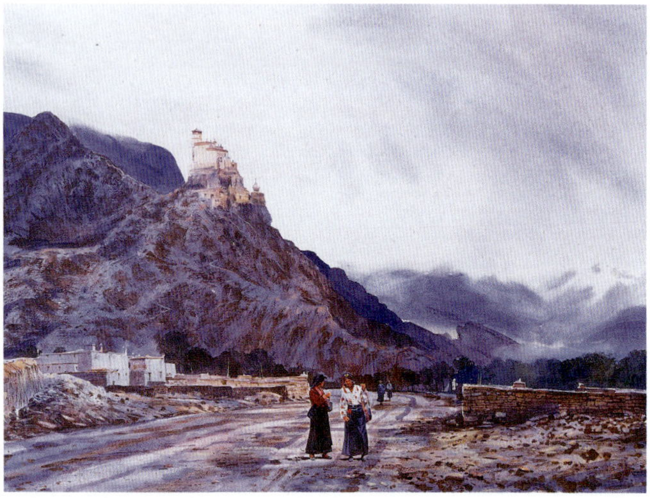

Yumbulagang Monastery, page 126

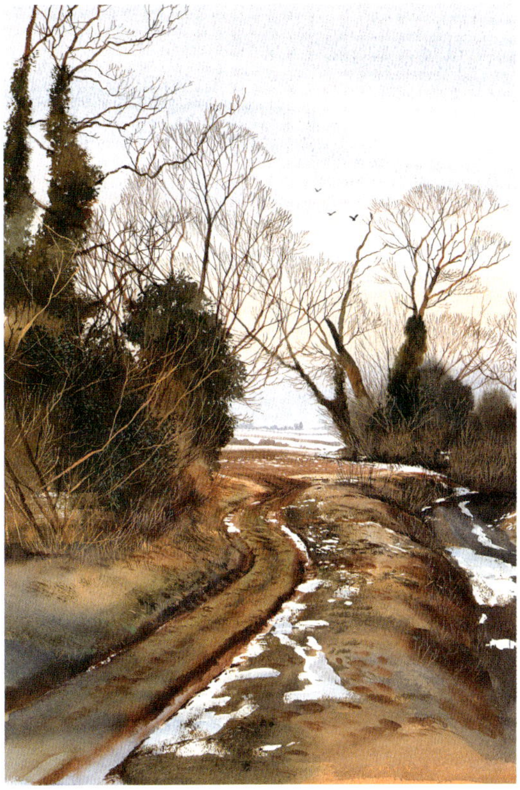

Snow Thaw, page 128

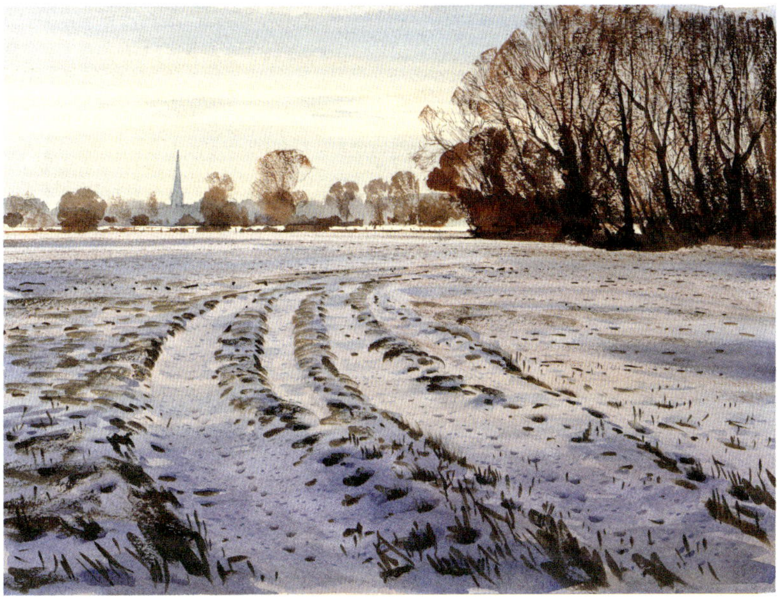

Tracks in the Snow, page 130

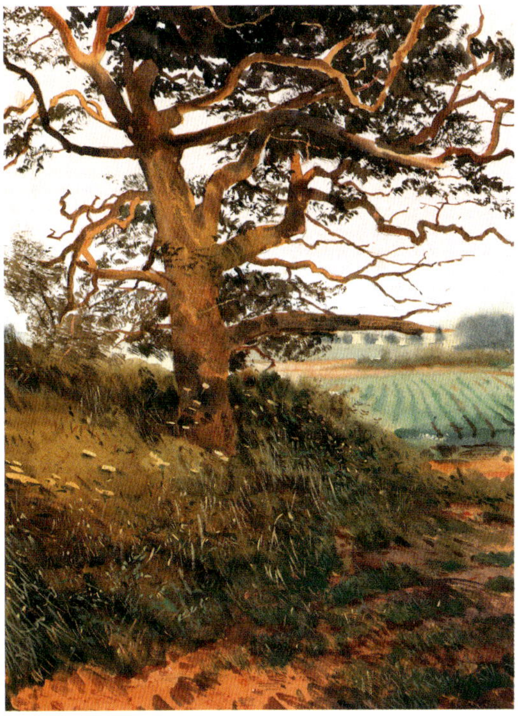

Summer Afternoon, page 132

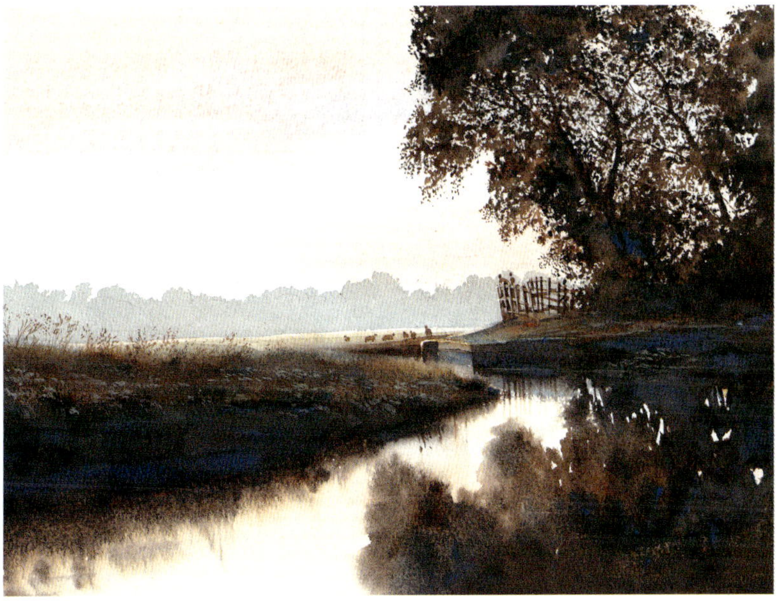

Reflections at Houghton Lock, page 134

OUTLINE 43

Undara Landscape

The savannah grasslands in Northern Australia contrast greatly with the kind of landscape I am used to in England. The reds and yellows in this outback scene have been used strongly to capture the rugged landscape. I used raw sienna as the main yellow, as it gives a good golden colour. Other hot colours were also used, including Indian red, burnt sienna and scarlet lake.

Palette of colours

- Yellow ochre
- Raw sienna
- Naples yellow
- Scarlet lake
- Indian red
- Burnt sienna
- Burnt umber
- Winsor blue
- Ultramarine blue
- Dioxazine violet
- Emerald green

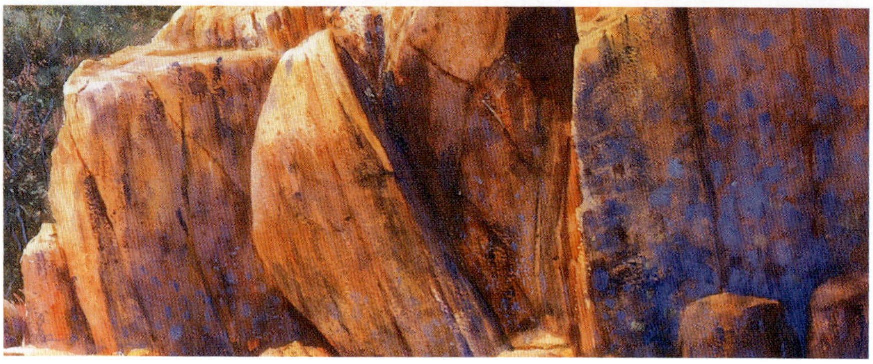

The rocky formation in the foreground required a lot of work to develop the patina of age. This was achieved by scrubbing the paint on, using the dry brush technique to give textures, and then working in the shadows with ultramarine blue and dioxazine violet.

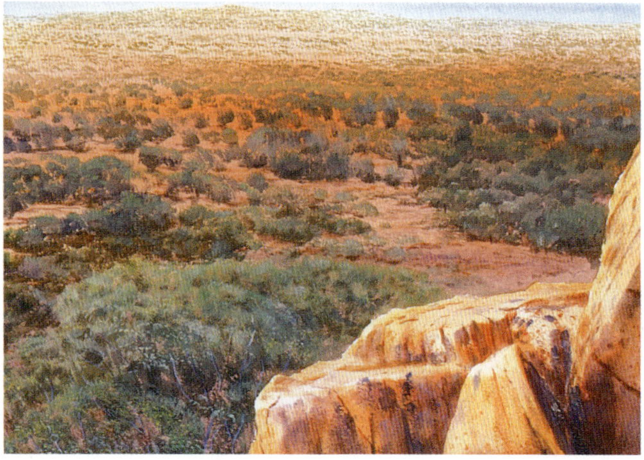

In the distance, the hot colours in the landscape get paler and cooler. On the horizon, the land and vegetation are close to the pale tone of the sky.

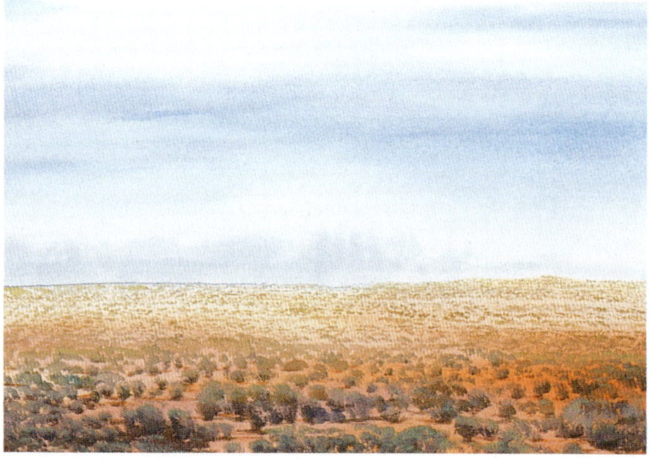

I found the blues in my paint box were not blue enough for the Australian sky, so I added the strong and vibrant Winsor blue.

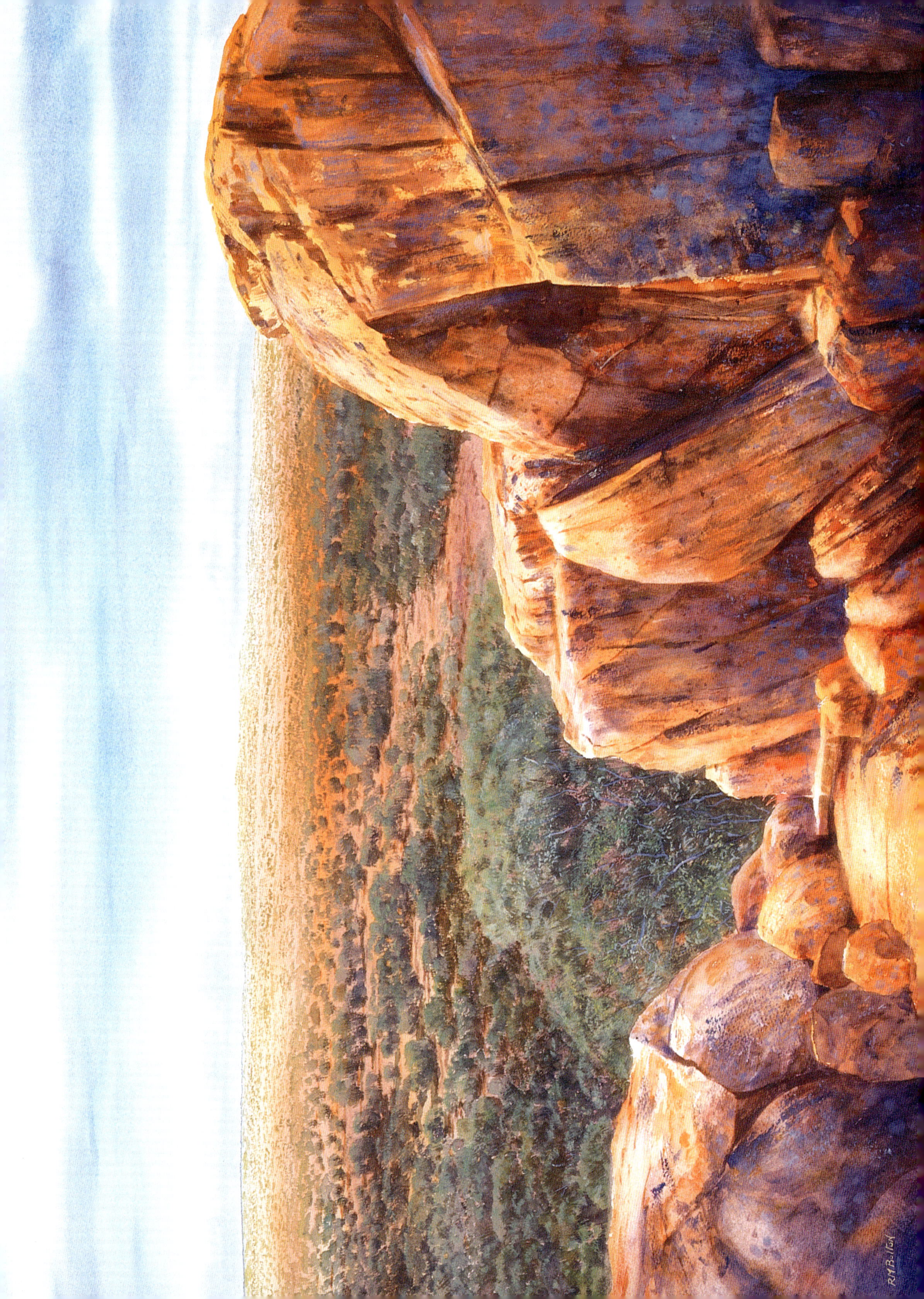

Farmhouse

Buildings can be a great help in a landscape setting: the contrast between the regular lines in architecture and those of nature can enhance a painting and give a useful focal point to a scene. As is often the case, small details can bring a painting of this kind to life. Patches of rust on a tin roof, the fine woodwork round a window or the texture of brickwork can all be used to great effect. In this painting, the dark clouds contrast with the face of the old farmhouse to dramatic effect.

Palette of colours

- Raw sienna
- Naples yellow
- Alizarin crimson
- Indian red
- Burnt sienna
- Ultramarine blue
- Cerulean blue
- Viridian
- Emerald green

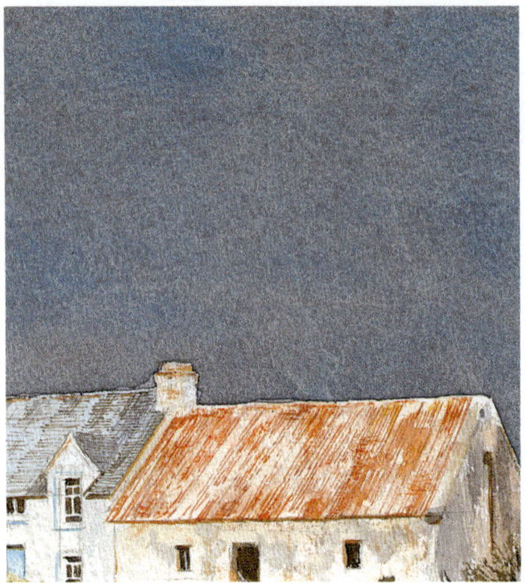

Masking fluid was used to paint out the farmhouse before I started working on the sky. The sky was completed in a couple of washes: firstly cerulean blue and a little alizarin crimson, which, when dry, was followed by ultramarine blue, alizarin crimson and a little burnt sienna. The darkest part of the sky wash appears behind the house to emphasize the contrast.

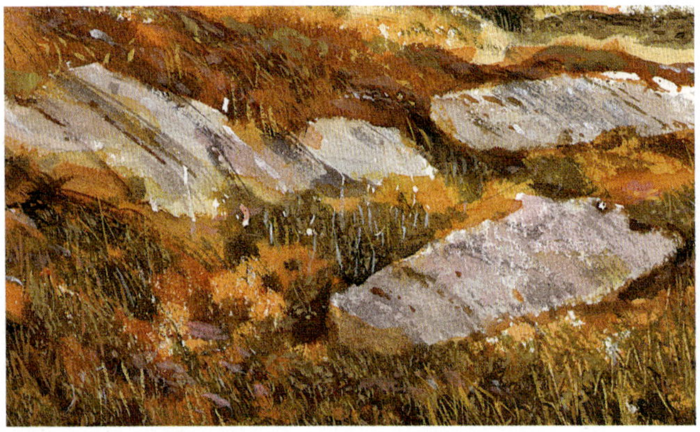

Wax resist and then masking fluid were applied to the foreground to give texture to the rocks and to mask them against a couple of brushfuls of raw sienna.

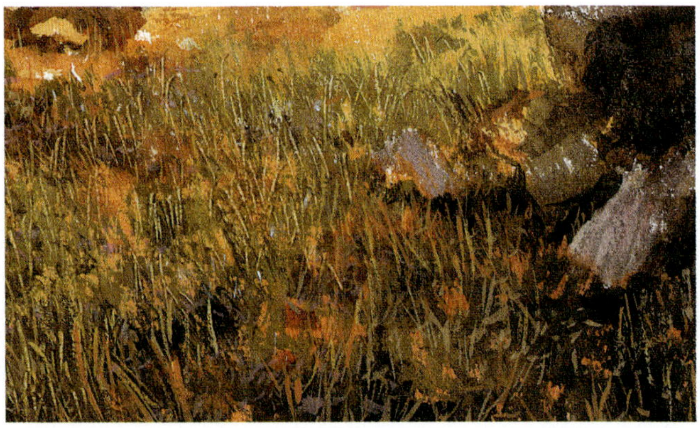

Indian red and burnt sienna gave me the rust colours amongst the heather, and this was followed by some scratching out with the corner of a razor blade while the colours were still damp, to introduce the fine stalks of grass.

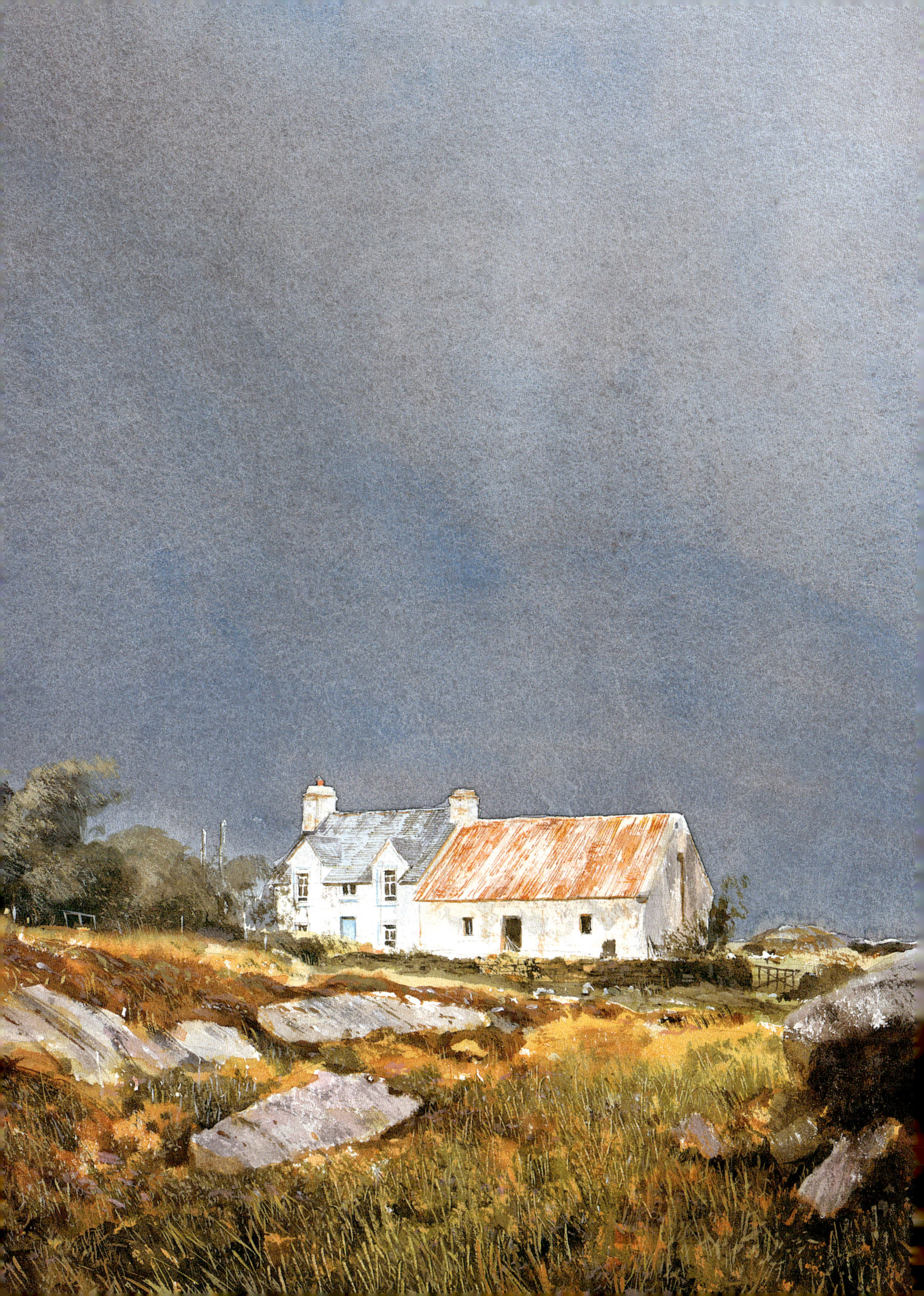

Reflections in the River Wye

Atmosphere can be found in many ways and here it is the grey, overcast day that has given the painting its tranquil, cool quality. The rocks reflected in the river are called 'the devil's shoes', and were a favourite spot for me to scramble up as a child, to see if I could spot a trout.

Palette of colours

- Naples yellow
- Burnt sienna
- Ultramarine blue
- Cerulean blue
- Emerald green
- Sap green

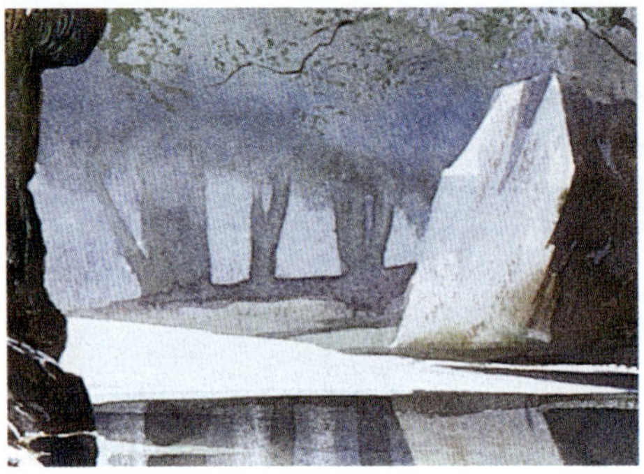

Many of the greys are made from a mix of burnt sienna and cerulean blue. Cerulean blue is a pale blue and is very effective for creating these cool shades. In the background, the paper was brushed with water before applying the colour, so that the colours would feather out and give soft edges.

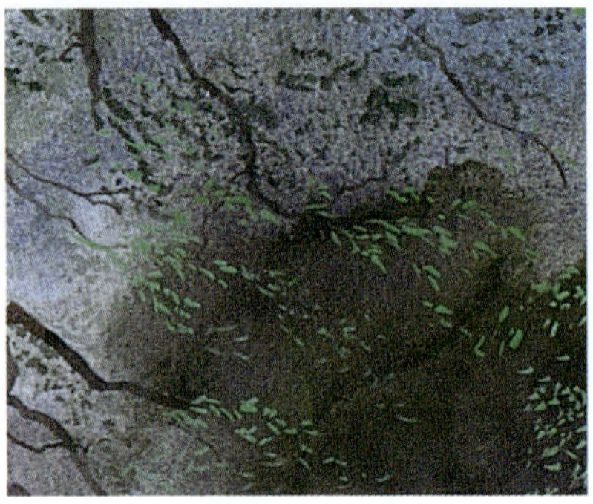

The burnt sienna and cerulean blue mix was also used to give shape to the background foliage, while the lighter green was mixed from emerald green and Naples yellow, and painted on with a small brush.

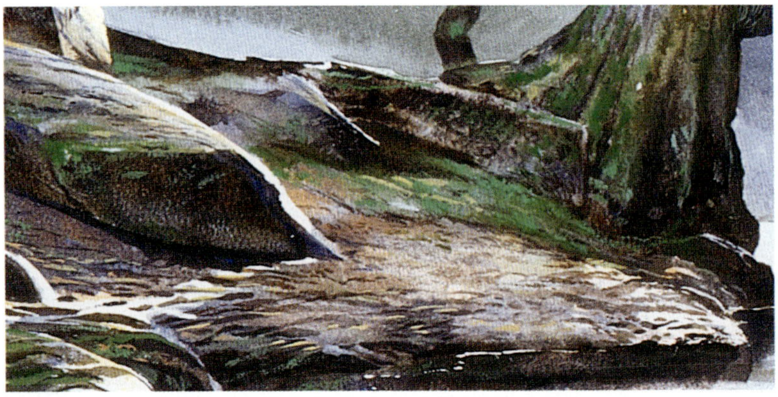

In the foreground, ultramarine blue was mixed with burnt sienna to paint the tree trunks and riverbank. Attention was given to the trees to give them shape by adding colours wet into wet and lifting out colours with a small brush to define the crevices and bumps in the bark. There was a lot of green moss on the trunks, and this was added by mixing sap green with burnt sienna and applying the mixture wet into wet.

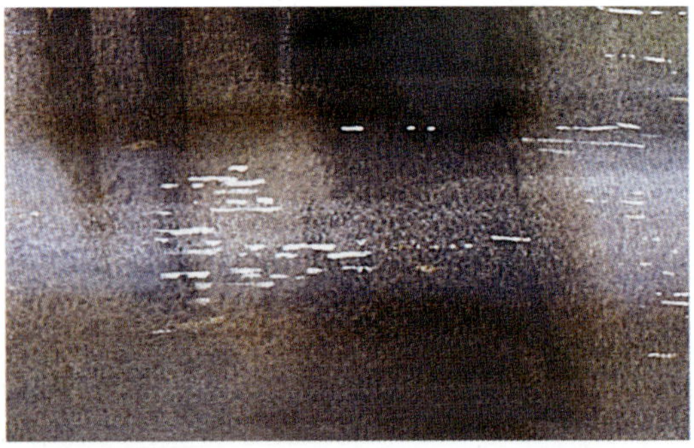

The river is mostly a mix of burnt sienna and ultramarine blue. A little masking fluid was used to touch out some fine highlights near the foreground. The bands of light across the water were added when the painting was dry. This was done by scratching the paper with a razor blade and using the edge of a ruler to keep the lines straight.

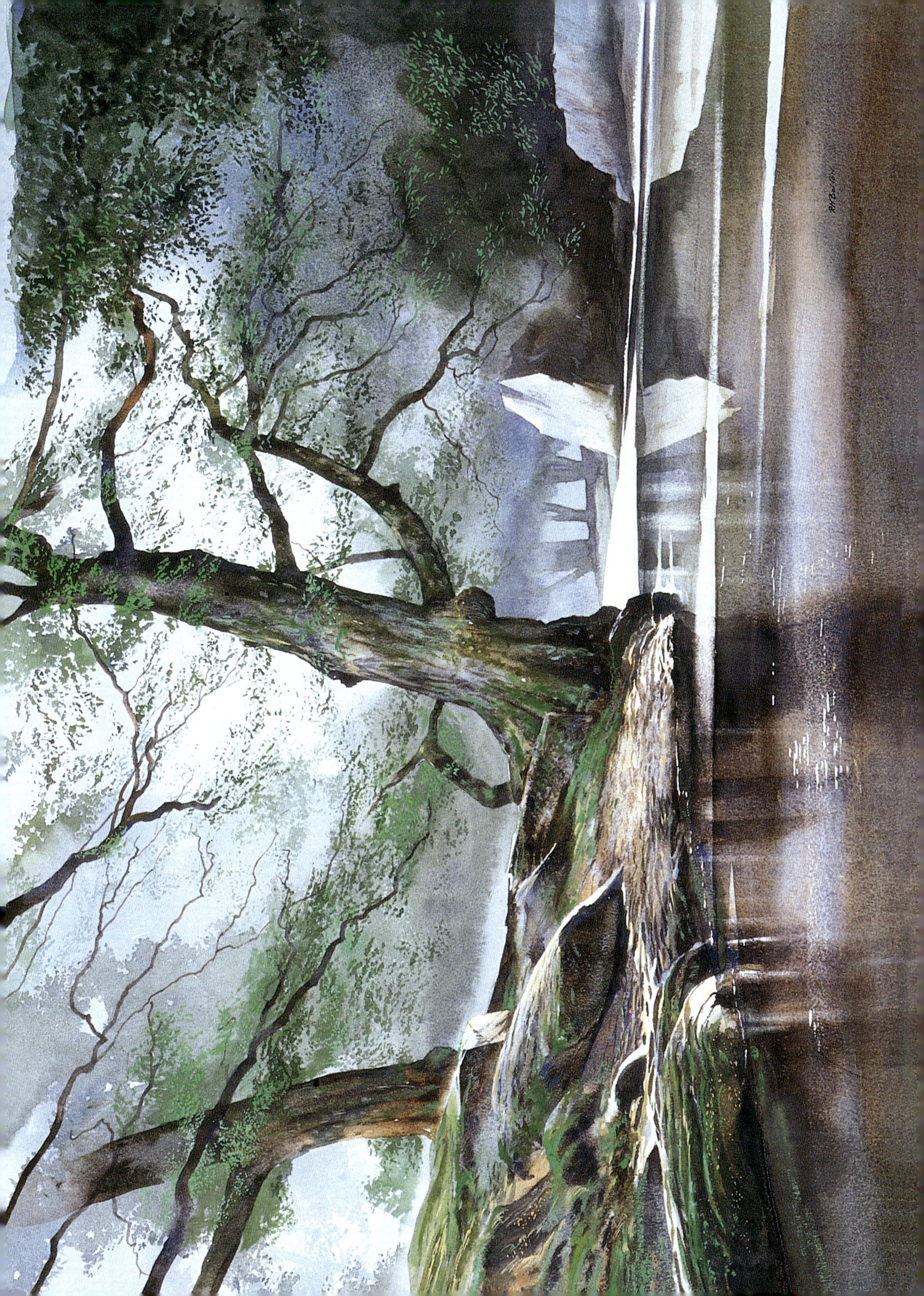

OUTLINE 46

Yumbulagang Monastery

Situated on a rocky peak, this Tibetan monastery presents a dramatic outline against the sky, while the figures add a welcome touch of colour. Figures are also useful indicators of scale in a landscape.

Palette of colours

- Raw sienna
- Cadmium yellow
- Naples yellow
- Alizarin crimson
- Indian red
- Burnt sienna
- Burnt umber
- Ultramarine blue
- Prussian blue
- Viridian

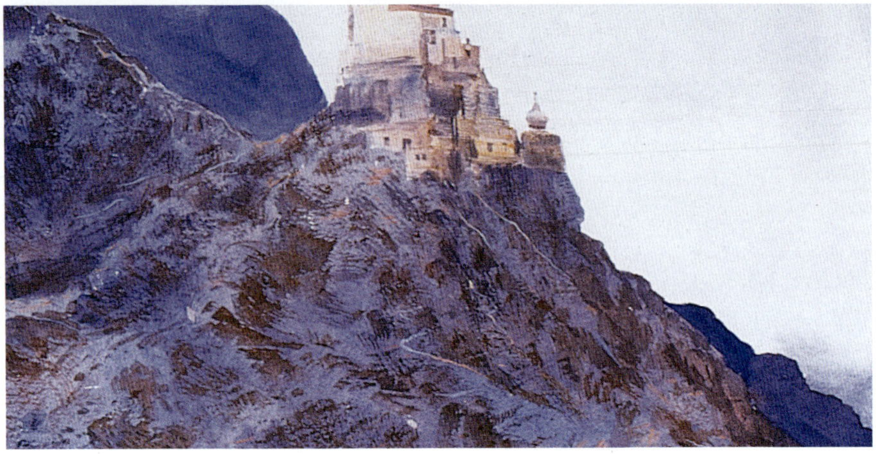

The mountains in the foreground were painted in broadly with a mix of ultramarine blue and Indian red, and then the rough texture of the rocks was scrubbed in using the dry brush technique, with a lot more Indian red in the paint mix.

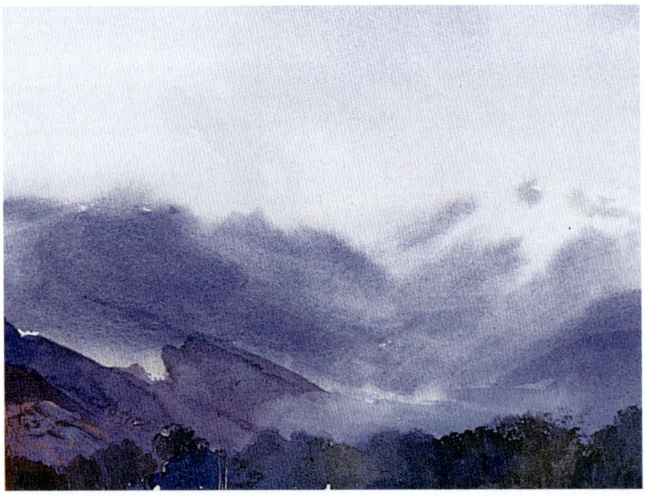

The background was painted with speed and vigour to keep the painting lively.

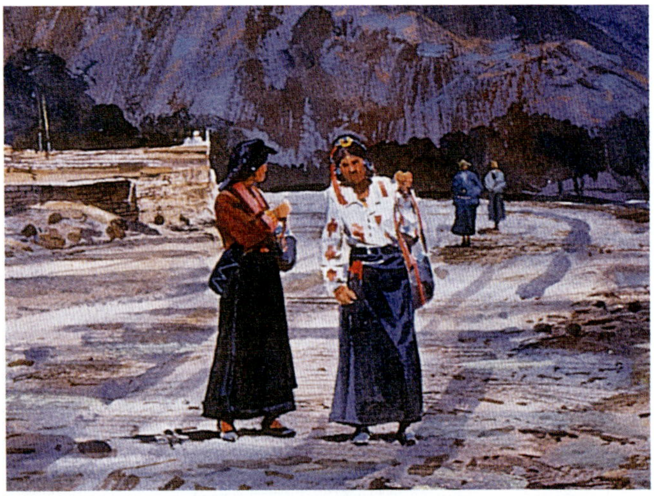

Since the girl is wearing a white shirt, I had to use masking fluid at the outset to prevent losing the white of the paper during painting. Masking fluid was also used for the hands and faces. The darker colours of the skirts and headgear were overpainted.

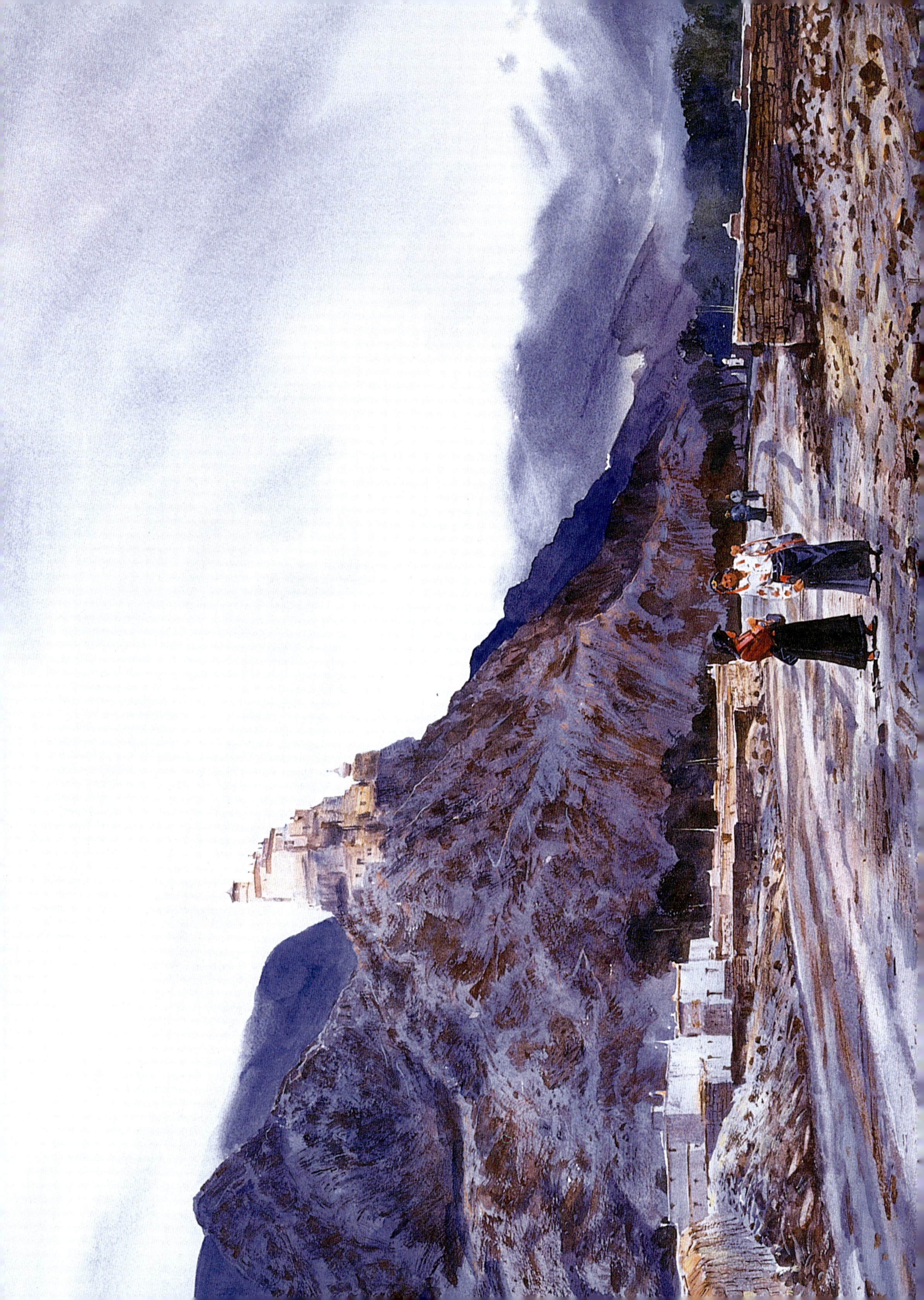

Snow Thaw

OUTLINE 47

Snow can be very dramatic in watercolour as the white of the paper shines through, giving the scene luminosity. In a painting like this, where the snow has thawed to leave only patches of snow, white areas are best masked out from the start.

Palette of colours

- Yellow ochre
- Naples yellow gouache
- Scarlet lake
- Alizarin crimson
- Burnt sienna
- Burnt umber
- Ultramarine blue
- Cerulean blue
- Viridian

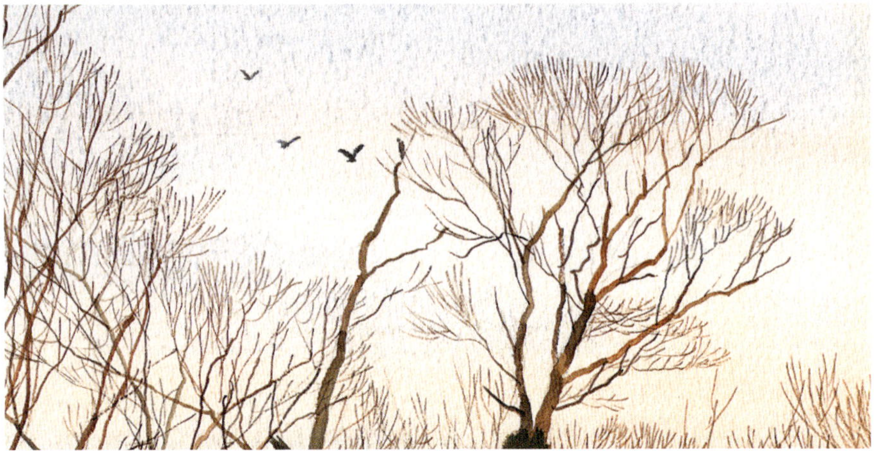

The branches and twigs are a good subject to paint with the rigger brush. The long, thin hairs are ideal for sweeping in the many long, fine lines. In the same manner, some lighter blades of grass and twigs have been overpainted with a mix of Naples yellow gouache and a little burnt sienna.

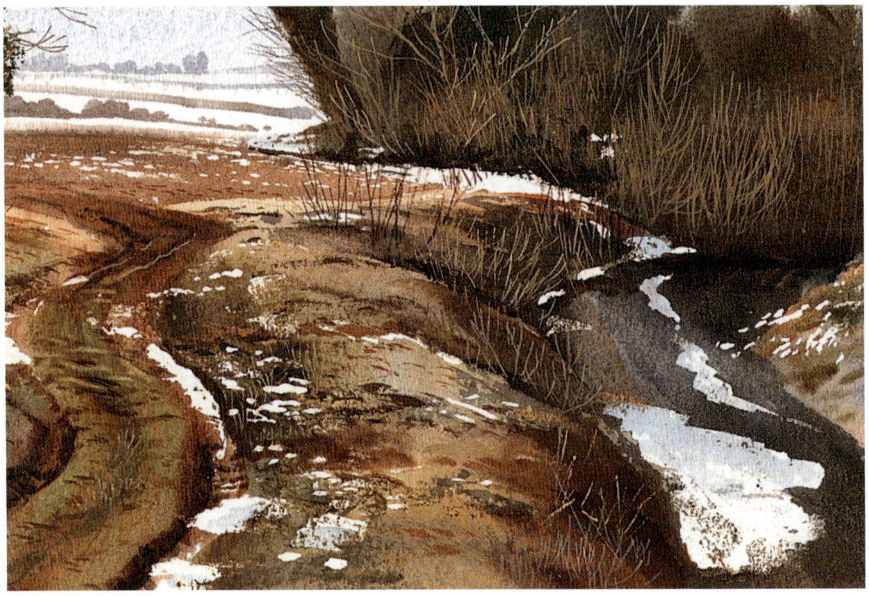

The great advantage of masking fluid is that it can be painted on in broad areas, but it can also be used for quite detailed work. In the field in this painting, small spots have been masked out to create the distant specks of snow.

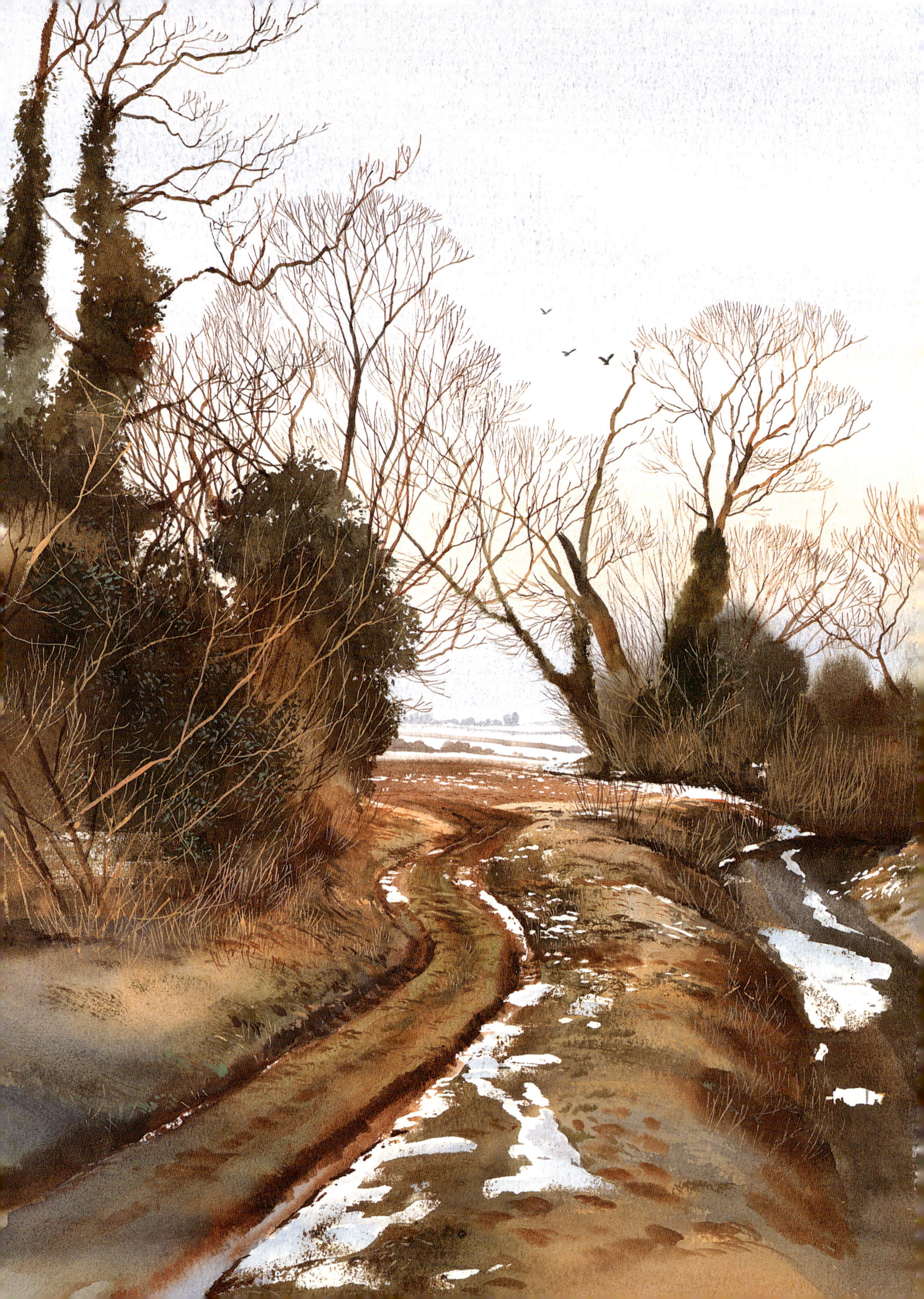

OUTLINE 48

Tracks in the Snow

Simple scenes can take on great charm after a fall of snow. Even these tractor tracks in the mud look picturesque filled up with snow. Snowy landscapes combined with brightness in a winter sky can create subtle and unusual lighting effects.

Palette of colours

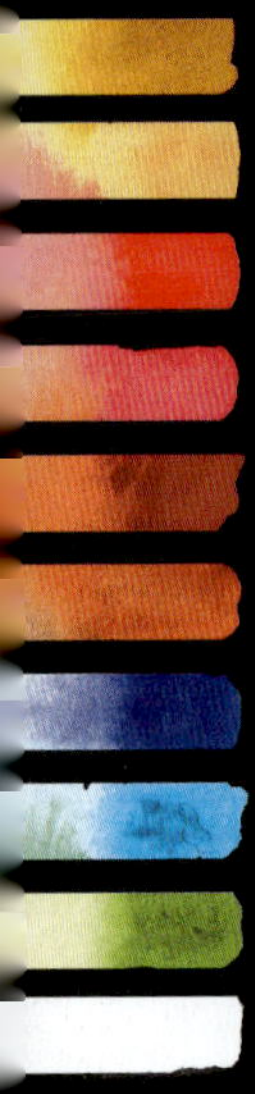

- Cadmium yellow
- Naples yellow
- Scarlet lake
- Alizarin crimson
- Indian red
- Burnt sienna
- Ultramarine blue
- Cerulean blue
- Sap green
- Chinese white

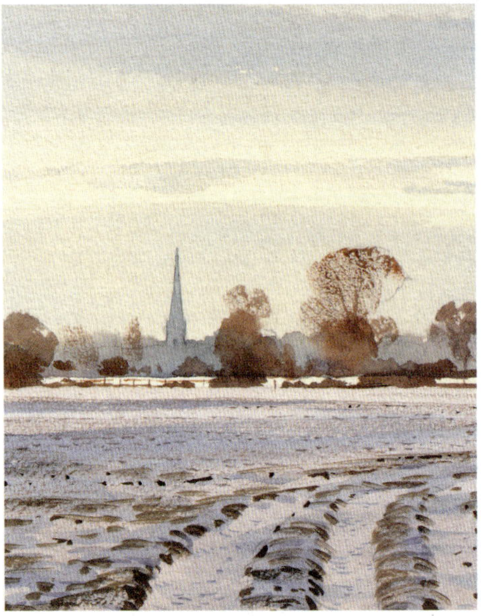

Four successive washes were used for the subtle lighting here, starting with a wash of a mix of Naples yellow, cadmium yellow and a touch of scarlet lake over the whole background; then a second wash of the same mix with more scarlet lake over the sky; a third of ultramarine blue with a little alizarin crimson; and finally a wash of stronger ultramarine and alizarin crimson over the field.

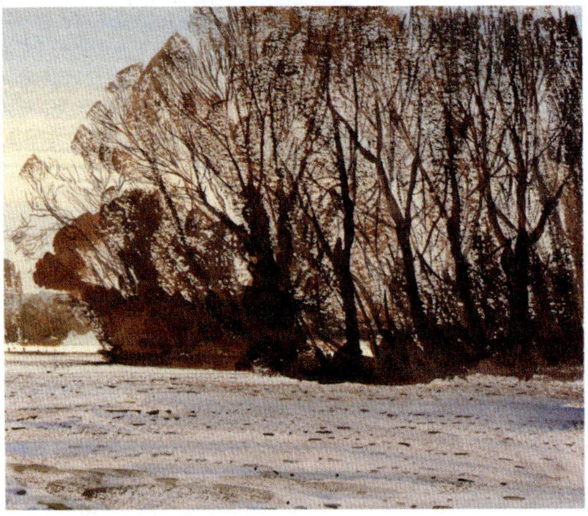

Use a strong mix of burnt sienna, ultramarine and alizarin crimson to build up the large tree with the side of a size 12 brush to create the ragged edges, then pick out the branches with a smaller brush. Work quickly to avoid becoming bogged down in the detail.

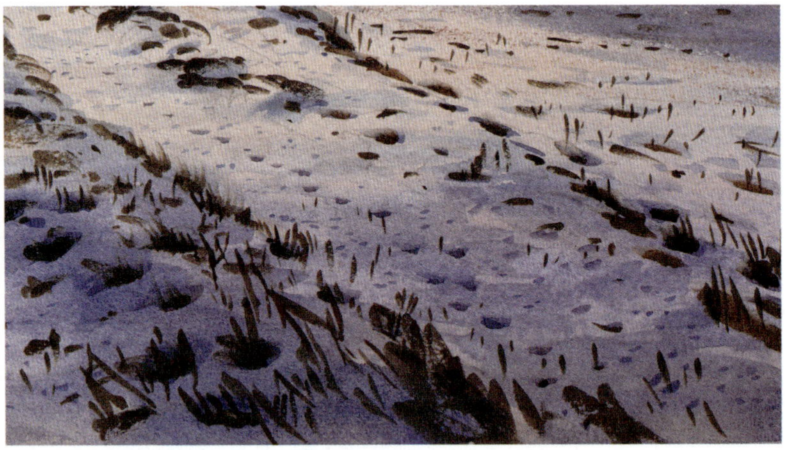

The tyre tracks and shadows on the snow are painted using ultramarine. Vary the depth of colour to suggest the dappled effect of light and shadow on the snow. Use a mix of sap green, burnt sienna and ultramarine to paint in the areas of earth showing through the holes in the snow. Soften the top edges with a wet brush to make it look as though tufts of wintry grass are growing through the holes. In the foreground, strengthen and warm the colour of the grass by using Indian red mixed with sap green.

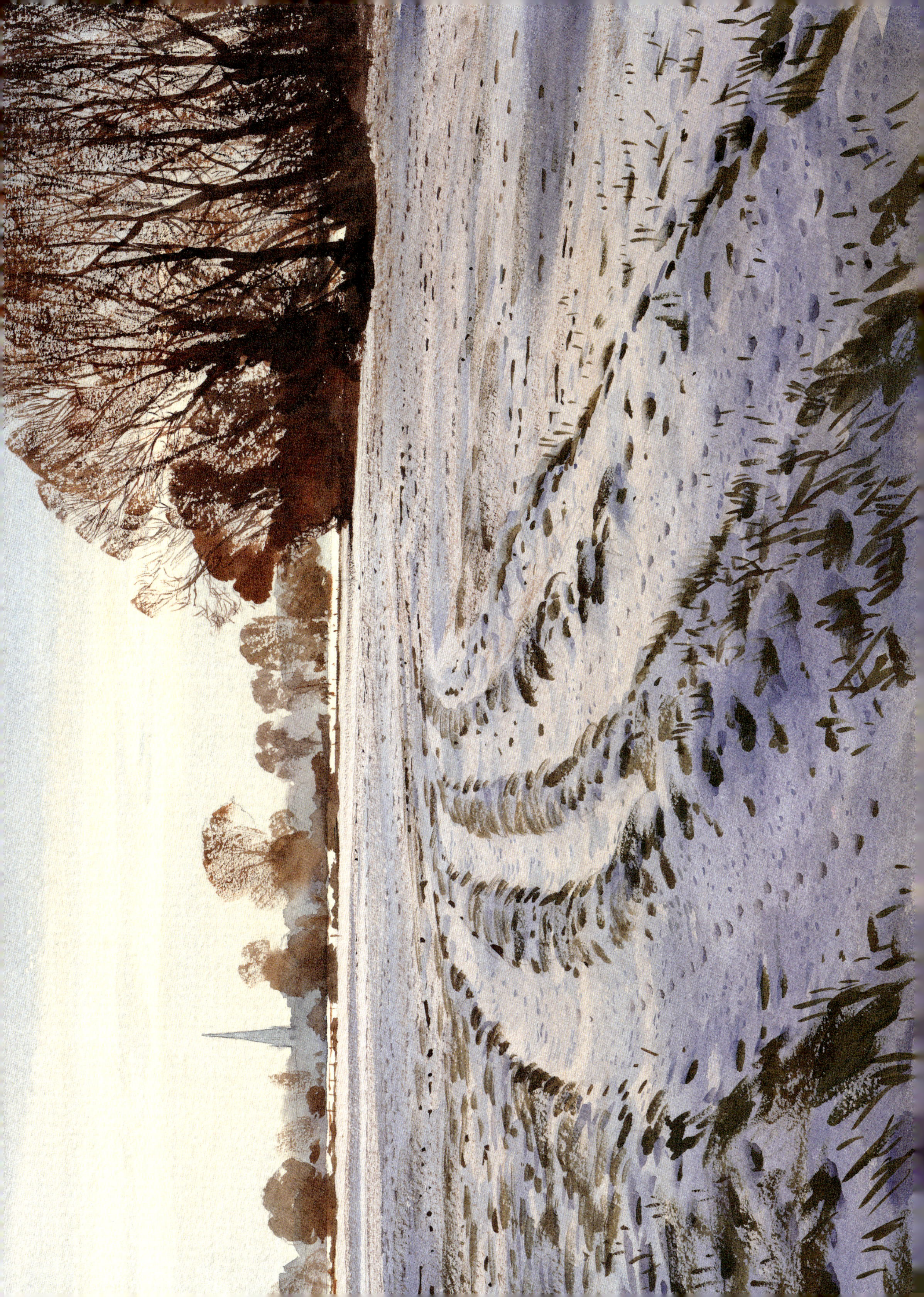

OUTLINE 49

Summer Afternoon

I was attracted to this scene by the rosy glow from the sun, picked up on the trunk of the tree. The golden tones of this scene seemed perfectly to catch the atmosphere of a summer afternoon. I kept the detail to a minimum in favour of a lively approach.

Palette of colours

- Raw sienna
- Naples yellow
- Scarlet lake
- Alizarin crimson
- Indian red
- Burnt sienna
- Ultramarine blue
- Viridian
- Emerald green

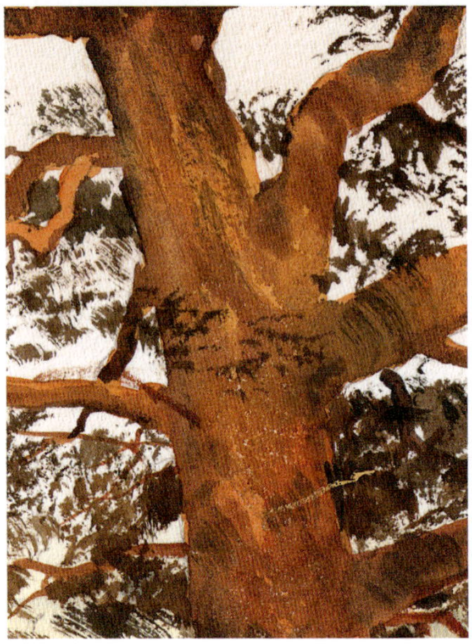

Rub candle wax on to the tree trunk at the start of the painting – as you add washes (a mix of raw sienna, burnt sienna and scarlet lake initially, followed by touches of viridian and ultramarine and alizarin crimson), the texture will emerge.

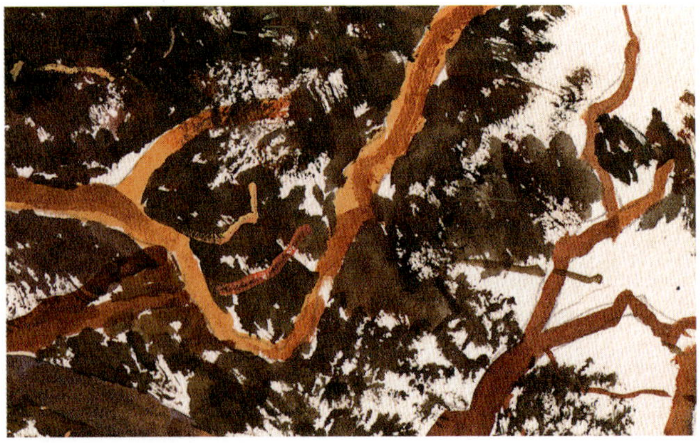

Start the foliage with the shadows, using a mix of alizarin crimson and viridian. Use a mix of alizarin crimson, ultramarine blue, viridian and raw sienna for the areas in the light.

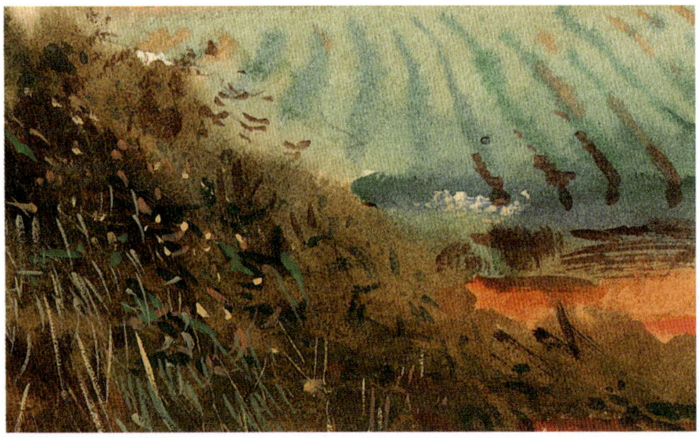

Contrast in the greens helps to build a sense of distance, with warm greens in the foreground and cooler greens further back.

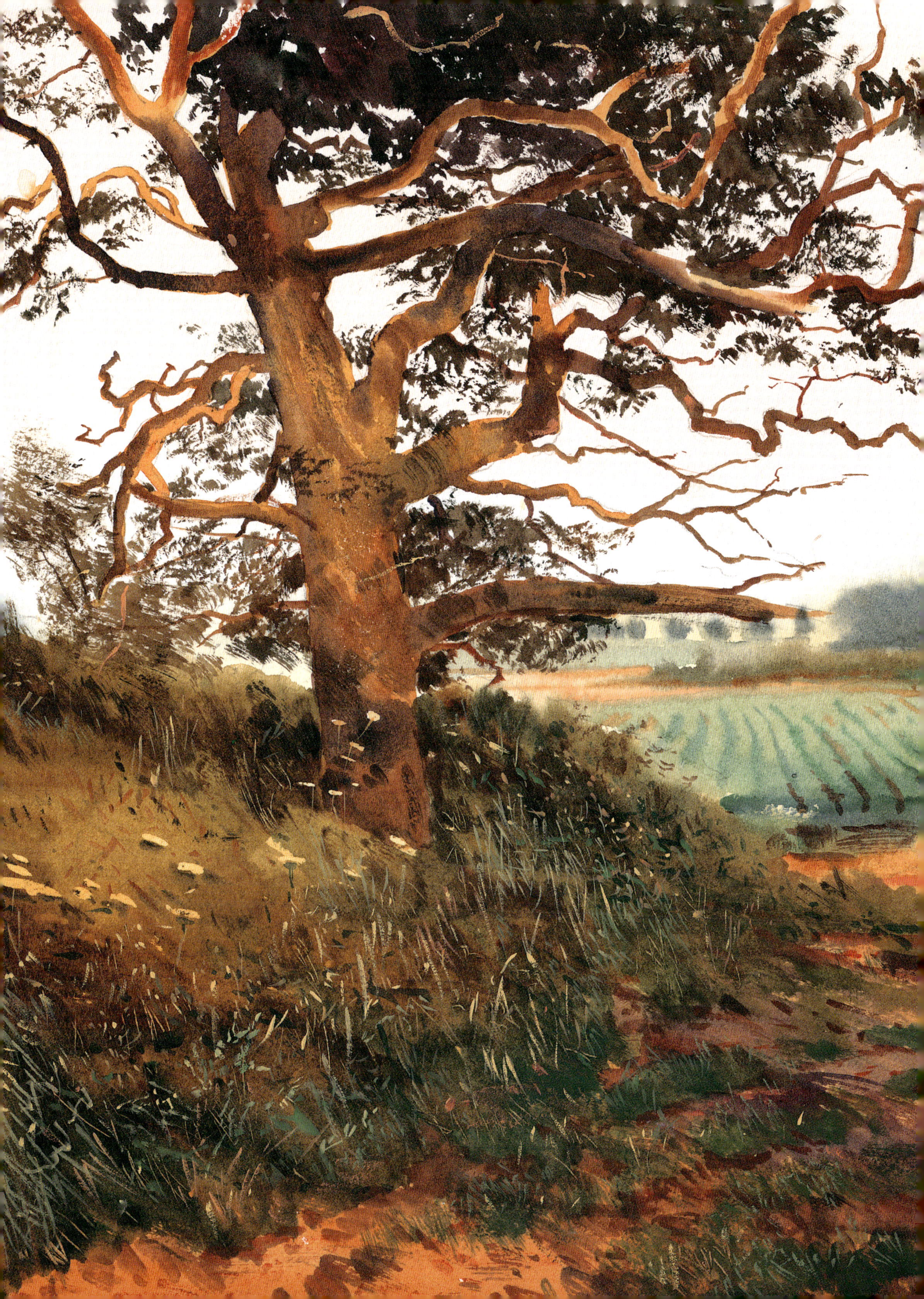

OUTLINE 50

Reflections at Houghton Lock

There is something very special about water. I have the feeling that I can always construct a painting if there is water involved. Its fluid nature, the colours and reflections, and its abstract quality can always lift a painting.

The water in this scene has that dark, inky quality which I find irresistible in watercolour.

Palette of colours

- Naples yellow
- Alizarin crimson
- Burnt umber
- Cerulean blue
- Prussian blue
- Sap green

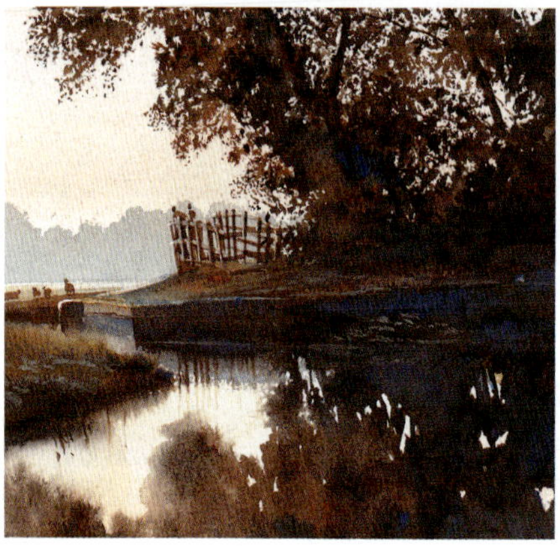

There is little colouring here: the bank and trees form dark shadows of burnt umber and sap green against a background wash of Naples yellow with traces of red and blue.

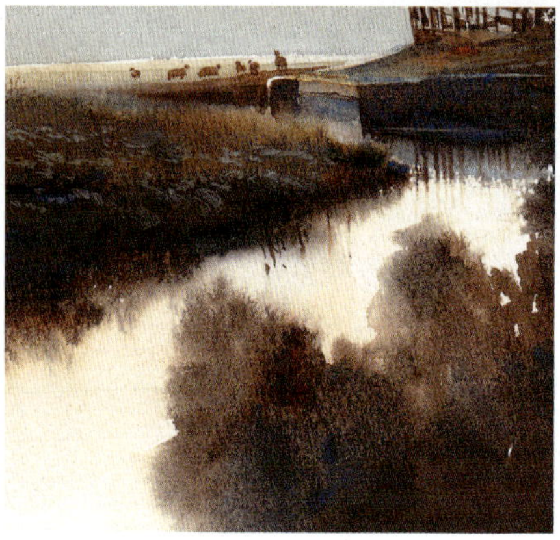

The reflections are painted wet into wet and softened away with clean water for a diffuse effect.

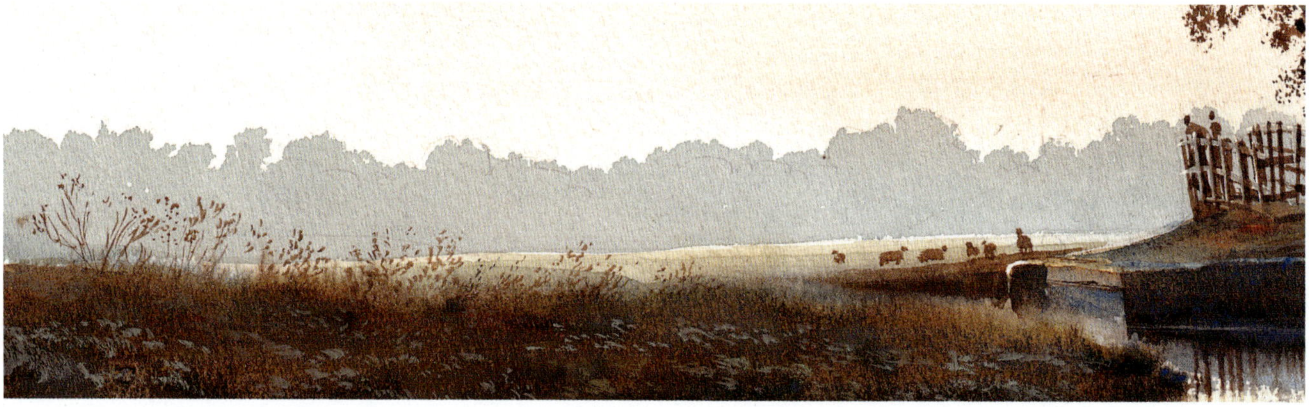

The distant tree line is a cool blue-grey – a mix of cerulean blue and Naples yellow.

Index

The outlines

You can use scissors or a craft knife to remove the outlines from the book to use them, or you can work directly from this book.

If you prefer, you can photocopy or scan the outline first, and transfer the outline from a copy. See pages 8–9 for how to transfer the outlines, and pages 10–11 for more ideas.

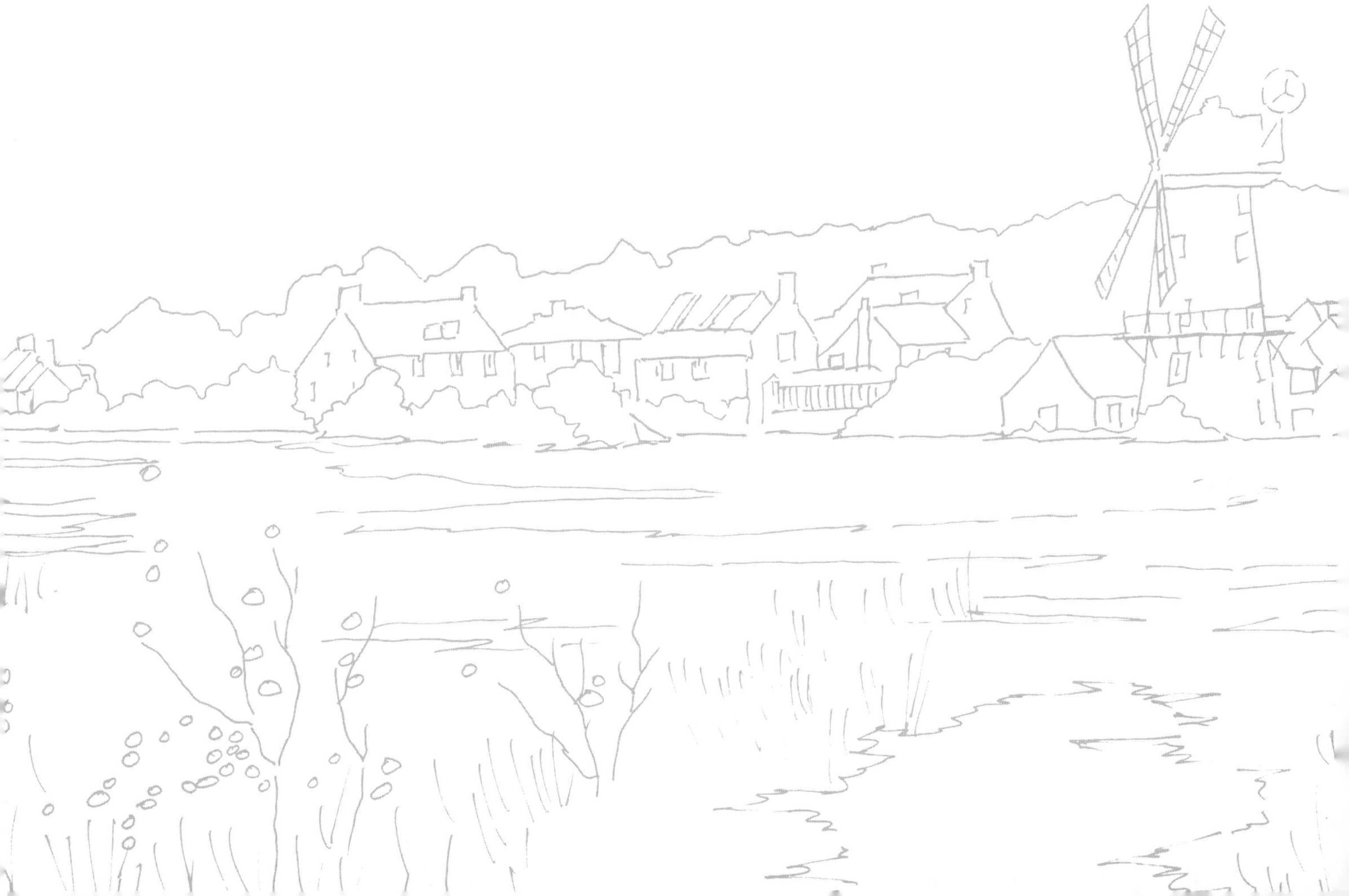

1

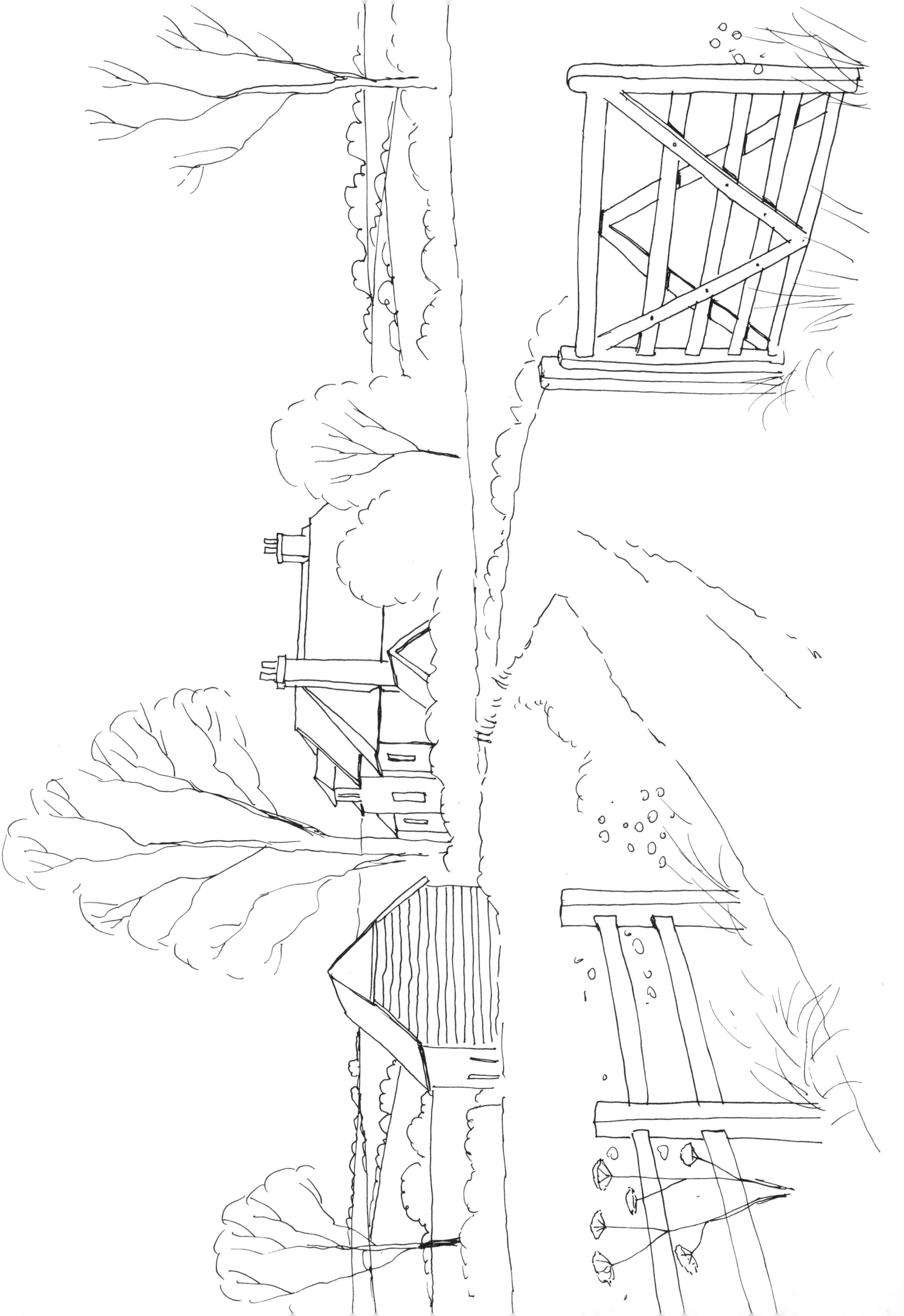

2

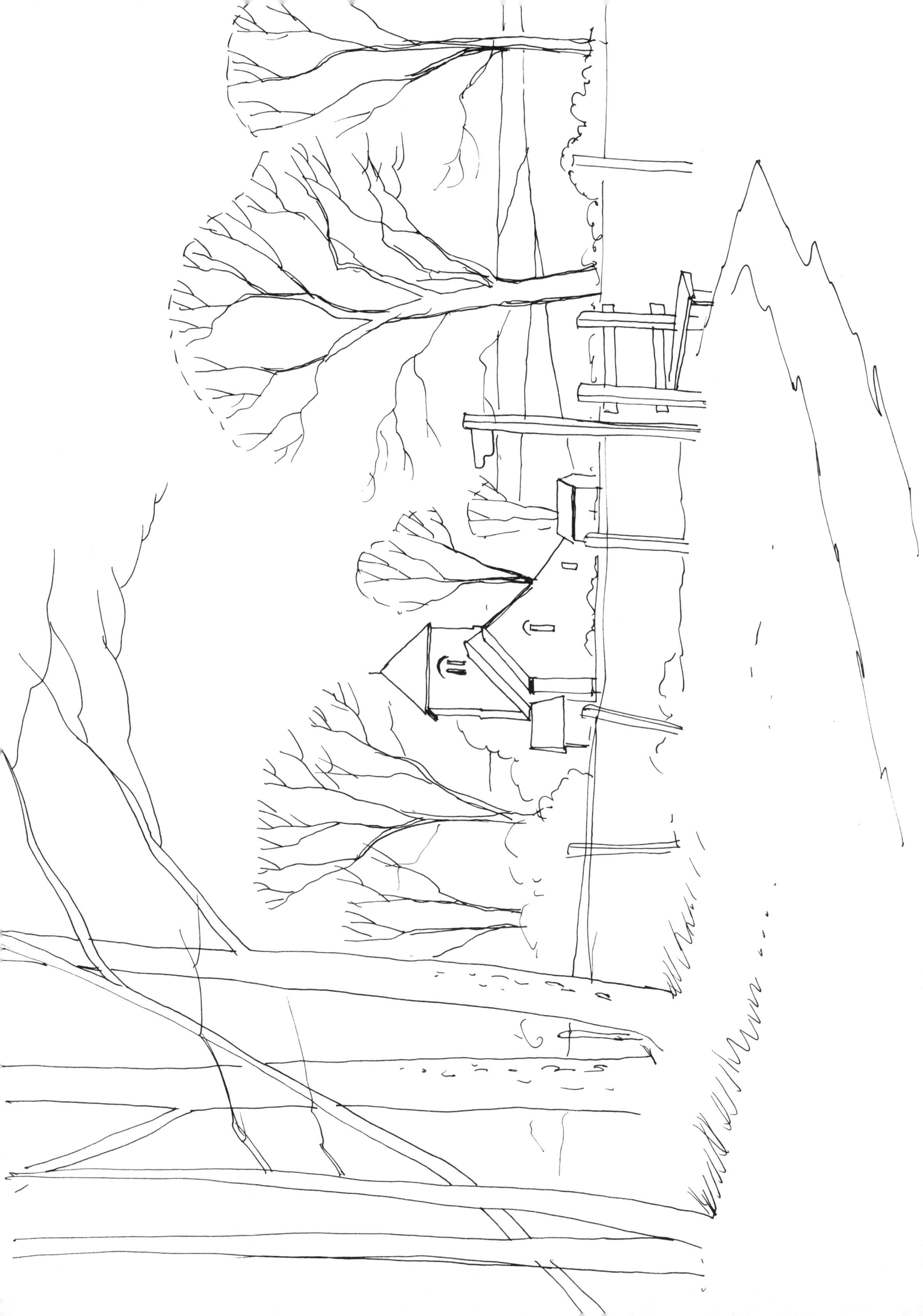

3

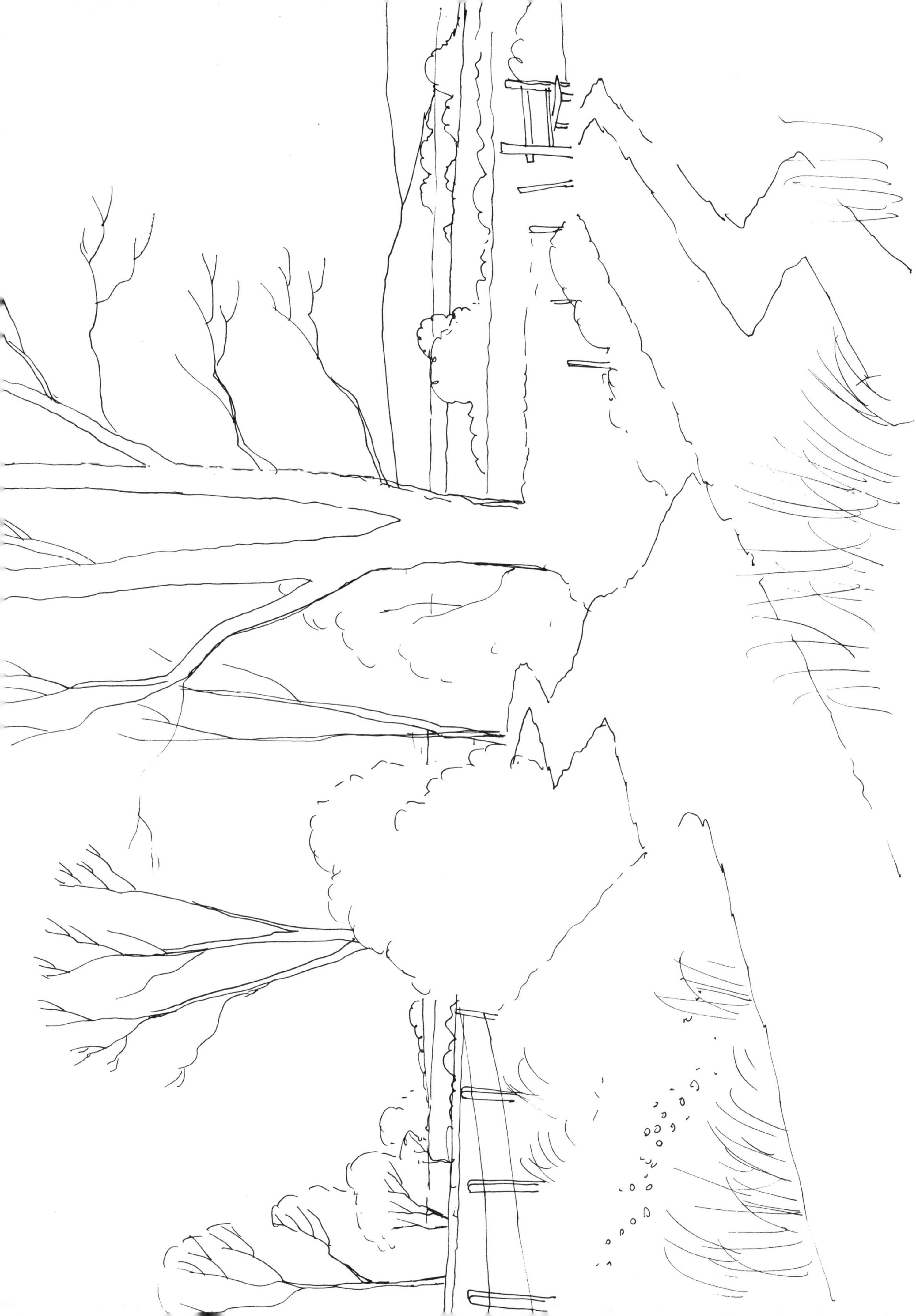

4

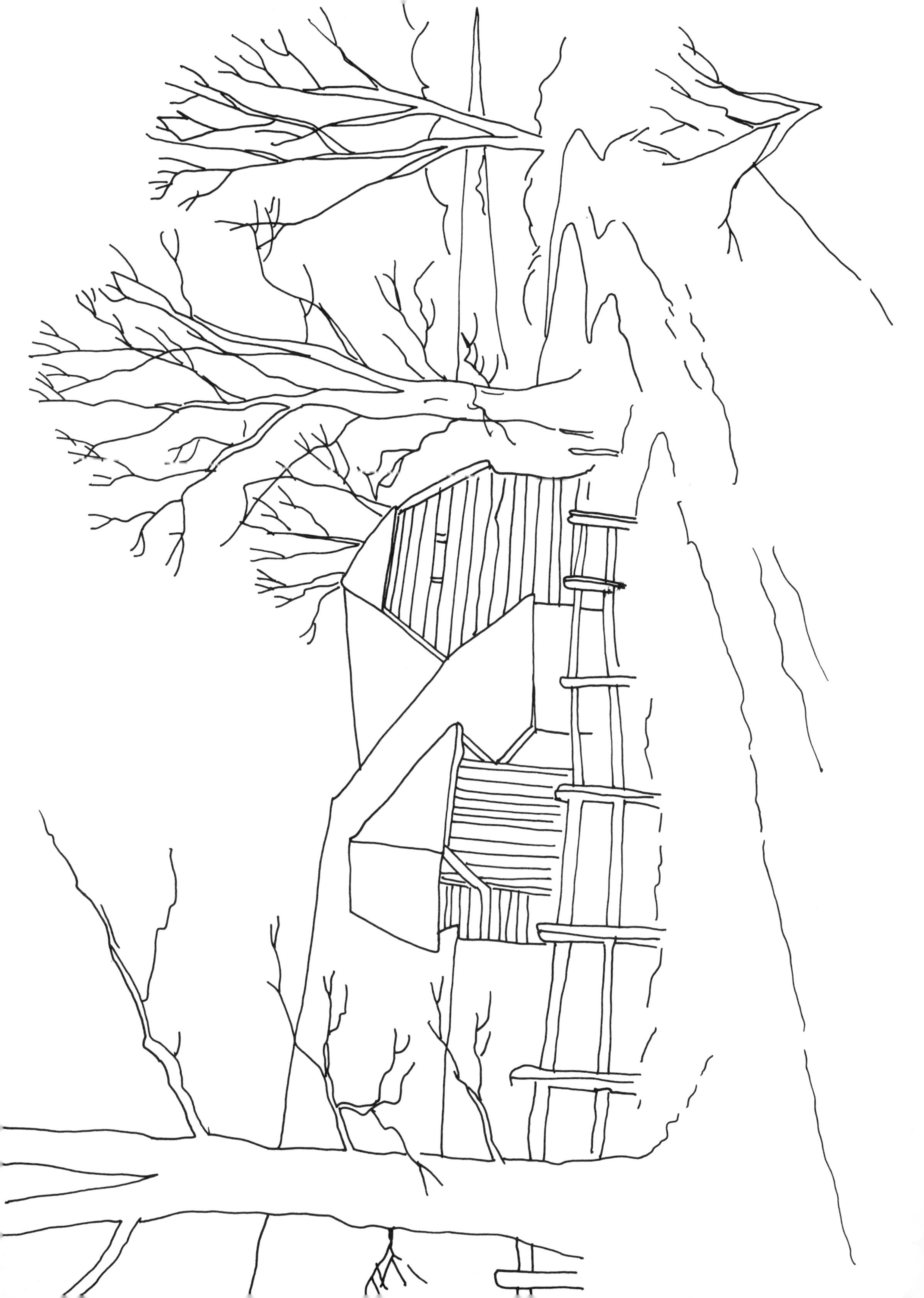

5

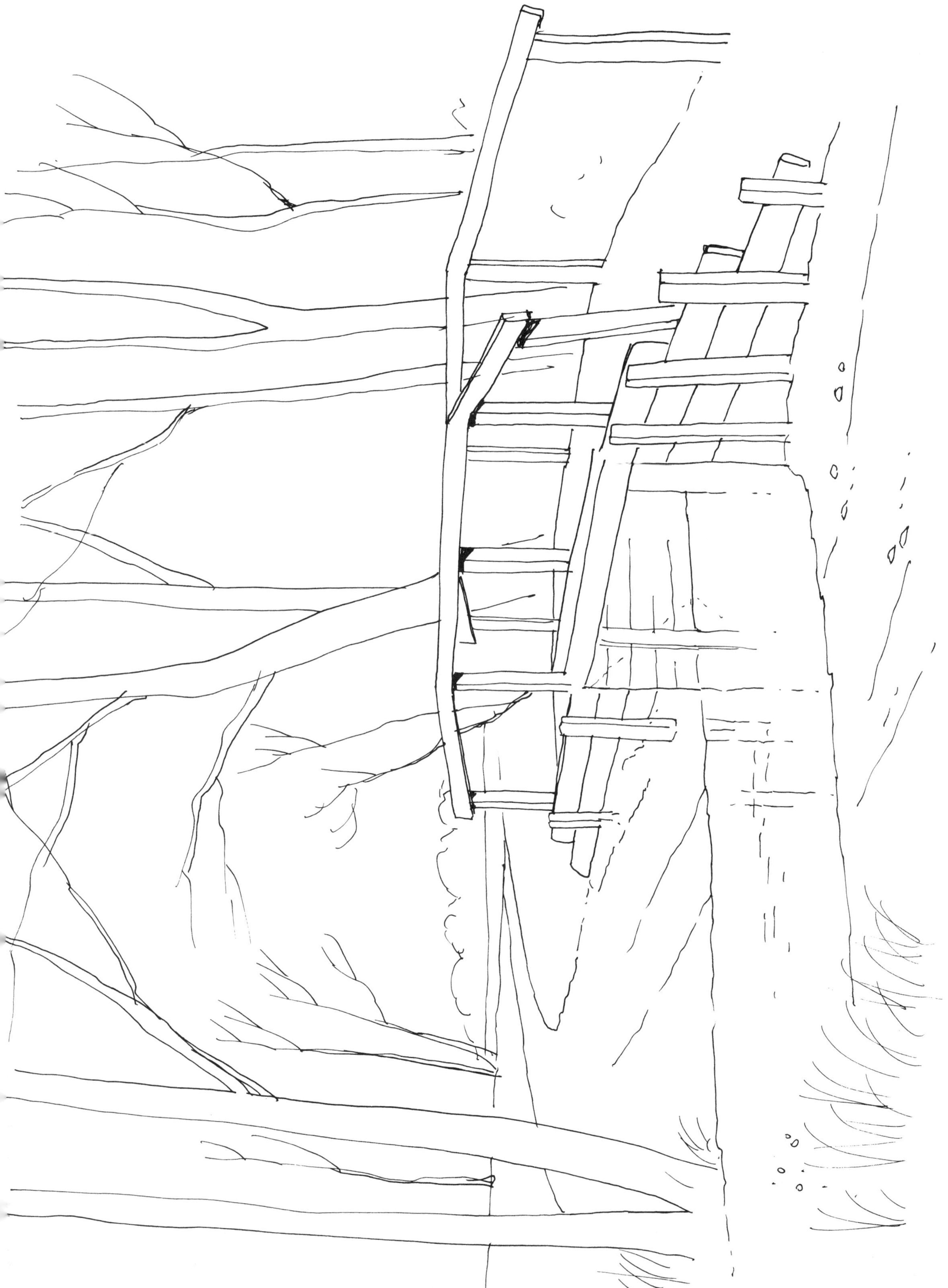

6

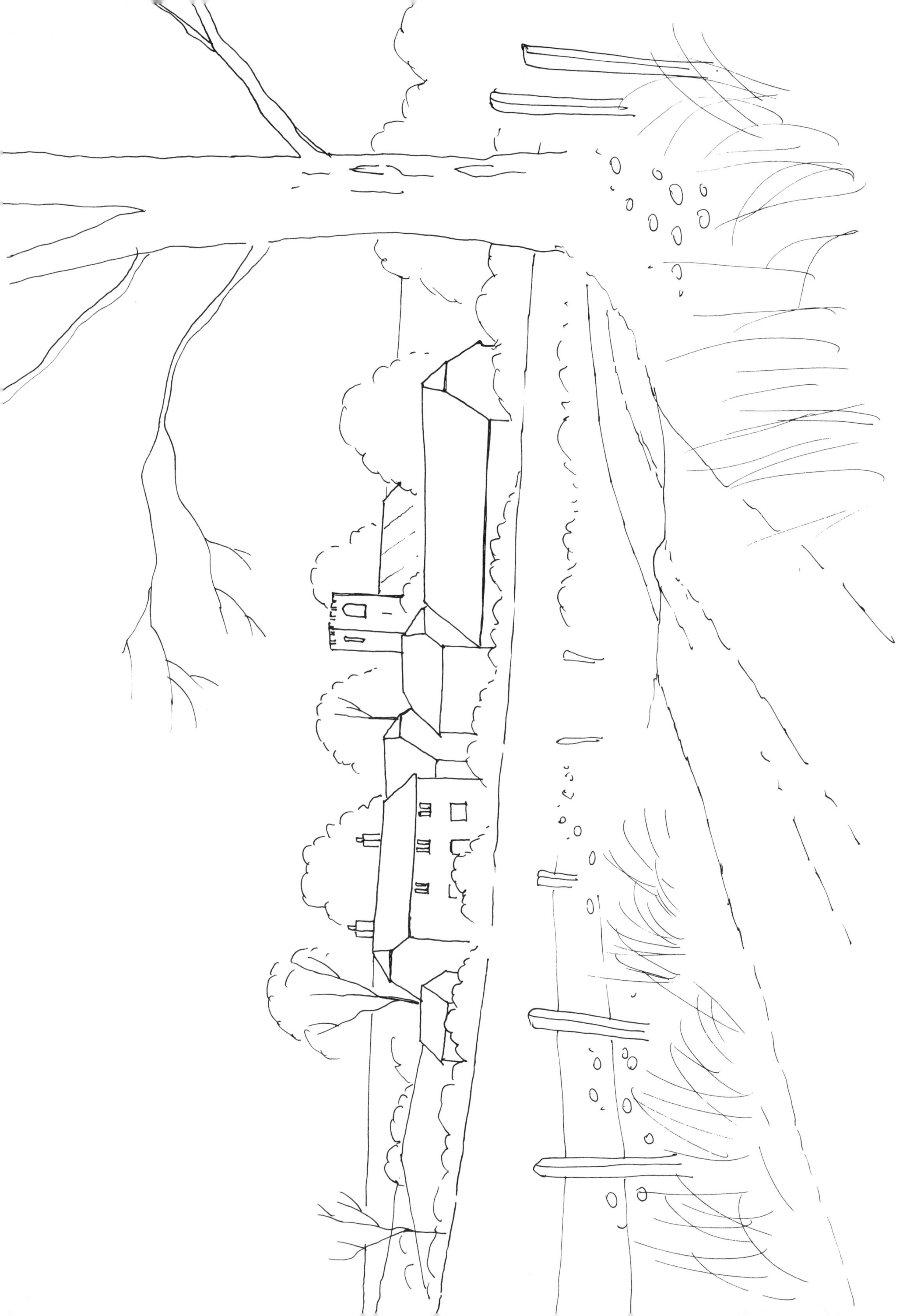

7

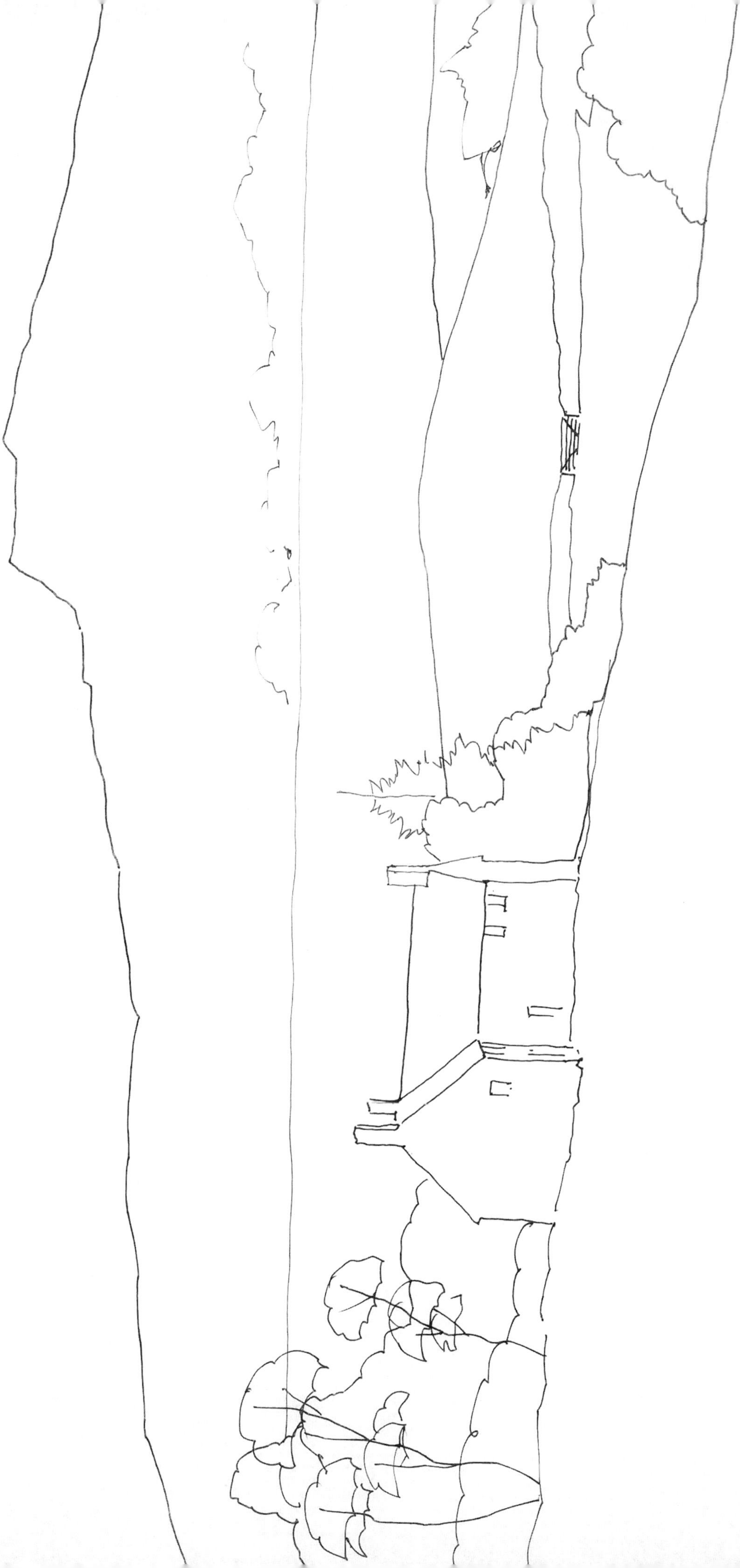

8

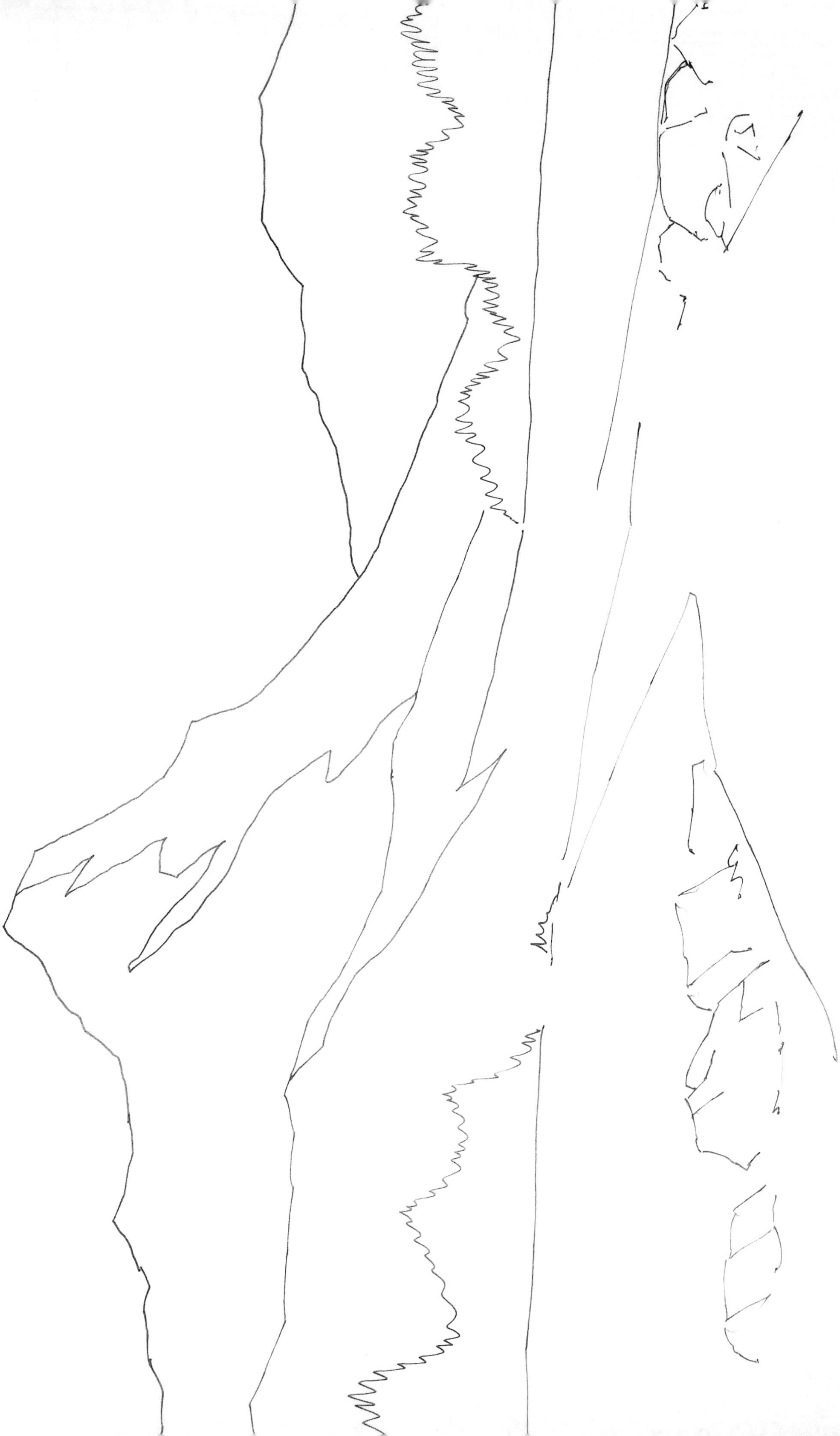

9

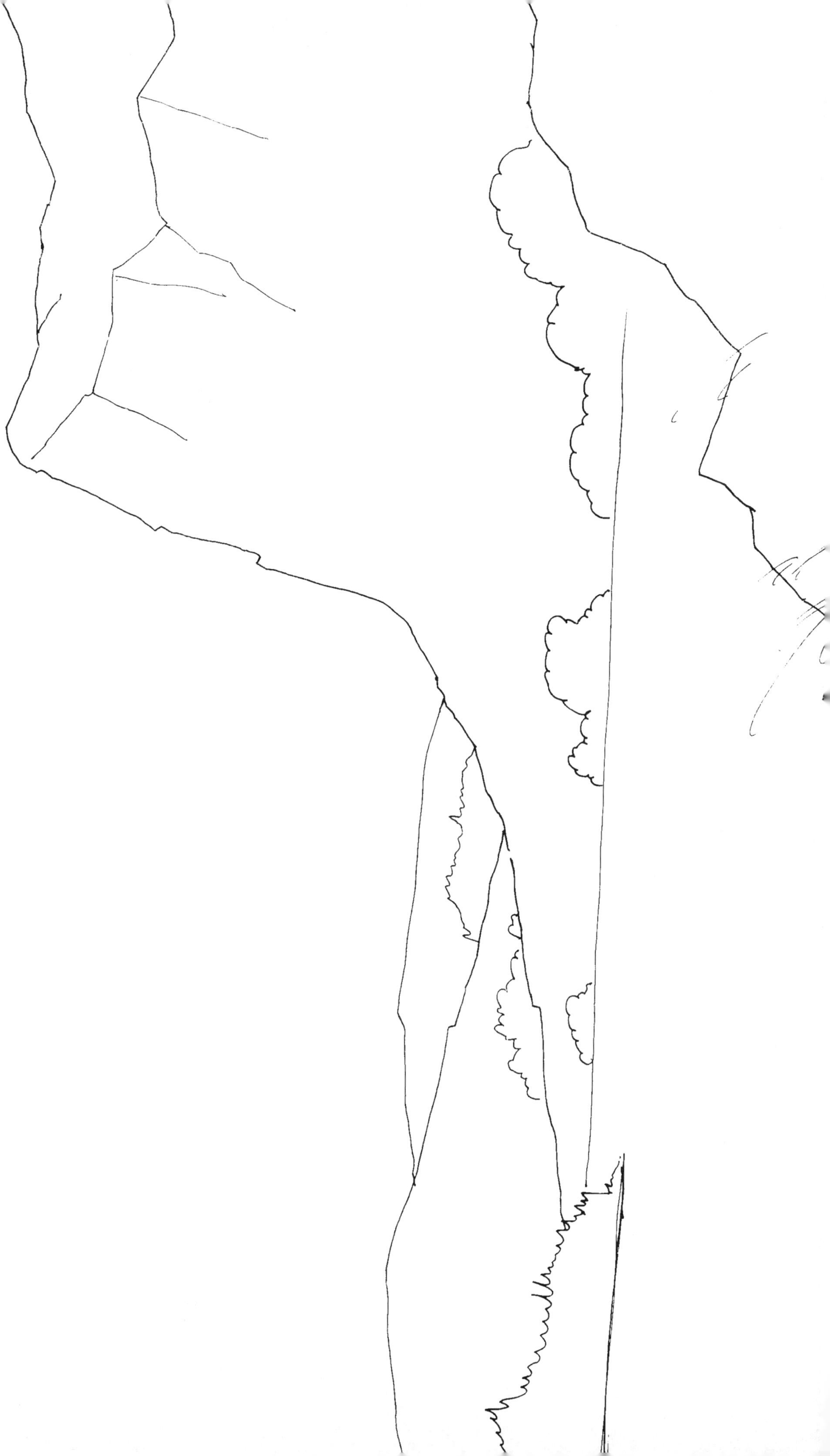

10

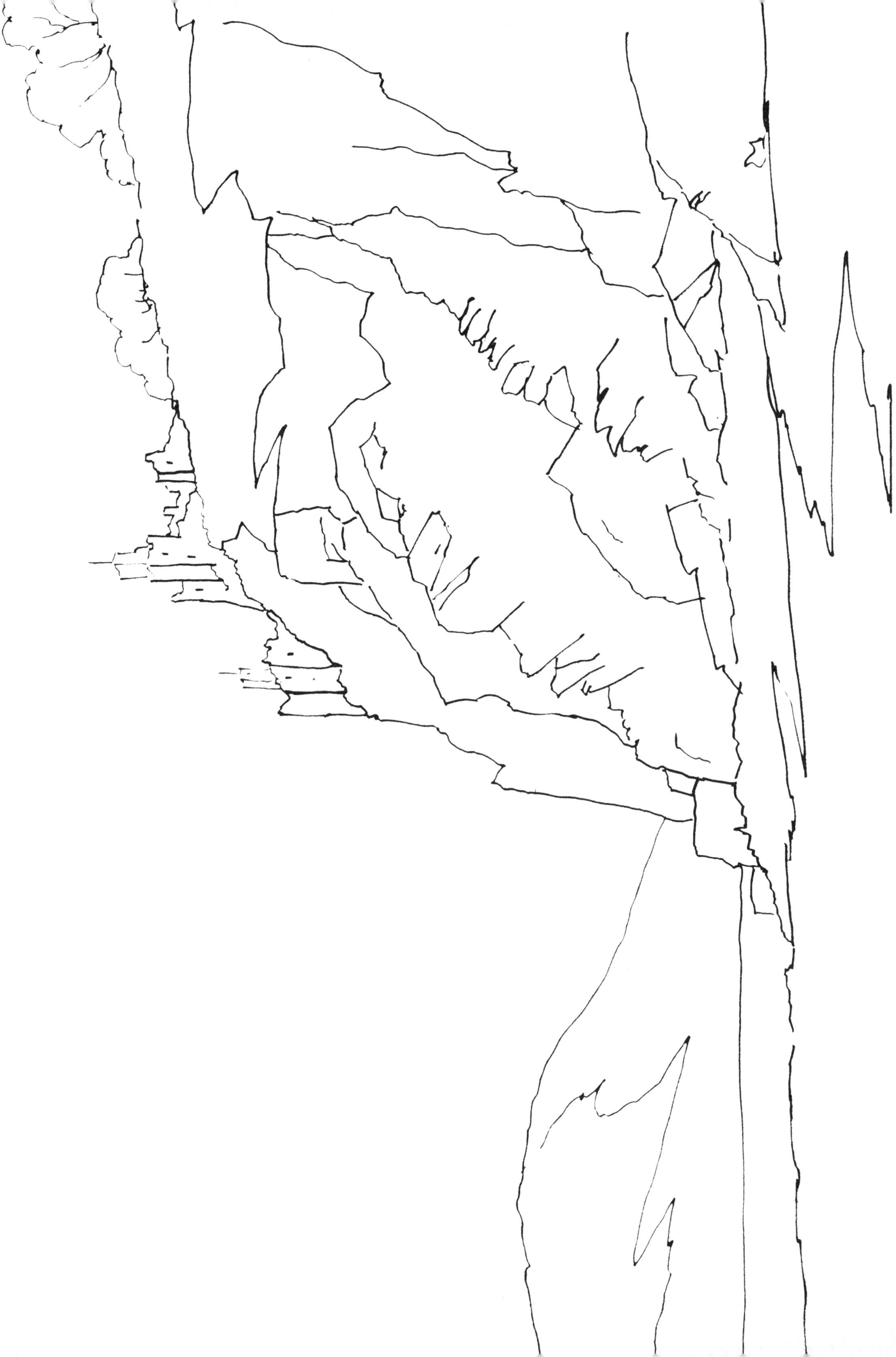

11

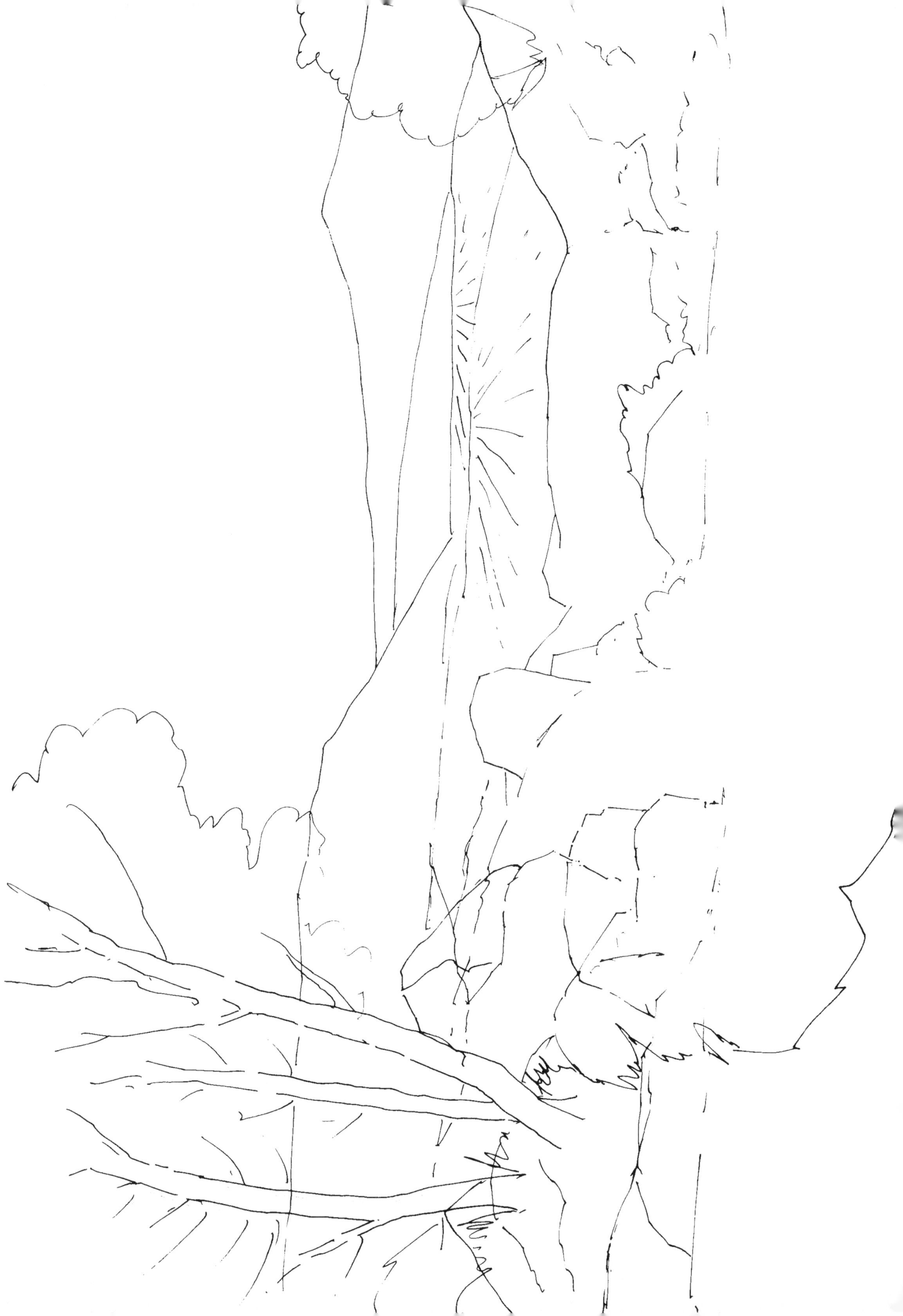

12

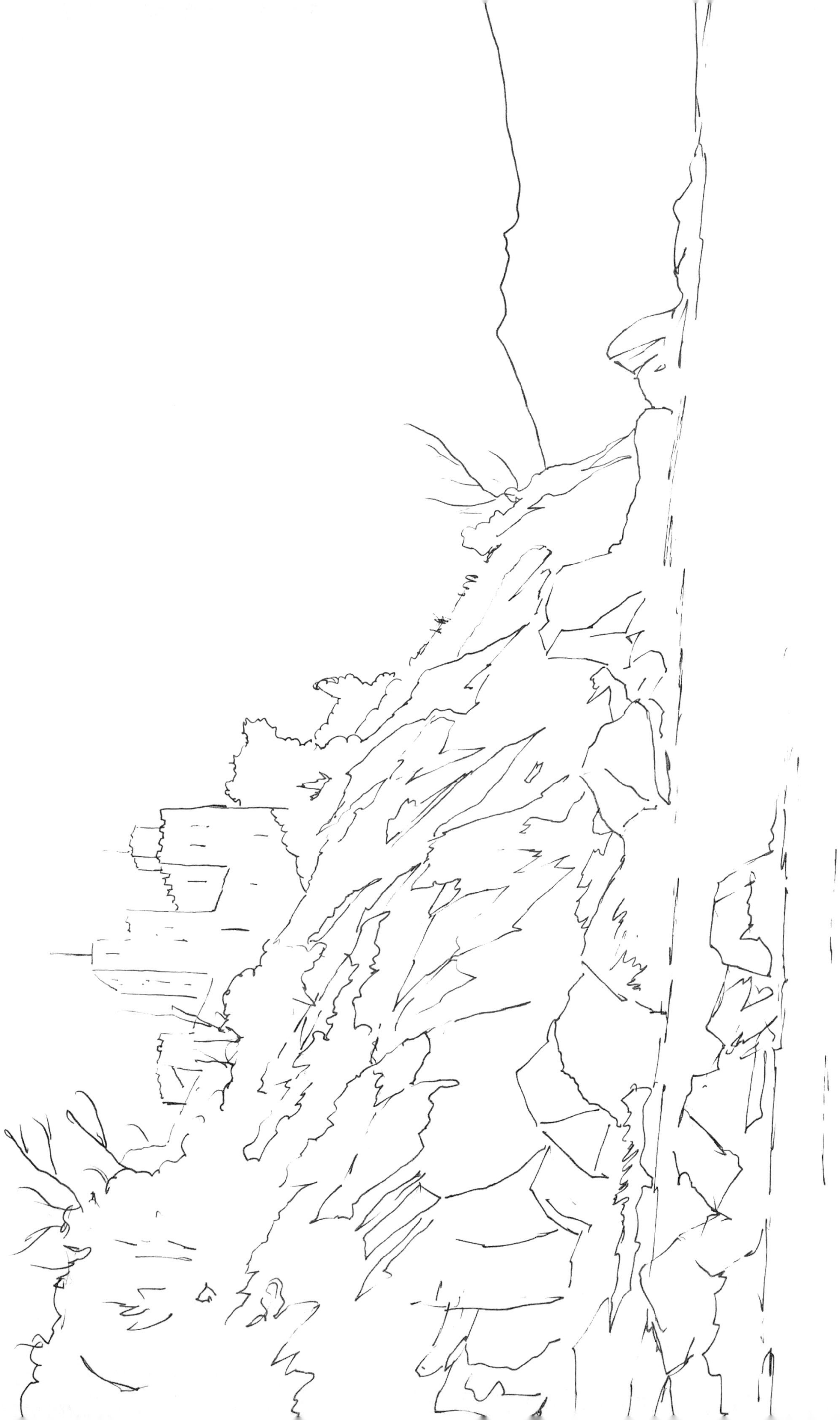

13

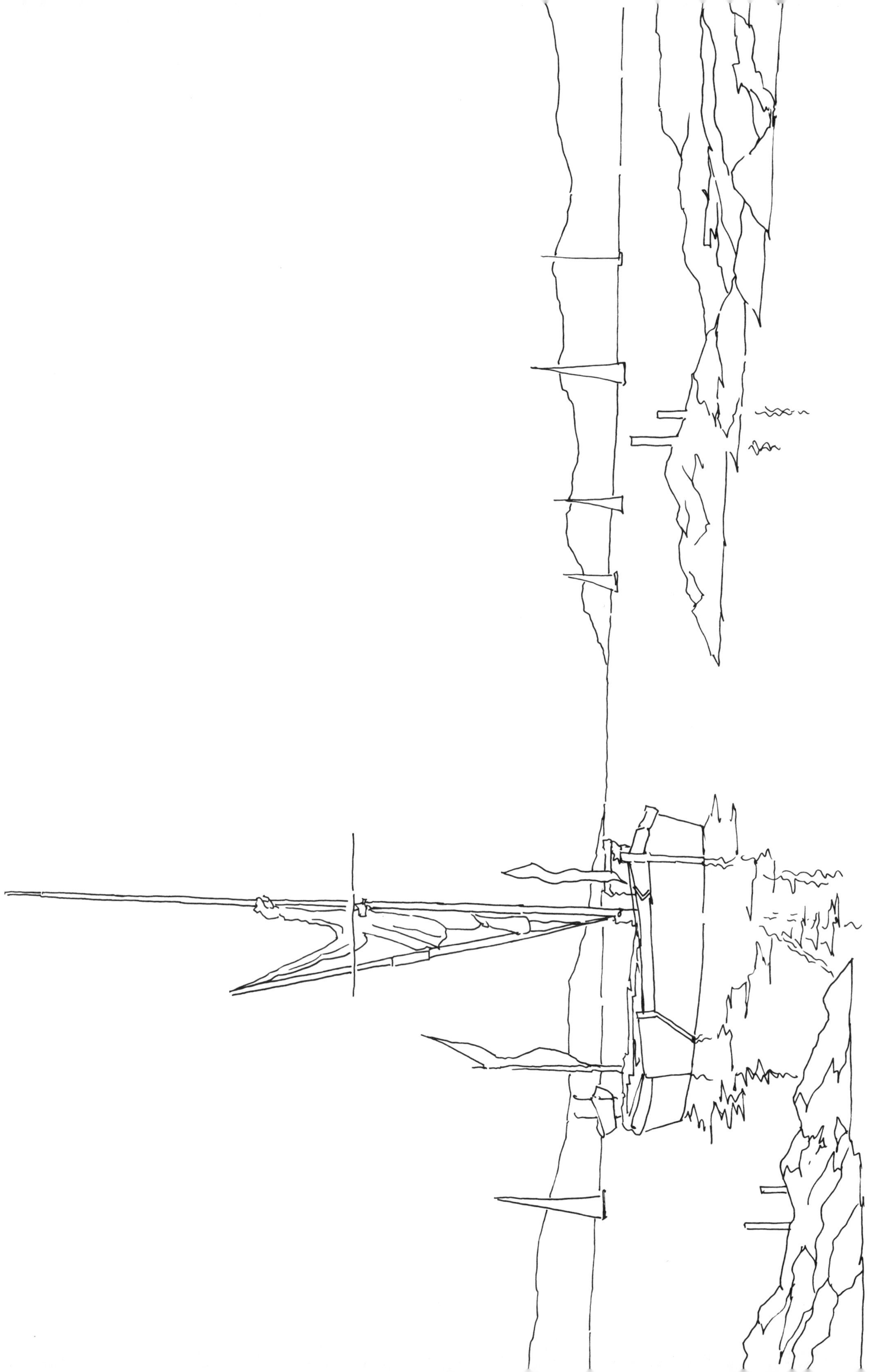

14

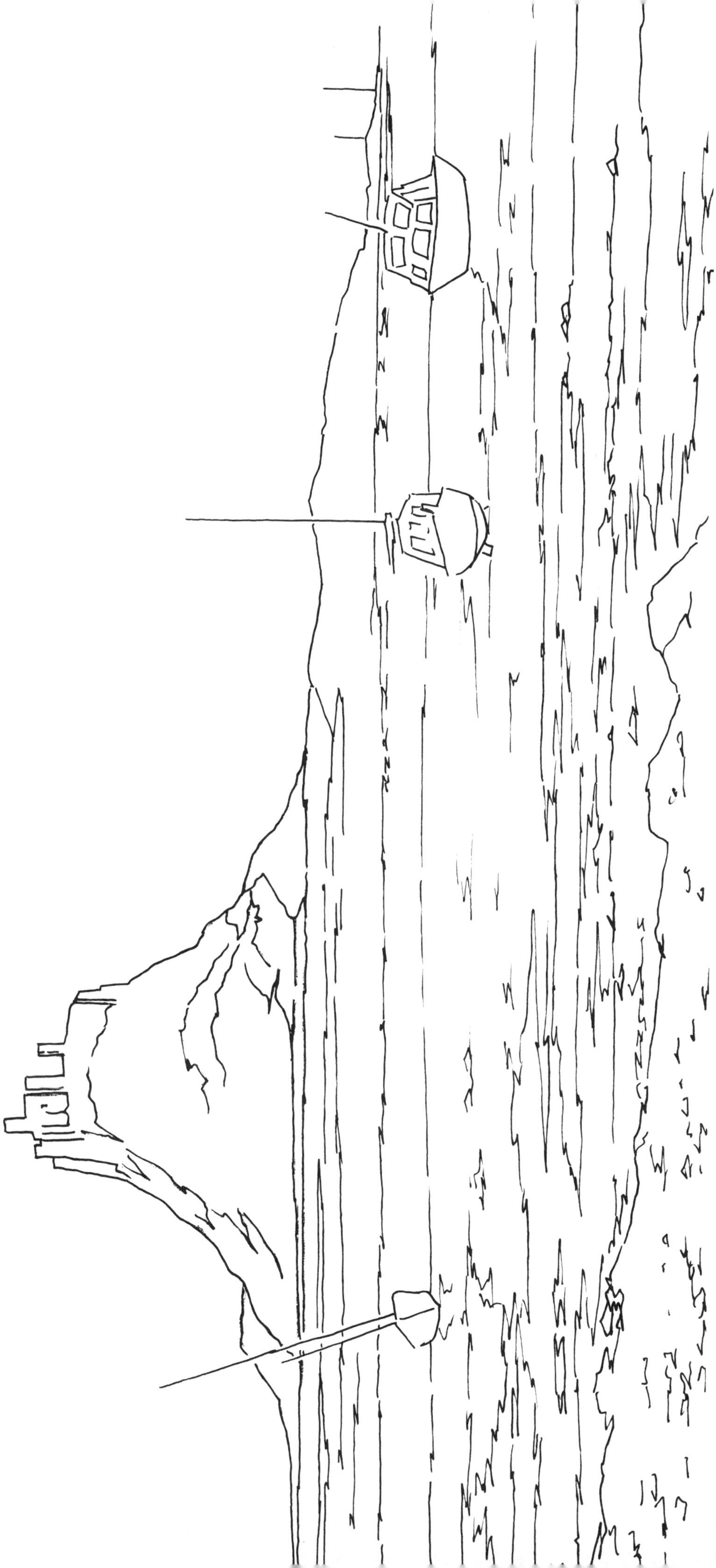

15

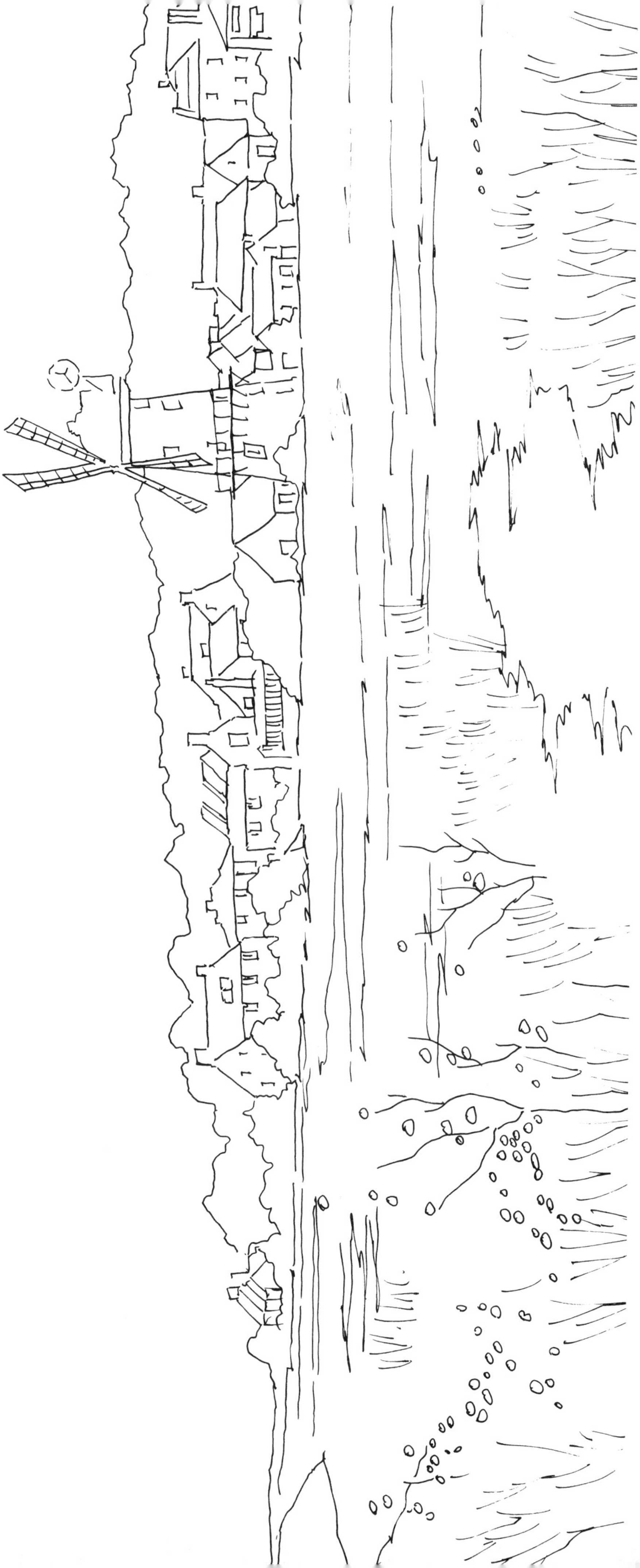

16

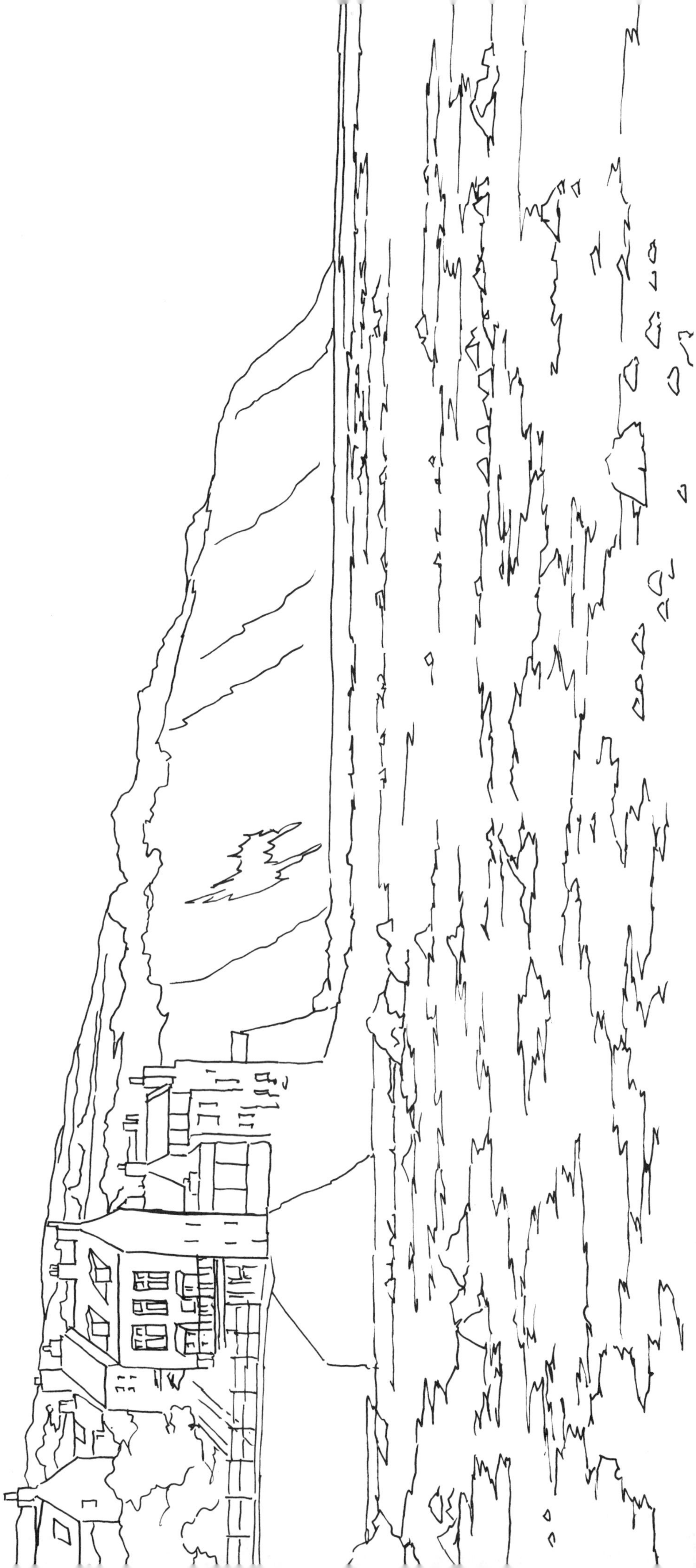

17

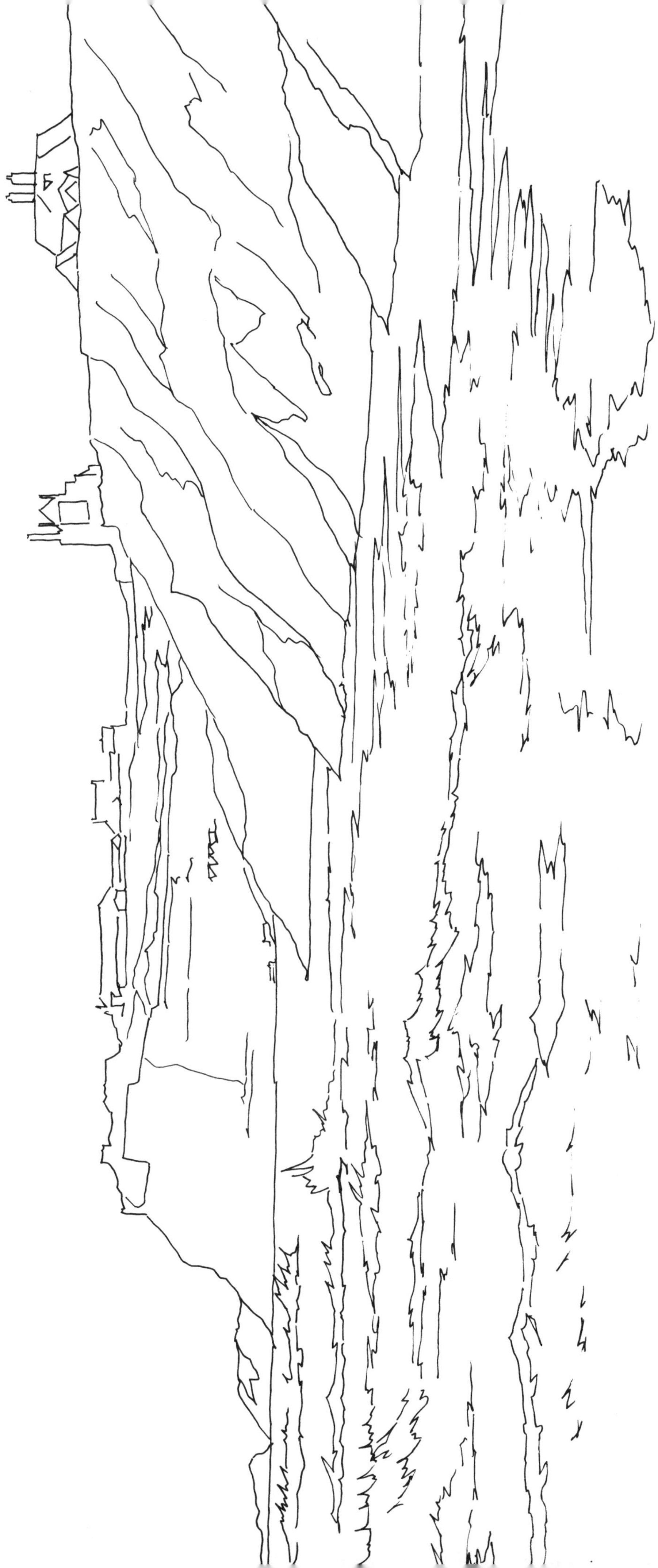

18

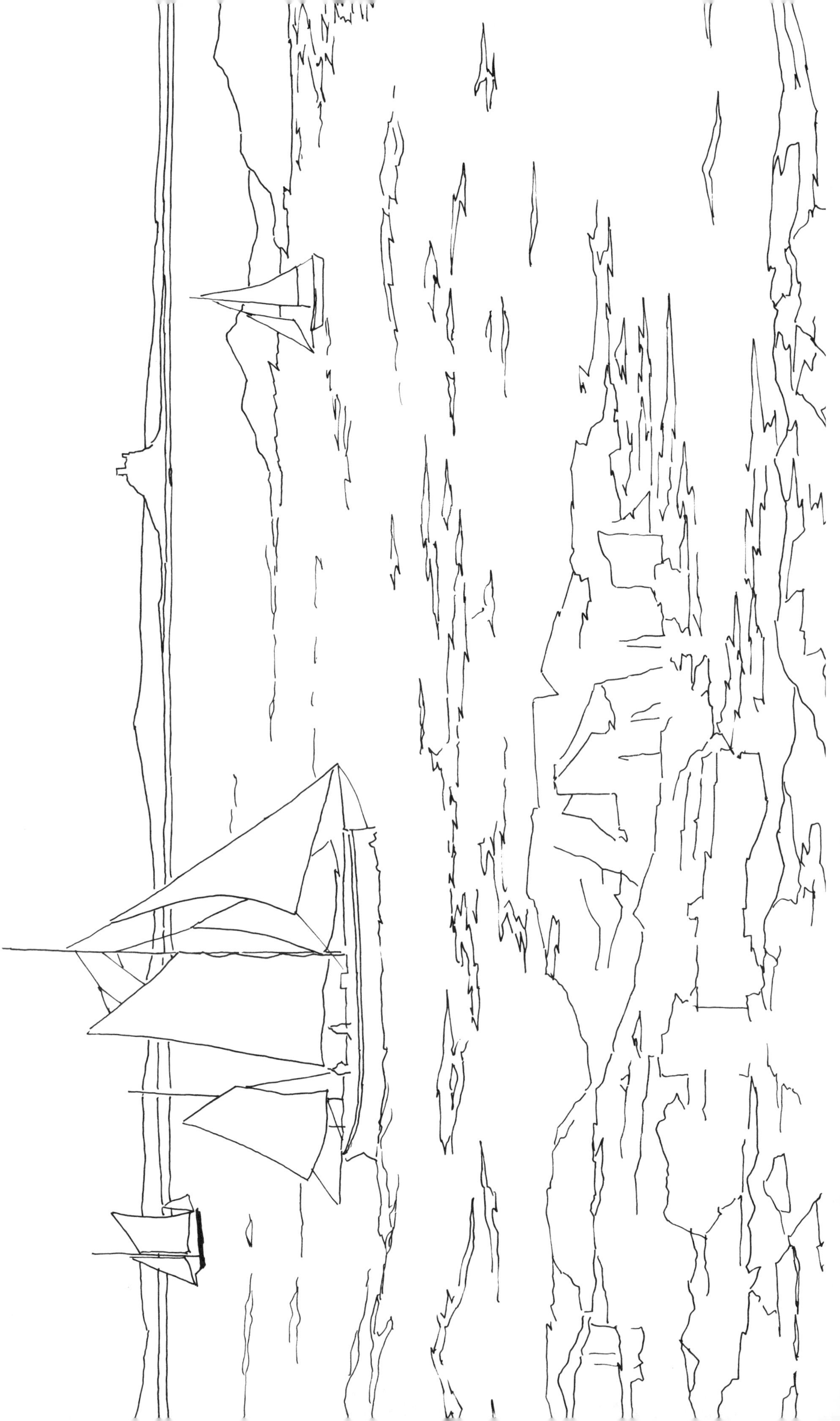

19

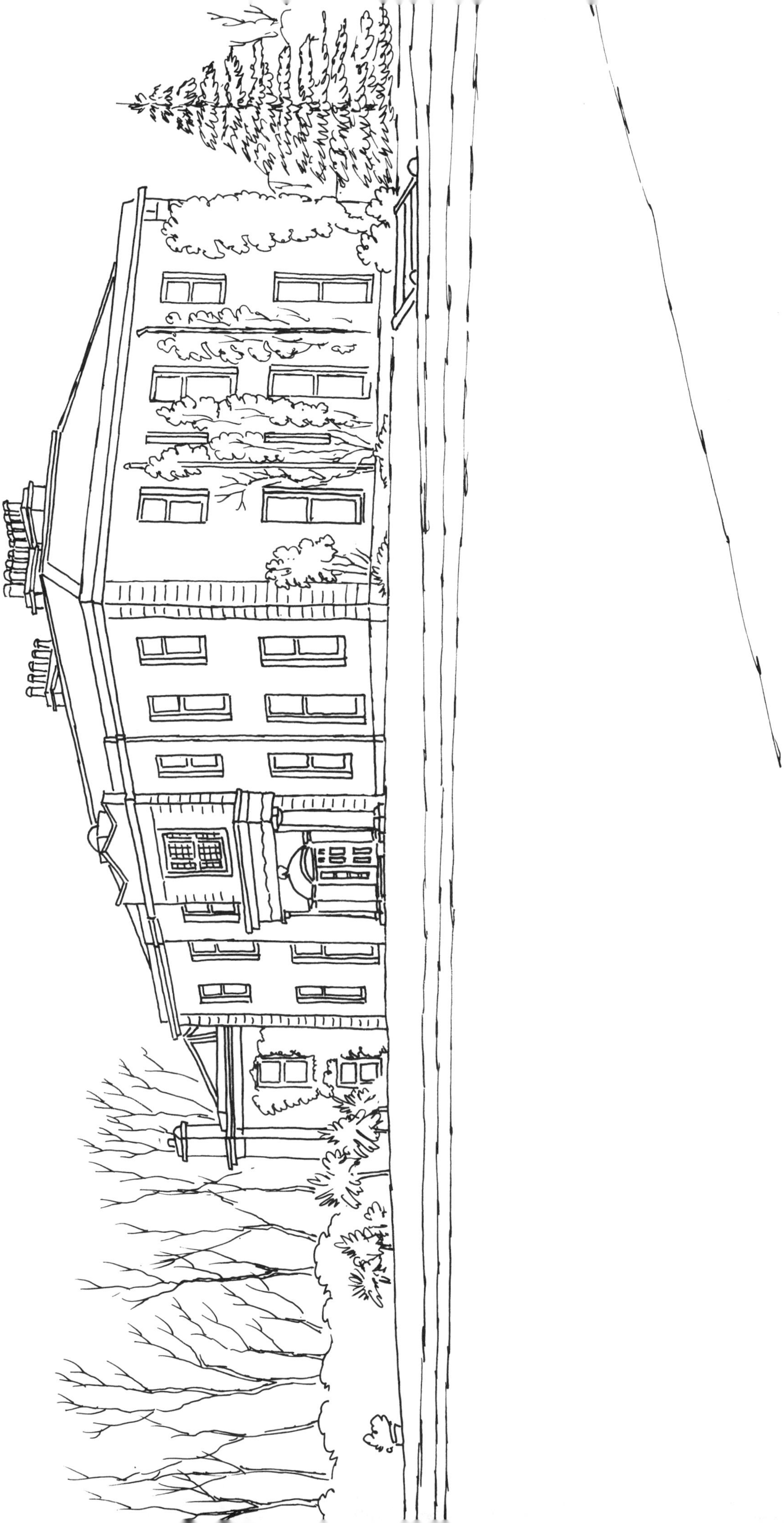

20

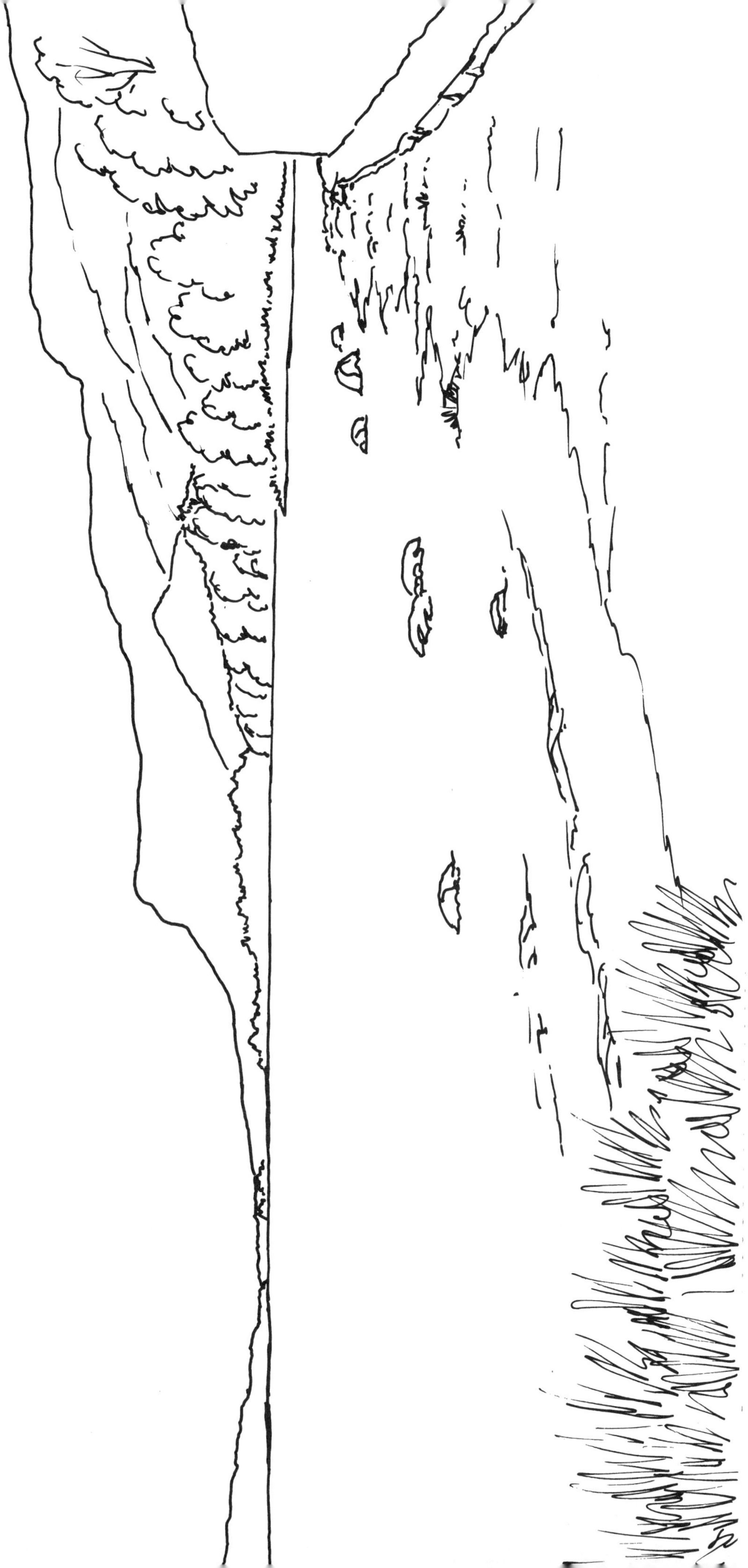

21

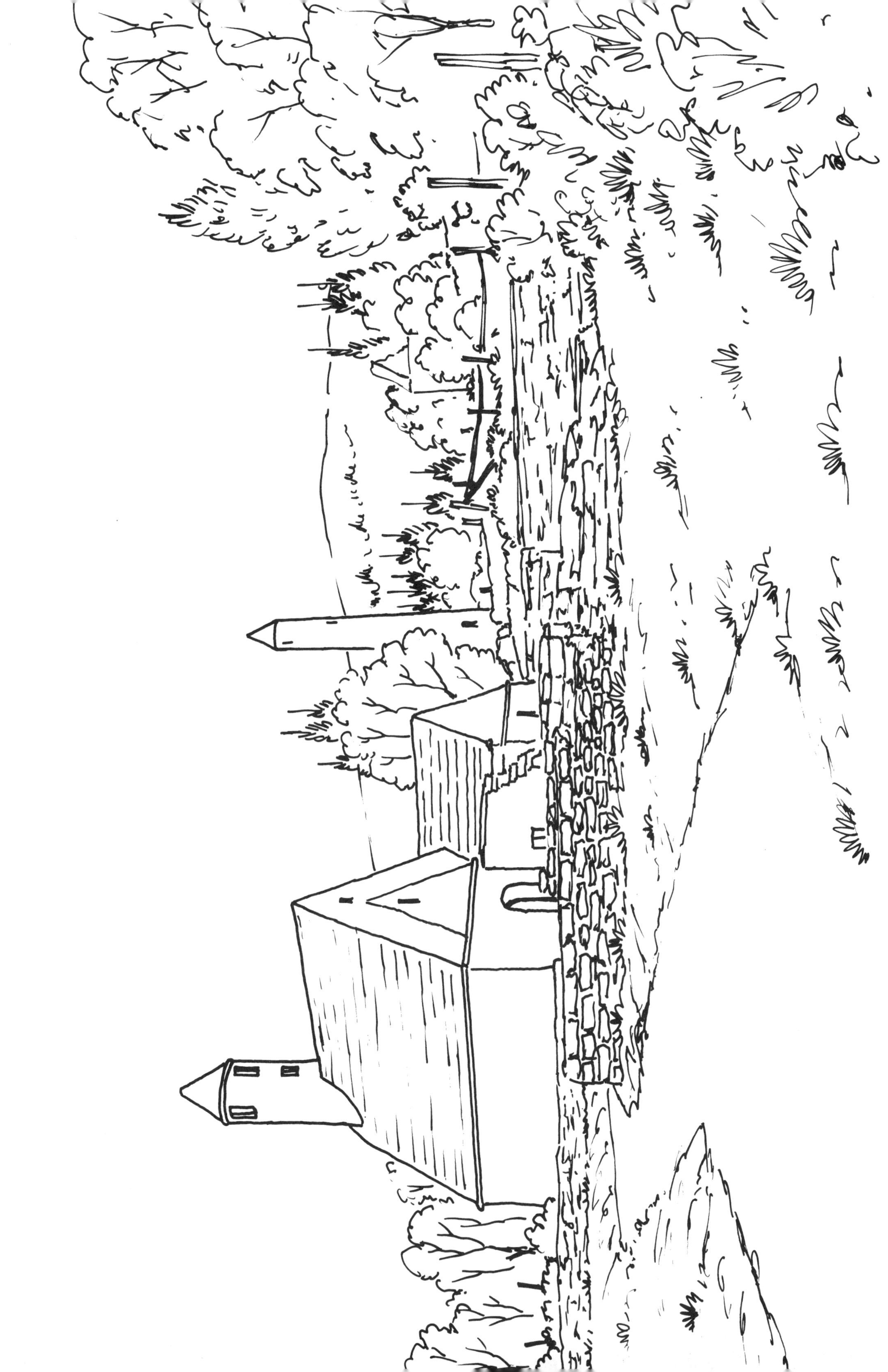

22

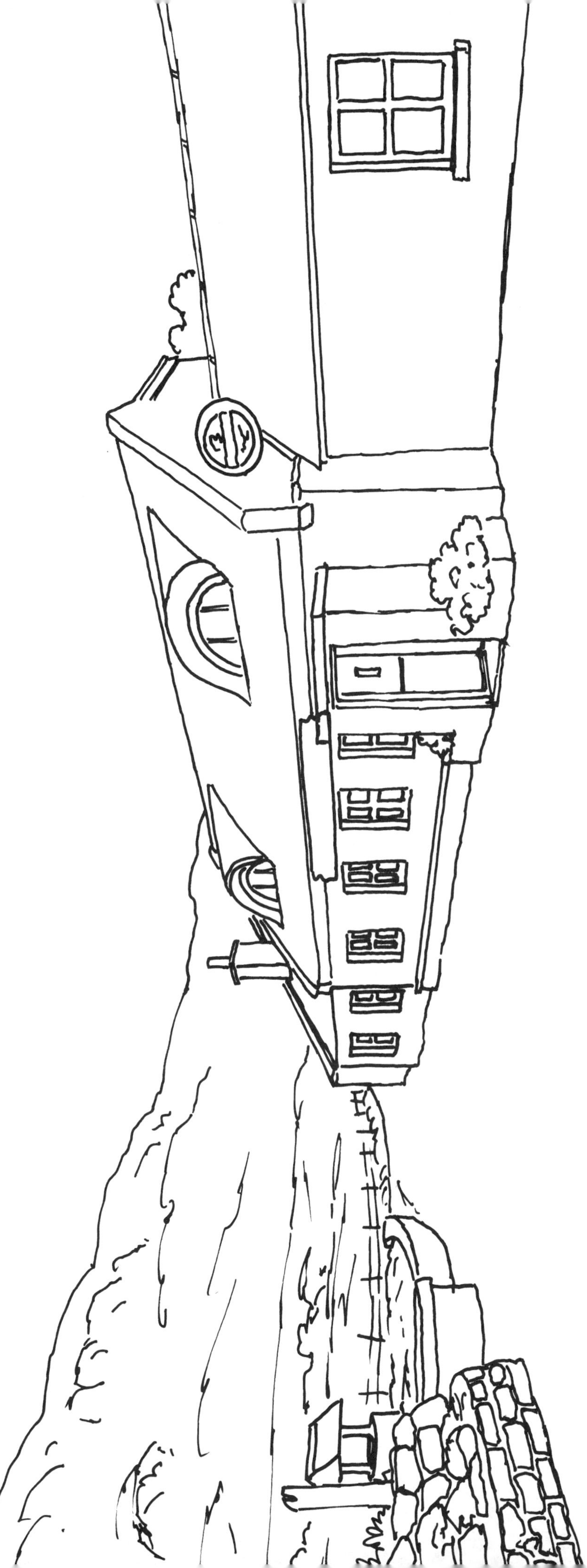

23

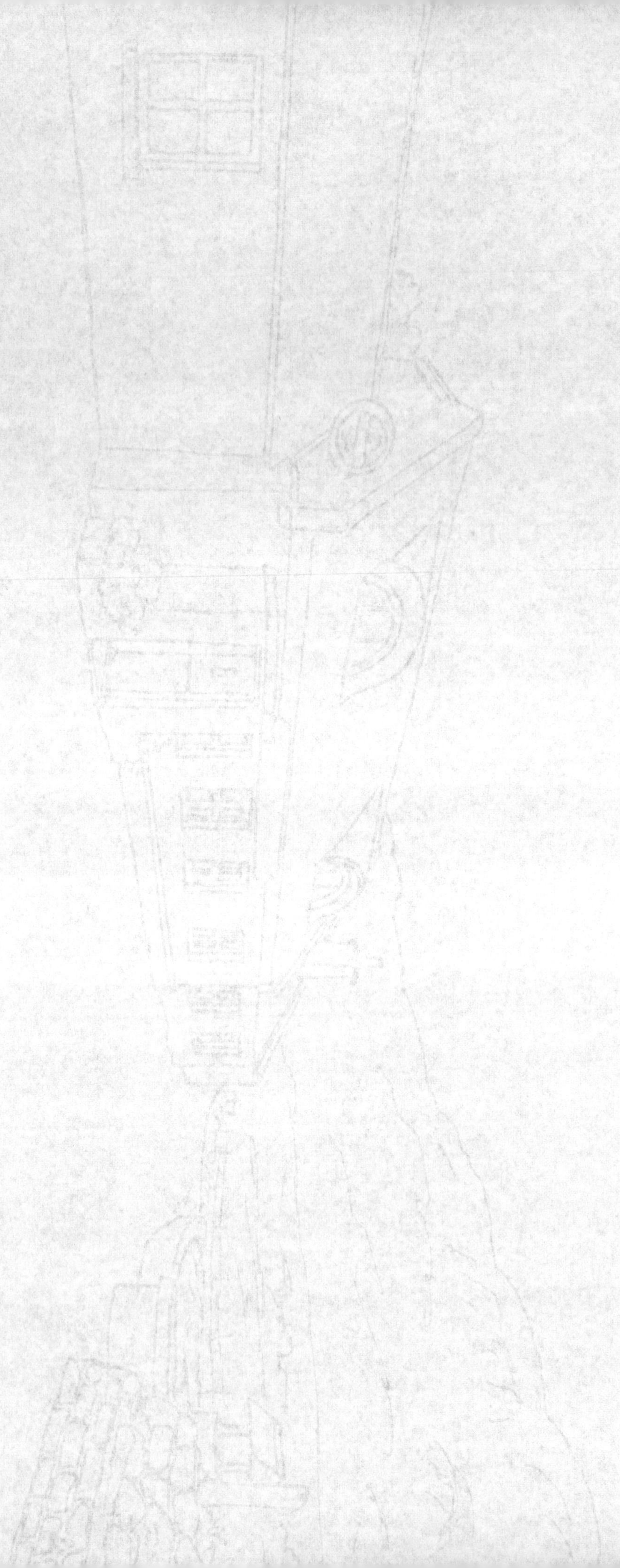

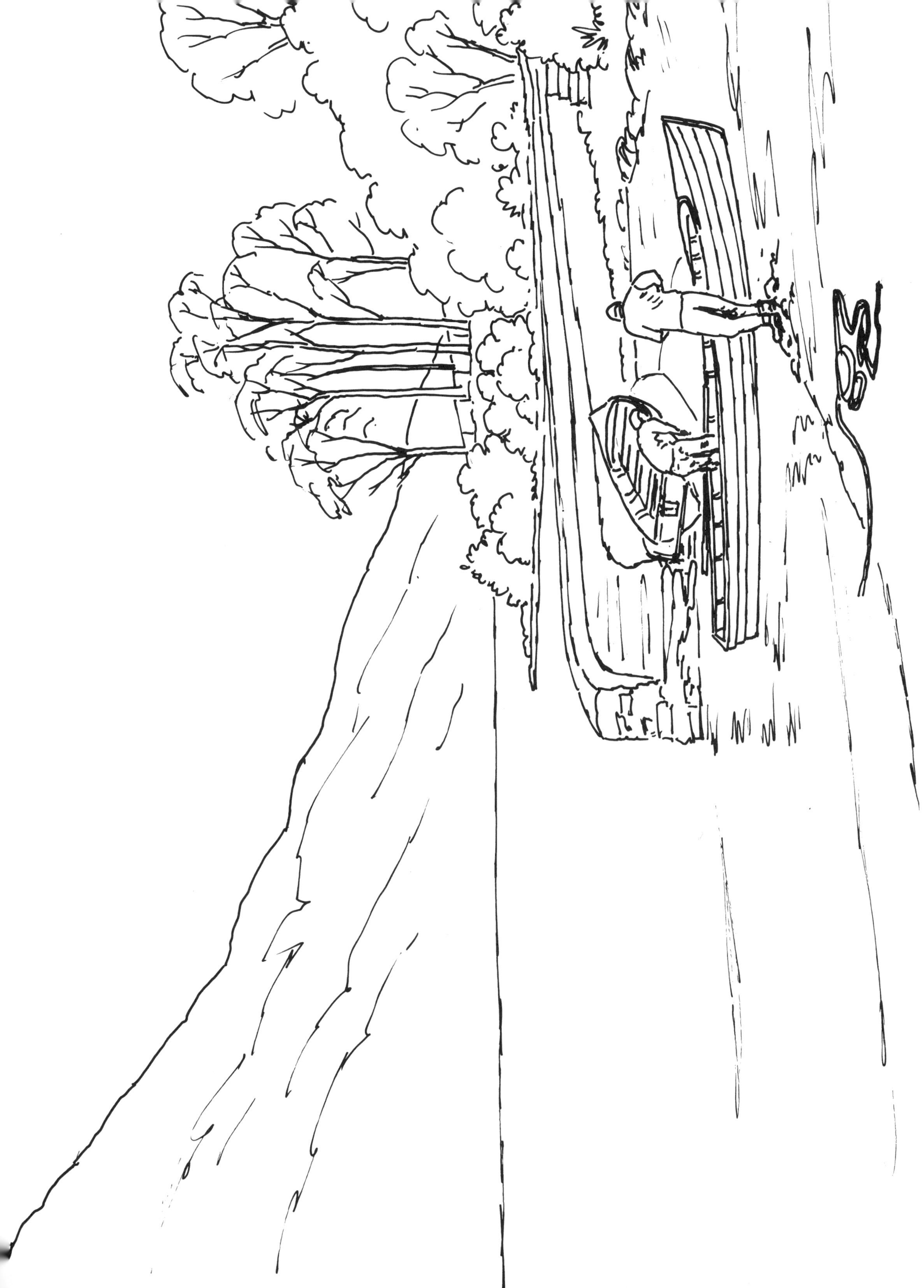

24

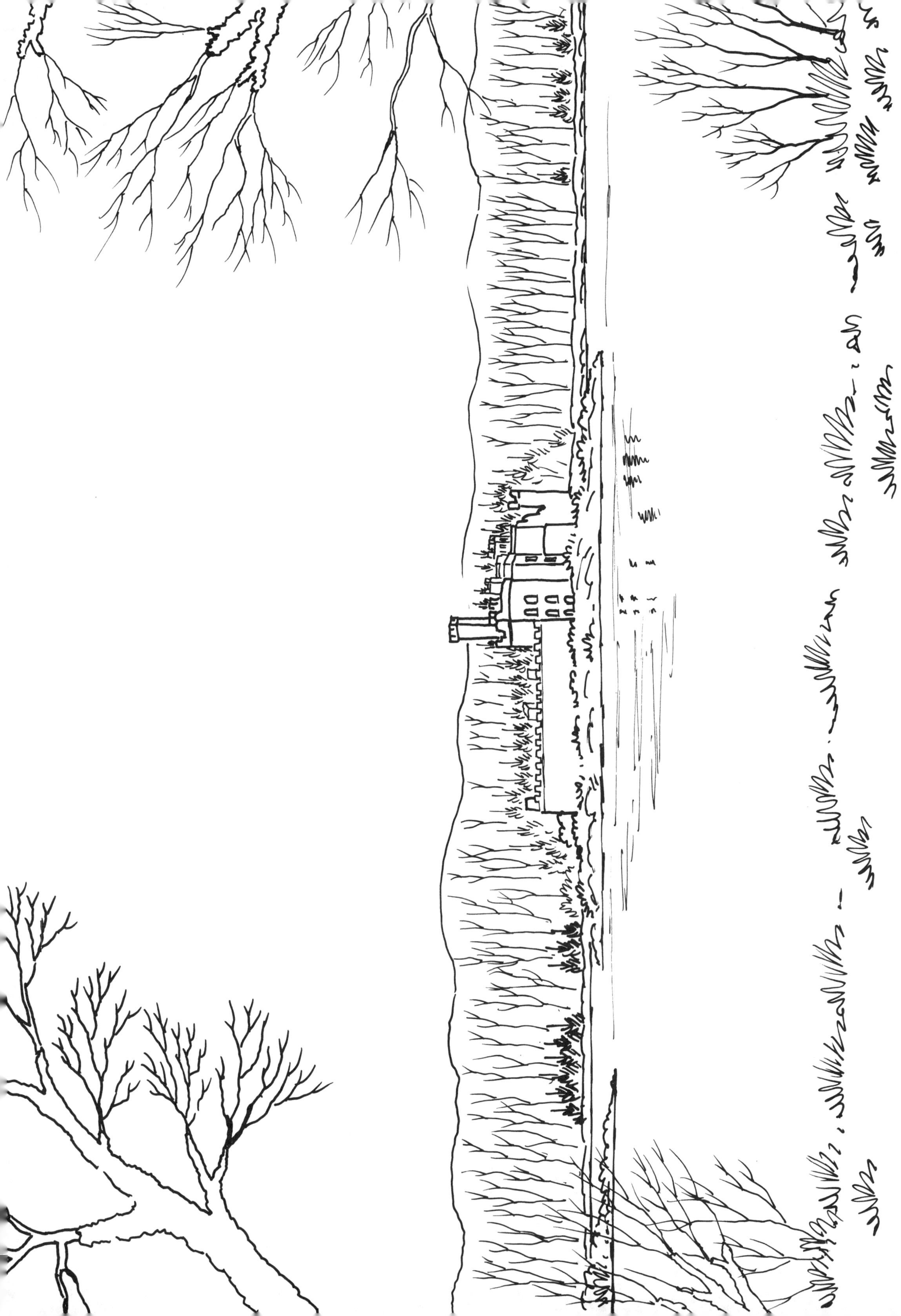

25

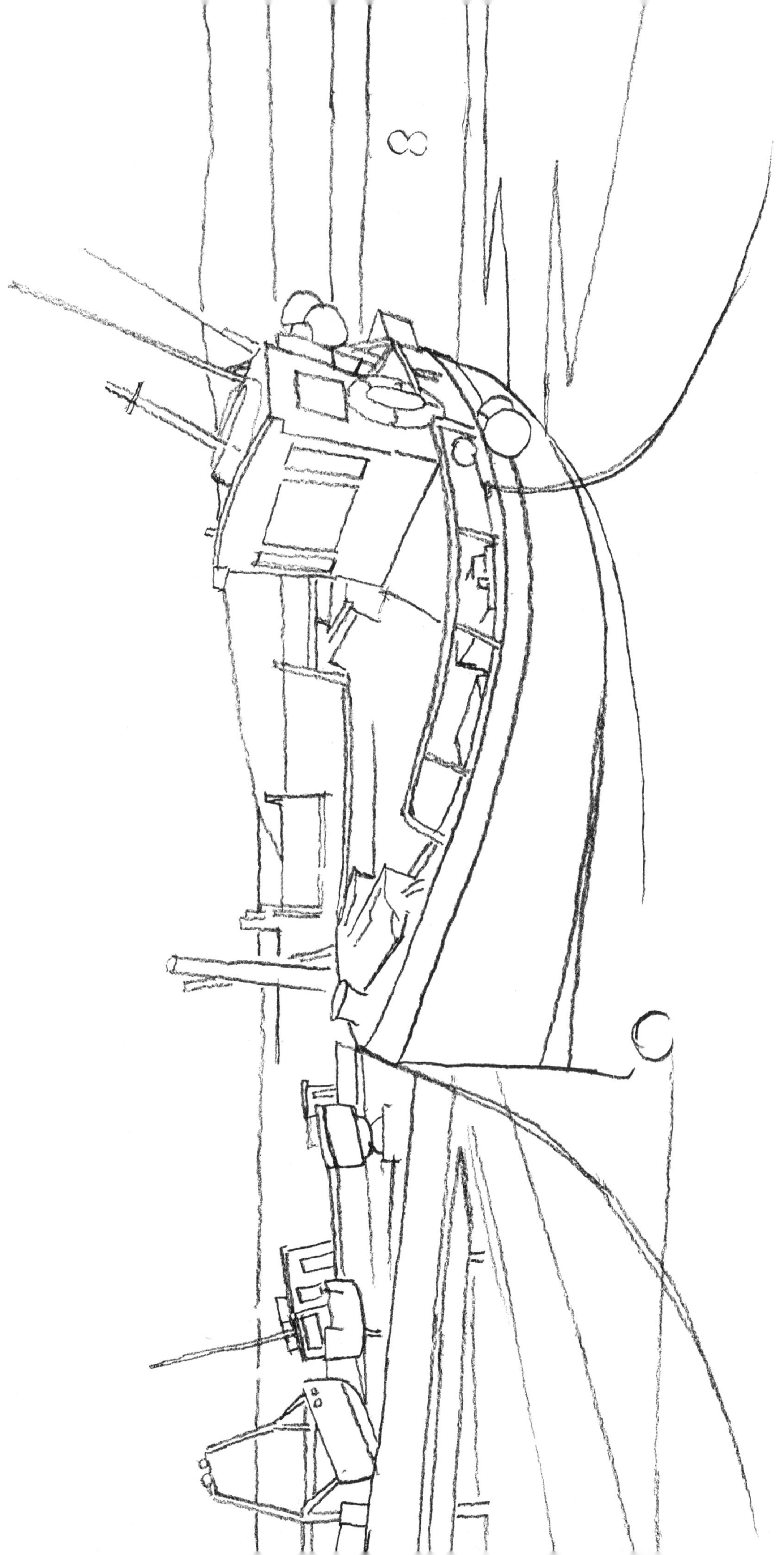

26

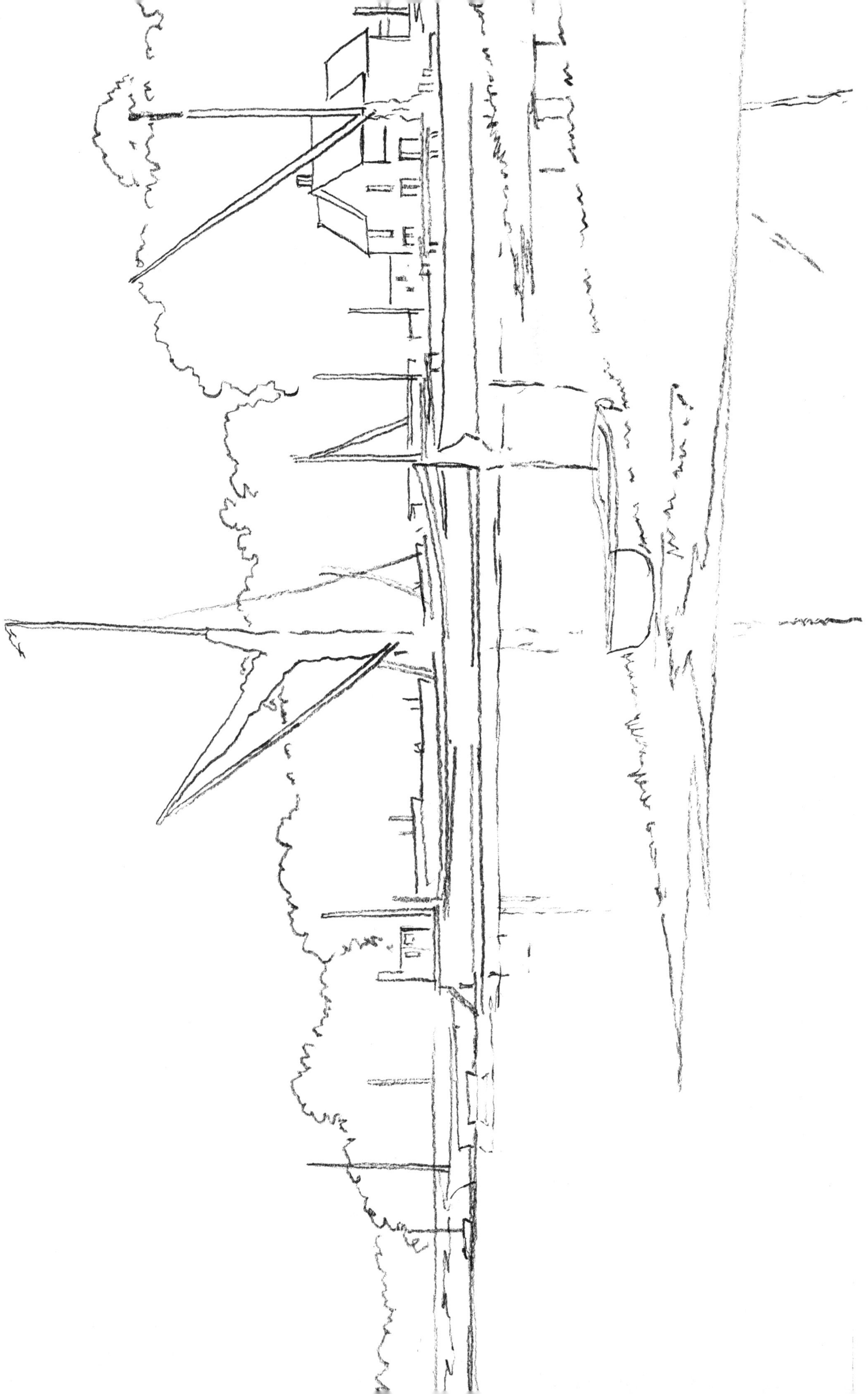

27

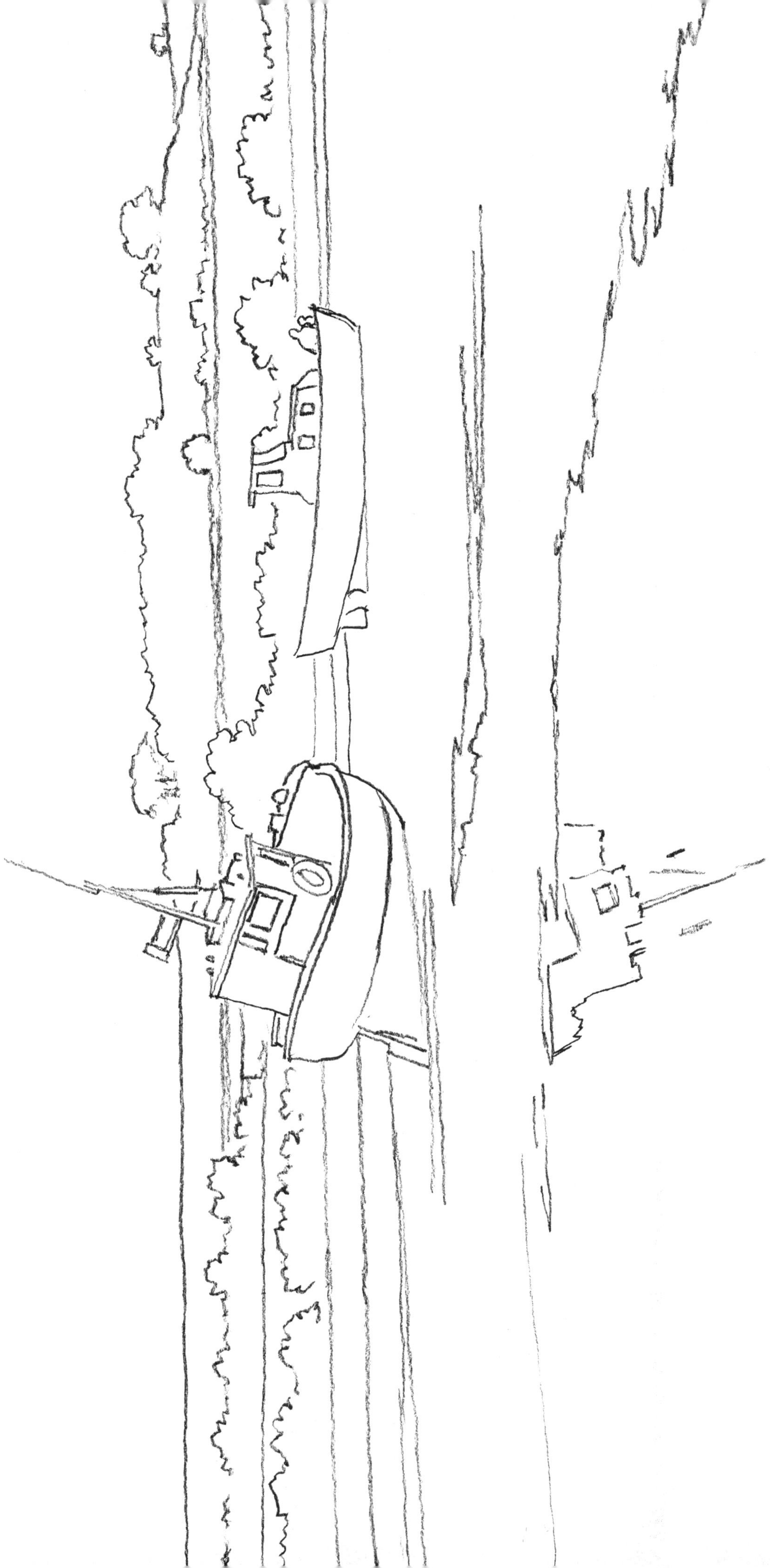

28

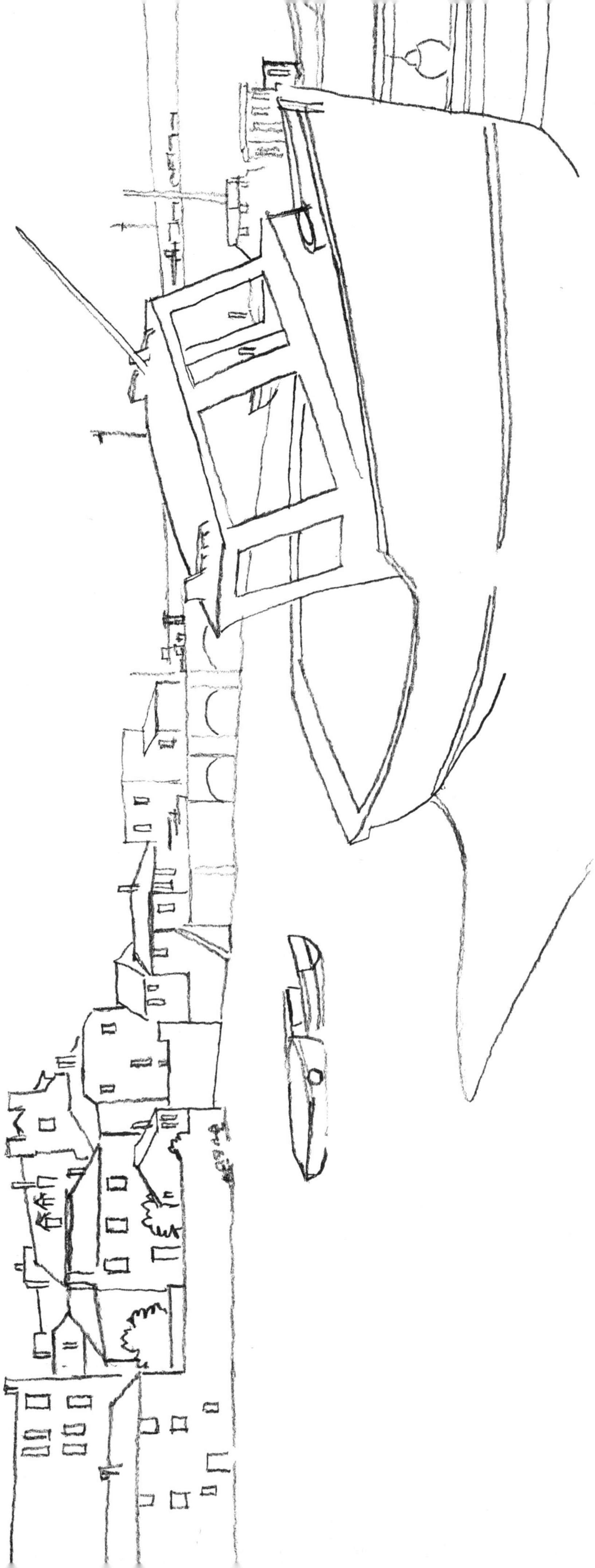

29

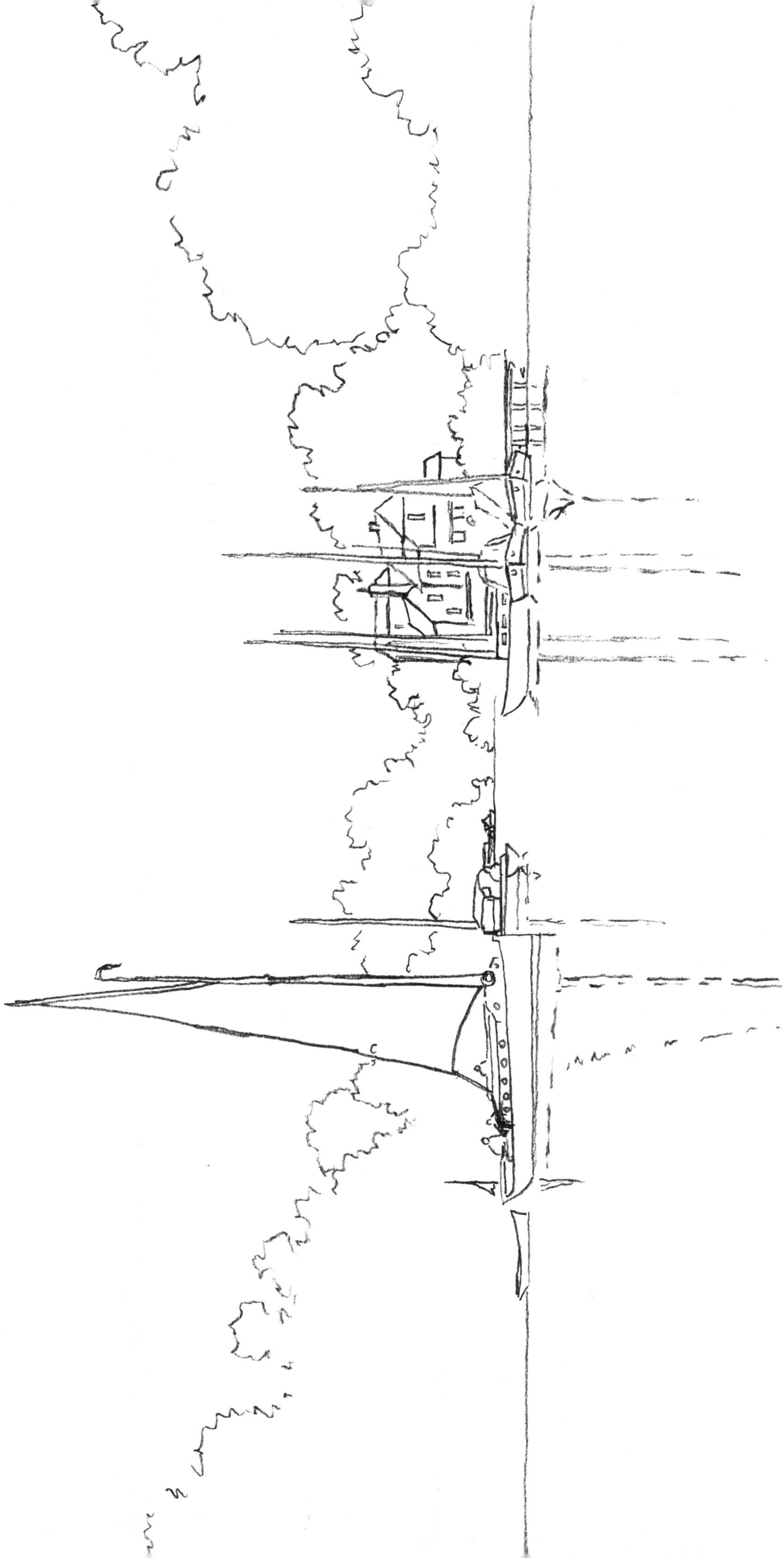

30

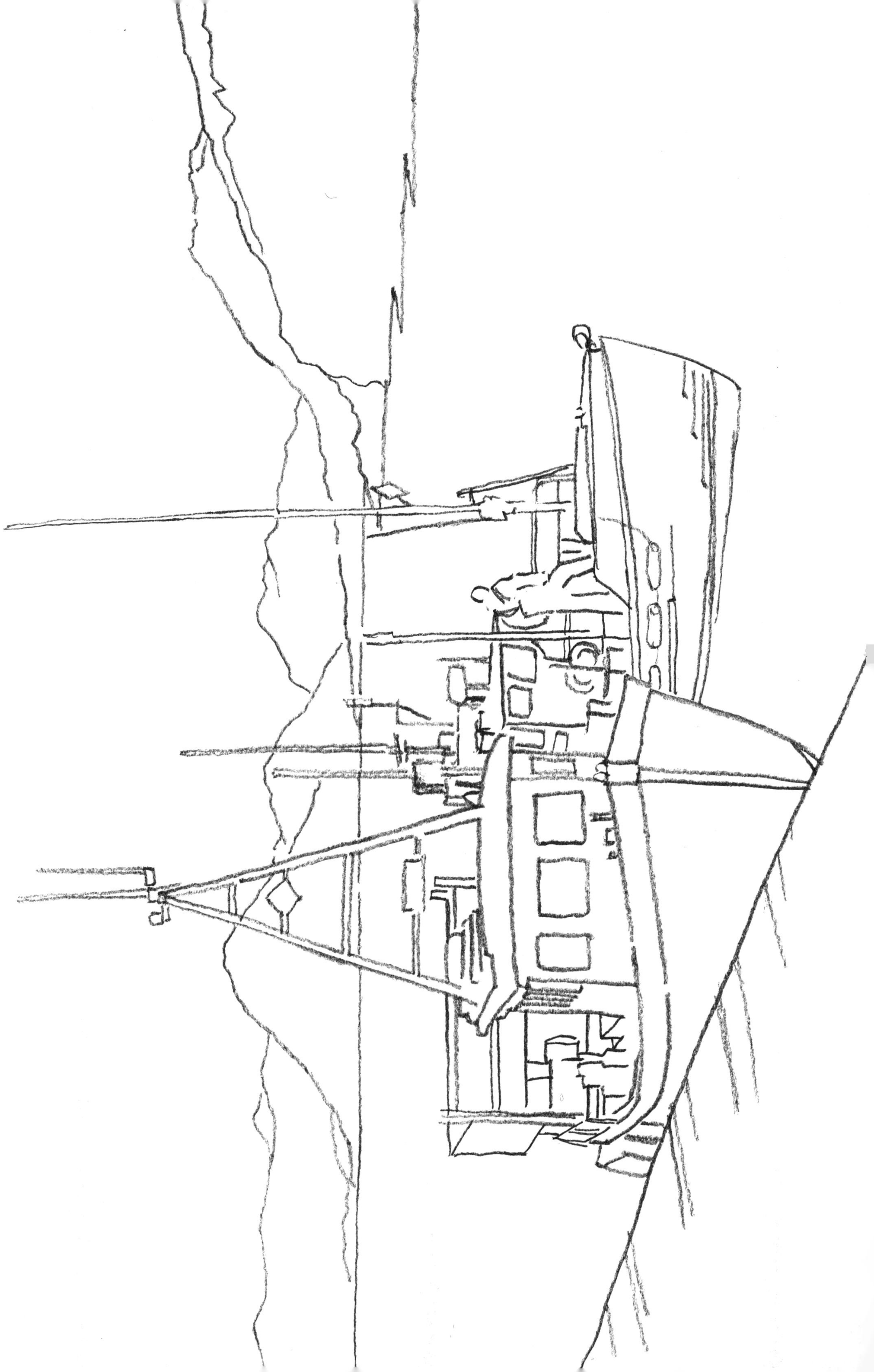

31

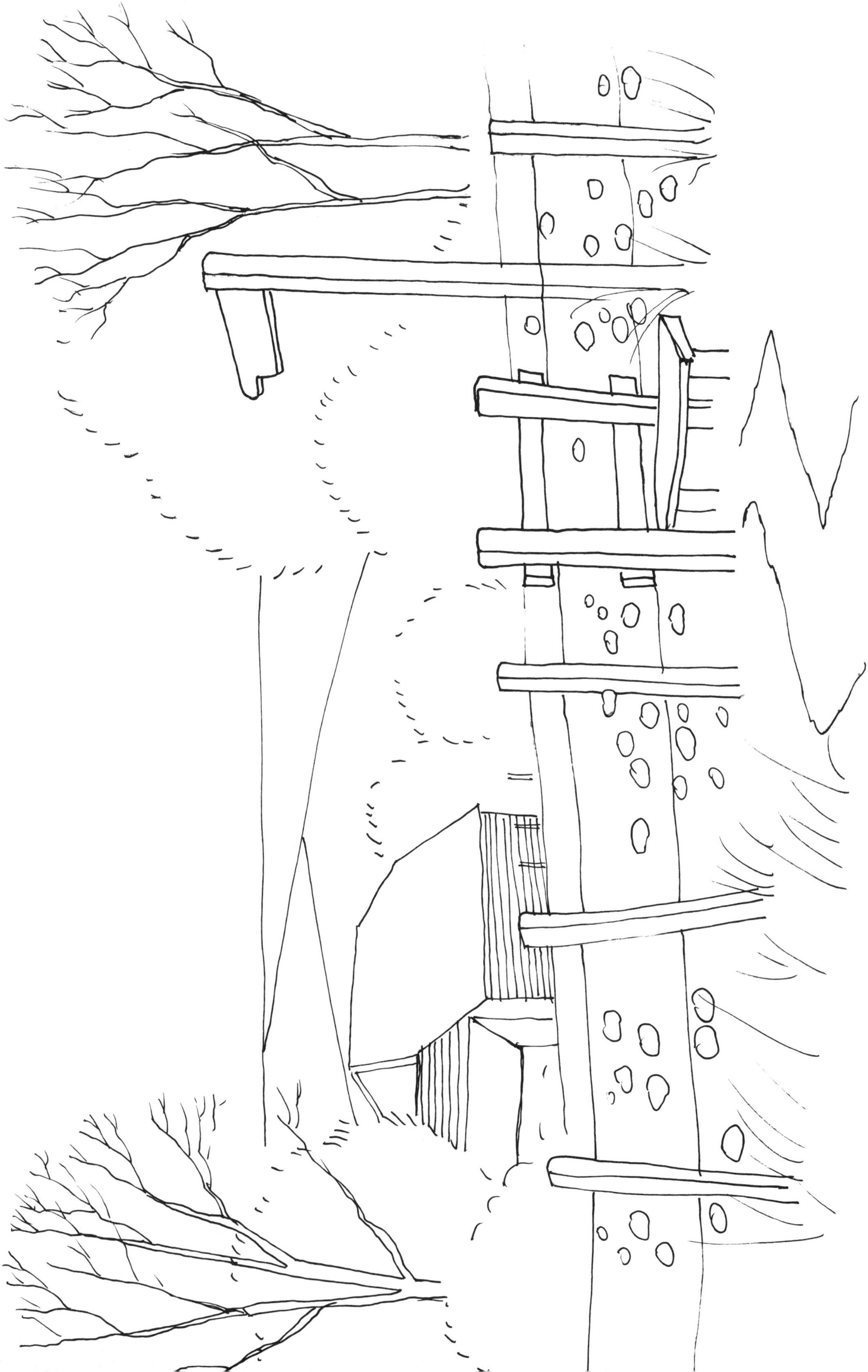

32

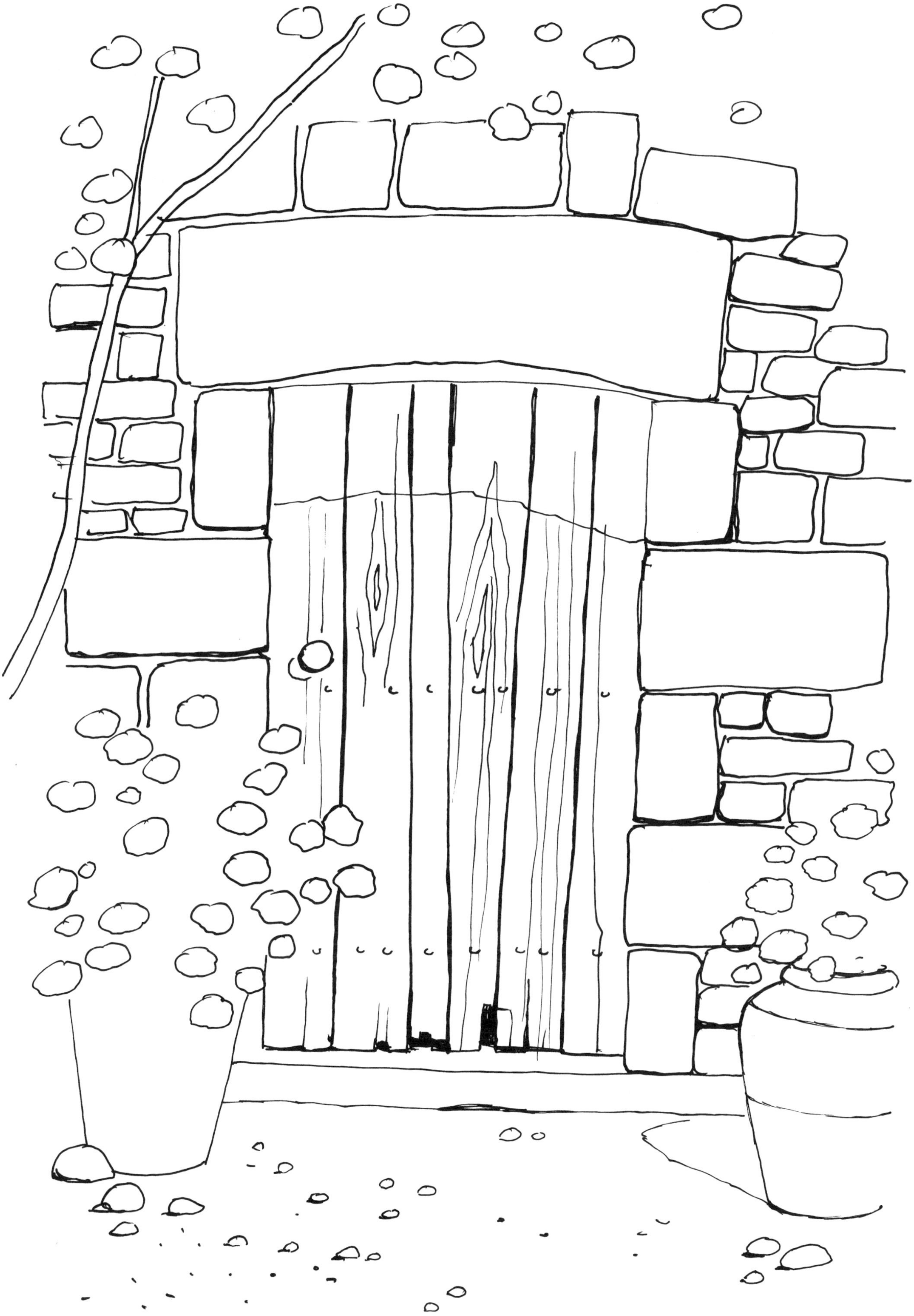

33

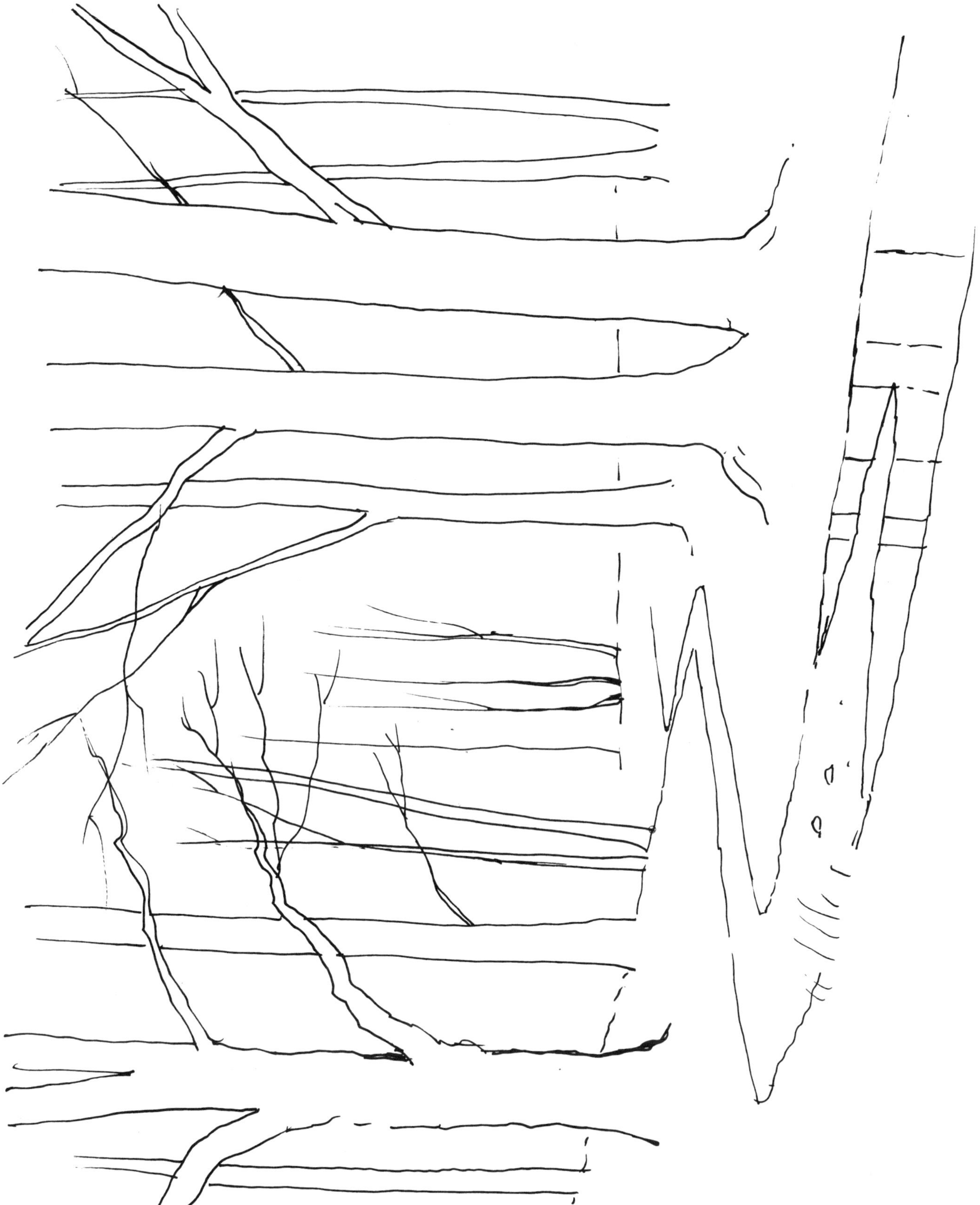

34

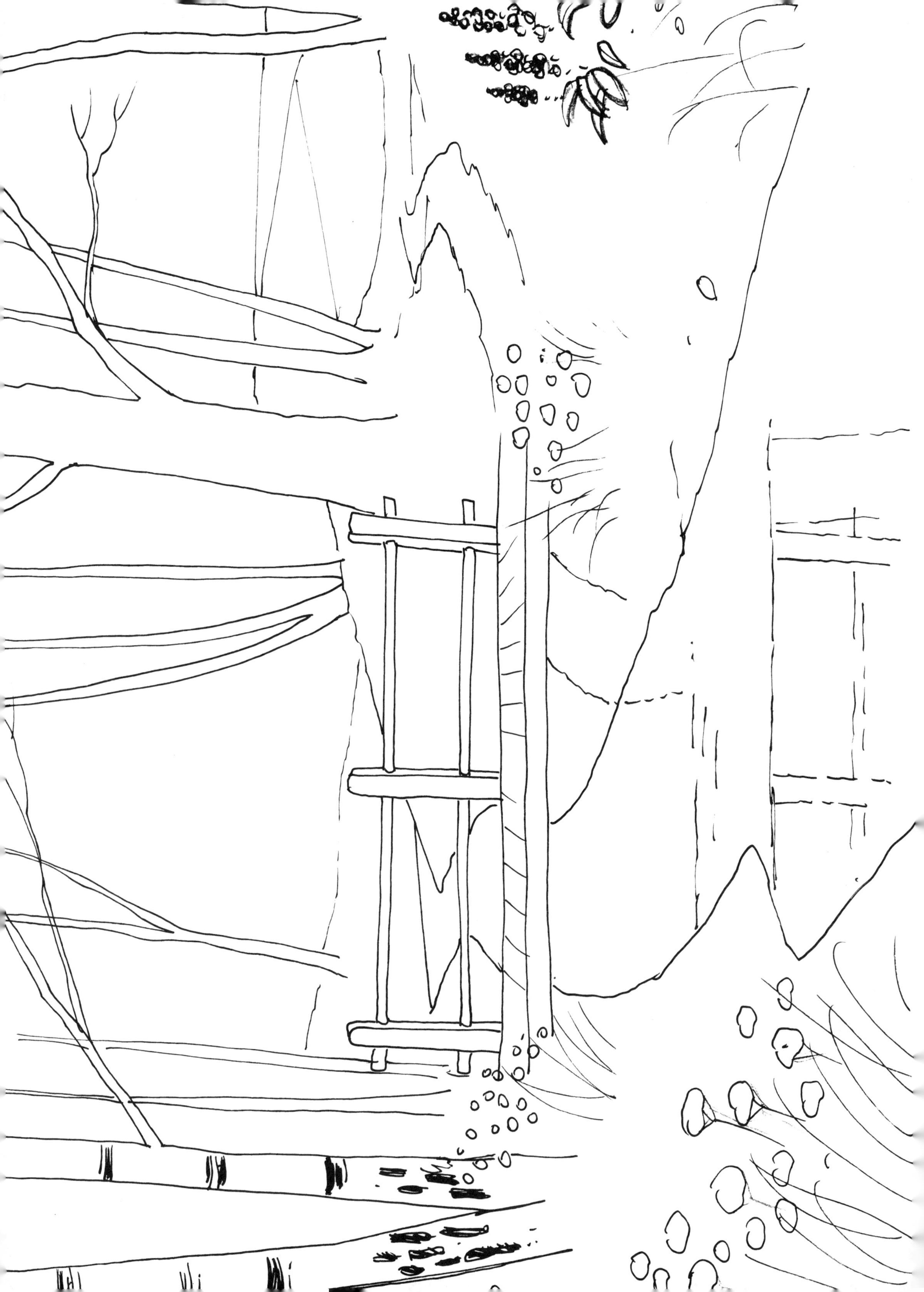

35

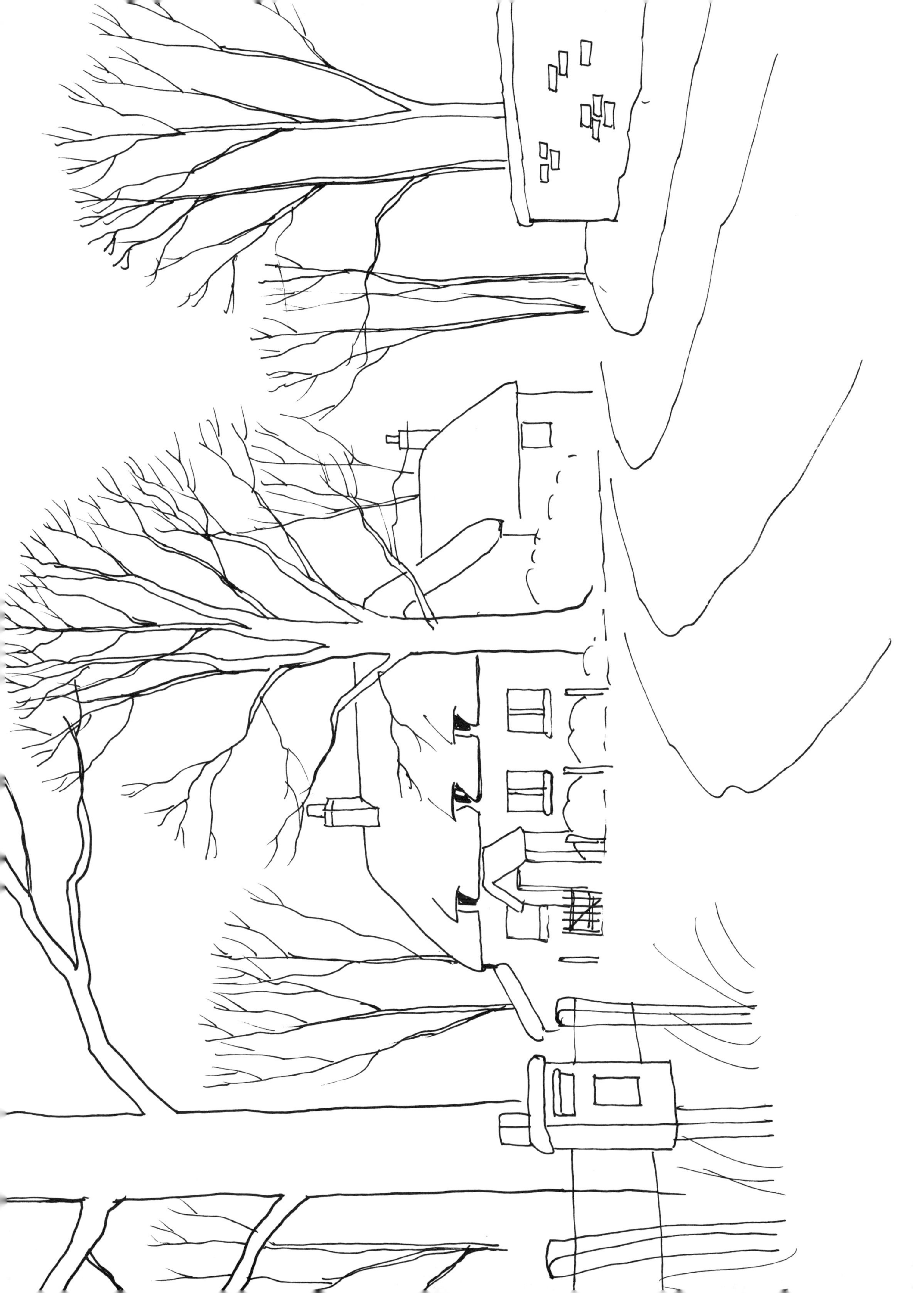

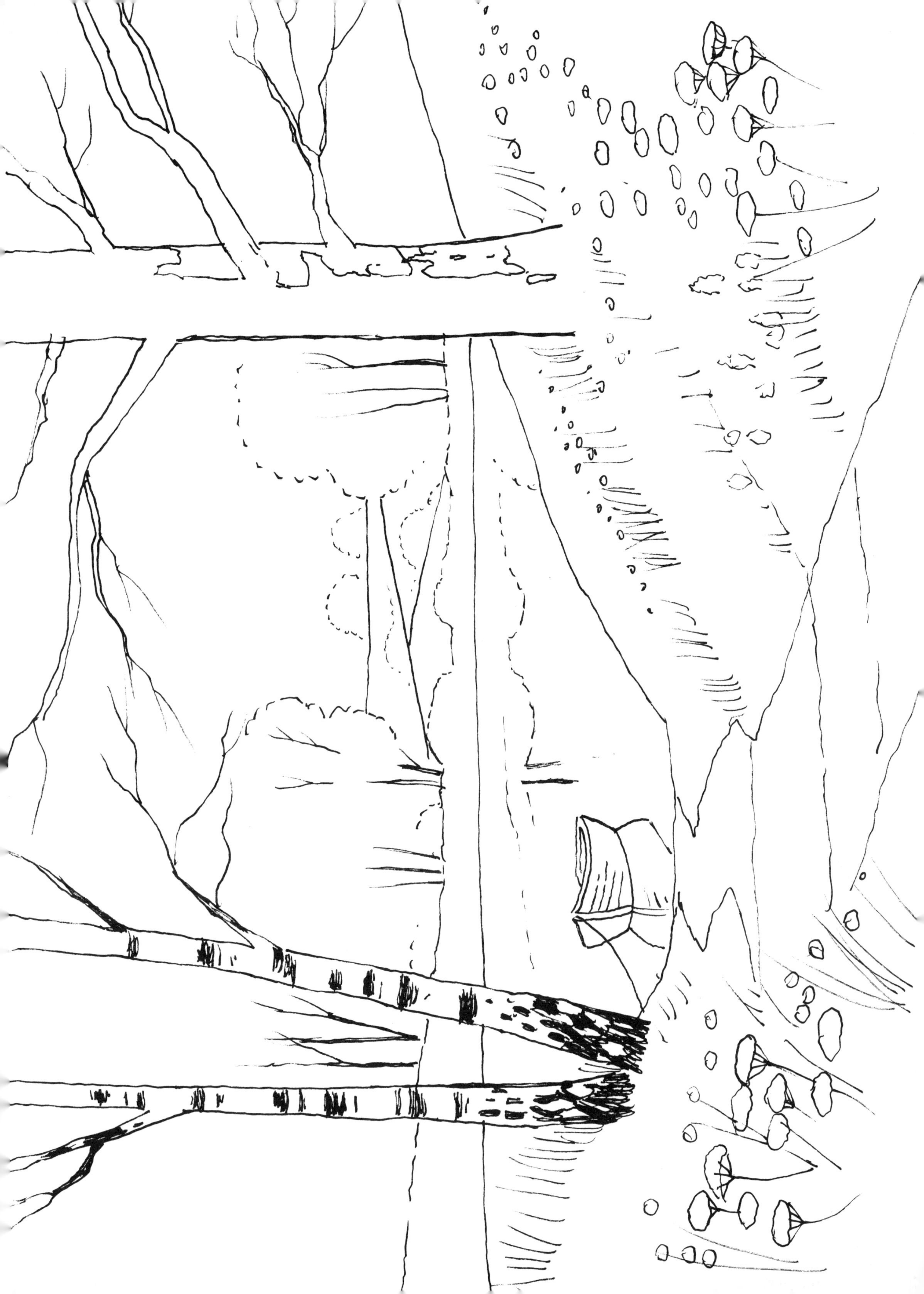

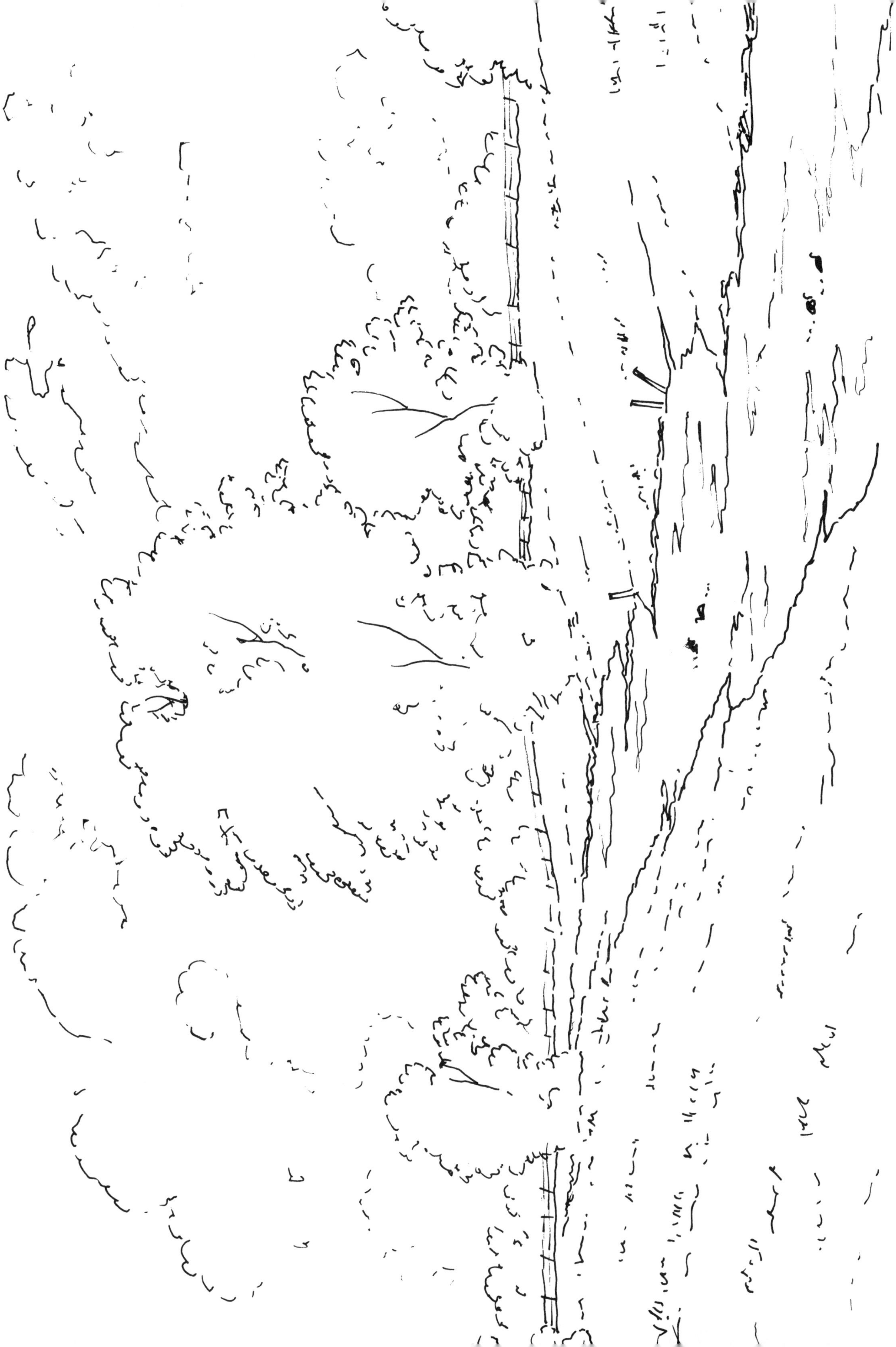

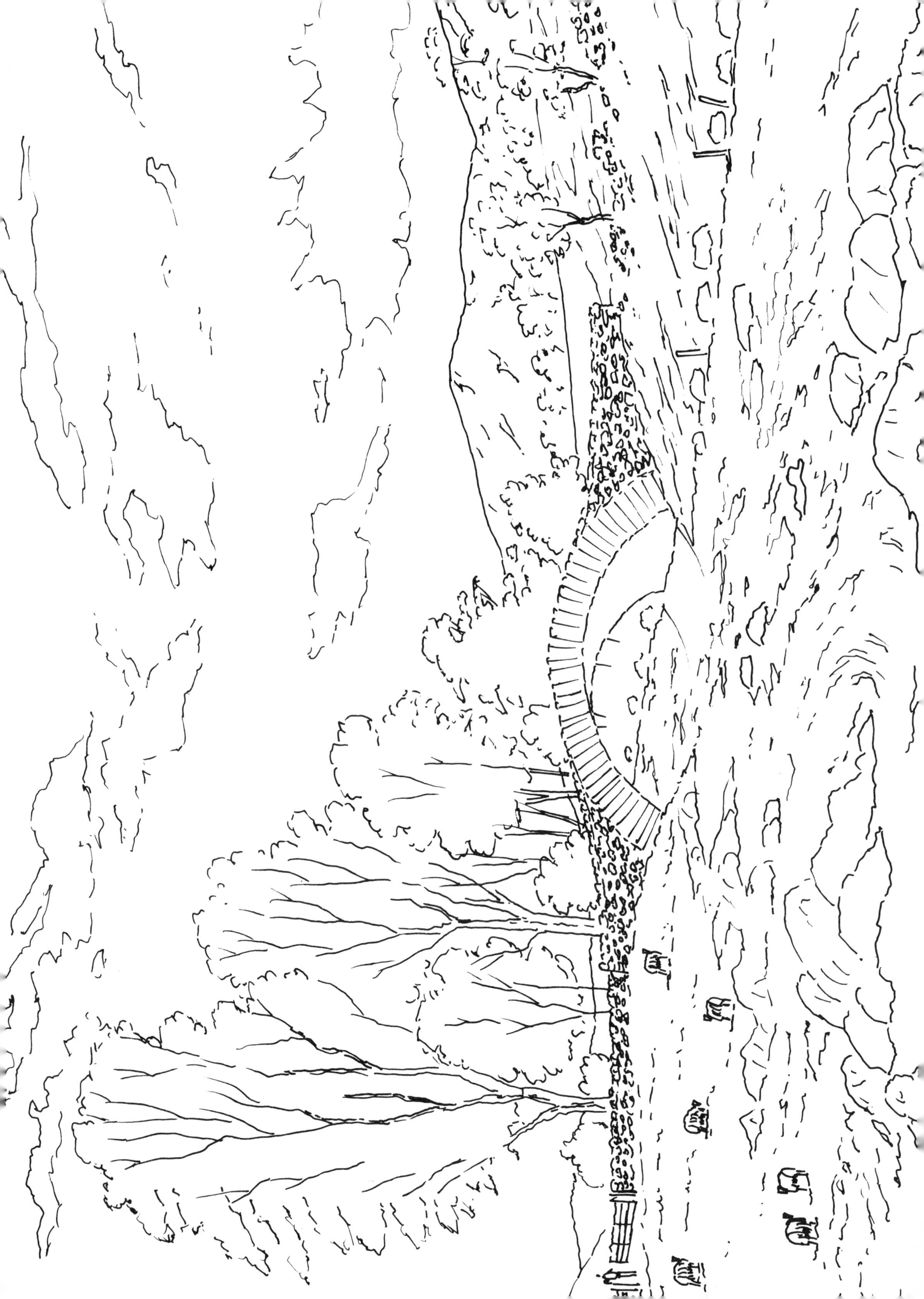

39

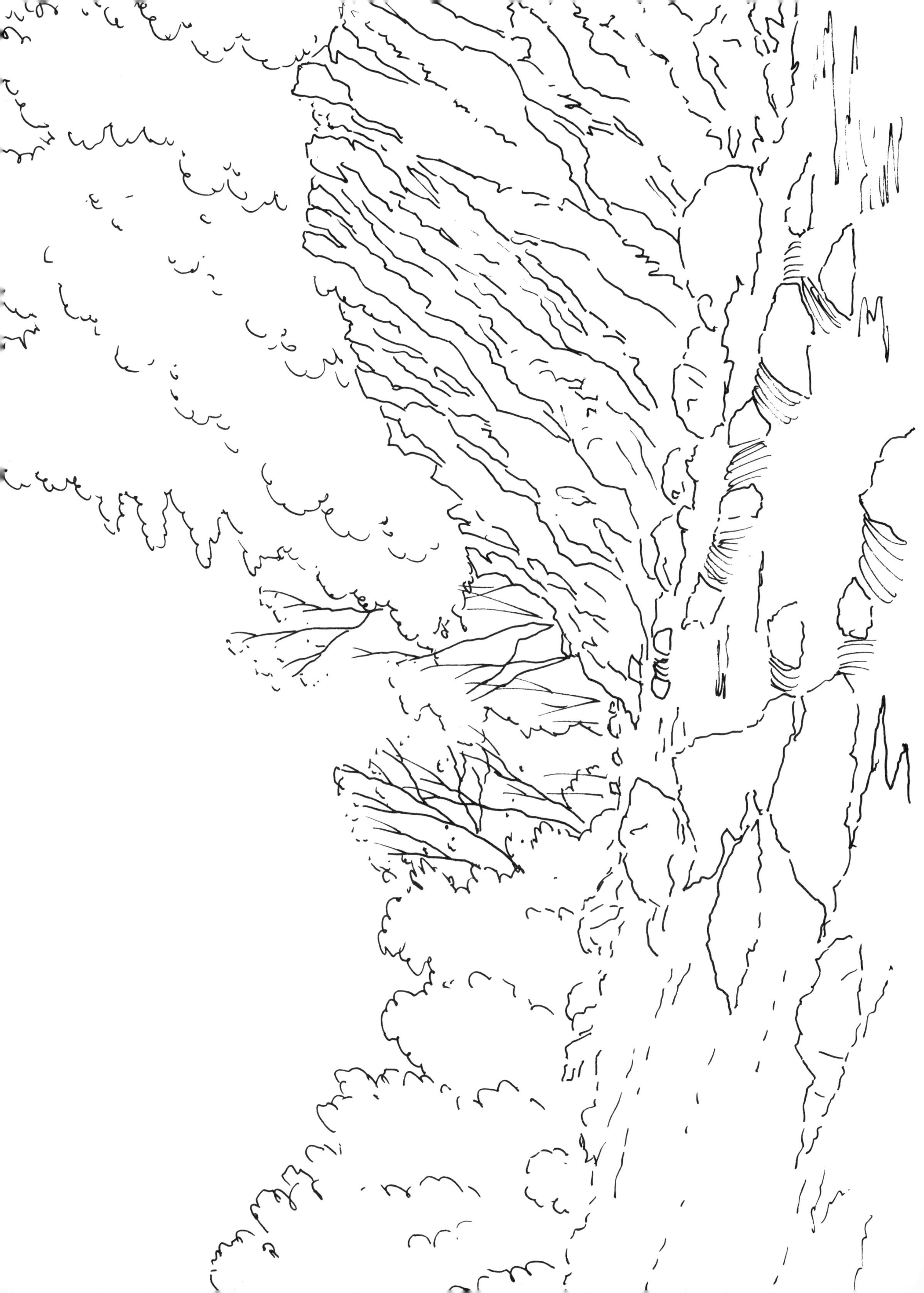

40

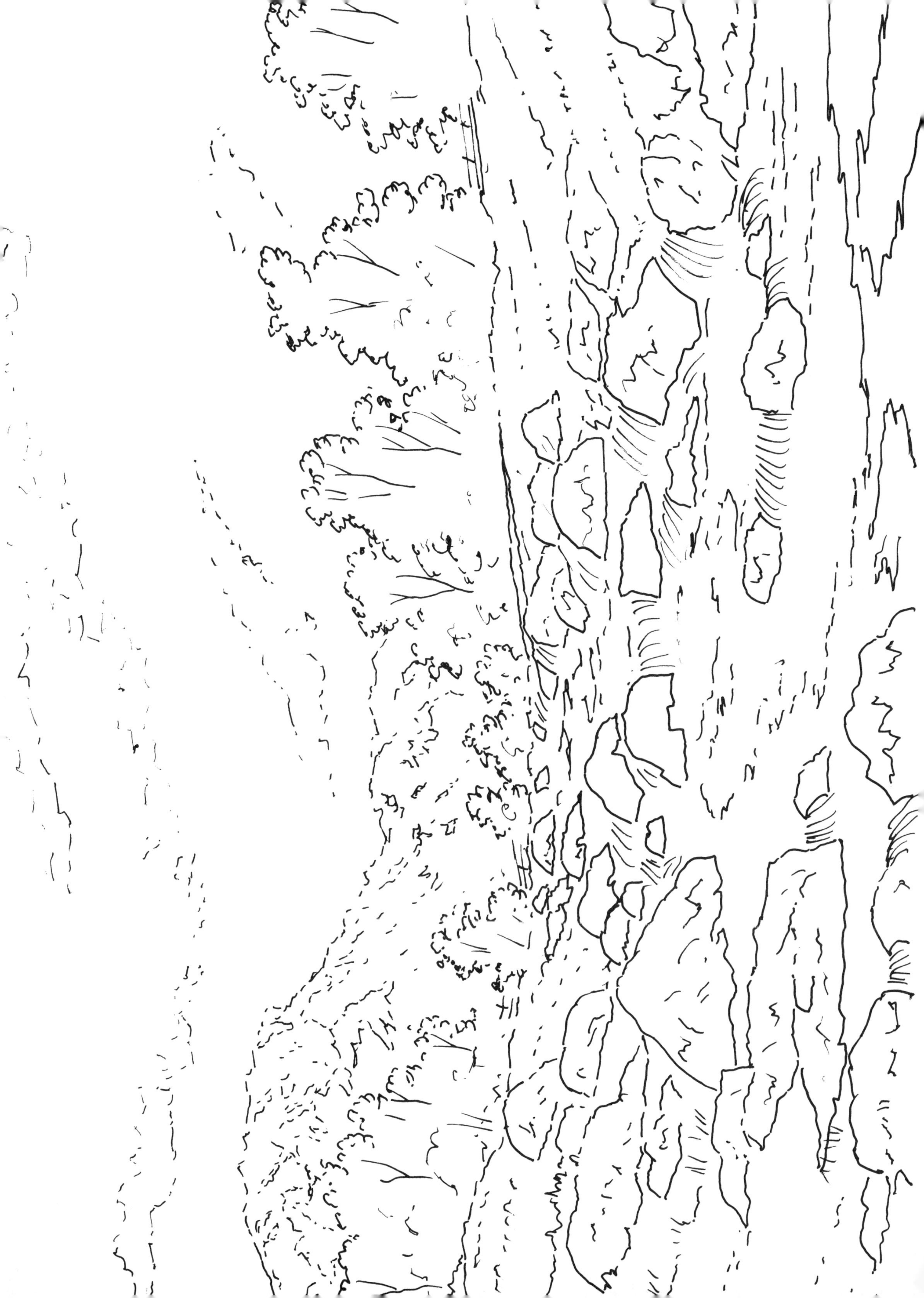

41

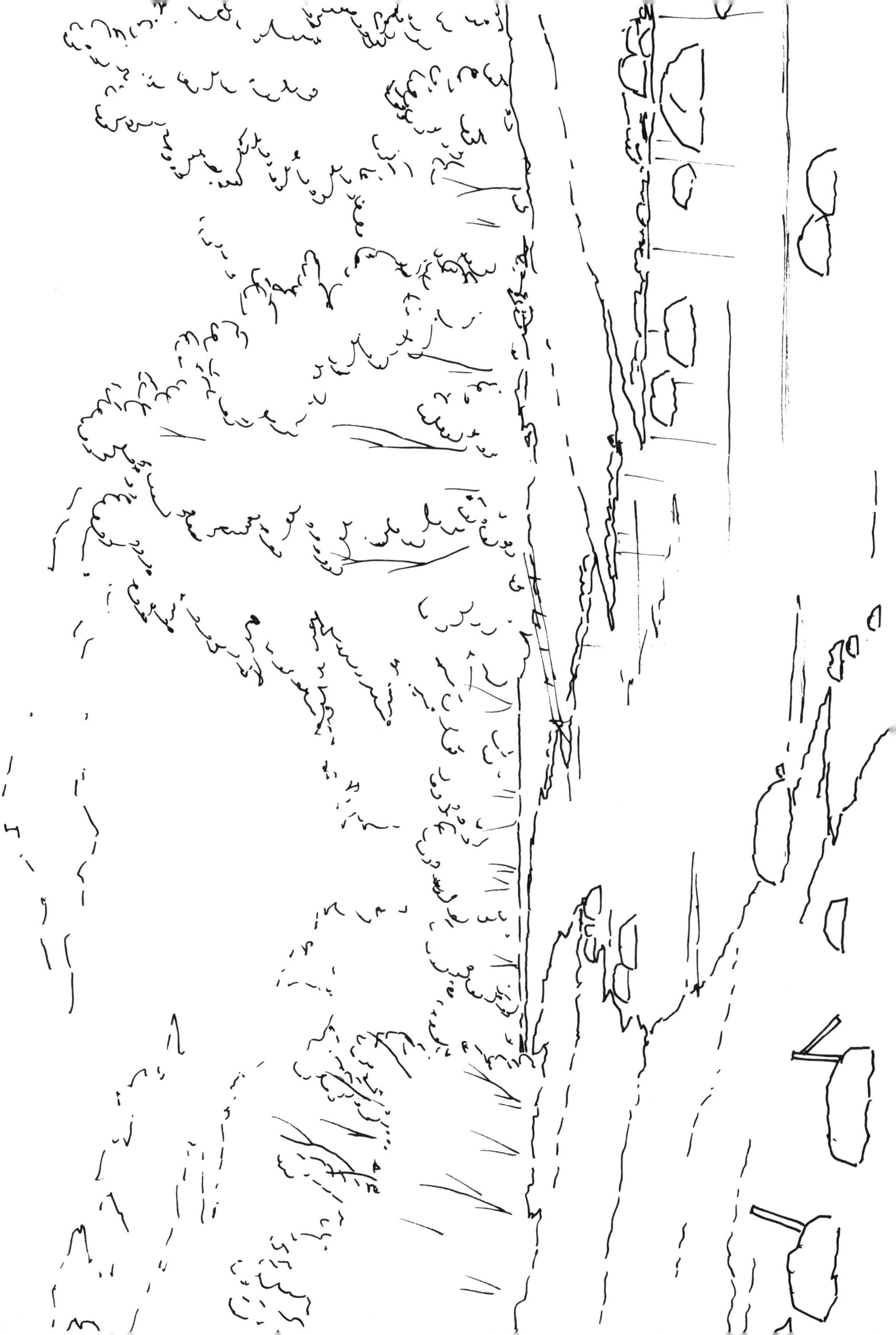

42

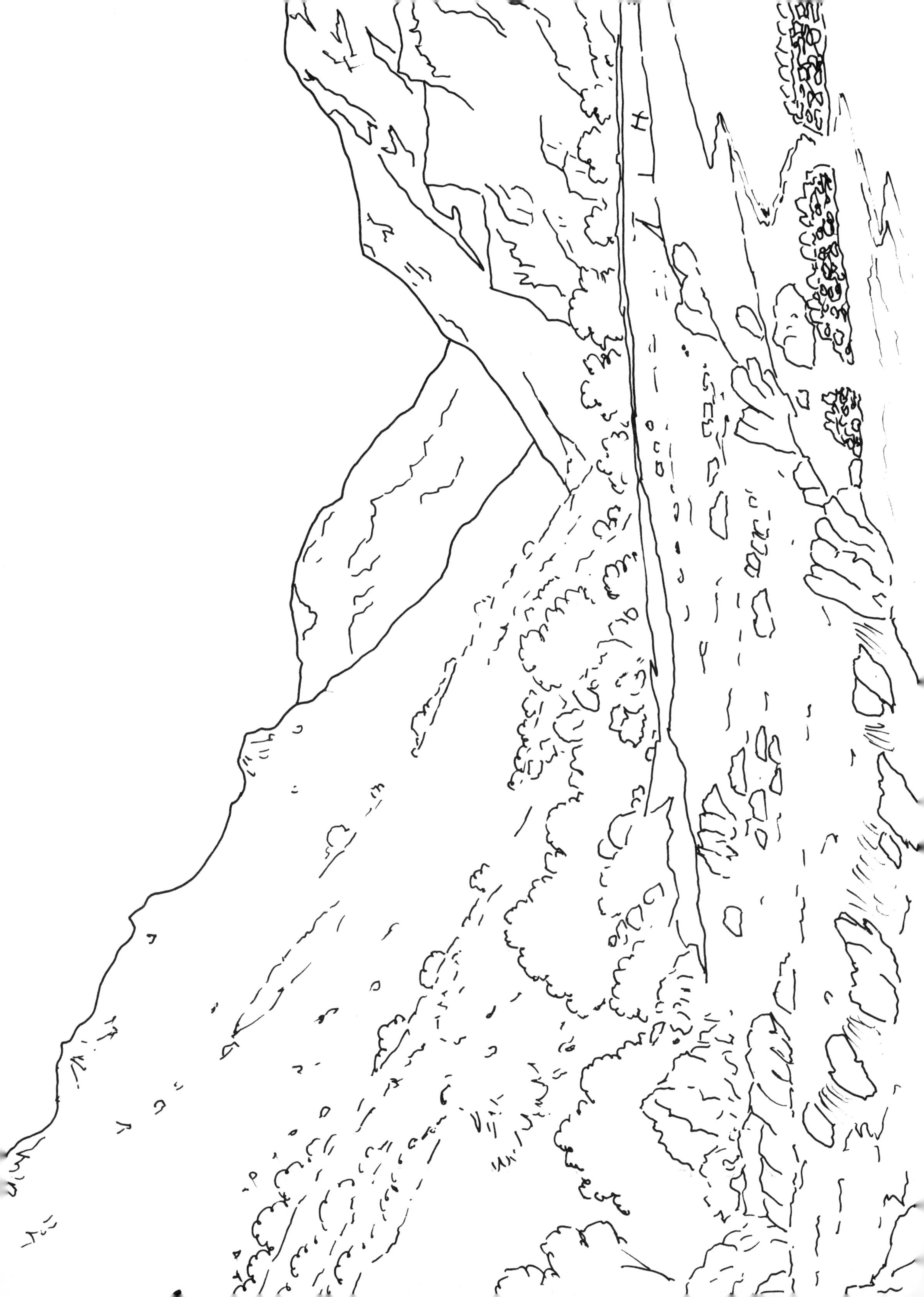

43

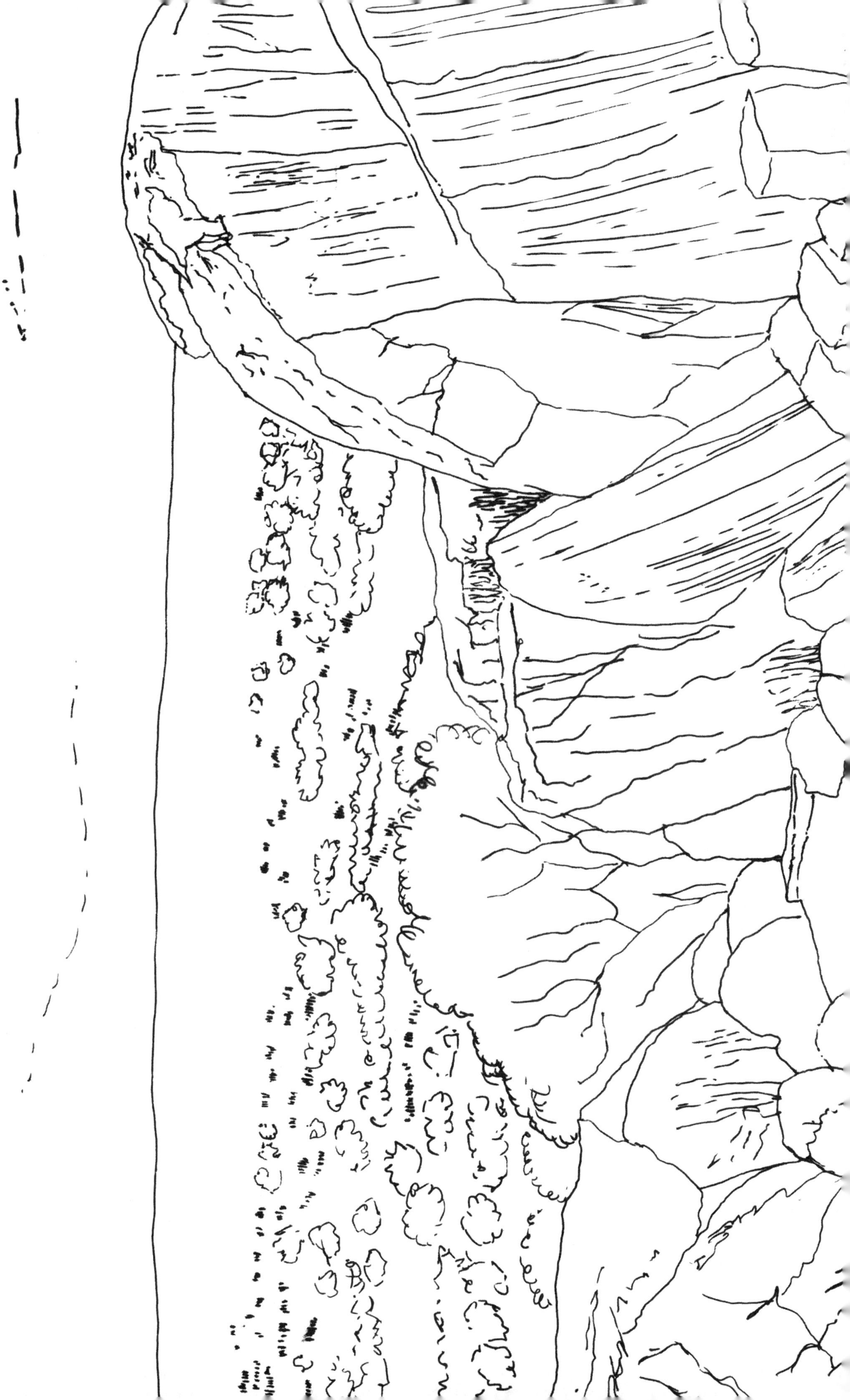

44

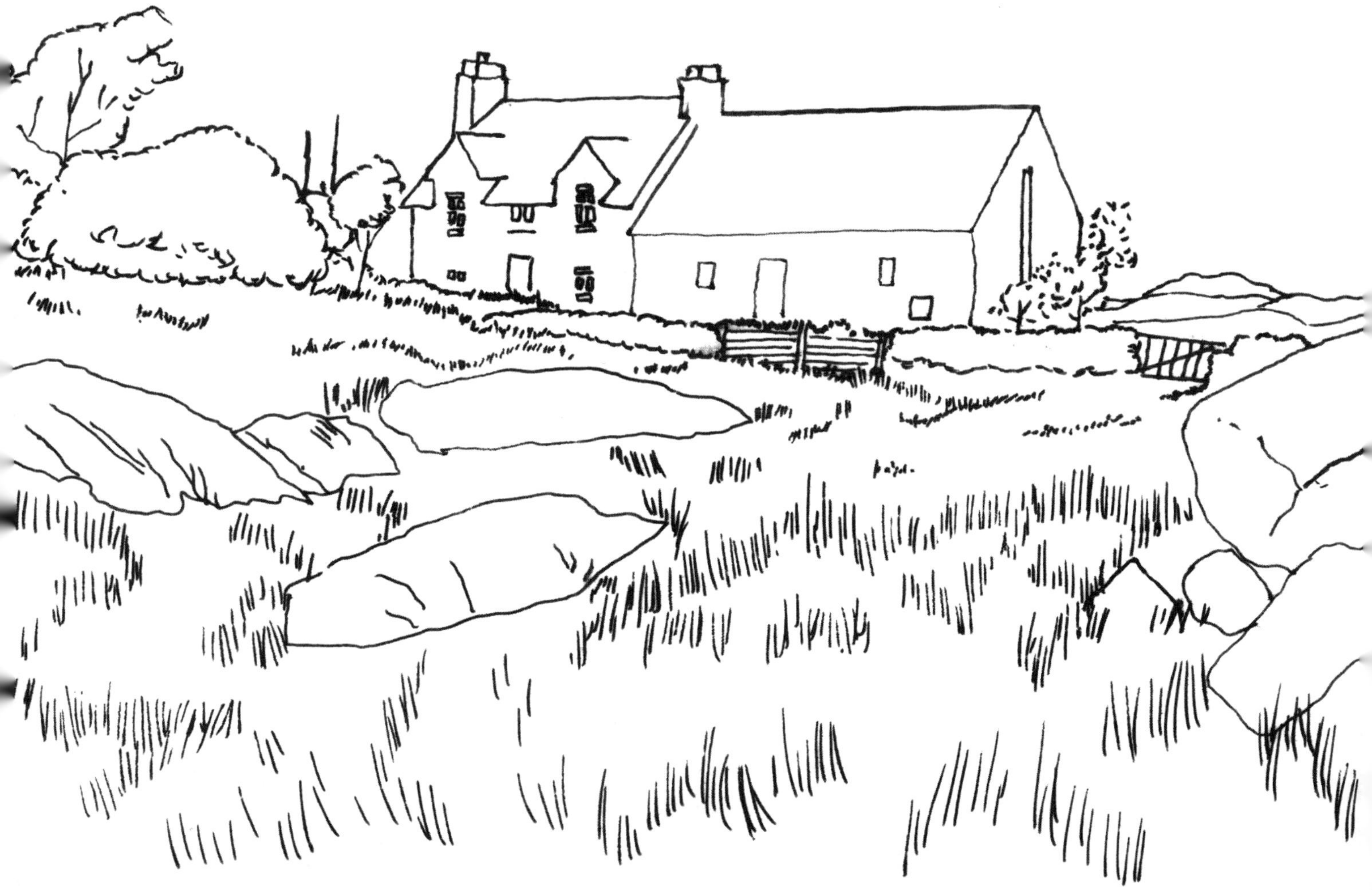

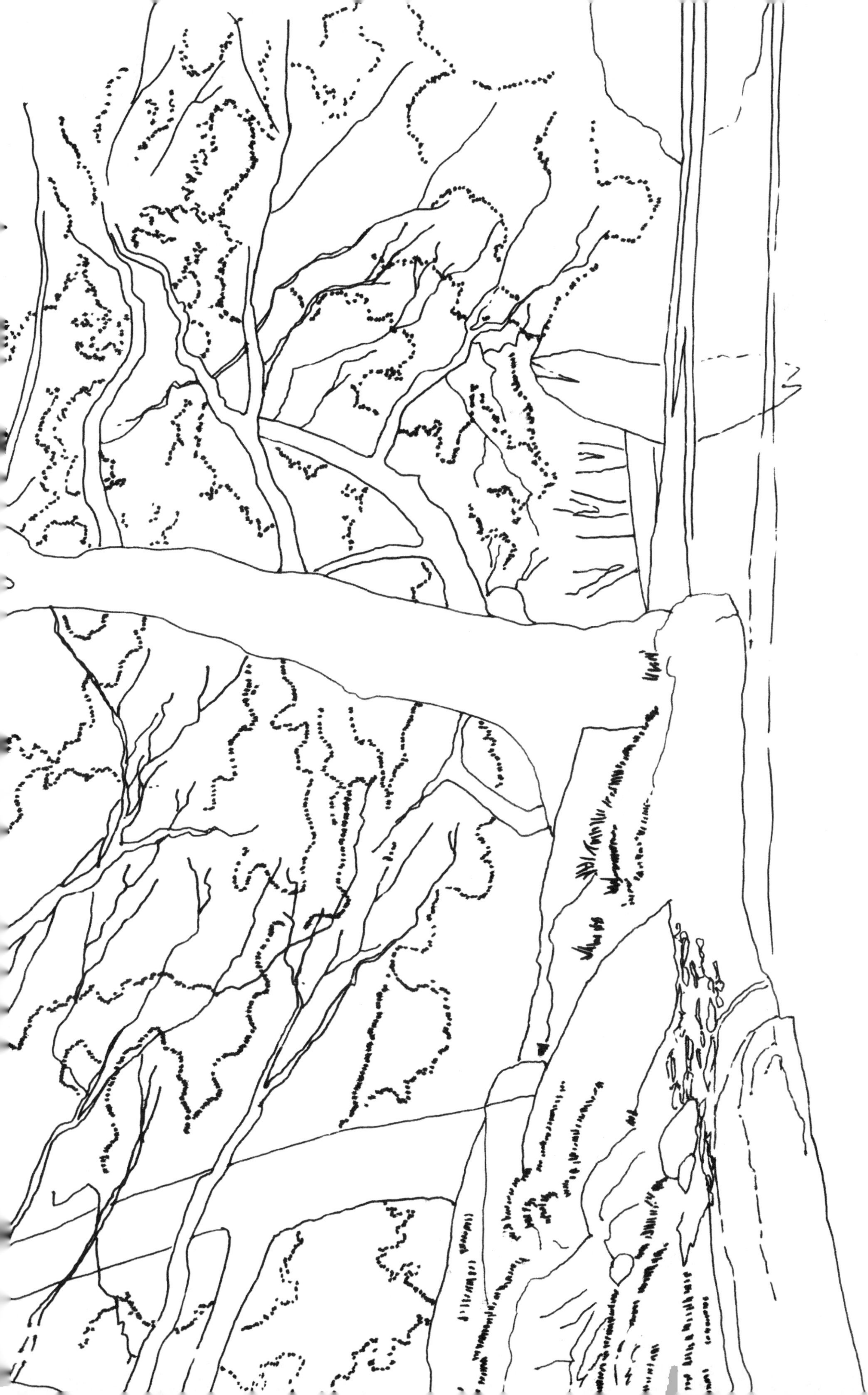

46

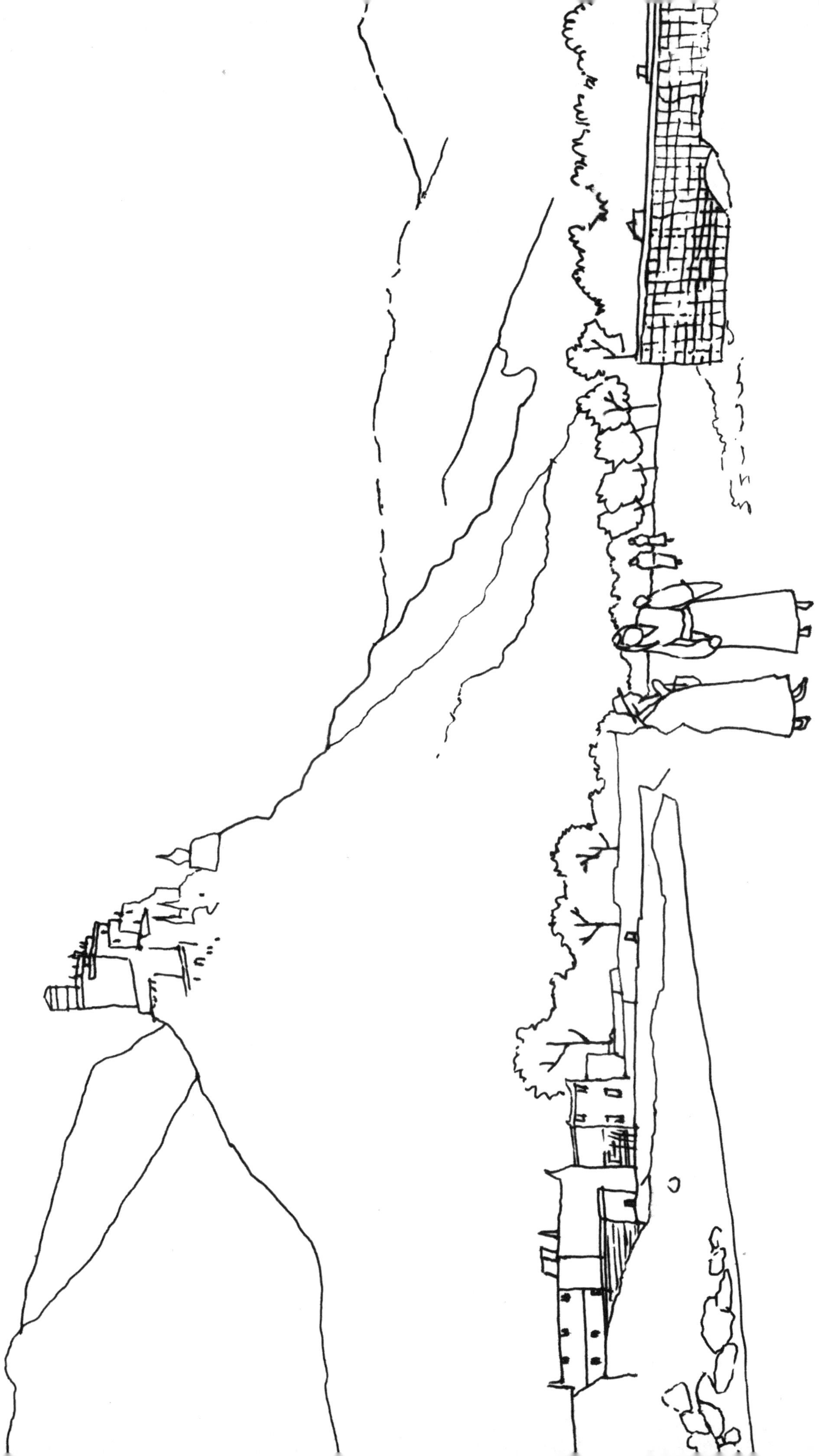

47

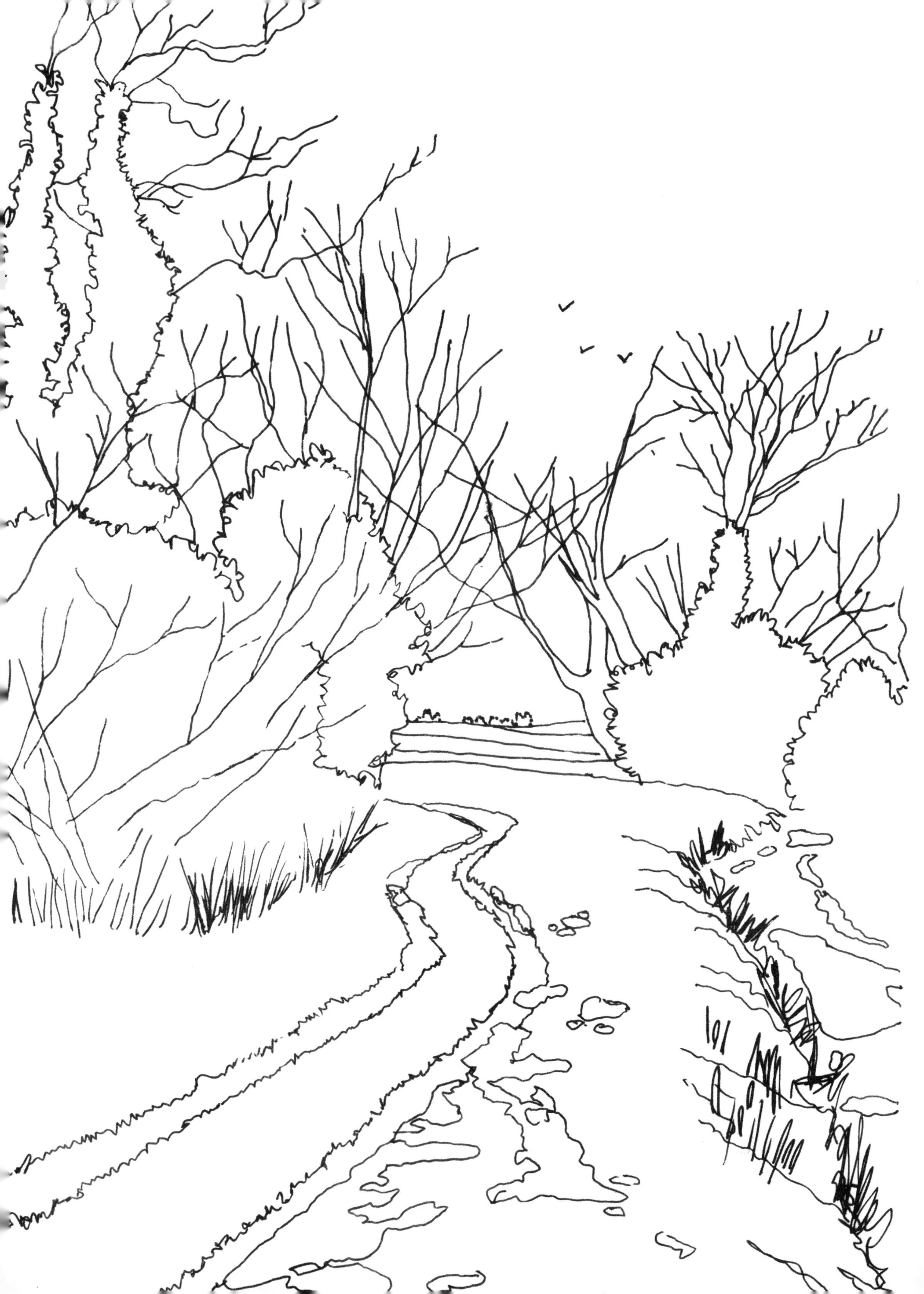

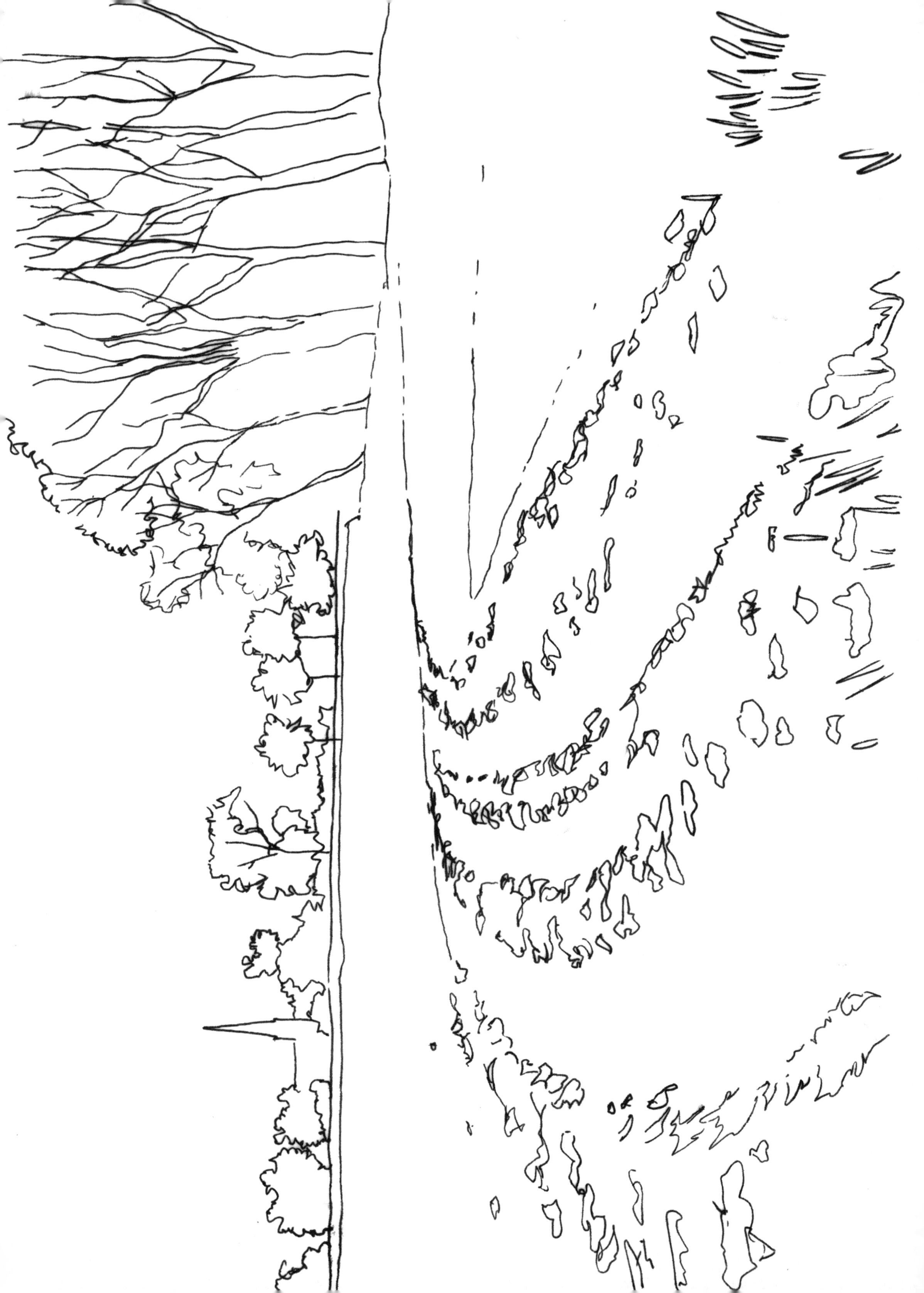

49

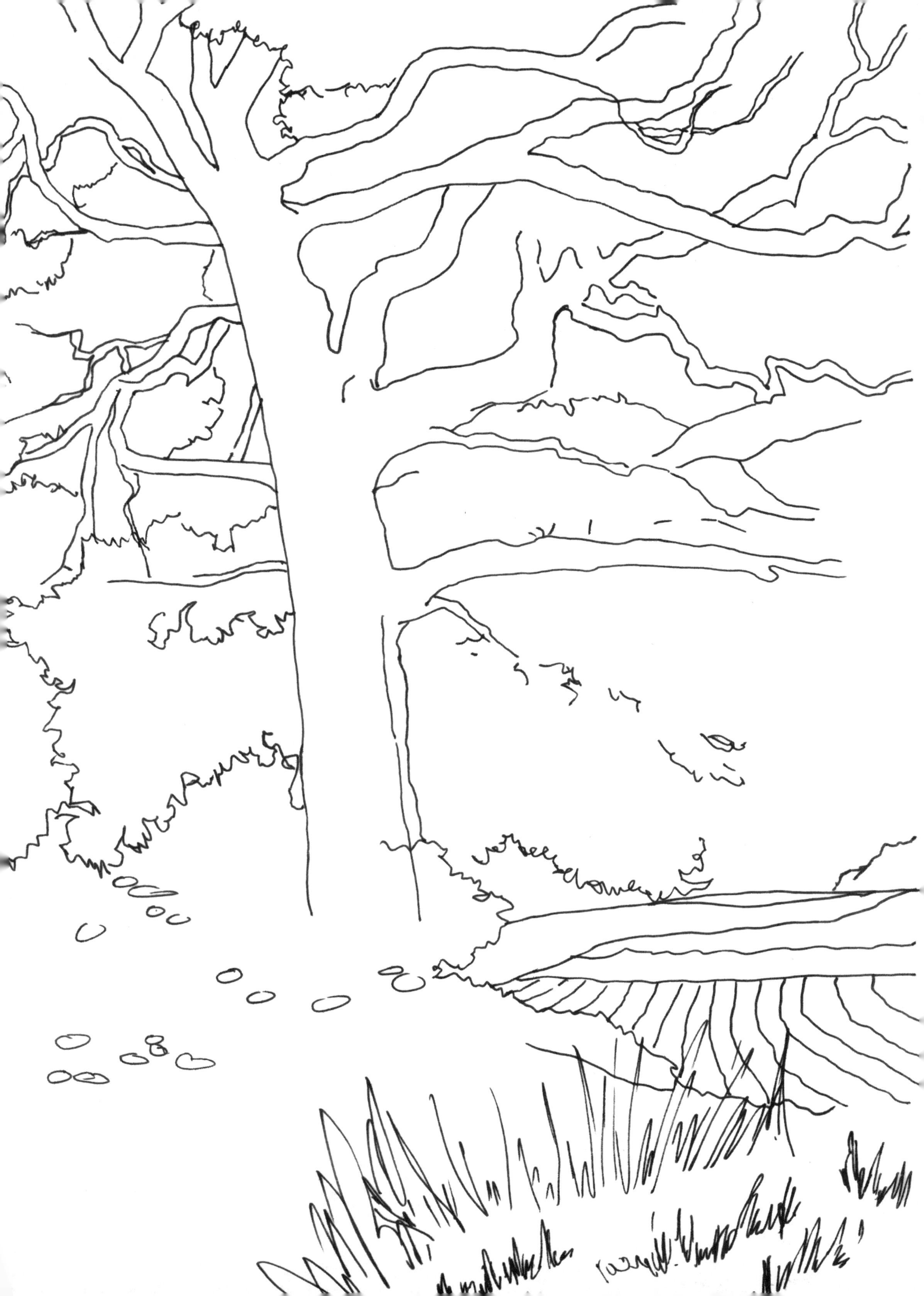

50

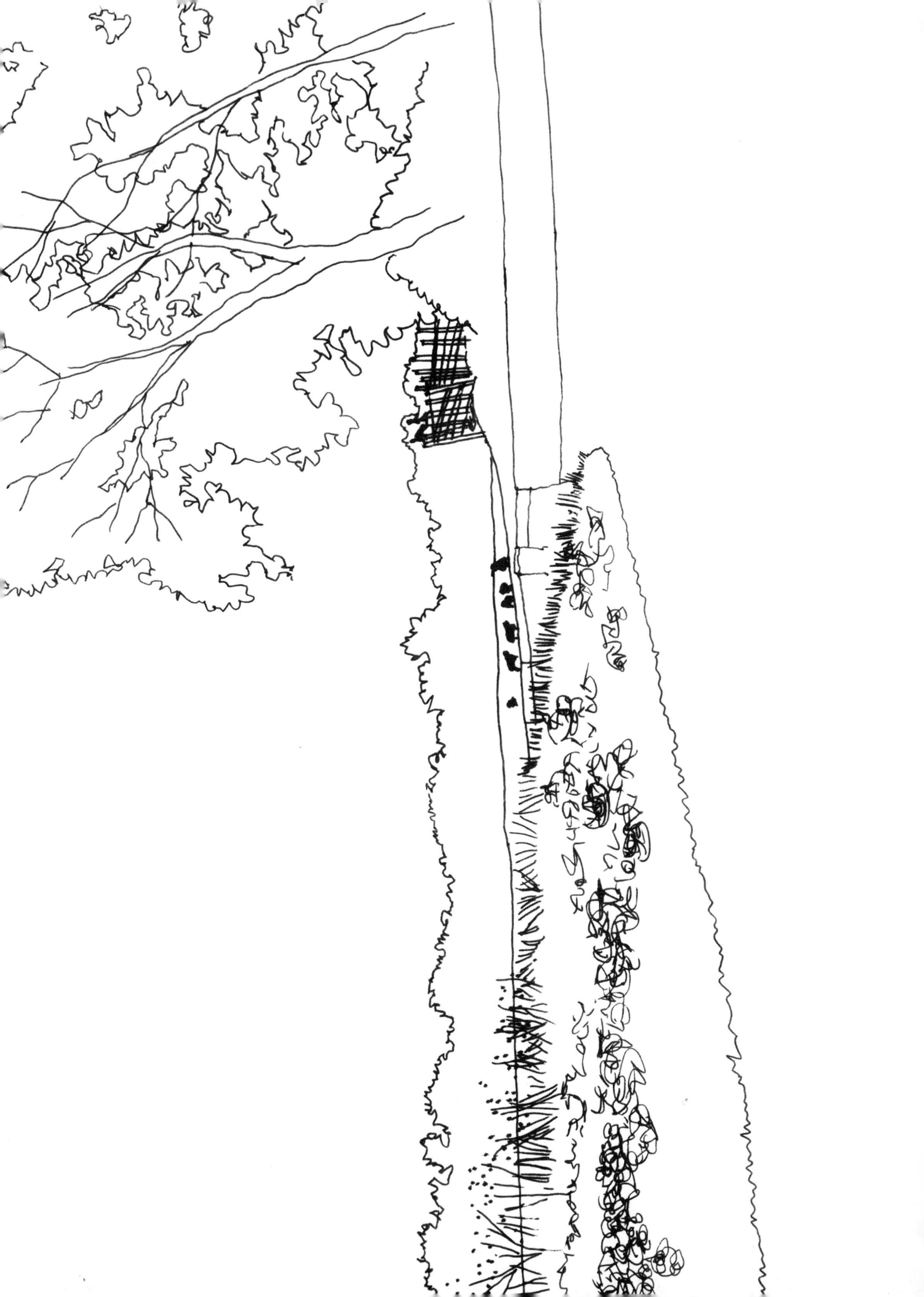

Looking for more?

Extra copies of the outlines are available to download for free from the Bookmarked Hub. Search for this book by title or ISBN: the files can be found under 'Book Extras'.

Membership of the Bookmarked online community is free: www.bookmarkedhub.com

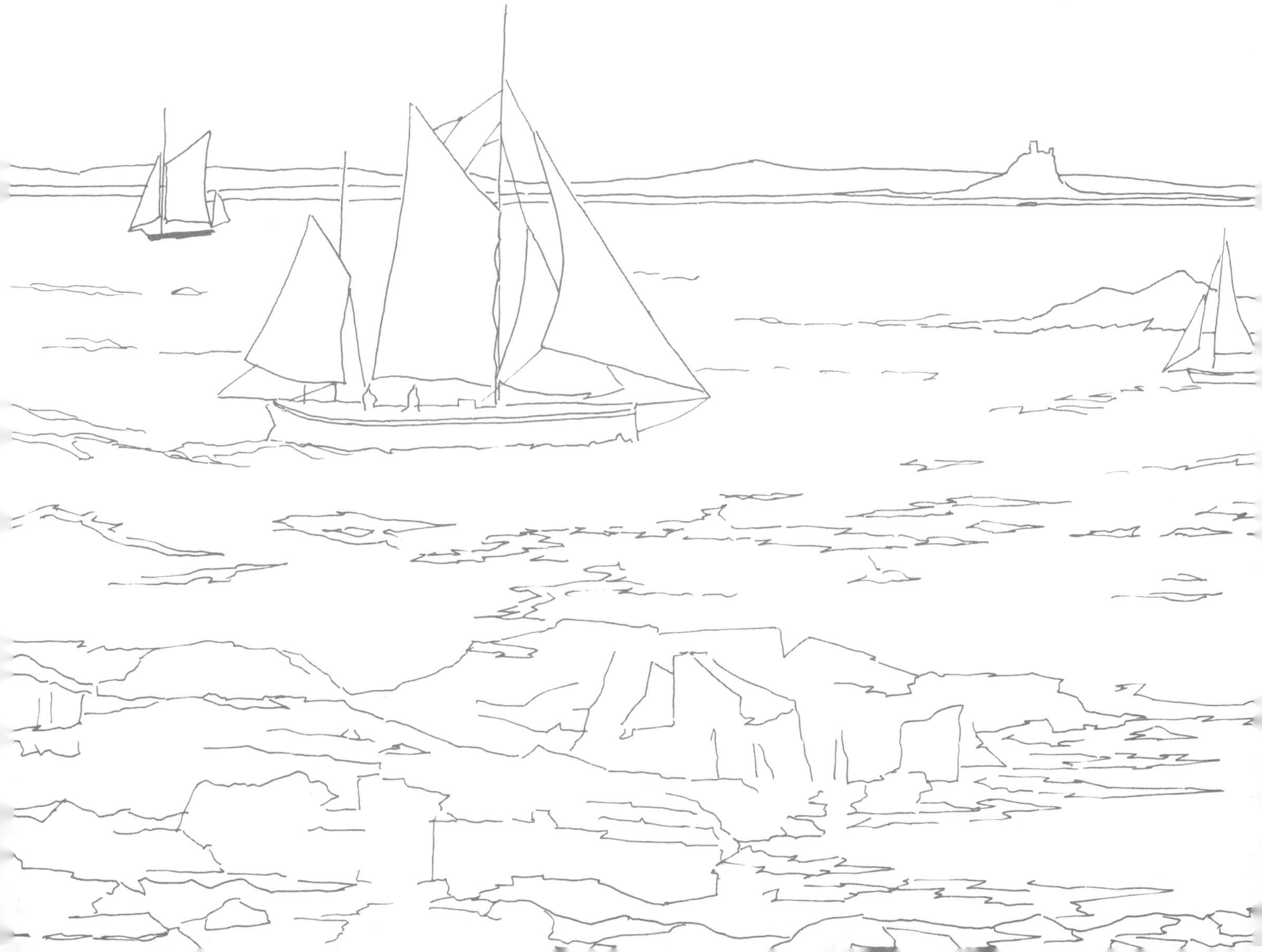